A NEW DEAL IN ENTERTAINMENT
Warner Brothers in the 1930s

NICK RODDICK

A NEW DEAL IN ENTERTAINMENT
Warner Brothers in the 1930s

First published in 1983 by the British Film Institute
127 Charing Cross Road
London WC2H 0EA

Cover design: John Gibbs

British Library Cataloguing in Publication Data
Roddick, Nick
 A new deal in entertainment: Warner Brothers in
 the 1930s
 1. Warner Brothers, *Firm* — History
 I. Title
 384'.8'0979494   PN1999.W

ISBN 0 85170 125 6
ISBN 0 85170 126 4 Pbk

Typeset and printed by
Garden House Press, London NW10

Contents

Acknowledgments

There are numerous individuals and institutions without whom this book would have been very different and in some places impossible.

I should like formally to acknowledge financial help from the Area Studies Fund at Manchester University and from the British Academy's Small Grants Research Fund in the Humanities. More personally, I want to thank Ken Richards, Professor of Drama at Manchester, for support and encouragement, and Ralph Duckwall, Chairman of the Department of Theatre Arts at California State University Long Beach, for giving me a timetable which allowed me two clear days a week for research. I also want to thank former students and colleagues in both Manchester and Long Beach for all sorts of suggestions, most of them useful. Finally, a personal thank you to Stanley, Charlene and Geoffrey Kahan for making my year at CSULB possible: without it, I could never have written this book.

I am grateful to the staffs of the British Film Institute Library in London, the Margaret Herrick Library of the Academy of Motion Picture Arts and Sciences in Beverly Hills, and the outstanding library at CSULB. I am particularly indebted to Janet Lorenz, Robert Knutson and other staff in the Special Collections Department at the Doheny Library at the University of Southern California, and to Leith Adams, who looks after the Warners Archive and deserves more help.

Without three film archives, I would have been able to see less than a tenth of the films discussed in this book: the National Film Archive in London; the UCLA Film Archive, particularly Abbe Wool down in the crumbling vaults of the old Technicolor plant, who had the next can of film ready before I even knew I needed it; and above all Maxine Fleckner and her staff at the Wisconsin Center for Film and Theater Research at Madison, which has to be the world's nicest and most efficient film archive. I should also like to record a number of other places and organisations which (probably unwittingly) helped me see or re-see several films: Manchester University, Cal State Long Beach's Department of Radio/TV; the Aaben Cinema in Hulme, Manchester, the Nuart in West Los Angeles, the Fox Theatre in Venice, California and the Vagabond Theatre in downtown Los Angeles; BBC Television; and Channels 5 (KTLA) and 11 (KTTV) in Los Angeles.

Acknowledgment for the stills reproduced in the book is made to Warner Bros. Inc. (and particularly Eric H. Senat), United Artists Corporation, the Wisconsin Center for Film and Theater Research, the Stills Library of the British Film Institute, and the Special Collections Department at the Doheny Library of the University of Southern California.

I should also like to make a point of thanking Joan Cohen and Stephen Hanson for advice, contacts and friendship. And I owe a particular debt of gratitude to Hal B. Wallis for agreeing to an interview at a time when he was only partly recovered from a serious car accident, to his secretary Marge for taking care of the details, and to Martha Hyer Wallis and Mr Wallis himself for their hospitality during my visit to their Rancho Mirage home.

Finally, I must thank David Wilson, my editor at the BFI, for general advice, gentle pressure and for helping steer the book through a major crisis in its final preparatory stages about which I should probably remain discreetly silent.

NICK RODDICK
London, 1983

PART ONE

The Studio System

1 Hollywood

Almost from the start, the American film industry has been the model for the rest of the world's cinema; and at the base of the American film industry lies (or at any rate lay) the Hollywood studio system. The hegemony of Hollywood was established in the decade between 1910 and 1920, during a period when most potential competitors were geared to a war economy and had little interest in a fledgling industry whose product was regarded as frivolous and marginal. By the time Europe recovered from the First World War, the stylistic and above all economic dominance of Hollywood was firmly established, and other national industries began to ape the Hollywood system and the Hollywood product. In the case of the rare pockets of avant-garde film practice, film-makers consciously rebelled against them. In either case, the result was the same: Hollywood was taken as the dominant model, and the methods and movies that characterised it were openly or tacitly acknowledged as the constituent factors in what most people, inside the industry and out, understood by 'cinema'.

American industry, like that of most developed nations, has tended to concentrate production of a particular commodity in one geographical area – Detroit for automobiles, Pittsburgh for steel, Milwaukee for beer. But it is hard to think of another industry whose output has, like the film industry's, been so totally associated with so limited an area (Hollywood is a comparatively small Los Angeles suburb), and certainly impossible to cite another on the same scale: during the 1920s the film industry was, in a period of rapid economic expansion, one of America's top growth industries. From the early 1930s onwards, of course, the exclusive association of film production with the suburb of Hollywood was more a matter of myth than a geographical reality. From 1931, Warners' Sunset Boulevard studio became secondary to the First National lot in Burbank and turned into little more than a rental facility. MGM was located in Culver City six miles to the west of Hollywood. Universal City had always been north of the Hollywood Hills. The 20th Century-Fox lot was on the fringes of Westwood in what has now, since the sale of large sections of it for real estate, become Century City. Columbia and Goldwyn still continued to operate from Hollywood itself, but the groundwork was laid even before the golden age of Hollywood for the situation which now exists, where only one of the major studios, Paramount, still operates from the Hollywood side of the hill.

Why, then, did the myth of intense centralisation survive for so long? And why, even now, is the word 'Hollywood' still more or less synonymous with the American film industry, and still capable of being regularly used as a term of undefined but real glamour in the trade names of make-up, candy bars and quiz shows? In part, of course, Hollywood is not a myth. Even if the activities of the American film industry were, within fifteen years of its move to the West Coast, spread over a larger area than merely Hollywood, the concentration of output and decision-making was still intense: all but a handful of American films were planned, scripted, shot and edited within a very limited section of what was, in the early 1930s, still not really a major city. What is more American cinema accounted, during the same period, for over three-quarters of the world's total motion picture footage. Hollywood became, with some justification, synonymous with the notion of a worldwide entertainment industry, a situation which the implantation within the same general area of a high proportion of subsequent entertainment activities – notably television and the record industry – has done much to perpetuate. The fact that the word 'Hollywood' has, in general usage, become another name for such activities is in many ways more significant than the tenuous geographical concentration on which such usage is based. Throughout the 1930s, all major production decisions continued to be taken in the Hollywood area – it was indeed the 'entertainment capital' of the world – even if the enormous loans the studios had required to expand and to effect the conversion to sound in the late 1920s had meant that *financial* control of the industry was effectively centred in Wall Street.

Moviegoers, however, were not concerned with financial control: they were concerned with the product, and the product bore the unmistakable stamp of 'Hollywood'. It is worth considering for a moment just what that stamp entailed, since in the entertainment industry carefully fostered and disseminated images are as vital a part of the product as the more tangible material manufactures on which that image is built. The structural film movement in Europe in the late 1960s and early 1970s devoted much of its energy to breaking down the notion that film was a magic beam of light which threw an unproblematic or idealised picture of the world on to the world's screens and into the minds of the world's audiences.[1] But the majority of the moviegoing public, for whatever reasons and with whatever justifications, preferred – and still prefers – to think of cinema as just that: a flow of images in whose method of manufacture, assemblage and projection they are not interested, beyond the level of gossip and personality cult which 'behind the scenes' stories in newspapers and fan magazines are prepared to reveal.

A considerable part of Hollywood's dominance relies on the perpetuation of this idea of a Hollywood style (lifestyle, moviestyle, storytelling style). Hollywood, as Hortense Powdermaker was among the first fully to realise over three decades ago,[2] is a word which carries many implications: wealth, sin, glamour – a dreamworld offering reassurance about the real world and any number of apparent lessons about our day-to-day hopes and fears. Much has been made of the attempts to clean up Hollywood's image in the wake of the Fatty Arbuckle and Wallace Reid scandals in the early 1920s, and especially through the more or less rigorous application of the Production Code from 1935 onwards. But even the most conservative executives knew that it was primarily a cosmetic exercise, a form of self-protection on a market vulnerable to the attacks of religious and moral pressure groups: the continued promise of forbidden fruits remained an essential part of Hollywood's marketing policy, conflicting with but never quite cancelled out by the image of wholesome family entertainment. One has only to look at some of Warner Brothers' titles during the period with which this book is concerned to realise that one of the marketing strategies adopted by distributors of soft-core porn movies in the 1970s – the choice of a title which promised something that the movie did not and, in many cases, could not possibly contain – was not a device invented for the porn market: *Dancing Sweeties* and *The Matrimonial Bed* (both 1930), *Misbehaving Ladies* (1931), *She Had to Say Yes* (1933), *The Merry Wives of Reno* (1934), *Don't Bet on Blondes* (1935) and *Naughty but Nice* (1939), to take a selection largely at random, all promise something vaguely risqué, and are all aimed at audience expectations which, as with striptease and soft-core porn, can only be kept alive by never being entirely fulfilled.

But Hollywood also means something much more than a hint of glamour. To any moviegoer who grew up in the 1950s or before, the name carries a promise (generally fulfilled) of slick, fast-moving entertainment, high production values and a series of hero and heroine figures who act as models for our behaviour. They can do this either because they present idealised versions of ourselves or because our idealised self-images are already to some extent modelled on them. This ambiguity – do we model ourselves on our movie heroes or are they modelled on us? – is one that is crucial to any understanding of the movies as a social force. Moreover, the ability of such idealised images to act on us is dependent precisely on the stylistic slickness – the seamless transparency – of the vehicles in which those images are conveyed. As critics have become increasingly aware over the past decade, Hollywood is a style before it is a content. And, though moviegoers in the 1930s may not have seen it in precisely those terms, they could not have failed to be aware that the roles played by James Cagney and Bette Davis – Cagney as the brash, self-centred hero who belatedly, and sometimes too

5

late, discovers the value of consideration and friendship; Davis as the emotional innocent whose feelings, due to circumstances more beyond than under her control, turn destructively inwards – vary far less than the often rather strained plots within which those roles were contained.

The classic Hollywood style rested upon the individualising of social issues. Problems which appeared general at the outset would be resolved only at the level of the central character (Cagney's cowardice in *The Fighting 69th*; Bogart's fascism in *Black Legion*; Muni's Luddite tendencies in *Black Fury*; even, in a slightly different way, Davis' frustrated maternal instincts in *The Old Maid* and *The Great Lie*), but in a way which appeared to imply a more general resolution. The cinematic means of expression – shot, framing, camera movement, editing and music track – were tied to the trajectory and destiny of the central character. If nothing else, the traditional terminology of shot description – close-up, long shot, three-quarter shot and so on – makes this clear by being entirely determined by the camera's distance from the human subject. Our knowledge of a situation – the Georgia penal system in *I Am a Fugitive From a Chain Gang*, the FBI in *G-Men*, Mexican history in *Juarez* – is restricted stylistically and narratively to one or at the most two persons' experiences of and within that situation. Even Warners' more apparently documentary forays of the decade, *20,000 Years in Sing Sing* and *Confessions of a Nazi Spy*, are hung explicitly and decisively on the peg of an individual experience. The audience was intended to identify, and the style was designed to make that identification as easy as possible. It would probably not be going too far to say that the major part of Hollywood's collective energy was devoted to exercising the maximum control over the audience's perception of the story, while disguising such control to the greatest possible extent. The trick was to make it seem obvious.

But Hollywood's international dominance, though it may have relied to a considerable degree on the establishment of a style presented (and accepted by other national film industries) as the only possible way to tell a story, was obviously not achieved entirely by stylistic or even ideological methods. It was achieved above all by economics. Although it is still a recurrent belief in the American film industry that a movie can only be adjudged a commercial success or failure on the basis of domestic (i.e. US and Canadian) box office returns, everything else being traditionally regarded as icing on the cake, there can be no doubt that all the majors, from the early 1920s onwards, devoted considerable time and money to establishing themselves on the foreign markets. The fact that, at the outset, they had product to market when no one else did clearly helped such establishment. But they were quick to capitalise on it, setting up powerful marketing organisations in every national capital which, through a series of more or less scrupulous practices ranging from superior advertising campaigns to block-booking clauses, soon implanted the notion that American films were better – indeed, the only genuinely entertaining form of cinema – and that the national product was a parochial, shoestring operation best suited to the bottom half of the occasional double bill. No European country during the inter-war years was successful in setting up a national film industry which could seriously rival Hollywood on its home market, let alone on the international or American markets. The only possible exception was the Italian cinema under the control of Vittorio Mussolini, the Duce's son, which managed to some extent to protect the home product. Outside Europe, only two national film industries, those of India and Japan, have been to any real extent successful in establishing a viable national product. But again, to all intents and purposes the frontiers of those industries were the frontiers of the country itself. In the past decade Hong Kong has perhaps succeeded, through production methods common to most of the colony's other industries, in establishing a foothold on the world market. But it is only a foothold.

Basically, then, Hollywood, through a complex mechanism of stylistic and economic implantation, placed itself in a position where it became the dominant model for world cinema for at least four decades (from 1920 to 1960). And though the power of Hollywood to control world cinema may have waned with the power of cinema itself as a form of mass entertainment, the model that was established during that time (almost half the medium's life to date) still to a very large extent determines the production and consumption of image-based narratives.

One of the striking things about Hollywood, in an industry whose 85-year history has been marked by a quite unusual degree of organisational fluidity, is that one basic system of organisation – the studio system – should have held sway for quite so long and should, for that matter, have left its indelible mark on all subsequent organisational structures, not just in the film industry itself, but in its offspring, the television industry. It is tempting to argue that this happened because such an organisational structure was the only one that really met the particular needs of film-making. But the studio system is, in fact, a product of a particular economic history – that of the American film industry: it is not found to anything like the same extent in other national film industries. They may have adopted the central core of the Hollywood system – the specific organisation, crewing hierarchy and scheduling of the actual period of shooting. But they did not – or, more accurately, they could not afford to – back it up with the overall economic infrastructure which was typical of Hollywood: writers under contract; a constant pool of talent, technicians and managers who moved from picture to picture and whose focus was, therefore, not the individual film but the company they worked for; an advertising, marketing, distribution and exhibition network of epic proportions; and perhaps most importantly, a back-up industry outside the immediate control of the major studios but closely geared to their needs – an industry which perpetuated the image of Hollywood as a dream factory and the crucible of the nation's (if not the world's) desires, fears and efforts at public self-examination. This back-up industry, which encompasses everything from trade papers like *Variety*, *Hollywood Reporter* and *Motion Picture Herald* to the fan magazines and the gossip columns, was an essential part of the Hollywood system, relied upon to keep alive a general desire for the industry's product: no one who did not have to would have put up with Louella Parsons and Hedda Hopper for long.

The system was integrated on a vast scale. It owed its economic ascendancy not only to the vertical integration (one company exercising control over the entire range of activity, from production through distribution to exhibition) which characterised Hollywood from the late 20s to the early 50s. It was also integrated in a much wider sense: it was able to create, meet and adjust its own demand thirty years before any other major industry, with the advent of large-scale advertising in the 1950s, was really able to do so. What Hans Magnus Enzensberger has to say about the influence of advertising in the past twenty years – that it is not the creation of a false need, but the false meeting of a real need[3] – could be applied to Hollywood throughout its golden age. Hollywood did not engage in sinister activities, but it undoubtedly engaged in manipulative ones: gauging and responding to audience needs was essentially a manipulative process.

It was a system of, in a manner of speaking, perpetual feedback. The producers knew which of their products the audience was responding to, the exhibitors and distributors knew well in advance how their marketing campaigns would have to be geared, and the various ancillary industries whose existence depended on the production industry were available to provide fine tuning. Though it was not a monopolistic system in the true sense, it was not really a competitive one either. Each studio kept a close eye on what the others were doing, and the kind of duplication of effort that tended to characterise the American film industry in the 1960s and 1970s was largely unknown. What is more, each studio tended to specialise in – and audiences tended to associate it with – a particular kind or style of film. Studio styles were made easier to identify by the fact that individual theatres, being owned by one or other of the majors, would show that studio's films almost exclusively. To a considerable extent it is the breakdown of this system of feedback, partly as a result of government anti-trust legislation, partly as a result of the shift in leisure habits in the 1950s, that has now left the American film industry with only a slight advantage over that of other nations. The advantage is provided more than anything else by the scale of available investment capital: the majors are otherwise floundering in an unaccustomed darkness with, seemingly, only the vaguest ability to

8

correlate massive investment with massive box office returns. In the 1930s, a major feature might do disappointing business, but it could never do worse than a programmer; whereas nowadays, small budget features regularly (though not, of course, predictably) do big business, while $20-, $30- and $40 million epics regularly flop.

Although the studio system held sway in Hollywood for a remarkably long time, it did not, of course, remain constant in its details. Nor did it spring into existence fully formed at the outset. The industry's first fifteen to twenty years were characterised by a very different form of organisation. The debate will probably go on for many years as to who, precisely, invented cinema; but from the American point of view it was invented by Thomas Edison. As an inventor, Edison was naturally more concerned with the machine he had invented than with the art form it gave birth to.[4] Accordingly he viewed films largely as disposable products necessary to maintain demand for and promote sales of the major product, the machine. In the years before 1900, Edison directly controlled the major part of the American film industry. In the first decade of the twentieth century, he and his associates found it necessary to institutionalise that control through the setting up of the monopolistic Motion Picture Patents Company. Eventually an anti-trust suit was filed against the MPPC but, as Tino Balio points out,[5] the trust was a dead issue long before it was technically laid to rest.

The emergence, evolution and corporate histories of the major studios which have dominated Hollywood since the early 1920s are complex developments which it is not within the scope of the present book to examine in detail,[6] but there can be no doubt that the studio system was born out of a revolt against the MPPC. The origins of MGM, Paramount, Fox, Universal and, to a lesser extent, Warner Brothers can be found in the attempts of theatre owners like Louis B. Mayer, Adolph Zukor, William Fox, Carl Laemmle and the Warners to find ways of evading the restrictive practices instituted by Edison and, in the classic tradition of American enterprise, to ensure for themselves profits greater than those potentially available to them as mere purveyors of somebody else's product. Their experience was in exhibition and distribution (William Fox was the only major film exchange owner to refuse to accept the MPPC's ultimatum) and, if they were to continue to exist on an independent basis, they realised they would have to go into production as well. This sequence of events is crucial to the evolution of the studio system. For Edison, exhibition was a licensed outlet for the chief product, distribution a way of servicing that outlet. The manufacture of machinery was the main focus of his activity; film-making was secondary. It was, to start with, a very profitable activity. Edison was an inventor who was more interested in the potential profitability of his brainchildren than in their cultural potential, and if it had not been profitable he would not have pursued it. But whether he simply failed to foresee how things would develop, or whether his experience in the traditional world of late nineteenth-century capitalism prevented him from grasping the growth potential of the film industry, he (and with him the other early production companies) showed very little interest in developing it as an entertainment business. As a result, the early American film industry quickly reached a point of stagnation.

The new breed of independents who, within fifteen years, would become the prototypical Hollywood moguls, however, had direct experience of audience reactions and geared their organisations accordingly. The fact that they came from exhibition and distribution rather than production (of the Warner brothers, only Sam, who died in 1927, had even the vaguest interest in the technical side of the business) meant that they saw the industry as a way of meeting audience needs, whereas Edison had viewed the audience as anonymous consumers of his product. The whole rationale of the studio system – economically, stylistically and artistically – stems from this change in perspective: there was an identifiable audience need to be met, and the studio system was designed to meet it as economically – and therefore as profitably – as possible. It took the independents rather more than a decade to establish control of the industry, and the period between 1912 and 1925 is characterised by a series of crises, realignments, mergers and splits. But by the late 1920s the pattern was firmly established. The five majors, MGM, Paramount, Fox, Warners and RKO, exercised a substantial degree of control over the three crucial stages of their business operation: production, distribution and exhibition.

The advent of sound on a large scale in 1928-9 brought about two major adjustments in the system, one economic, the other stylistic. Sound contributed to the economic adjustment and directly caused the stylistic one. Economically, it created a need for huge amounts of investment capital (from the Wall Street finance companies) to extend the theatre chains, thereby consolidating the industry's economic base, and to equip the theatres and studios with the expensive new facilities necessary for the talkies. Films now cost more to make and there was, in addition, the interest on the various development loans to be met. This situation was accentuated by the largely coincidental disarray that Wall Street found itself in over the same period. Since budgets could not continue to spiral and since the actual physical cost of filming had increased, a proportional reduction had to be made in the non-technical costs – that is to say, in sets, schedules, stars and story material. Erich von Stroheim was perhaps the most spectacular victim of this changeover, but he was scarcely alone. The new Hollywood could not afford another *Greed*, whoever the director was. The new cost-conscious budgeting and meticulous planning that would characterise the studio system through the 1930s had come to stay.

The stylistic effect of the change was less immediate but more far-reaching. Like most studios, Warners continued for a while to make the kind of extravagant historical or exotic epics whose predecessors can, lovingly restored and with full orchestral accompaniment, still fascinate modern audiences: they made *Noah's Ark* in 1928, for instance, and *The Desert Song* in 1929. But by the early 1930s Warners and all the others were making a very different kind of movie – movies which were, in a word, more realistic. For all its exaggeration and whimsy, MGM's 1953 musical *Singin' in the Rain* pinpoints this development fairly exactly: audiences could accept the exaggerated posturings of the people who occupied the dream world of the silent screen, but once those characters began to speak they had to speak credible dialogue. As long as they could imagine the words The Red Shadow said to Margot Bonvalet in *The Desert Song* moviegoers, traditionally less sophisticated than theatre-goers, had no problems. But as soon as they had to listen to them, a different set of expectations – and a more critical response – came into play. In the final analysis, the major shift in Hollywood production between the mid-20s and the mid-30s is perhaps not so much towards more realistic subjects (the silent cinema dealt with its fair share of realistic subjects) as towards a more realistic style and above all decisively away from exotic subjects. Such a development did much to consolidate the already well-established studio system. If audiences were presented with a picture of a world they knew (or thought they knew because they could recognise its externals – modern cities, modern dress, contemporary apartments), their responses were likely to be more uniform: what is or is not realistic depends on much less flexible criteria than what is or is not artistically valid. This was a development which could only help to perfect the perpetual feedback which was the system's base and its single greatest strength. No studio made this shift more decisively than Warner Brothers.

This changeover is the basic reason why I have chosen, in this book, to concentrate not only on Warner Brothers but on the 1930s. But there is a secondary reason, closely related to the first but giving rise to a phenomenon of a quite different kind. In the early 1930s, Hollywood was providing America with an image of itself on a scale and with a degree of apparent precision which no culture had previously known. Not only did the average twice-weekly visit to a movie theatre by an American family provide that family with fictionalised reports on the more dramatic events of recent American history such as gang wars, prohibition, newspaper scandals and the birth of the aviation industry. It also gave them a regular view of other families apparently just like them facing day-to-day emotional and social problems not unrelated to theirs. As a result, the American film industry in the 1930s provides the first instance of a process which has by now become a crucial social factor in modern life: the ideological impact of the mass media. The trends and events of public life provided the story material for and therefore strongly influenced the output of Hollywood; in turn, the image of themselves which the movies reflected back to the moviegoing public exercised an influence on the same trends and events which had given birth to the image. For the first time, the circle was closed: the entertainment industry was no longer simply a source of relaxation, as it had been, perhaps, to Edison. It was also a major ideological force. The rationale of the studio system was based on its ability to manipulate that situation, not in any sinister sense, but simply by giving the public what it appeared to want.

The implications of this development, in terms of creating powerful social norms, not simply of dress or lifestyle but of the correct behaviour in a given situation and of the correct response to social and emotional problems, have generated a situation which we still do not really understand. Since the mid-nineteenth century, we in the West have grown used to having the external events of our lives controlled by the needs of industry (via employment and the industrially-based growth or recession of our national economies). But it is only since the 1930s that we have had to get used to – though we may not always know how to cope with it – the ways in which our inner lives (our self-images and many of our more private desires and aspirations) are strongly influenced, and at times almost controlled, by another industry. And an industry which is, moreover, geared precisely if not explicitly to doing that.

The importance of the relationship between the economic organisation of the film industry and its ideological impact has not received anything like the necessary critical attention. In the brief history of film criticism, critics have approached Hollywood slowly and with considerable caution. It is not my intention to summarise the trends in film criticism,[7] merely to indicate an area which seems to me, perhaps because it falls between the traditional domains of criticism and history, to have been somewhat neglected. In its early days film criticism operated as a sub-division of aesthetic theory, with a strong influence from art criticism most notable in the writings of Rudolf Arnheim; or, in the case of the Russian constructivist critics, a tendency to view film as the most extreme, because least definable, stage in the development of modernism. In either case, the focus was firmly on film as an art form – a means of expression whose specifics had to be fully understood if they were to be more effectively manipulated by film-makers or perceived by audiences. The result was in most cases strongly normative: if the full potential of the new art form was to be realised, it would have to perform certain transformations on itself and develop along certain lines. Dogmatic statements about the nature of film are common in pre-war film criticism.

Most post-war film criticism was a reaction against this. Starting from the premise that films produced in Hollywood were in many cases as interesting as – if not more interesting than – those produced by the more overtly art-oriented industries of Eastern and Western Europe, critics set out to identify just what it was that made the Hollywood product so dynamic and so fascinating. A number of possibilities were advanced, the most radical and still the most influential of which was the *auteur* theory. This involved suggesting that, despite the fact of working within an industrial system which appeared to give fairly little scope to individual creative urges, a number of key directors none the less managed to imprint a style, be it visual or thematic, on the films they made. The effect of this development was less radical than it seemed. True, it recognised that, within a system we had been taught to regard as philistine, there existed any number of vital and unique works of art. But this recognition depended to a considerable extent on denying the specificity of the medium, and on restoring the traditional literary notion of the single author to a field from which, since the early films of D.W. Griffith, it had been notoriously absent. The strength of the *auteur* theory was that it accorded serious critical attention to films which had deserved but not previously received it. Its weakness – a weakness which laid it open to constant ridicule from those who saw its efforts as merely pretentious – was that it transferred much of the language of traditional literary criticism more or less intact to film criticism. To do so it was forced to deny not only a large number of the other creative energies that went into film-making (writers, producers, cameramen, editors, actors), but also the entire structure into which the activity of the director was inserted. Above all, the studios were allotted an almost entirely negative role in the process, as obstacles which the creative *auteur* had to overcome in order to make his statement: he triumphed in spite of them; when he failed, it was because of them.

A secondary aspect of *auteur* criticism was the barely concealed contempt with which it regarded the mass moviegoing public. It was a critical approach for initiates who, because of their familiarity with the overall opus of the director, could spot the enduring values of the Hawksian style in *Hatari!* or *Red Line 7000*, while the rest of the audience just enjoyed the action.[8] That *auteur* criticism should be elitist would matter less (criticism is almost by definition an elitist activity) if it were not for the fact that one of the prime stimuli for the critical approach had been provided by a desire to give serious consideration to films which were (a) commercially successful and (b) commercially produced. None the less, *auteur* criticism helped shift film criticism from the fringes of film production to the centre. And above all it was descriptive rather than normative: it looked closely at how films were rather than declared what they ought to be.

Genre criticism followed hard on the heels of *auteur* criticism, but in retrospect appears to have been more an offshoot of it than a new departure, partly because most of its original practitioners were trained in an *auteur*ist approach, and partly because the key films in any particular genre usually turned out to have been made by already respected directors. But the major departure from *auteur*ism made by genre criticism was that it forced critics to recognise that genre was defined by audience expectations. If *High Noon* fails to fit many of the established criteria for a Western, it remains none the less a Western. Conversely *Easy Rider* manifests many of the traditional structural and narrative features of a Western, but quite obviously is not. One of the problems with genre criticism – and the one which probably resulted in its comparatively short life other than in the field of coffee-table picture books – is that it adopted the predominantly descriptive approach of *auteur* criticism without fully examining the theoretical and other reasons for the existence and perception of the genre itself. Too often, therefore, it tended to become a list of films, some better, others worse, some more purely generic, others manifesting only certain features of the genre. In many ways, it was *auteur* criticism without an *auteur*.

The film industry, as I have tried to suggest above, is a massively integrated activity in which individual creative energies are harnessed to a complex production process. It is, moreover, since it relies on fulfilling the entertainment needs of a mass public, a closed process in the sense that the needs which are fulfilled feed back into the production process. This is, after all, a normal industrial pattern: the market determines what is manufactured and not vice versa. And only by denying the basically industrial nature of film production can film criticism manage to ignore this fact. The market can be analysed, even influenced, but it can never be entirely predicted, nor even controlled other than under the most extreme of monopoly conditions. And film production has never been a monopoly industry: it is neither entirely controlled by one company nor does it account for the entirety of the entertainment market. Even more importantly, it supplies a notoriously fickle need: the entertainment, relaxation and self-reflective – in short, the aesthetic – needs of the public. That is what makes it risk-dominated and, of course, so potentially profitable. But however impossible it may be to provide a model which will adequately explain the workings of the industry, any critical approach to film, and above all to the American film industry, which fails to take into account the huge areas of activity which precede and shape the final film cannot hope ever fully to understand that film.

Recent developments in critical writing on film have gone some way towards tackling the entirety of the cinematic apparatus. Semiological and structuralist criticism has increasingly addressed itself to the problem of how and what an audience perceives when confronted with a flow of narrative images. And recent historical and critical works operating outside this discipline (though often strongly influenced by

14

it) have devoted more attention than ever before to those areas of film production not controlled by the director: screenwriters, cinematographers, stars who are the dominant message in their own films, producers and the studios themselves. The economic structure of the industry has been analysed and documented with increasing thoroughness. But bridges still need to be built between the various areas. Theorists theorise about film rather than particular films, which is scarcely surprising. Studio histories, probably because of the economics of contemporary publishing, are lavish picture books more anecdotal than analytical. And treatments of the industry's economic history prefer, again for obvious reasons, to devote very little space to the artistic or even the ideological content of individual films produced within that industry.

This book is clearly not going to build the bridge referred to above. Equally clearly, many of the confident criticisms of the shortcomings of previous approaches will become self-referential in the pages to come. But to look at the operation of the studio system through an examination of some of the most successful films produced during the 1930s by one of the most dynamic of the Hollywood majors, and to look at them in the context of their production, their social background and their reception, is something which needs to be done. Until we understand just what it is that is specific about cinema – cinema as industry, cinema as art, cinema as entertainment – we are unlikely to have a form of film criticism which is anything other than a poor relation of some other area of activity, be it literary criticism, linguistics, psychology or Keynesian economics. Nor, perhaps, do we stand much chance of grasping the forces which, through cinema and its present successor in the mass entertainment field, shape more of our attitudes towards life than we are often prepared to admit.

2 Warner Brothers and the Studio System

Of the five majors who dominated Hollywood production during the 1930s, three – MGM, Paramount and Fox – were in one way or another well established in the film business by the time World War I broke out in Europe. So, too, was Carl Laemmle, future head of Universal. A fourth major, RKO, was formed much later, in 1928, as the result of a series of corporate manoeuvres designed to exploit RCA's patents in sound reproduction. Only Warner Brothers, among the majors, combined elements of both these histories. And it is quite possible that it is this combination – a long, direct experience of the distribution and above all exhibition businesses, coupled with a rapid capitalisation and expansion just prior to the coming of sound – which accounts for the studio being the most distinctive film producing company in Hollywood during the 1930s. It was not, as was RKO, run by a board of directors more committed to a return on investment than to a particular style of film-making. Nor was it, when talkies revolutionised the industry in 1927-8, strongly committed in terms of equipment and organisational practice to a particular way of running its business.

In 1914, the Warner brothers were still operating on a relatively small scale. By 1918, although they were getting involved in production as well as distribution and exhibition, there was little to suggest that, within ten years, they would be in a position to compete with the companies headed by Adolph Zukor, Louis B. Mayer, Samuel Goldwyn and William Fox. This is not to say, of course, that the four brothers – Harry (b. 1881), Albert (b. 1884), Sam (b. 1886) and Jack (b. 1892) – were without experience of the film business: by the time Warner Brothers began to emerge as a major studio around 1925, the brothers had been in the business on and off for 22 years. In 1903 they pioneered screenings of Edwin S. Porter's *The Great Train Robbery* in the Youngstown, Pennsylvania suburb of Niles; and for the next four years they had a degree of success with touring movie shows and with running Newcastle, Pennsylvania's first permanent nickelodeon, the Cascade Theatre. From this experience in exhibition, they took the logical next step by opening a film exchange, the Duquesne Amusement Supply Company, with offices in Pittsburgh and Norfolk, Virginia. Duquesne started trading in 1907 and ceased in 1909 when Edison moved against the newcomers. The Warners were neither well enough established nor adequately financed to combat the MPPC as the other, larger independents began to do. For a while they abandoned the movie business, but soon returned via a route which, although it put them decisively outside the Trust, did not guarantee them any real freedom of initiative or operation: importing foreign films from countries where the Trust was not yet established. These they distributed and exhibited along with movies produced by the largest of the independents, Carl Laemmle's Independent Motion Picture Company (IMP). In 1912, they moved to the West Coast – a location which became the centre of operations for the independents both because of its climate and because of its geographical distance from the New York-based Trust. Between 1915 and 1918 they attempted, largely unsuccessfully, to go into production. With somewhat greater success they operated a Los Angeles film exchange. As a florid 1929 press release put it, 'with that sturdy pioneer spirit which refused to acknowledge failure, the brothers stood together'.[1]

Pioneer spirit or no, there is little before 1918 to distinguish the activities of the Warner brothers from those of any number of small-time movie companies. In 1918, however, they produced their first major feature, *My Four Years in Germany*, based on the autobiography of US Ambassador to the Kaiser, James W. Gerard. The picture is significant because it is Warner Brothers' first success; in other respects, it was a big picture produced by a small company with all the attendant problems of distribution and exhibition. None the less, the film grossed $1,500,000 and is probably the real starting point for the process of growth and consolidation that, over the next seven years, was to lay the foundations for the future of the company as a Hollywood major. Although Warner Bros. Pictures Inc. was formed in 1923, the crucial formative years were 1925 to 1928. There are two versions of this three-year period. According to the authorised romantic version enshrined in the 1929 press release ('A depression hit the entire business. But their difficulties only bound the four brothers more closely together') and repeated with variants over the years, Warners teetered on the verge of bankruptcy and saved itself by gambling everything on the popularity of talking pictures. Such a version is hard to reconcile with a closer look at the various financial moves undertaken by Harry Warner during the three years in question – moves which, though admittedly risky, suggest a fairly consistent programme of expansion culminating in (rather than being rescued by) *The Jazz Singer* and the company's emergence as the pioneer of talkies.[2]

In 1925, two loans of well over $1 million enabled Warners to increase production and to acquire the old Vitagraph studios in Brooklyn, in addition to their West Coast studios on Sunset Boulevard. The Vitagraph deal also brought Warners control of Vitagraph's thirty-four North American film exchanges. The Brooklyn studios became Sam Warner's base for experimentation with the sound-on-disc system that would enable the company to produce the first two successful sound features, *Don Juan* in August 1926 and *The Jazz Singer* in October 1927. The increased working capital and distribution network gave them the base which was necessary if their pioneering talkies were to be anything other than gimmicks. Almost a year after *The Jazz Singer*, in September 1928, they raised a further $100 million to buy the Stanley chain of movie theatres and the following month acquired a controlling interest in First National Pictures, one of the big five of silent film production and distribution. The acquisition of First National was completed on 4 November 1929 when, for a further $10 million, they bought out the remaining one-third share from Fox West Coast Theatres.

The acquisition of First National was important for a number of reasons. Firstly, it provided Warner Brothers with a second, better equipped West Coast studio at Burbank in the San Fernando Valley. In the early days, sound recording facilities remained in the old studio on Sunset Boulevard and a number of films were shot at Burbank with the sound recorded over a telephone line link to Sunset Boulevard – an arrangement which obviously continued only until proper recording facilities could be installed at Burbank. After that, the Sunset studios continued to be used intermittently – most of the early Busby Berkeley musical numbers for *42nd Street* and *Gold Diggers of 1933* were filmed there – but from late 1933 onwards they were used as a rental facility and as the base for Warners' animated cartoons. Throughout the 1930s, however, Warner Brothers continued to release films under both their own banner and that of First National, at first because the terms of the takeover required this (two separate programmes had to be made up for each year), later for tax purposes. All the major features bore the banner 'Warner Bros. presents', but a considerable number still remained technically First National pictures: even as late as 1941, thirteen films out of a total output of fifty still appeared nominally under the First National banner, though the cinemagoer would have needed good eyesight and an exceptional degree of attention to the small print on the credits to have been aware of the fact.

In addition to production facilities, the acquisition of First National enabled Warners to compete on a more or less equal footing with the huge Loews, Fox and Paramount-Publix theatre chains. In terms of production, distribution and exhibition Warners was, by the start of the 1930s, sufficiently capitalised to be indisputably regarded as one of the big five. The First National deal also brought them a number of much needed box office stars, including Douglas Fairbanks Jr., Billie Dove, Loretta Young, Richard Barthelmess, Kay Francis and Constance

Bennett. By the time Wall Street crashed on 28 October 1929, Warner Brothers was firmly established as both a typical Hollywood studio and one with a unique history and, therefore, unique possibilities. The company would continue to hold this position up to (and of course beyond) 7 December 1941 when the Japanese airforce attacked Pearl Harbor, thereby ushering in a new era in American history. It is with the activities of Warner Brothers between October 1929 and December 1941 – dates which, to all intents and purposes, limit the '1930s' – that this book is concerned.

Three things remain to be dealt with in this chapter. First, how did Warners fare economically during the 1930s? Secondly, just what was it that was unique and what was typical about the studio – what, in fact, makes Warners a studio particularly worth studying during this crucial period of American film history? Thirdly, in what way did the system itself influence and determine the kind of films that were made and, perhaps, the way in which audiences perceived them? A full answer to the final question can only come from a detailed study of the films produced by Warner Brothers, but it seems none the less important to map out some kind of theoretical framework into which that detailed study can be inserted, as well as to look at the more quantifiable questions of economics and organisation.[3]

Warners' economic health and sickness during the 1930s can be dealt with fairly simply. Although a fuller understanding of the various trends and decisions should emerge from later chapters, the bare facts of the studio's activities can best be expressed in figures. The following tables concern annual profit and loss figures as declared to the company's stockholders, and annual production of features. Appendix I indicates how the studio fared in the various annual polls. Between them, Tables 1 and 2 and Appendix I are designed to cover the three areas which, in different ways, were crucial to the studio's economic life: profitability, production and critical respectability.

I do not propose to analyse Tables 1 and 2 in detail, but they do call for some kind of comment. The dive from profit to loss between 1929 and 1933 – a drop of $28½ million in four years – was clearly caused by the Depression, and the gradual climb back into profit over the next five years parallels the economic recovery of the nation under Roosevelt's NRA. Warner Brothers took longer to feel the Depression than the other majors because of their very strong position in 1929, but the fact that this strength was heavily dependent on loan capital meant that, when the Depression did hit, it hit Warners harder than most of the others (though they did not go into receivership, as did Fox). At the same time, the basic health of their operations enabled them to climb steadily back into profit as the economy strengthened, and the brief slump in 1938 seems to have been more of a liquidity problem than anything else. The fluctuation in feature production figures is less

Table 1. Annual Profit and Loss Figures, 1929-1941
(in millions of dollars)

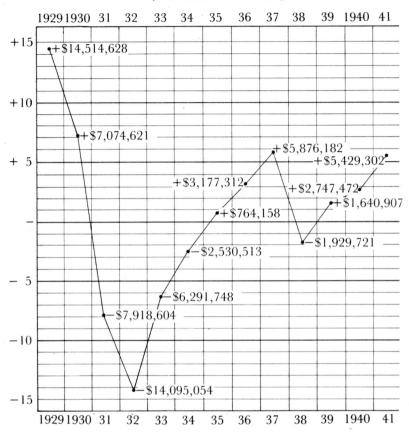

dramatic, though also to some extent caused by the Depression. But from 1931, the number stayed remarkably constant: around 55 features a year. The cutback from 1929 to 1931 also necessitated an adjustment in the number of first-run theatres operated by Warners in New York. At the beginning of 1930 they had four; a fifth opened at the end of April 1930. By the end of 1934, only one of these – the Strand, at Broadway and 47th – was still operating full-time as a first-run movie theatre.[4] The number of features was by then down to about one a week and any interference with this steady flow of product (if a picture was held over for one or more extra weeks at the Strand, for instance) was offset by the fact that at least ten of the 55 or so features produced each year were not considered suitable for Broadway openings. Similarly, a number of

Table 2. Feature production, 1929-1941

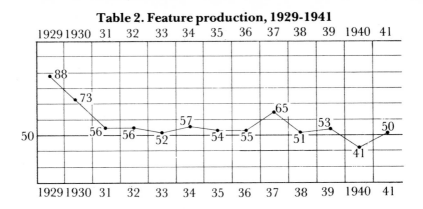

the more prestigious features were given roadshow openings at the Radio City Music Hall.

The figures for profit and loss and feature production are not markedly different from those of any other major studio: Warners was a typical Hollywood studio. It was also, however, one with unique features. The most important of these, of course, was that it began as a family business and, despite heavy financial dependence on a number of merchant banks, essentially remained a family business. True, family considerations were important at other studios, where more or less advanced forms of nepotism were not unusual. But only Warners was run throughout the 1930s by a triumvirate of brothers (Sam Warner died 24 hours before the premiere of *The Jazz Singer*). Of the three surviving brothers, only two were closely involved in the day-to-day running of the company. The third, Albert Warner, nominally Vice-President of Warner Bros. Pictures Inc., and always referred to as 'the Major' (a title whose origins are now obscure), led 'more of a gentleman's life'[5] with a stud farm in North Carolina. Harry M. Warner was the New York-based President of the company and the one most directly concerned with the studio's financial liquidity. And it was, of course, Harry Warner who was responsible for negotiating the loans which enabled the company's expansion between 1925 and 1928. Of the three brothers, Jack Warner was nominally the least powerful. His sole title was Vice-President in charge of Production: even the Major, in addition to being a Vice-President, was also Treasurer and Vice-President of Warner Bros. Artists Bureau Inc. But Jack Warner was the one who had the most direct and powerful influence on the films produced by Warner Bros. And he is the only one of the trio who belongs in that mythical company of moguls so beloved of Hollywood chroniclers – a myth which he did much to perpetuate with his autobiography, *My First Hundred Years in Hollywood*.[6]

It is difficult to gauge exactly how much influence the family connections had on the running of Warner Brothers. But it seems likely that, together with the comparatively recent evolution of the company's corporate structure, it contributed towards making the studio the most tightly run, economical and streamlined of the big five during the 1930s. The thing which ensured this efficiency of operation was, of course, the structure that Warners shared with every other major company: the structure which I have referred to earlier as the 'studio system'.

Warner Brothers/First National had, like most studios, two main offices: a West Coast Production Office, initially located on Sunset Boulevard in what is now the headquarters of Gene Autry's Golden West Broadcasters, and subsequently on the First National lot in Burbank; and a New York office at 321 W. 44th St. which, in addition to being Harry Warner's base, was the headquarters of the legal and advertising departments. This last fact deserves some comment. The location of the advertising department (headed by Charles Einfeld) on the other side of the continent from the product it was involved in advertising necessarily slowed down the post-production side of the operation; it nevertheless represented the continued acceptance of the fact – not just through the 1930s but well into the post-war years – that, although Hollywood was the movie capital, Broadway was still the place where movies had their public premiere. The location of the financial and legal operations in New York was simply a recognition of New York's *de facto* dominance of the nation's business affairs. A certain amount of the studio's legal work – partly for convenience and partly because a lot of it came under the provisions of California law – was handled on the West Coast. This was taken care of by R. J. Obringer (whose name will appear with some frequency on the memos quoted later in the book), working in conjunction with Ralph Lewis of the Los Angeles law firm of Preston and Files.

The Burbank studio was Warners' largest and most important single asset. Throughout the 1930s, almost all the footage which appeared in Warner Brothers' pictures was shot there. Such location work as was needed was done wherever possible on company land: the Warners Ranch at Calabasas or the Sherwood Forest site at Chico, 350 miles north of Los Angeles, which, strangely enough, carried that name long before *The Adventures of Robin Hood* was shot there. There was also the First National 'trainshed' which could be used for various kinds of process work as well as the obvious railroad scenes. In addition, the Burbank backlot contained a number of standing sets – the New York Street, the Dijon Street, the Viennese Street, the Tenement Street, and so on – which, with some redressing, appeared in film after film: Emile Zola battled with his umbrella, the Fighting 69th marched and Bette Davis, in *All This and Heaven Too*, was taken off to jail along the same piece of street frontage. Occasionally an outside location would be

Hal Wallis (far left), Jack Warner (2nd from right) at the Warners studio in the 1930s

rented for extensive use, such as the Providencia Ranch in the Simi Valley, which provided the battlefield for *Sergeant York*. Other locations were used only when it was totally unavoidable, like the Navy Air Force Base in San Diego for *Devil Dogs of the Air* and *Dive Bomber*: not even the ingenuity of Warner Brothers could enable them to land planes on the backlot. The reason for this avoidance of location work is simple: it cost money. Cast and crew had to be paid from the moment they reached the studio, and travel between studio and location was on company time. Outside locations were also liable to disrupt the schedule, since the weather could not be counted on to perform as planned, and the schedule was all important.

Production in general was organised on a factory basis, with as little waste of time and equipment as possible. Wherever possible, sets were recycled: Fred Jackman's miniature for *Captain Blood* was adapted into the long shot of Leghorn in *Anthony Adverse*, and the *Anthony Adverse* sets were used again in *Hearts Divided*. The only real exception to this process was *A Midsummer Night's Dream*, where the massive forest set was a one-off, built across three sound stages with a connecting ramp to enable the necessary depth. It is not surprising to find that this extravagance became one of the major foci of the film's advance publicity: if Warners was going to break its own rules and spend lavishly, it wanted to make sure everyone knew.

23

Human beings were used with the same determination to maximise their productive potential, and it is this more than anything else that makes Warners a classic example of Hollywood studio organisation. The studio system is, in its simplest form, a classic management pyramid. As Vice-President in charge of Production, Jack Warner was ultimately responsible for the choice of stories, casting, budgeting and approval of the final print. In practice, however, most of these responsibilities were delegated. Hal Wallis tells the story of sending Warner an early copy of the best-selling novel *Anthony Adverse* with the suggestion that he should read it. It was returned with a note saying 'Read it? Hell, I can't even lift it!'[7] In reality, production was organised by the studio executive who was head of production. At the beginning of the 1930s there were two: Darryl F. Zanuck, production chief at Warners; and Hal B. Wallis, head of production at First National. When Zanuck left in 1933 to set up his own production company (Twentieth Century Films, later merged with Fox[8]), Wallis became overall production chief for the studio. Looking through the memos for the period, it is sometimes difficult to believe that one man could have done so much, from reading original story material, supervising casting and contractual negotiations, attending writers' conferences and commenting on the scripts, through budget approval and scheduling, to viewing the day's rushes and making extremely detailed cutting notes (six pages is not unusual) on the post-production phase. If there is one person who left his mark on Warner Brothers in the 1930s, it is not Jack Warner, it is Hal Wallis: the 1930s at Warners were the Wallis years.

But Wallis himself, of course, did not function as sole producer on individual films (though towards the end of the decade his name begins to appear on the credits as Executive Producer): this was the responsibility of a stable of 'line' producers directly responsible to Wallis – Henry Blanke, Robert Lord, Sam Bischoff, Lou Edelman and others. Occasionally a director would be credited as producer on his own film – this was the case with Howard Hawks, William Wyler and, at times, Mervyn LeRoy and Anatole Litvak – but the ultimate production responsibility remained Wallis'. In the virtually unique case of *Sergeant York*, Jesse Lasky brought the idea to the studio and shared the executive producer function with Wallis.

The line producer was drawn from a pool of personnel which also included directors, cameramen, contract stars and players, and technicians of all kinds. The stage at which a director was assigned depended on both the status of the director and the importance of the project. A director might express interest in a particular property; he might also decline an assignment, but only if another assignment was likely to become available shortly afterwards. Otherwise, he would be given an unpaid lay off.[9] A director had limited right of approval on script, sets and costumes, but basically he remained a studio employee

24

like any other. His services were used in much the same way as those of the art department, the music department, the research department, the titling department and so on. In this factory system, Wallis and the line producers played a supervisory role. So, too, did the Studio Manager, Bill Koenig, and the overall Production Manager, T.C. ('Tenny') Wright. So, in a different way, did Bryan Foy, who was responsible during the second half of the decade for the production of the studio's low-budget programmers. Occasionally Foy would find himself with a property which he felt deserved large-budget treatment, as with *The Fighting 69th*, and relinquish it to one of the A-team.[10]

The Hollywood studio system as exemplified by Warner Brothers was a mass-production system. In so far as we tend to associate the creation of an art work with the notion of an individual expressing him- or herself in circumstances largely free from outside interference, it was not a system designed to produce 'works of art'. It was a factory geared to turning out product on a regular basis. But the product was in a sense artistic: if a work of art is defined not by the conditions of its production but by the circumstances of its consumption, then the product manufactured by Warners (and the other studios) was undoubtedly art. Even with a more rigorous definition, it is hard to deny the status of 'work of art' to at any rate some of the films produced by Warners during the 1930s – *The Life of Emile Zola*, perhaps; *Dark Victory*, *High Sierra* and *The Letter*. And if to some, why not to all? *The Life of Emile Zola* was produced in the same way as *Happiness Ahead* and *Nancy Drew, Detective*. And however they may have been produced, *all* films made by Warners were consumed as art – popular art, mass art or entertainment art, but art nevertheless. Their relationship to the real world in which the audience lived was not a direct one: it was an aesthetic one. What is more, the terms in which the films are discussed in the studio memos – structure, balance, impact, pacing, credibility – are terms which are basically concerned with the artistic, not the physical nature of the product. Even in cases where financial considerations are clearly the origin of the memo, the aim is always to get the best effect in the most economical way. The criterion remains, in the final instance, artistic. How else is 'the best effect' to be designated?

The studio system, as represented by the Executive Producer, the line producer, writer, production manager, director, editor, studio head and advertising department personnel (as well as, in different ways, the cinematographer and even at times the research department), has to be admitted into any consideration of the creation of the film work. To allocate sole artistic responsibility to the director, while more convenient from a critical point of view, in no way reflects the specific conditions under which the film was created. What is more, it is time film critics stopped giving in to the temptation to regard studio executives as philistines. The irresistible conclusion that comes from any extended

DAILY PRODUCTION AND PROGRESS REPORT

Day **TUESDAY**   Date **11/12/35**

Name of Production	"ANTHONY ADVERSE"	No.	**958**	Name of Director	**LE ROY**
Number of Days Shooted	**60**	Production Started **11/6/35**	Days Elapsed Since Starting	No. of Scenes Necessary Daily	Average No. Scenes Taken

Estimated Finish Date **1/18/36**   Status as Regard Time   LOCATION OF WORK **Back Lot**   Exteriors **X**   Interiors

Company Called	8:30AM	**SCRIPT REPORT**	EXT. ROAD DECK & STREET (Day)
Time Started	8:20AM	No. of Scenes Original Script **414**	LEGHORN, 1794 & 1796
Lunch Called	12:45PM	No. of Scenes Previously Taken **11**	
Time Started	1:45PM	No. of Scenes Taken Today **11**	EXT. PRADO & STREET-LEGHORN 1796
Dinner Called	5:40PM	Total Scenes Taken to Date **22**	
Time Started	6:30PM	Balance to Be Taken **392**	EXT. LEGHORN STREET- 1773 (Night) (Day)
Time Finished	11:00PM	No. of Added Scenes Taken **54 18 69**	

CAST			EXTRAS	Record No.	No. of Takes	Time of Ok Takes	STAFF		Time Started	Time Finished
W-Worked H-Held		Time Started / Time Finished	**108 Extras**							
March	W	8:30A 5:40	**d Standing**	N69	3		Supervisor	Blanke		
A. LLOYD	WF	8:30A10:45	**11 Horse-**	70	2		Director	Le Roy	8:15A 11:00P	
GATESON	WF	8:30A10:45A	**men**	71	2					
Crehan	W	9:00A12:45P		72	3		Dial Dir.			
Gwenn	W	10:00A12:45P	**1 Double**	73	5		1st Asst.	Cannon	8:00A	"
deHAVILAND	H W		**for Sancho**	74	8		2nd Asst.	Lueker	8:00A	"
ALBERNI	H			75	2	0'50"		Tyler	8:00A	"
SONDERGAARD	H		**21 live-**	76	2		Tech. Man			
WOODS	SW	10:30A 3:40	**stock**	77	2		Art	Grot		
			8 carts &	78	2		Unit Mgr.	Alborn	8:00A	"
			carriages	79	2	1'00"	Script	Ross	8:15A	"
			STILL REPORT	80	5		Cam'rm'n			
10 CHILDREN				81	1		Head	Gaudio	7:30A	"
CARUSO, F	H		Prev. Taken **60**	82	1	1'00"	2nd	Guthrie	7:30A	"
CARUSO, A	H		Taken Today **14**	83	1		Jkman	Wimpy	5:00P 9:35P	
SYRACUSE	H		To Date **74**	84	2		" Asst	Kraus	5:00P 9:35P	
EPPOLITS	H			85	3	0'45"	Asst.	F. Gaudio	7:00A 11:00P	
COOPER, L	H			86	1					
DUGAN	H		MINUTES							
DANNY	H						Prop Men	Edwards	7:00A	"
COOPER, C	H		Total Today **4'10"**					Wiley	7:00A	"
WAXMAN	H		Prev. Taken **16'25"**							
FIDONE			Total to Date **20'35"**				Electricians	Riggs	8:15A	"
			OK'd Records to Date					Scheid	7:30A	"
								Brown	8:30A	"
								Weixal	7:30A	"
							Gaffer	Johnson	7:30A	"
							Grip	Harris	7:00A	"
							Stills	Marigold	8:30A 10:30P	
							Wood.			
							Hair	Romaine	7:30A 3:40P	
							Wdrbe	Greenfield	7:30A 11:00P	
							Makeup	Dudley	7:30A	"
							Hair	Falker	6:30P	"
							Cutter	Dawson		
							Music	Carossio		

Script Scenes Taken							
235	180	181	182	183	184	185	
186	187	188	82				

Added Scenes Taken							
157R	157S	157T	157V	157W	157Y	O.K.	
225A	225B	225C	180A	180B	180C	82A	
82B	82C						

REMARKS: **1½ Days behind schedule.**

     Scenes 181 to 188 inclusive omitted.

         2915
         13610

NOTE—Kindly indicate above—When finished with set: WHEN STARTING OR FINISHING WITH ANY ACTOR OR ACTRESS. If any artist delays director starting work or arriving later than time called, state reason, or any mechanical delays.

Daily production report for *Anthony Adverse*

CAMERA CREW ½ HOUR LUNCH	CALLED ON SET 8:30AM
1 HOUR DINNER	LINING UP 7:30AM
	REHEARSING 8:20AM
Marigold, stills, 1 hour lunch	FIRST SHOT 8:35AM
1 hour dinner	LAST SHOT 11:00PM

N69 8:30 - 8:45
1 0'35" NGT
2 0'40" Held
3 0'30" Print

70 8:45 - 9:00
1 0'40" Hold
2 0'40" Print

71 9:00 - 9:15
1 0'20" NGS
2 0'20" Print

72 9:15 - 10:10
1 0'30" NGA
2 0'30" Hold
3 0'30" Print

73 10:10 - 10:20
1 0'50" Hold
2 0'30" NGA
3 0'30" Print

74 10:20 - 10:50
1 0'20" NGA
2 0'20" NGA
3 0'20" NGT
4 0'20" NGT
5 0'20" Hold
6 0'20" NGA
7 0'20" NGA
8 0'30" Print

Costume Change Year 1796

75 10:50 - 11:40
1 0'50" Hold
2 0'50" Print

76 11:40 - 12:10PM
1 0'35" Print
2 0'40" Held

77 12:10 - 12:30
1 0'35" Hold
2 0'30" Print

78 12:30 - 12:45
1 0'20" NGS
2 0'40" Print

LUNCH 12:45 - 1:45

N79 1:45 - 2:50
1 1'00" Print
2 1'00" Hold

80 2:50 - 3:20
1 0'50" Hold
2 0'20" NGC
3 0'45" NGT
4 0'20" NGA
5 0'50" Print

81 3:20 - 3:40
1 0'35" Print

Lining up nite shots
Call back crew
5:30PM shooting 6:30PM

Supper 1 hour.

82 6:30 - 7:40
1 1'00" Print

83 7:40 - 7:50
1 1'00" Print

84 7:50 - 9:35
1 1'00" Hold
2 1'00" Print

85 9:35 - 10:50
1 0'50" NGA
2 0'45" Hold
3 0 Print

86 10:50 - 11:00
1 0'40" Print.

familiarity with the Warner Brothers production files is that the executives – Zanuck, Wallis, Blanke and the others – were closely and committedly concerned with the artistic values of the films on which they worked. To see them as merely money men whose only interest was that a certain number of feet of film should be produced for as few dollars and sold for as many dollars as possible is not only insulting to the executives involved; it is a serious misrepresentation of the methods of production of a major art form. The fact that that system was organised along lines which more closely resemble a factory than the traditional artist's garret should not blind us to the nature of the work involved.

How this system worked in detail will be examined in the case history of the production of *Anthony Adverse* which constitutes the next chapter. What its implications were in terms of Hollywood in the 1930s and the ideological impact of film on American life during that decade will be the focus of subsequent chapters. All that remains by way of introduction is to reiterate one point. The kinds of films which were made by Warners (and other studios) during the 1930s were strongly influenced by the economic and organisational system under which they were produced. The classic Hollywood style, with its insistence on the unproblematic, seamless narrative whose advancement is controlled by the destiny of one or more individual characters, was determined by the economics of the production system. The need to mass-produce art necessitated a certain approach to storytelling. Studio practice required an economy of production method which in turn created an economy of narrative method. The studio system dictated, by its structure and its gradually established orthodoxies, the making of a particular kind of movie. Formula it may have been, but it is a formula which is now clearly established as the standard approach to movie-making, and it continues to exert its influence on any number of independent film-makers working under very different circumstances from those which produced the formula. It is, simply, the archetypal form of cinema, the model for most films that have come after it, in the same way that Dickens is still to a large extent the model for the socially realistic novel. Hollywood movies are, with due allowance for variation and reaction, still what we understand by 'movies'. And Hollywood movies are a product of the Hollywood studio system.

3 Anthony Adverse: A Casebook

I have chosen *Anthony Adverse* as an example of Warners' production methods partly because it comes in the middle of the period covered by this book, and partly because it marked a turning point in the studio's production programme. Partly, also, I have chosen it because it is well documented. It was the studio's biggest production of 1936. It had a running time of 136 minutes (very few of Warners' films from the 1930s ran for two hours, let alone longer) and was based on a 1,200-page best-seller by Hervey Allen.[1] It tells the story of a foundling child in late eighteenth-century Europe who rises to a position of prominence in the Leghorn business of his adoptive father, John Bonnyfeather, but is constantly thwarted by the wicked manoeuvres of Don Luis, the cuckolded husband of his natural mother (who dies in childbirth), and by Faith, Bonnyfeather's scheming housekeeper, later Don Luis' mistress, who is eager that none of the money she stands to inherit should fall into Anthony's hands. Anthony's adventures and misfortunes take him to Cuba and Africa (where he becomes involved in the slave trade), and finally to Napoleonic Paris, where he discovers that his childhood sweetheart, who had borne his son but whom he had lost through bad luck and misunderstanding, is now the Emperor's mistress. Anthony and his son set sail for the New World.

Anthony Adverse was made for the fairly large budget of $1,050,500, with a shooting schedule of 60 days (i.e. ten weeks), about double the average. The subject was something new for Warner Brothers, the kind of costume epic with which the studio had not previously been associated. The only real forerunners were the previous year's extravagant prestige production *A Midsummer Night's Dream* (which had cost some $300,000 more), and two epic tales, *The World Changes* in 1933 and *Oil for the Lamps of China* in 1934. But *A Midsummer Night's Dream* had been very much a special subject, the two epics had not been costume dramas, and none of the three had been outstandingly successful at the box office.[2] It is tempting, therefore, to wonder whether the success of *Anthony Adverse* may not have set Warners on a course of large-scale costume pictures which would continue through to the end of the decade and include *The Charge of the Light Brigade* (1936), *The Prince and the Pauper* (1937), *The Adventures of Robin Hood* (1938), *The Private Lives of Elizabeth and Essex* (1939) and *The Sea Hawk* (1940) – all of them starring Errol Flynn (who would undoubtedly have played Anthony if the film had been made a year later), and all but one of them starring Olivia De Havilland, the discovery of *A Midsummer Night's Dream* and an actress whom Hal Wallis seems initially to have had difficulty envisaging in anything other than period costume.[3]

Anthony Adverse opened at the Carthay Circle Theatre in Los Angeles on 29 July 1936 and ran there for just under eight weeks, an unusually long run for the middle of the decade, when roadshow audiences seem to have dwindled and weekly changeovers of double bills were becoming the rule. Its East Coast premiere was just over a month later, on Wednesday 26 August, at Warners' New York showcase, the Strand Theatre on Broadway; it ran there for 31 consecutive days, the year's longest run at the theatre. The film was also successful enough to be returned to the company's main Los Angeles theatres, the Warners Hollywood and the Warners Downtown, for a two-week run starting on Thanksgiving Day 1936 – an opening date traditionally reserved for sure-fire entertainment pictures. In terms of first runs in New York and Los Angeles, *Anthony Adverse* was by far the most successful Warners feature of the year, notching up a two-city total of 100 playing days, more than double that of its nearest rival, the comedy *Three Men on a Horse*.[4] It received seven Academy Award nominations and came away with five Oscars: Best Supporting Actress (Gale Sondergaard), Best Cinematography, Best Film Editing, Best Score and Best Assistant Director.[5] It came eighth in the *Film Daily* Critics' Poll, with 231 votes from 523 voting critics. As usual, MGM dominated the Poll, with 1st, 3rd, 4th and 7th places; but 1936 was an exceptionally good year for Warner Brothers, with four films in the Top Ten. *Anthony Adverse* also featured in the National Board of Review top tens for 'Popular Appeal' and 'Young Reviewers' choices', though it did not feature in the 'Exceptional Photoplays' category.[6]

All in all, then, *Anthony Adverse* was a big-budget picture and a success in both box office and critical terms. It may not be a film which has weathered well – it frequently appears turgid, with rather too many moments of unintentional humour – but its production does provide an excellent example of the studio system in operation at Warners in the middle of the decade. In the following casebook of its production, I have divided the process into its three most clearly defined phases: pre-production, production and post-production. Pre-production covers the period from when Warners acquired the rights to the novel (September 1933) until shooting began in November 1935. Production – shooting – was between 6 November 1935 and 31 January 1936. Post-production continued from then until the preview at the Warner

30

Theatre in Hollywood on 8 May 1936, after which no major changes appear to have been made. In each phase, rather than stick to an absolute chronology, I have organised the stages of work into headings which, although they may overlap, give a clearer idea of how the production system operated. Rather than attempt to construct a narrative round the process, I have simply noted the dates of significant meetings, decisions or contracts, and introduced comments and conclusions where they seem appropriate. The information contained in the following pages is based on material in the Warners Archive at the University of Southern California which, although extremely detailed, is not always complete. Some of the following casebook, therefore, involves conjecture. The cast and crew of *Anthony Adverse* may be found in the Filmography. A number of other names recur in the following pages. They are: Hal B. Wallis, Production Chief at the studio; Maxwell Arnow, head of the studio Casting Department; Bill Koenig, Studio Manager; R. J. Obringer, Head of the West Coast Legal Department; T.C. ('Tenny') Wright, Studio Production Manager.

PRE-PRODUCTION

1. Story

9 September 1933: Warners acquire the rights to Allen's novel for $40,000. The contract gives them the right to include up to eight musical compositions and songs in the final screenplay (in the wake of *42nd Street* and *Gold Diggers of 1933* earlier that year, was Warners perhaps contemplating making *Anthony Adverse* as a musical?). Warners' rights extended only to that portion of the novel used in the screenplay, and expired if the film was not made within three years. The finished film was to be at least 5,000 feet (approximately 55 minutes) in length.

20 September 1933: Cable to Wallis from Pandro Berman at RKO: 'Would you be interested in selling Anthony Adverse or do you plan to produce it yourself?'

21 December 1933: Memo from Wallis to Brown Holmes, co-author of the screenplay of *I Am a Fugitive from a Chain Gang*: 'Will you please, immediately, read ANTHONY ADVERSE and begin preparing this.'

17 January 1934: The story department returns an unsolicited scenario to an agent on the grounds that it is 'nothing more than a lengthy synopsis of the novel; one of the most interesting episodes was omitted, probably for reasons of brevity'. Warners' plans for *Anthony Adverse* are obviously widely known (studio files contain other letters with advice and comments on script, casting, etc. from readers of the novel).

February 1934: Correspondence, letters and cables between Wallis and Paul Green, writer of such earlier Warners pictures as *Cabin in the Cotton* and *Voltaire*. Green assures Wallis he can 'write a good picture out of this for you'. Wallis asks him to come out to California from North Carolina. Green is unable to come immediately and suggests another writer start work on the project. Wallis cables back: 'NATURALLY ANXIOUS START ANTHONY ADVERSE IMMEDIATELY AND WILL PROBABLY GIVE THIS TO OTHER WRITER BEGIN BLOCKING OUT'.

16 March 1934: Memo to Wallis from writer Edward Chodorov commenting on a proposal sent in by playwright Owen Davis that Don Luis, not Anthony, should be the focus of the screenplay: 'A very interesting suggestion, except that it doesn't mean anything!'

2 April 1934: First memo to Wallis from Sheridan Gibney, indicating that he had started work on the screenplay. Previous writing credits include *I Am a Fugitive from a Chain Gang* (first draft, but no final credit), *The World Changes*, *The House on 56th Street* and *The Story of Louis Pasteur* (for which, with co-writer Pierre Collings, he got an Oscar); clearly, therefore, a top studio writer accustomed to 'large' subjects and complicated structures. Gibney writes that he has been told by a friend that the Hays Office will not allow slave-trading scenes on the screen. 'Two facts may help us, however: first, the slave traffic as shown is purely historical and has no relation to modern times; second, in treating these scenes, slave-trading will be consistently condemned and its demoralising influence upon those who engage in it will be fully shown. . . notably in the case of Anthony himself.' Wallis replies: 'I wouldn't worry too much about the slave trading episodes in ANTHONY ADVERSE, principally because it is historical, going back to 1797. I am sure we won't have any trouble on this score.'

30 July 1934: First draft of the screenplay completed and sent to Koenig by Wallis with a memo that it is 'absolutely confidential' and not to be sent out to department heads or anyone else. At this stage, Gibney seems to have suspended work on the screenplay for two or three months.

26 October 1934: Gibney cables Chodorov from New York that he is having trouble with the opening sequence.

7 November 1934: Memo from Chodorov to Wallis expressing surprise that Gibney should want eight days' salary for his extra work on the screenplay.

19 November 1934: Wallis to Obringer. Settle with Gibney: $1,000 for the extra work done. Gibney seems to have completed the major part of the screenplay between late March and late July 1934, and then to have been called back to write an additional opening sequence in October 1934. Although there are no records of it in the studio files, it seems almost certain that Gibney did some rewriting between October 1934 and April 1935.

17 April 1935: Wallis from Koenig, expressing concern that writers' salaries now total $17,000 for the picture. Wallis replies that this is 'not too much considering the Herculean task it is to adapt an immense 1,200 page novel of this nature'.

11 April 1935: Letter to Jack Warner from Jacob Wilk of the New York office stressing the need to 'get busy with the ANTHONY ADVERSE matter', otherwise the rights will expire. He suggests that Gibney should meet the novelist. (This had been suggested to Wilk earlier by Allen's publishers, Farrar and Rinehart, but Wallis had rejected the meeting as 'a little premature'. On the face of it, this seems strange, since a draft was already complete and it would seem to have made sense that writer and novelist discuss a first rather than a later draft. But subsequent exchanges of memos make it likely that there was another reason for the delaying tactics: Warners had no one to play Anthony and was therefore not keen to press ahead with production plans.)

16 April 1935:Wallis informs Koenig that Gibney is being sent East to meet Wilk and Allen 'at the end of this week'. Gibney is instructed to meet Wilk in Wilmington on 23 April, but this is subsequently amended to a suggestion that he first meet Allen's publisher, Farrar, in New York.

19 April 1935: Wallis reassures Jack Warner that they can complete the movie within the period laid down in the contract. But he suggests that, 'given our present casting difficulties', it might be wise for Wilk to attempt to arrange a year's extension.

26 April 1935: Airmail letter from Wilk to Jack Warner reporting enthusiastically on the meeting between Gibney and Allen which had taken place in the latter's home in Talbot, Maryland the previous day. 'Gibney's visit to Allen was a very wise move, and much good will come of it ... In a frank way, we have now secured Hervey Allen's complete co-operation with us in the preparation of the script.'

3 May 1935: Hervey Allen also makes a point of writing to Warner about the meeting: 'I wish to say that meeting Mr Gibney, going over the script in great detail and discussing it with him from every angle, firmly convinced me that Mr Gibney is peculiarly fitted to handle such a book as "Anthony Adverse" in preparing it for the screen. He has a thorough grasp, not only of the technical twists which are so essential, but from the author's standpoint I feel that he has really got the spirit of the novel and sees how it can and should be conveyed by the film ... I felt that you at least would not be indifferent to having me tell you that Mr Gibney's hard and excellent work has aroused my confidence in every way.'

29 April 1935: Gibney's account of the meeting, in a studio memo to Wallis, is far more businesslike. His introduction confirms Wilk's assessment of the meeting: 'Mr Allen feels that the structural development of the script is right as it is; consequently, he does not want us to use his suggestions if they are going to necessitate any important changes in the present set-up.' He then goes on to outline Allen's ten suggestions. Most of them are minor, but three are worth noting. 'Mr Allen,' declares Gibney, 'would like to inject into the script and especially the character of Anthony, something of the mystical element of the novel.' Judging by the final film, Allen's suggestions were incorporated, particularly where they involve the character of Brother François, whom Allen wanted to be - and the film portrays as - 'a more symbolic character, possibly even suggesting the supernatural'. Allen's second suggestion is that they should 'make cuts wherever possible in the African episode'. Allen shows considerable astuteness here: the African episode is a kind of 'season in hell' for Anthony, where his bitterness at the way in which he has been deceived by all and sundry (including, so he believes, his adoptive father) turns him briefly into a positively unpleasant character. It may have had a symbolic function in the novel, but in the film it appears improbable and even distasteful, largely because of an extraordinarily misjudged performance by Steffi Duna as a very Latin-looking half-caste girl who is Anthony's mistress and, by implication, the objective sign of his degradation.

Allen's third point – a proposed minor change in the Cuban episode – is less interesting than Gibney's reaction to it. To follow it, he states, would make Anthony 'again a passive character – the very thing I have tried to avoid in this script ... From the dramatic point of view, this is the chief difficulty with the character as drawn in the novel: events continually force him to act; he, personally, never motivates the plot.'

18 July 1935: First contact with the Hays Office which, in the time since work had begun on *Anthony Adverse*, had drawn up and issued its new Production Code. A temporary copy of the script was sent to Joseph I. Breen. His reaction, in a six-page letter, was strongly negative.

'Frankly,' he wrote, 'the present script suggests to us the kind of story which, if made into a picture, will have to be rejected under the provisions of our Production Code and the Resolution for Uniform Interpretation thereof.' Communications from Breen are expressed in a language all its own. The temptation to ridicule them is strong. But they are not ridiculous: they exerted a strong influence on Hollywood well into the 1950s. They are also, in their way, remarkably perceptive, ferreting out dubious implications in what might seem the most innocent of screenplays. For these reasons, I shall quote at length from the opening page and a half of Breen's letter on the draft script. The italics are Breen's.

34

'In spite of its spirit of romance and adventure, much charm and certain possibilities for spectacular presentation,' Breen declared, 'this story is definitely immoral. As we read it, it is the story of *an illegitimate son* who winds up alone in the new world with *his own illegitimate son*, on the way to America to face a new life. None of the principals – most of whom are immoral characters – with the exception of those who appear least in the story, suffer for their sins. Maria, Anthony's mother, a most sympathetic character whose sin we are tempted to condone, dies in childbirth. Denis, the illegitimate father, is killed by Don Luis, Maria's middle-aged husband. Don Luis, who is painted as a philanderer and an old "rounder" we find, at the end of the story, apparently happy and prosperous, with the housekeeper of Maria's father *as his mistress*. Angela, the mother of *Anthony's illegitimate son*, becomes a favourite of Napoleon. Anthony himself seems to have been regarded in the story as an unfortunate man, despite his illicit sex relationships – with Angela and, later, with the native woman in Africa – and suffers only the loss of Angela for his misdeeds.

'The danger of such a story lies in the fact that an attempt is made to conceal and dissipate its nakedness and rawness by a mass of nationalities and countries – by the quiet appeal of life in a convent – and by the glamour of Napoleonic revelries. We think, too, that all the business of the small statuette of the Madonna is invidious and potentially offensive to intelligent religious people. The idea of the Madonna hovering over a panorama of sin seems to us to be a kind of *pietistic fatalism*. The basic story of this play, in our judgement, is unacceptable despite the fact that the story is based upon a popular novel of wide circulation. It is our notion, however, that in adapting this novel to the screen you have hit upon these "high spots" of the story which have about them the flavour of illicit sex, and chosen to exclude from your screen play much of the book that might be more attractive and, certainly, less likely to give offence.'

The next four and a half pages of Breen's letter contain detailed objections to particular scenes or to single lines of dialogue. The objections concern six main areas: the recurrence of the statue of the Madonna and various other explicit religious images or actions; scenes of brutality; the inclusion of a scene apparently condoning revenge killing in a duel; the slave trade sequence which, Breen implies, should be suggested rather than shown; scenes of nakedness ('You will be careful, likewise, in shooting scenes of the natives not to indicate their *sex*. Keep in mind that, even though they be natives in Africa, they are not to be naked at any time'); and instances of suggestive dialogue and general moral turpitude ('The *details* showing the relationship between Maria and Denis are, in our judgement, very bad. If it be necessary for the proper telling of your story that Maria give birth to an illegitimate child, can it not be indicated that her liaison with Denis occurred *before* her marriage to Don Luis? It seems to us to be thoroughly offensive for screen presentation before mixed audiences for you to indicate a married woman, carrying an illegitimate child, and fondling and making love to another man behind her husband's back.')

In conclusion, Breen refers to a telephone conversation with Wallis and says that he realises the studio has paid a great deal of money for the rights and that the novel had had 'wide appeal'. All the same, the screenplay as it stood was 'totally unacceptable' under the provisions of the Production Code.

9 August 1935: Despite Breen's apparently insurmountable objections, Wallis does not appear to have been too concerned, since he sends Arnow a memo telling him to get hold of a copy of the script and be ready to discuss casting the following week.

7 September 1935: A revised temporary script is sent to Breen, who considers it a 'vast improvement' over the previous one. 'The basic story seems now to be acceptable under the provisions of the Production Code.' Since the basic story has not changed and since many of Breen's objections over the next three pages of his letter concern essentially the same points as before (with the exception of the religious material), it seems more than likely that some amount of behind-the-scenes discussion had taken place. A closer reading of Breen's letter of 18 July suggests that he expected this: although his objections to the basic story are very strongly worded – so strongly, in fact, that one might assume he believed the story could never be made into an acceptable film – the letter as a whole is based on the clear assumption that the film will be made (viz. phrases like 'You will be careful, likewise, in shooting scenes of the natives ...'). Breen's final approval would, as always, be dependent on his seeing the completed film. But his letter about the revised temporary script is a tacit go-ahead for *Anthony Adverse*, and his objections are now to details rather than to matters of substance, e.g. 'Page 44 Scene 117: You understand, of course, that the "low-bosomed gown" of Mrs Udney should cover her breasts entirely, and that these should not be emphasised'.

Further correspondence between Breen and Warners on detailed revisions and cuts is dated 14, 20 and 21 November 1935, and 20 January 1936. Some of this concerns proposals for 'protection shots' in case the scripted shots prove unacceptable.

September 1935: Detailed preparations for the production continue. A temporary schedule is issued on 25 September (see the section on 'Scheduling' below).

24 October 1935: A copy of the script is sent to Fredric March at the Waldorf Astoria for him to read on his train journey West.

6 November 1935: Shooting begins. Script revisions are clearly still being made by Gibney since Wallis sends a memo to Blanke instructing him not to issue 'blue pages' (final shooting script) on 'a picture of this importance' without checking with him first.

7 November 1935: Memo from Gibney to Wallis to the effect that he has submitted the second half of the final draft to Blanke, 'greatly improved … thanks to your suggestions'. Gibney asks permission to leave Hollywood at the weekend.

December 1935: Milton Krims, whose first screen credit for Warners will be the following year on *Green Light*, is brought in to do day-to-day rewrites. Wallis appears concerned that the rewrites may end up being substantial enough for Krims to be entitled to screen credit, and instructs him to do no more work without express permission. Krims responds by asking Wallis' permission to complete the rewrites agreed on with Henry Blanke and LeRoy.

15 January 1936: Blanke to Wallis: Krims is requesting screen credit.

30 January 1936: Wallis to Blanke: 'Under no circumstances do I want this matter [Krims' credit] taken up with the Screen Writers' Guild.'

11 February 1936: Academy Code of Practice signed – the equivalent to registering the film's credits – allocating sole writing credit on *Anthony Adverse* to Sheridan Gibney.

18 February 1936: Wallis to Blanke: be sure that Gibney sees the first rough cut and get him to write the intertitles so that they can be cut in in time for showing to the Sales Manager the following Monday.

3 March 1936: Picture run for Warner and Breen. Breen is sufficiently uncertain about the film to see it a second time, after which his conclusion is clear: 'I regret to advise you that it is the unanimous opinion of our staff that the picture, *in its present form*, is definitely in violation of our Production Code.' The objections now concern four main areas:

'1. Unnecessary details which emphasise the illicit sexual relationship between Denis and Maria;
'2. Too much emphasis on Don Luis' "delayed honeymoon";
'3. The definite and specific indication of an illicit sex relationship between Anthony and Neleta; and
'4. Too much emphasis upon the suggestion that Angela is the mistress of Napoleon.'

The next four pages of Breen's letter go on to demand twenty-one detailed cuts, or else the substitution of the protection shots discussed

37

in previous letters. The cuts range from small excisions ('Delete shot of Angela in Signora Bovina's house where her breasts are partly exposed') to fairly major changes. The two chief areas remain, of course, the affair between Maria and Denis, and the relationship between Anthony and Neleta. The former objection is a fairly straightforward question of illicit sex: 'It is our purpose to delete from your picture the too definite suggestion in Reel 1 that Denis and Maria are *actually indulging in a sex affair* while the camera is panning around the tree tops. We also think the line: "I'm yours – all yours" over-accentuates the point you wish to make.' The latter objection involves a section of the Production Code which is somewhat less savoury. 'It goes without saying that no censor board in the United States, at least, will allow any such suggestions of miscegenation. Further: any such suggestion in your picture is certain to result in running into enormous difficulty throughout the South.'

22 May 1936: Breen has seen a revised version of the film and now finds 'little, if anything, that is reasonably censorable'.

29 July 1939: Public premiere of *Anthony Adverse* in Los Angeles and certain mid-Western cities.

The scripting of *Anthony Adverse* is a fairly typical example of how Warners elaborated a screenplay for a major feature during the 1930s. A number of contract writers worked on the preparatory stages, blocking out a structure and pinpointing certain key scenes before a single writer (or occasionally two writers) was allocated full-time. Even while Gibney was working on the screenplay, it looks from some of the memos as though Edward Chodorov remained involved in the project in a kind of supervisory role on behalf of the story department. It is also clear that Hal Wallis retained final control over every stage of the scripting process, from initial structure through to final adjustments and rewrites. As in other areas of production, nothing happened without Wallis knowing and approving. The rare instances in other areas of the production where things were done without his knowledge are, as we shall see, signalled by a curtly disapproving memo.

Only two things are unusual about the preparation of the screenplay for *Anthony Adverse*: that it took so long; and the extent of the problems with the Hays Office. The first can be accounted for by both the size of the undertaking and the casting problems discussed in the next section. The second has to do with the relative newness of the Production Code: it had been in effect for less than a year and no one was sure exactly how it would work in a given instance. *Anthony Adverse* was clearly something of a test case for both Breen and Warners. Most of the problems faced by Gibney and by the studio in general as far as the screenplay was concerned arose out of the need to placate two opposing viewpoints: on the one hand, that of Hervey Allen and his readers; and on the other hand, that of Joseph Breen in his role as guardian of Hollywood's moral public image. It is fairly clear from the memos that Warners took both responsibilities seriously. It was important to them to do justice to Allen's novel – why else spend all that money acquiring it? – and not to produce the kind of trivialised hack script that the fulsome enthusiasm of Hervey Allen's letter to Jack Warner rather suggests he may have expected. Nor, I think, is this concern solely the result of *Anthony Adverse* being a prestige production. Wallis brought the same attention – the same notion of what, if the idea of industrial production is carried through, might be referred to as 'quality control' – to all the films whose production files I have been able to check. And the negotiations with Breen make it abundantly clear that the Production Code was not a form of externally imposed censorship but a protective operation self-administered by Hollywood: it was, after all, important that the finished film should be marketable throughout the United States, including the South. However absolute they may sound, Breen's statements are in fact the basis for negotiation. Hollywood's production machinery was designed to make this sort of adjustment, and to combine the best possible film with the best possible commercial possibilities.

One final point about the script memos: Gibney's determination in adapting the novel was to make Anthony 'motivate' the plot. *Anthony Adverse* is a modern picaresque novel, a popularised version of the initiatory voyage of the eighteenth-century innocent through the real world of passions, intrigue or cruelty – like *Candide*, perhaps, or *Joseph Andrews*, whose title Allen's novel perhaps intentionally recalls. As such, it jars with the instincts of a Hollywood-trained screenwriter like Gibney, for whom the hero is the initiator, not the initiated: he must control, determine – 'motivate' – the plot, rather than be simply swept along by it. It is interesting to compare Gibney's script for *Anthony Adverse* with his earlier screenplay for *The World Changes* where he was likewise faced with an epic saga, in this case concerned with the history of the United States between 1856 and 1929. *The World Changes* focuses very definitely on one character, Orin Nordholm Jr, who becomes the channel through which such experiences can be understood and assimilated, while at the same time remaining the master of his own destiny.[7] Such a procedure is far more difficult to apply to *Anthony Adverse*, where the central character is almost by definition a largely passive victim of the plottings of others. Gibney tries hard to make him active, but is not entirely successful, at any rate for Frank S. Nugent of the *New York Times*, who found the film 'aimless'. But it is clear that Gibney felt that the personalisation of the narrative – the creation of a clearly identified 'hero' – was an essential part of his job. A Hollywood picture required a hero.

2. Casting

Warner Brothers' main problem with *Anthony Adverse* was that they had no contract star suitable for the title role. James Cagney was clearly out of the question, and Edward G. Robinson was not physically suited to the role of Anthony. Paul Muni had just completed *The Story of Louis Pasteur* and did not regard the part as worthy of him. By late 1935 Errol Flynn was still an unknown quantity, since *Captain Blood* was not released until after shooting had begun on *Anthony Adverse*. This meant that a star would have to be borrowed from another studio. The first possibility was Leslie Howard, but this never became a serious prospect. Readers of the novel put forward other suggestions, such as John Barrymore or Lew Ayres. In the end, Fredric March was borrowed from Fox in exchange for Warners' top juvenile star, Dick Powell, who was to appear in Fox's *Thanks a Million*. The terms were the standard ones for a loan agreement: March was to get top billing, with his name appearing in letters at least half as large as those used for the picture's title; he was to be available to Warners for eight weeks from 1 October (this was later amended to 31 October, and the period extended to 8 January, with Warners paying March a weekly pro rata of his annual Fox salary). The casting of March was unpopular with at least one of the novel's readers, Carolyn Knowles of San Diego, who wrote to Mervyn LeRoy that March was 'too old, too short, too lacking in charm, too American'. There is no record of LeRoy's response.

Once the title role was cast, the rest of the casting procedure for *Anthony Adverse* could go ahead.

19 August 1935: A memo from Wallis to Koenig: 'This morning we had a tentative cast conference ... and we have listed about twenty people whom we want to test for various parts.' The tests were to start later that week, on 21 or 22 August.

22 August 1935: Koenig informs Wallis that tests cannot start until 3 September because make-up man Perc Westmore is too busy. Wallis responds that the picture is too important to delay, and that another make-up man should be hired. This does not seem to have happened and the tests appear to have been postponed.

24 August 1935: Wallis to Warner, asking him to call Mayer and see if he can get Freddie Bartholomew for the role of Anthony as a boy. 'He is absolutely essential to the story and will help our picture as much as he did *David Copperfield* – and he was about eighty per cent of that picture.' Mayer seems to have said no.

27 August 1935: Wallis tells Arnow to find out who played the little boy in *Dark Angel*,[8] but not to make the enquiry directly through Goldwyn.

10 September 1935: First tests run for Wallis and LeRoy.

26 September 1935: Wallis instructs Arnow to test Mary Nash for the role of Faith, and to let him see some film of Kitty Carlisle.

27 September 1935: Wallis advises Arnow and LeRoy to test Basil Rathbone for the role of Don Luis. 'While he isn't exactly the physical type, at the same time when you put a little goatee on him and age him a little bit, he can give you a hell of a performance.'

3 October 1935: Wallis cables Irving Asher at First National in London: 'WE STUCK FOR CHARACTER DON LUIS ANTHONY ADVERSE KNOW YOUR OPINION GIELGUD BUT PLEASE MAKE TEST THIS CHARACTER RUSH ALSO TEST GEORGE ROBEY SAME PART ADVISE REGARDS'

9 October 1935: Memo to Koenig from Wallis: has he arranged to test Bette Davis for Faith? 'Also, did you get it understood with her that when she gets a call it means she is to come in?' The studio's problems with Davis (and vice versa) are legendary; clearly, however, they started earlier than is generally believed.

10 October 1935: Blanke, Arnow and LeRoy told by Wallis to see *Bitter Sweet* at the Shrine Auditorium for cast possibilities.

22 October 1935: Wallis goes on record to Koenig admitting they are having great difficulty in casting Bonnyfeather, Don Luis 'and a couple of other important parts' (Faith, Denis and Anthony as a boy). This, he says, is not for want of effort, but because all the other studios are involved in big pictures.

23 October 1935: Memo to Arnow from Wallis about the need to discuss Claude Rains for Don Luis, since Edward G. Robinson has turned down the part.

26 October 1935: Edmund Gwenn is borrowed from MGM for Bonnyfeather on a four-and-three basis (four weeks, with the option of a further three) at his regular MGM salary of $1,250 per week. The main problem, according to Arnow, is billing, since MGM want 'very big billing in view of the fact that he was starred in a picture by them'. Warners want to give him fourth male billing, with the possibility of billing two women above him. MGM wants him third overall and ahead of Rains. The following day Wallis tells Obringer to be sure they can have Gwenn until the picture is finished. The final contract from MGM stipulates that they are to receive $4,500, plus $1,500 a week for Gwenn, with a minimum guarantee of four weeks. Billing problems are ironed out by a compromise. Gwenn gets joint second male billing (third overall) with Rains on printed publicity, but is billed fifth, below Donald Woods and Anita Louise, but above Rains, on the actual print.

5 November 1935 (the day before shooting starts): Wallis cables Asher in London to test Basil Sydney for Napoleon. 'ALSO ADVISE WHETHER HE WOULD ACCEPT A TWO WEEK GUARANTEE AND LOWEST SALARY'

20 November 1935: Despite the fact that shooting is now in its third week, the casting of various key minor roles is, very untypically for Warners, still not complete. John Carradine, originally cast as Ferdinando, has had to be replaced because of a 'prior lengthy engagement at another studio'. LeRoy wants Paul Sotoff (who ended with the part) but Wallis would prefer J. Carroll Naish (who finally played the part of Major Doumet). The concluding sentence of Wallis' memo to Arnow gives some idea of the nature of the problems faced by Warners in casting *Anthony Adverse*: 'As you know, on account of the peculiar nature of the schedule on a picture of this nature, I have been endeavouring to make deals in order to save money and, at the same time, get good actors.'

23 November 1935: Wallis putting pressure on LeRoy to recast some of the minor parts. They need a better actor than André Cheron for the small part of the coachman, and the 'Carlson boy' is not suitable for young Anthony. 'Make another attempt to get Freddie Bartholomew. Gene Reynolds will not do. Neither will the other boy with two teeth.'

26 November 1935: More tests.

27 November 1935: Akim Tamiroff borrowed from Paramount for the role of Carlo Cibo. Memo to LeRoy from Wallis that he has just seen a test done in New York of 'a boy named Billy Mauch' (one of the Mauch Twins who briefly became Warners' leading child actors). They would have to act quickly as MGM was also after him. Arnow is instructed to wire New York that they should hold on to Mauch.

9 January 1936: With shooting three-quarters complete, the last major casting deal is made: Louis Hayward is borrowed from MGM for the role of Denis Moore. The failure to find an actor for the part had led to the entire shooting schedule being reorganised so that the Maria-Denis sequences could be shot last. Hayward would need to wear elevator shoes to make him two inches taller.

Apart from the difficulty of finding an Anthony, the major problem facing Warners in casting *Anthony Adverse* was the episodic nature of the screenplay. There is a much higher than average number of secondary roles, since each episode of Anthony's life brings him into contact with a number of people who, briefly, play an important part in the story. Not only did this mean that the parts required good actors: it also made scheduling extremely difficult (see following section, memo of 7 November 1935). Actors might only be required for two or three days' work, which ran counter to two established Hollywood practices: firstly,

Anthony Adverse: Fredric March as Anthony, with Edmund Gwenn

contracts of actors of sufficient stature to play the parts generally carried four-week guarantees; and secondly, it was virtually impossible to be sure within two or three days what the exact schedule on a picture of this scale would be. Once again, as with the screenplay, Wallis had to balance in a very specific way the demands of quality against the demands of studio economy. Casting was not usually this much of a problem at Warners: the stock company of stars and supporting actors were used with greater consistency, inventiveness and, some might say, ruthlessness than was normal at other studios. But in *Anthony Adverse*, five of the top eight roles were taken by non-contract players. The combined processes of story development and casting made the film's pre-production period a particularly difficult one for Warners, and it was thus important that the scheduling should be as tightly controlled as possible.

3. Scheduling

The schedule and a rigid adherence to it were the cornerstone of the studio system. Going over schedule not only cost money, it set a bad precedent. Wallis, Blanke, Wright and Al Alborn therefore kept an iron grip on it. This does not mean, however, that the schedule is to be seen in an entirely negative light – as the oppression of the artist by the

43

administrator. It was also the structure within which the film, as discussed and planned, was to be made, and made to the highest possible standard.

10 August 1935: Memo from Wallis to Koenig: 'Beginning immediately, we want to start active preparation on ANTHONY ADVERSE. The starting date is October 10th.' This memo is the nearest possible indication of the date by which the screenplay was completed.

20 August 1935: A rough set list is drawn up: 42 exteriors, 39 interiors.

29 August 1935: Wallis asks Koenig to check whether March can postpone the agreed starting date. Obringer replies that LeRoy has talked to March and arranged to move the starting date back to 1 November. Until that time, March would be on vacation in Europe.

25 September 1935: A temporary schedule is drawn up, allowing for 25 days shooting between Monday 4 November and Monday 2 December. Koenig issues a memo to all department heads which, although it does little more than outline standard studio practice, does so with such force that it is worth quoting at some length. Referring to a meeting earlier that day in Wallis' office, Koenig officially announces the start of work on *Anthony Adverse*:

> Everything pertaining to sets, props and wardrobe must be completed one week in advance of the time the company goes into the set. All props must be ready and okayed by the director one week in advance. All of you people will have approximately four weeks time to do this. Am giving you this advance information *now*, so there will be no alibis later.
>
> Am also going to provide the necessary stage space, and we can start erecting the sets next week. As soon as the first set is ready you can immediately start to dress same. This will give you plenty of time to have the sets built, dressed and okayed by Mr LeRoy before he starts shooting in them.
>
> Tests are being made of the players and the parts will be cast this week. As soon as a person is definitely cast for the picture, want you to immediately start work on his wardrobe. Want the wardrobe all set way in advance of the picture's starting date. If we start now, we will have plenty of time to complete the wardrobe and make any changes that may be necessary before the wardrobe works on the set. We are *not* going to be delayed on the picture because of wardrobe.
>
> Want all wigs, costumes, etc. tested before we go into a set. Want you to understand right now that we will not tolerate any delays caused by your departments not being prepared in time, nor will we accept any alibis or excuses from you as to why you were not ready.

If every one of you will follow out the instructions herein enclosed, there will be no reason for delays. Each department head is going to be held personally responsible for any delays caused by his department.

Am going into great detail in giving you this information because this is one of the biggest pictures we have ever attempted, and there is more detail to same than in any other picture we have made. We do not want you to come to us when it is too late and say there is something you do not understand. Therefore, am giving you all the necessary information in writing; the date we start, the date the sets will be used, and everything that will be necessary to work in the sets. The script you now have is practically final and you can follow it to the letter.

The schoolmasterly tone of Koenig's memo is unusual: I have not come across another one quite like it in the Warners' Archive. Yet he is not saying anything that the department heads would not already have known. He is merely making it plain that there is no room for hitches. The reason is obvious enough: *Anthony Adverse* was, as Koenig says, outside the normal run of Warners pictures and the studio was beginning to get panicky about it by late September 1935. Panic forced it back to a restatement of basic operational principles.

28 September 1935: A studio production number is assigned to *Anthony Adverse*: 958. Every production had a number, and its allocation was traditionally the moment at which the production became definite.

3 October 1935: A meeting between Wallis, Koenig and the department heads to discuss models and plans.

11 October 1935: Wallis informs Koenig of a major change in the schedule: the Maria-Denis scenes would be left until last, and the picture would start with Anthony grown up (because Denis was not yet cast and because March was due to start on 1 November).

19 October 1935: Wright from Wallis: 'We will definitely start shooting on Monday 4 November. There will be no further postponements.'

Late October/early November 1935: A series of detailed memos from Wallis to various members of the production staff, comprising the basic mechanics of the studio system and the bread-and-butter side of Wallis' job as executive in charge of production:

— to Koenig, 18 October: Why not use the same sort of miniatures that Jackman made for the Port Royal set in *Captain Blood*? The same one, plus a few boats, might do for the major Leghorn set. 'We could undoubtedly use the same set and save a fortune.'

45

— to Koenig, 18 October: Get Carossio to work immediately on the music for the opera sequences. Was he going to use 'some of the old operas' or would they have to write music?

— to Koenig, 24 October: Querying Anton Grot's budget on a number of the sets that would only appear in 50-100 feet of film. 'It seems unnecessary to go into the tremendous amount of detail that we usually do.'

— to Blanke, 24 October: Check on some of the stock shots of the theatre used in Columbia's *Love Me Forever* for the opera sequences.

— to LeRoy, 4 November: The Anita Louise and Gale Sondergaard costumes need to be toned down. A virtual duplicate to Milo Anderson.

— to Blanke, 5 November: A detailed request for a number of cuts in miniatures, sets and costumes. 'I see no reason for sitting in meetings for two or three hours and then have the Art department come in with budgets of this kind in spite of our talk.'

— to Fred Jackman, 6 November: After seeing his Rin Tin Tin shots.[9] 'I'm sure you can do ANTHONY ADVERSE 100% better.'

— to Wright, 7 November: Querying the half-day locations in the schedule. 'We want the picture scheduled the most economical way, so far as the company is concerned, and we are not going to worry about shooting in continuity.'

5 November 1935: Official cast and crew list issued.

15 November 1935: The working budget is finalised. Adjustments will be made later, notably because of the need to extend March's contract and because the film went slightly over schedule.

1.	Story	$40,000
	Gibney	24,667
	Added dialogue	2,060
	Other	1,507
2.	Director*	45,933
	Supervisor*	3,000
3.	Assistant directors*	10,651
4.	Camera: Gaudio 13 weeks @ $425*	5,525
	Other*	6,962
5.	Cast: March	12,480
	De Havilland*	2,375
	Louise*	4,000
	O'Neill*	2,570
	Woods*	3,500
	Crehan*	315

	Alberni*	5,000
	'Denis'	2,000
	'Lucia'	1,500
	Rains	16,000
	Sondergaard	6,825
	Gwenn	10,625
	Other	39,767
	Talent on day check	13,480
6.	Extras	42,473
7.	Musicians/Song releases	39,000
8.	Props labour	10,102
9.	Set Construction	145,300
10.	Stand-by labour	20,000
11.	Electricians	18,890
12.	Striking	15,000
13.	Make-up	13,715
14.	Art department salaries*	25,000
15.	Cutters' salaries*	6,000
16.	Prop Rental and Expenses	24,485
17.	Electrical Rental and Expenses	10,000
18.	Location Expense	10,107
19.	Tricks, miniatures, etc.	16,535
20.	Wardrobe	47,000
21.	Negative film	16,000
22.	Developing and printing	20,000
23.	Other	30,380
	DIRECT COST	770,729
	Studio Overhead: 31%	248,942
	Depreciation: 4%	30,829
	TOTAL	1,050,500

(*indicates portions of studio contract salaries carried in the *Anthony Adverse* budget).

The budget also contains a breakdown of set costs, indicating their overall cost (i.e. not simply that of construction). Those that come to over $5,000 are:

Interior Maria's bedroom: $11,079
Interior lower floor Casa Bonnyfeather: $16,461
Interior Opera House Leghorn: $9,269
Interior Paris ballroom: $18,004, including $5,500 for
    extras
Interior Opera House promenade: $13,070, including $7,000 for
    extras

Exterior Anthony's home Gallegos: $11,521, including $3,870 for extras

Exterior jungle: $10,564

Exterior road Alps: $8,819, including $2,177 for location expenses

Exterior French chateau: $8,249, including $1,469 for location expenses

Exterior old mill and forest clearing: $5,323

Exterior convent courtyard: $6,629, including $3,545 for location expenses

Exterior Casa Bonnyfeather and street: $44,032

Exterior Bonnyfeather courtyard: $6,375

Carriages crashing in the Alps: $5,350, all for trick work.

18 November 1935: Even after shooting has started, Wallis is still keeping a close watch on cost. Memo to Blanke and LeRoy about the exaggerated costumes for the Napoleon tests: 'Let's not go daffy on these costumes.'

23 November 1935: Wallis to Blanke and Wright: The schedule needs to be more economical.

21 December 1935: Wallis to Wright (the clearest indication of all that Wallis continues to keep a tight grip on production details):

My purpose in writing this note is because I feel that I have been double-crossed again and I am getting a little tired of it. The last time we had a meeting on the opera sequence I gave positive instructions to Grot that for this sequence we were to build two boxes – on the first floor and on the second floor – and that this would be sufficient for our reverse shots. In other words, we would confine our audience shots to the section that would be backed up by two boxes, and that was all we were going to build. This would have been plenty, because our shots towards the stage could have been shot over the people in the box ... as they were in the dailies.

Instead of the above, I find that we have built almost a complete theatre, with boxes along one whole wall ... and running round to the back, with the whole back of the theatre re-built, and consequently we have a reverse shot in there that was filled up with people and all we're going to use of it in the picture is about four feet, so that somebody has criminally wasted thousands of dollars ... why I don't know! There is no God damned reason for things of this kind happening, and I'm going to do something drastic about it if I have to fire four or five Art directors, and whoever else is concerned in it, because I'm getting disgusted with having meetings and telling people what to build, and then finding the stuff coming out on the screen with thousands of dollars spent uselessly. I don't object to spending money when it is going to be shown on the screen, and when it is necessary for the action, but I do object to a reckless, inconsiderate, ridiculous waste of money on a case such as this. There is absolutely no necessity for a reverse shot such as was made in this picture, with a hundred or two hundred people in costume, sitting in a theatre looking at the stage – a dead cut that doesn't mean a damn thing, and it was only shot because the set was there for it, and that was my reason for NOT building a set, because if we hadn't we wouldn't have filled it up with people.

I think you were present when we decided that we would build two boxes and our action would be confined in this manner, and I want to know Monday why these instructions were disregarded.

It seems to me that anyone who is able to read a plan would have known that there was too much set being built, and I have been depending upon you to follow through after we have these sessions, and to see that plans were executed according to our discussions.

If it is going to be necessary for me to okay plans in the future, it is alright with me, but these fellows will either do what we tell them to or they're not going to work here any more.

I want to know what the cost was on the Paris Opera House set; also, how many people worked in the audience.'

Wallis' memo is a key document in any understanding of how Hollywood worked. Obviously, as Bill Koenig wrote in his schoolmasterly memo, *Anthony Adverse* was a large and complicated production. For this reason, control of budget and schedule were more than usually important. But the pre-production stage of *Anthony Adverse* followed what was otherwise a fairly set pattern in studio practice: a series of meetings designed to make sure that every stage of the production process was meticulously mapped out in advance and that there was as little room for deviation as possible. Because of the scope of the production, certain choices had to be made. The story and cast were particularly expensive, and savings had to be made wherever could possibly be used again. The studio system was not geared to because of its episodic structure, called for a large number of sets, savings on set and costume were not easy to make. But they were essential: hence Wallis' final memo. Hence, also, the occasional memo during shooting to the effect that sets were not to be scrapped since they might be able to be used again. The studio system was not geared to producing single movies. Throughout work on *Anthony Adverse*, Wallis and others would have been working on other productions. Warners was geared to the production of annual programmes of pictures: investment in a large-budget picture could be partially recouped in other, smaller productions.

49

All things considered, the cast for *Anthony Adverse* came remarkably cheap. None of the contract artists was expensive in terms of the proportion of their annual salary borne by the film's budget (certainly not if one compares the $85,667 borne by the budget of *Angels with Dirty Faces* two years later for the services of James Cagney[10]). Nor, given the success of Wallis' deal-making, did the outside talent cost anywhere near as much as it might have done. All in all, the studio came close to producing an MGM picture at Warners prices. And it was the efficiency of their production system that enabled them to do so. The pre-production work on *Anthony Adverse* shows this system in operation at maximum force. Wallis took the decisions, with frequent reference to Jack Warner; Blanke, Koenig and Alborn put them into effect, relying on the skilled operation of a number of integrated departments. The tone of Wallis' final memo makes it clear that deviation from well-established practice was not merely unacceptable but downright surprising. In this process, the director, Mervyn LeRoy, was another employee, highly skilled in his particular area – an area which, like those of other studio staff, basically involved realising a pre-planned scheme.

This is not to deny a creative input to LeRoy. Clearly, his work on *Anthony Adverse* was creative and contains a number of his trademarks as a director, notably a fondness for a mobile camera in fairly tight interior scenes where other directors might have relied on shot/reverse shot set-ups. But as a work of art *Anthony Adverse* depends for its creative achievements and shortcomings on multiple decisions taken by a number of people within a well established and smoothly functioning system, not on its being the expression of one man's artistic sensibility. Relations between Wallis and LeRoy were obviously of a different kind from those between Wallis and other studio personnel. This can be seen from the tone of the memos they exchanged – they are those of one production executive talking to another. And that, within the studio system, is what the director was: a top production executive taking executive decisions in a different area, but not really of a different kind, from those taken by Wallis, Koenig or (in the case of *Anthony Adverse*) Blanke. In fact, the hierarchy of salaries – director, writer, star – is, even allowing for the fact that it was determined more by the amount of time worked than by any absolute value system, a fairly exact indication of Warners' overall hierarchy of creative values. Even so, Mervyn LeRoy's freedom of movement was fairly strictly limited. That was the way it was supposed to be: that was the way the studio system worked.

PRODUCTION

Once the schedule was established, the shooting of a picture became a question of sticking as closely to it as possible. The schedule was designed to allow the best possible film to be made within the limits of the time (and therefore, of course, the money) available; it was not designed to allow self-indulgence, on the part of the director or anybody else (though it couldn't always prevent it[11]). Throughout the decade, every film had a Daily Production and Progress Report prepared by the Unit Manager which was submitted, with comments, to the Production Manager, Tenny Wright, with a copy to Wallis. The Report was extremely detailed and always typed up in full: it was, after all, an essential part of the studio system. The illustration on pp. 26-27 shows both sides of an actual Daily Production and Progress Report from *Anthony Adverse*. What follows is an edited compilation of those Reports.

(a) Tests

Date	Location	Artists tested and other work done
1935		
October		
1	Stage 18	Anita Kerry, Ann Schoenmaker, Pedro Cordoba, Joe Sawyer, Ann Howard
2	Stage 18	Katherine De Mille, Henry Walthall, Siegfried Rumann, Fritz Leiber
3	Stage 18	Donald Woods, Alma Lloyd, Rafaelo Ottiano
4	Stage 18	Marilyn Knowlden, Douglas Scott, Kitty Carlisle. Recorded aria from *Carmen*
8	Stage 18	George E. Stone, John Carradine
10	Stage 18	Dickie Jackson, Bobby Bizzett, Carli Russell (children), Steffi Duna, Pedro Cordoba, Eily Malyon
11	Stage 18	Bette Davis. Lackeys. Wardrobe.
14	Stage 18	Billy Burrud, Ashley Feltas (children), Anna Demetrio, Jocelyn Birse
15	Stage 1	Joseph Crehan, Olivia De Havilland, Dorothy Libaire
17	Stage 1	Several tests of Claude Rains in different costumes and make-up, ages 43 to 70
18	Stage 1	J. Carrol Naish
November		
1	Stage 18	Olivia De Havilland, Fredric March, Gale Sondergaard, George E. Stone
2	Stage 6	Edmund Gwenn, Mathilde Comont
4	Stage 6	David Holt, Clare Blandick, Olivia De Havilland. Jackman shooting key shots.
11	Stage 6	Alma Lloyd, Marilyn Knowlden, Edmund Gwenn, Olivia De Havilland

(b) **Shooting**

1935

November

6	9.00-18.15	Stage 14	Bonnyfeather ext. & int.
7	9.00-17.45	Hastings Ranch	Country road, Leghorn
		Stage 6	Anthony's bedroom (¾ day behind schedule)
8	13.30-18.45	Trainshed	Ext. road
		Stage 6	Bonnyfeather int.
9	9.00-17.40	Stage 6	Bonnyfeather int. (1 day behind)
10	Sunday		
11	9.00-16.50	Back lot	Deck of boat. Leghorn street.
12	8.30-23.00	Back lot	Leghorn street (1½ days behind)
13	13.00-3.30	Back lot & Stage 6	Night scenes: Gate and patio Bonnyfeather int. & ext.
14	18.30-2.30	Back lot	Bonnyfeather ext. night
15	18.00-1.20	Back lot	Bonnyfeather ext. night (2 days behind)
16	10.30-18.40	Stages 14 & 16	Bonnyfeather int.
17	Sunday		
18	9.00-18.35	Stages 16 & 6	Signora Bovina int.
19	9.00-18.00	Stage 6	Bonnyfeather int.
20	10.30-23.25	Ranch	Convent wall, Signora Bovina's doorway, Stage door
21	13.00-16.45	Back lot	Havana ('Called off Ext. patio Havana because of bad weather and change of cast member.') (3 days behind)
22	9.00-21.10	Stages 14 & 16	Signora Bovina int. Trading post.
23	9.00-18.00	Stage 14	Trading post & Anthony's house, Gallegos
24	Sunday		
25	9.00-16.30	Ranch	Ext. trading post & stockade
26	8.30-16.15	Ranch	Ext. trading post & stockade
27	8.30-16.30	Ranch	Ext. trading post & stockade
28	No shooting because of bad weather		4 days behind schedule
29	12.30-14.50	Stage 5	Jackman unit: keys for Anthony's carriage

	9.00-18.30	Ranch & Stage 14	Ext. trading post. Int. Anthony's house. ('All NG sound takes NG because of plane noise.')
30	9.00-19.07	Stage 2	Ext. François' colony

December
1	Sunday		
2	9.00-21.15	Ranch, Stages 2 & 14	Ext. trading post & jungle Int. Anthony's living room
3	9.00-18.50	Stages 2 & 14	Int. Anthony's living room (5 days behind)
4	8.00-18.05	Trainshed	Ext. jungle. Ext. carriage. Leghorn. ('Completed all African sequences')
5	9.00-18.55	Backlot & trainshed	Leghorn exteriors & quay
6	9.00-17.50	Stage 2	Bonnyfeather int.
7	9.00-17.25	Dijon St. & Stage 2	Bonnyfeather int. & Bonaparte's study
8	Sunday		
9	9.00-17.30	Dijon St. & Stage 2	French village street. (6 days behind)
10	9.00-17.40	Dijon St. & Stage 2	Bonaparte's quarters & village
11	9.00-18.00	Dijon St. & Stage 4	Bonaparte's quarters & Vincent's library
12	9.00-17.50	Stages 4 & 16	Int. Vincent's library, Bonaparte's room in Tuileries & Leghorn inn
13	9.00-18.20	Vitagraph Theatre	Int. Leghorn Opera House
14	9.00-17.20	Stage 14	Int. Angela's cottage
15	Sunday		
16	9.00-18.00	Stage 1	Int. Paris ballroom. ('150 extras. 100 dancers. 2nd unit rehearsing Paris Opera.')
17	13.00-22.40	Stage 1	Int. Paris ballroom.
18	7.00-15.30	Sherwood Forest	Jackman unit: Dusty road & bridge
	10.00-21.15	Stage 1	Int. Paris ballroom & Opera
19	7.30-14.45	Sherwood Forest	Jackman unit as before ('Delayed waiting for sun.')
	9.00-17.20	Vitagraph Theatre	Int. Paris Opera. Glass shots, 250 extras)
20	9.00-18.10	Vitagraph Theatre	Int. Paris Opera
21	9.00-16.00	Stage 1	Promenade & foyer
22	Sunday		
23	9.00-16.10	Back lot	Ext. Havana quay, patio & street
24	9.00-15.00	Stage 5	Ext. Havana quay, patio & street

25	Christmas Day		
26	13.00-2.30	Back lot & Stage 6	Int. Bonnyfeather & ext. Havana
27	19.00-2.00	Trainshed	Coaches
28	14.00-18.40	Stage 4	Int. Vincent's library
29	Sunday		
30	9.00-22.30	Trainshed & Stage 6	Ext. road in Alps. Int. Bonnyfeather.
31	9.00-16.40	Back lot	Ext. Havana & ext. Alps

1936

January

1	New Year's Day		
2	9.00-17.00	Sherwood Forest	Ext. Angela's cottage. (7 days behind)
3	9.00-23.00	Trainshed & back lot	Ext. Alps & ext. Havana patio ('Scotty Beckett ill')
4	10.00-17.40	Stages 3 & 5	Ext. boat to America
5	Sunday		
6	9.00-18.10	Stage 6	Int. Bonnyfeather
7	9.00-17.50	Stage 7	Int. Bonnyfeather courtyard
8	9.00-20.55	Back lot & Stages 14 & 6	Ext. Bonnyfeather courtyard
9	9.00-17.55	Stages 18 & 16	Int. chateau
10	9.00-18.00	Stage 16	Int. chateau (8 days behind)
11	9.00-17.00	Stage 6	Int. chateau
12	Sunday		
13	9.00-18.20	Stage 16	Int. chateau ('Mr Hayward rehearsing duel. Mr O'Neill taking Latin lessons.')
14	9.00-22.00	Pasadena Bush Garden	Ext. chateau
15	9.00-17.45	Pasedena Bush Garden	Ext. chateau
16	9.00-18.05	Trainshed & Stages 18 & 16	Int. cell, int. coach, Issoire inn. (9 days behind)
17	9.00-22.45	Stages 16 & 6	Int. & ext. cell, int. Royal Baths & int. inn
18	10.00-17.00	Ranch	Ext. mill
19	Sunday		
20	9.00-17.25	Ranch & Stage 18	Ext. mill & int. inn
21	9.00-20.30	Ranch & Dijon St.	Ext. convent & ext. inn
22	9.00-16.30	Ranch	Ext. convent
23	9.00-17.45	Stage 18	Int. inn
24	9.00-17.35	Stage 18	Int. inn (duel scene)
25	9.00-16.50	Stage 18	Int. inn
26	Sunday		
27	9.00-0.40	Ranch & Stage 14	Ext. convent & int. library
28	9.30-17.35	Stages 14 & 18	Int. library, int. dining room & ext. Swiss chalet

29	9.00–17.15	Stages 18 & 6	Int. chalet, int. convent (10 days behind)
30	9.00–16.30	Back lot	Ext. Bonnyfeather (11 days behind)
31	9.00–16.20	Stage 6	Int. Bonnyfeather ('Picture closed today, 12 days over schedule.')

(c) Additional footage

February

| 3 | 9.00–16.30 | Santa Susanna Pass | Opening shots (dir. Michael Curtiz) |
| 14 | 9.00–12.25 | Stage 6 | Mother and baby ('no longer under the lights at any time than 30 seconds') |

Scheduled 60 days. Took 72, not including two days extra work after the picture had officially closed. Total hours worked 693 (approximately five hours work for every minute of film in the release print).

Obviously a lot of the decisions that were taken during the shooting are not recorded in studio memos:[12] Blanke and LeRoy were on the set, and are likely to have talked rather than written to one another. Throughout the shooting of *Anthony Adverse*, however, Wallis continued to exercise the same degree of control and close surveillance as he had done during pre-production. His memos concern everything from minor background details to important matters of scheduling and performance. Since each was occasioned by looking at the dailies or by reading the Daily Production and Progress Reports – the furious memo about the Opera House set makes it clear that this, rather than visits to the set, was his main source of information – I shall simply list them in order of date. The reader can, if desired, check them against the Report.

20 November 1935: to LeRoy. Concern about Olivia De Havilland's performance. 'You have to watch her on the delivery of some of her lines. She becomes a little theatrical and takes the reality out of the scene. The scene between March and De Havilland at the window was very nice until the last line, where she says: "Oh, Anthony, I love you!", and then it sounded as though she was back in MIDSUMMER NIGHT'S DREAM. She has a way of shaking her head and punching the line over that becomes theatrical and takes the kick out of the scene. She could have spoken it, I think, so much more simply and very quietly … just looking at him … but she acts with it and to me spoils it. Don't you agree with me?'

21 November 1935: to Blanke. A title will be necessary to introduce the character of Faith.

22 November 1935: to LeRoy. On De Havilland again, this time about the neckline of her dress: 'It is better to have a little less body showing and keep the shot in the picture.'

23 November 1935: to Blanke and Wright. 'I know that we have run into tough breaks on ANTHONY ADVERSE and that for one reason and another we have had short days.

'However, there has been so little stuff coming through the last few days that we should make an effort to pick up some time on this picture. I don't know if we're still trying to shoot in continuity, but going outside for – for instance, the Convent Wall, and waiting for light for two or three hours, and then making a couple of entrances and exits and killing a day – that way certainly isn't economy, and if we keep scheduling in this manner we are going to be on the picture for five months.

'We must do something about this, and I want you to get hold of Mr LeRoy and Bill Cannon and go over this schedule and see if we can't schedule some full days' work, and stop these half-days ... these late calls ... on account of night work and all of that. I'm not satisfied with the progress of the picture lately.'

4-5 December 1935: to LeRoy. More detailed comments on the dailies (Wallis was taking up to eight cans of film home with him at night)

6 December 1935: to Wright: 'Mervyn tells me he was held up a half-hour this morning because Westmore told Fredric March he was too busy to make him up when March came in. Let me know what this is all about.'

16 December 1935: to Blanke and Wright. This time it is Gale Sondergaard's neckline. 'We don't want to lose scenes out of the picture because the dresses are too low. Of course, we want a certain amount of this, but we don't have to go to extremes.'

23 December 1935: to Nathan Levinson, the studio's chief sound man. The playback is audible in some of the dialogue scenes. 'Your mixers must not do these things if they know they are wrong.'

26 December 1935: to Wallis from Wright. 'As you know, ANTHONY ADVERSE shoots Ext. Carlo Cibo's patio tonight and tomorrow night, and at present time I understand it is Mr LeRoy's intention to stop shooting if the breath of any member of the cast picks up photographically. At the time this set was discussed, we decided we would not tarp it due to the prohibitive cost, and that we would shoot it whether the breath showed or not. Would suggest you send a note to Mr LeRoy and to the cameraman that they are to shoot regardless of the breath, if this is your wish. As you know, we are six days behind on this picture, and the cost at the present time is $822,033, and the company is behind schedule six days now, with from five to six weeks left to finish the picture. From present indications, the company will be over schedule about two weeks, when finished.

'If there are any cuts in the beginning of this story, that is from Page 1 to 35 inclusive, which you could o.k., we would probably save time and money.'

Wallis sent the requested memo to LeRoy, pointing out that the nights would be cold until spring; whatever happened, he was not to call the company and then decide not to shoot.

28 December 1935: Wright to Wallis. LeRoy wants to use process, not moving backing, for the 'boat to America' scenes.

'A season in hell': Fredric March as Anthony, Steffi Duna as the native girl in the African episode

8 January 1936: to LeRoy. Problems with shots of the boy, Billy Mauch. 'Why weren't tests ordered on him?' The same memo to Wright, rather more forcefully expressed.

14 January 1936: to Wright. Strike as few of the sets as possible: they can be used on other pictures.

18 January 1936: to LeRoy. 'Have just spoken to JL and he is very worried about how long it is taking and how much it is costing. Please schedule two nights a week from now on.' A handwritten note on the bottom of the memo reads: 'Dear Hal: It shall be done. Merv.' (It wasn't: the company worked only one night in the remaining two weeks!)

20 January 1936: to LeRoy. Please stop printing two takes of every shot.

24 January 1936: to LeRoy. More concern about Billy Mauch: he needs to speak more clearly.

One thing emerges fairly clearly from the memos on the dailies. Once the production was under way, the bulk of Wallis' concern was no longer with the time and money aspects: that was now the responsibility of Tenny Wright. Instead, Wallis paid more attention to the artistic quality of the film, making detailed suggestions to LeRoy on how certain things might be improved. On one occasion (memo of 18 January) he appears to act as a buffer between LeRoy and Jack Warner, whose chief concern *was* with cost. Thus while the evidence of the pre-production stages of *Anthony Adverse* may be that the studio system as it operated at Warner Brothers was mainly concerned with the nuts and bolts of the production process, and was content to leave the more nebulous artistic factors to writer and director, the creation of an art work that would be both acceptable to the American public and consonant with a certain set of artistic values became the main focus once the production was under way. The studio system, in other words, was geared to the production of art, but art at a profit; without the profit, the art would never have existed. Not that the profit had always to be made on an individual picture: *A Midsummer Night's Dream* is a fairly clear example of a film where a loss was envisaged for prestige purposes. But the constant emphasis on schedules make it clear that pre-production planning and a system determined to ensure that the planning was followed during shooting were the areas in which financial considerations were foremost. Hollywood was a factory production system, but the product was artistic. Most of Wallis' memos to LeRoy during the actual shooting of *Anthony Adverse* concern artistic matters. As in other areas of the production process, the responsibility for the artistic side of the production was delegated to the executive appointed to deal with it: the director. Wallis did not exactly interfere. But he did keep a close eye on LeRoy's work; that, too, was a part of the system.

58

POST-PRODUCTION

Post-production is the least important phase in the Hollywood studio system, since the system was geared to producing a predictably controlled product. There was little or no room in it for the notion of a film that was brought into existence (or, for that matter, rescued) only in the cutting room. Editing was an important process, but the material which was presented to Warner's chief cutter, Ralph Dawson, was already pre-selected and shaped in such a way that his responsibility was to assemble it along lines of narrative flow and visual continuity whose principles were well established in Hollywood. He also received copious cutting notes from Hal Wallis who, in editing as in every other stage of the operation, continued to exert a strong influence.

Anthony Adverse was no different from any number of Warners features in its post-production. The phase involved a number of clearly defined areas. One of them – dealings with Joseph I. Breen – has already been dealt with. The others were:

(i) *Film editing.* Although the basic editing of *Anthony Adverse* was largely done while the picture was in progress, the final stage – the preparation of a release print – took about three weeks. Wallis would take cans of rough-cut home with him at night and screen them. The next morning, Dawson would receive copious notes advising him to cut a few frames here, alter a transition there: 3½ closely typed pages on 3 February, a further 3½ on 7 February, 2½ more on 10 February, 2 on 13 February. A print of the film was ready to be run on 14 February, just two weeks after the final day's shooting. Further adjustments were made in the following week: another 4½ pages of notes were dictated by Wallis on 18 February. A print was available for screening to the Sales Manager on 25 February. The previous day, Wallis had given the go-ahead for the film to be sent to Pacific Title for the credit sequence to be completed.

(ii) *Music.* Detailed work on the music score did not begin until after the picture was completed. A memo from Wallis to Leo F. Forbstein on 10 February reminds him that Korngold should not still be over at Paramount now that he is on salary at Warners. The screening on 14 February was primarily to enable Korngold to become familiar with the shape of the picture. And a memo from Blanke to Dawson on 3 March instructed him to make sure that Korngold had a dupe track as well as a dupe picture so that he could get *Anthony Adverse* scored, as Wallis wanted, by 10 April. A memo from Wallis to Forbstein a week later tells him that this date will have to be pushed forward to 5 or 6 April, since Wallis has to leave town earlier than anticipated, and that the studio preview, therefore, would have to be on 8 April – a little more than nine weeks after the shooting was completed.

(iii) *Credits and billing*. Most decisions on credits had been taken before shooting began (as a result of contract negotiations), or else followed practices so long established that they did not need discussion. There were, however, one or two minor incidents. As we have seen, Milton Krims requested – and was refused – screen credit for his re-writes. Korngold's credit was altered on 9 March from 'Musical Arrangement by' to 'Music by'. And there were some minor problems over the rights to the music composed by Aldo Franchetti for the Paris Opera sequence. A memo to Forbstein from Obringer on 10 February tells him to get hold of Franchetti and find out what the situation is, 'even though he is hard to understand'. Otherwise, advertising billing had been approved by Jack Warner on 6 December 1935:

Warner Bros. presents	50%
Anthony Adverse	100%
by Hervey Allen	50%
Starring Fredric March	50%
With Olivia De Havilland	50%
Edmund Gwenn	25%
Claude Rains	25%
Louis Hayward	10%
Akim Tamiroff	10%
Directed by Mervyn LeRoy	20%
A Warner Bros. picture	5%

On the main title of the film, the cards are allocated as follows:

1. Warner Bros. presents
2. Anthony Adverse – A Warner Bros. picture
3. by Hervey Allen
4. Starring Fredric March
5. With Olivia De Havilland
       Donald Woods
          Anita Louise
             Edmund Gwenn
                Claude Rains
6. Louis Hayward
       Gale Sondergaard
          Steffi Duna
             Akim Tamiroff
                Ralph Morgan
                   Fritz Leiber
                      Luis Alberni
7. Directed by Mervyn LeRoy
8. Screenplay by Sheridan Gibney

    9. Music by Erich Wolfgang Korngold. Operas by
        Monteverdi and Aldo Franchetti
  10. Photography by Tony Gaudio
        Art Director – Anton Grot
        Opera sequences staged by Natale Carossio
        Film Editor – Ralph Dawson
        Gowns by Milo Anderson
        Cosmetician – Perc Westmore
        Special Photographic Effects – Fred Jackman

A titled print was available for screening to Breen on 3 March, and adjustments took until 22 May to finalise.

(iv) *Preview*. The preview, heavily papered with studio personnel, took place at 8.20 p.m. on Friday 8 May at the Warners Theatre, Hollywood. This must have been in a version as yet without final Hays Office approval, but agreement was so close that there was clearly no risk involved. Previews were sometimes designed to test audience response, but the Hollywood Theatre previews reserved for Warners' major features were more in the nature of publicity exercises.

(v) *Advertising campaign*. The publicity campaign for *Anthony Adverse* was, as one would anticipate, on a fairly major scale. In addition to the usual large handbook produced for theatre managers (consisting of synopsis, credits, production stories, serialisations and biographical snippets for planting in local newspapers, and a selection of foyer and newspaper ads of various sizes), there was also a *Handbook of Advance Information* – the kind of thing Warners reserved for the biggest of their productions. The *Handbook*, compiled by Arthur Zellner, contained:
— a Foreword, describing the film as 'one of Warner Bros.' million dollar productions';
— an 11-page plot synopsis;
— a chronology of important historical events from the period during which the action was set (1775-1801);
— biographies of Mervyn LeRoy, Hervey Allen, Sheridan Gibney and Technical Consultant Dwight Franklin;
— details of the 131 settings, with the claim that four of the nine new sound stages were reserved exclusively for the film;
— a section on costumes, stressing the authenticity of the details and (generously) estimating the cast at 1,600;
— a section on props, pointing out that the carriages were specially built;
— a section on the cast, indicating that there were 98 roles and 78 important speaking parts.
    As with *A Midsummer Night's Dream*, Warners' major selling angle was the alleged extravagance of the production, together with a stress on the

popularity of Allen's novel. A press release issued just before the premiere drew attention to several of the points that have already been discussed. 'There is always a danger in a production like *Anthony Adverse*,' it declares, 'of a director who goes arty and in his attempts to do a class picture forgets the more practical principles of entertainment. This may account for Mervyn LeRoy's getting the assignment.' LeRoy himself is quoted as saying: 'The publicity men can talk about it being a sensational bestseller, an artistic masterpiece and a literary milestone, but Jack Warner and I like it for the same reason. Because it's perfect picture material.' Sheridan Gibney returns to a favourite theme: 'In the novel, Anthony was a passive character. Everything happened to him. For the purposes of drama it was necessary to show him as a man who sought adventure, rather than a man to whom adventure came.' '*Anthony Adverse*,' the press release ends, 'is the biggest picture to come out of Hollywood. It had to be.'

(vi) *Release.* Unusually, *Anthony Adverse* was shown on the West Coast and in selected theatres throughout the mid-West before it was shown in New York, which tends to suggest that Warners may have seen it as a big-budget entertainment picture rather than a prestige production. It may also mean that they simply did not want to open in New York in the middle of the summer. At all events, the film received an excellent review from Edwin Schallert of the *Los Angeles Times*,[13] but was less favourably received by Frank S. Nugent in New York. 'A few years back,' he wrote, 'we devoted the better part of a British weekend to the reading of Mr Allen's little pamphlet and we enjoyed it. Yesterday we spent only a fraction more than two hours watching its progress on the screen and we squirmed like a small boy in Sunday School.' None the less, overall critical response was favourable, as the *Film Daily* poll suggests, and the film did exceptionally good business.[14]

(vii) *Follow-up.* On 26 February 1936 Wallis wrote to Wilk in New York asking him to check with Allen about the possibility of a sequel. And on 28 August he sent a confidential memo to Blanke saying that a deal had been worked out with Allen for a sequel. No sequel was made. The studio files also contain letters from moviegoers pointing out errors in the film: Mrs Adeline Lewis Pritchett of San Diego noticed a Spanish belltower on an Italian convent; Helen Steese of Allendale, N.J. spotted a modern '4' on the Cuban clock instead of the more appropriate Roman 'IV'; and R. Glover Miller, Editor of the Anderson (S.C.) *Daily Mail*, wrote in to point out that the word 'harassed' was misspelled in the intertitles. Apart from this, Warners' only real problem in the aftermath of the film's release – hardly worth mentioning by comparison with the protracted lawsuits they faced over *The Life of Emile Zola* and *Juarez* – was that they had to pay $500 to cover breakages in an antique Chinese chess set. The possibility of tie-ins with the novel's publisher was excluded because March was under contract to Fox. In fact, there are only two minor details of interest in the slim correspondence following the picture's final release – a whimper on which to end this chapter. Efforts were made, when the picture was re-released in 1948, to remove Gale Sondergaard's name from the credits because she was married to one of the blacklisted Hollywood Ten. And a request was received in 1972 to use the book as a prop in Robert Mulligan's film *The Other*, proving that Warners still held the motion picture rights to *Anthony Adverse*.

4　The Crash to Pearl Harbor

This book is about Warner Brothers in the 1930s. Decades are rarely discrete units and neither 1 January nor 31 December are particularly significant dates in terms of film production, even when they come at the beginning and end of a decade. So I have been slightly more flexible in my definition of the 1930s, allowing the decade to run from the Wall Street Crash on 28 October 1929 to the Japanese bombing of Pearl Harbor on 6 December 1941. Both those dates changed American history. The 1930s was, of course, a significant decade for the American film industry: Hollywood passed through its organisational heyday in that twelve-year period. The studio system was consolidated, economically and artistically, by the coming of sound; in the early 1940s, it began to be undermined by a change in movie markets and a shift towards more autonomous production units, at first working within the studio system, later largely by-passing it. In the same twelve years, however, America as a whole underwent an equally important change. The collapse of the stock market ended a period of optimistically uncontrolled growth – the Jazz Age, the Coolidge years – and ushered in the Depression and the New Deal. It also left a gaping hole in the American Dream, making it painfully clear not just to the millions of unemployed but to the nation as a whole that market forces, left to their own devices, could not guarantee the universal prosperity which had long been their alibi: the proper business of American government was plainly more than just business.

As any number of subsequent commentators have pointed out, Roosevelt's solutions to America's problems were a good deal less radical than they seemed.[1] Despite the socialistic trappings of the National Recovery Administration launched by FDR during his first term of office, the basic philosophy remained remarkably similar to that of previous presidencies. The appeals to national unity and co-operative effort are misleading: individual initiative together with the incentives of personal and family prosperity were the virtues most consistently appealed to. It may not have been quite as crude as a morale-boosting insert which appeared occasionally in the *New York Daily News* during 1930 urging Americans to 'End the Depression: Buy now!', but the principle remained the same. America would be saved by restoring, not revolutionising, her economic base. Redistribution of wealth on a large scale and a radical change of direction were not part of the programme.

Of all the studios, Warner Brothers was the one whose production programme most enthusiastically reflected the New Deal, both before it officially came into existence – in facing up to the social crisis in a more direct way than any other studio – and after, adopting the Roosevelt administration's terminology (for what it is worth, *42nd Street* was billed as a 'New Deal in Entertainment'), placing its symbol, the NRA Eagle, on the main title card of its films, and preaching the paternalistic concern which was a feature of the FDR years. To see Warners as a studio committed wholeheartedly to socially conscious movies is, of course, a mistake: the studio turned out as many bromides such as *Flirtation Walk* and *Happiness Ahead* (both 1934), as it did 'social conscience pictures'. But a certain similarity does exist between American social history and the themes of the films produced by Warners during the 1930s. In that decade, the United States passed through severe depression to recovery, growth, complacency and finally into a new crisis as the economic isolationism on which the New Deal's successes had been built came into conflict with the principles of morality which had been its official ideology: could Roosevelt's America adopt towards the rise of fascism in Europe and the annexation of Austria, Czechoslovakia and Poland the attitude of non-intervention which its economic interests seemed to dictate?

Over the same period, the films produced by Warners changed along similar lines. The bleak portrayal of losers in a lost world which characterises *Doorway to Hell* (1930), *The Public Enemy* (1931) and *I Am a Fugitive from a Chain Gang* (1932) gave way to a kind of determined optimism, expressed through the all-pulling-together-to-make-it-work philosophy of the 1933 musicals, through the images of problems being faced and solved, either with the help of Federal authority – in *Wild Boys of the Road* (1933), *Massacre* (1934) and *G-Men* (1935) – or through the reassertion of an individual conscience, as in *Black Fury* (1935) and *Bullets or Ballots* (1936). This in turn gives way to a more general assertion of individualism, either equipped with a social conscience (*The Story of Louis Pasteur*,1936; *The Life of Emile Zola*, 1937; and *Juarez*, 1939) or largely free of one (*Kid Galahad*, 1937; *The Adventures of Robin Hood*, 1938; and *Knute Rockne – All American*, 1940). The regaining of confidence was also reflected in a flood of pictures about a variety of institutions in which American individuals served the community. In *Here Comes the Navy* (1934), *Devil Dogs of the Air* (1935), *Code of the Secret Service* (1939), *The Fighting 69th* (1940) and *Dive Bomber* (1941), conflicts between high-spirited individualism and service to one's country were ironed out in military settings, while *Brother Rat* (1938) and *Brother Rat and a Baby* (1940) completed a cycle of college pictures which dealt with similar themes. And *Ceiling Zero* and *China Clipper* (both 1936) are the most typical of the flying pictures which reaffirmed a belief in American technology, know-how and the spirit of innovative adventure. The crisis towards the end of the decade was dealt with either directly – as early as 1937 in *Black Legion* and as unequivocally as in *Confessions of a Nazi Spy* (1939) – or else through the gradually refined metaphysical despair of *film noir*, from *Angels with Dirty Faces* in 1938, which still looks back to the problem pictures of the first half of the decade, to *They Drive by Night* (1940), *High Sierra* and *The Maltese Falcon* (1941), which anticipate the flourishing of the genre later in the decade.

Clearly such a 'history' of Warner Brothers is both over-simplified and tendentious, and the rest of this book will, through closer analysis of a number of films, introduce important qualifications. But the relationship between the studio's output and the world into which it was released – America in the 1930s – does need to be stressed. Warners both reflected and reflected on the society in which they operated, and their films contain many of the ideological features which characterised Roosevelt's first two terms of office. Above all, they contain many of the same contradictions. The strongest of these was the need to deny that there was anything fundamentally wrong. The Depression, it was implied, had been a passing malfunction in an otherwise efficient system, brought on, perhaps, by greed. There were lessons to be learned from this, but they were lessons of adjustment, not radical change. What this meant in terms of movies was that the same values which had caused the crisis in the first place – rugged individualism; economic incentive as a basis for general growth – continued to be asserted as ways of resolving the crisis.

The contradictions in this belief are, on a wider scale, those of capitalism itself; and they are contradictions with which, against most of the odds, capitalism has so far managed to cope (thanks not a little to the ideological superstructure of 'commonsense' attitudes and undefined beliefs which it has generated). In a similar way, we are used to movie plots having, if not a happy ending, at least a smooth resolution, and we tend to be obscurely upset when they do not. Nor do we always notice the structural and narrative inconsistencies when they do. Like those of any other studio, Warners' films from the 1930s repeatedly sacrifice realism to resolution. This is not, it should be stressed, because the scripts are bad. It is because the prevailing and unshakeable belief was that a film which tackled a problem had to offer a solution, even if the real-life problem seemed likely to remain unsolved for some time to come. If an unemployed man finds employment in the course of a film, the problem of unemployment has, within the context of that film, been solved. What is more, on a broader scale the contradictions of American society in the 1930s were the material on which the studio drew, not something it necessarily set out to highlight. Art, least of all commercial art, is not designed to make fundamental

Billboard promotion in hard times

changes in society, nor is it capable of doing so. The most it can hope to do is to indicate those areas in which changes are necessary. Warners' movies undoubtedly did this during the 1930s – *Massacre*, a 1934 film about the systematic oppression of the native American, is one of the most striking examples[2] – even if the dominant ideology as reflected in the details and structure of their plots meant that the final effect was one of reassurance.

During the Wallis years, Warners produced around 65 features a year and a comparatively small number of shorts. For the record, the company also distributed two outside films under its banner: *The Mad Empress* (1939), as a result of a court case concerning *Juarez*,[3] and a British documentary, Harry Watt's *Target for Tonight* (1941). In the whole of the period covered by this book, Warners released 751 features. Since studio records for the early part of the period are not complete enough to determine exactly which features were planned or started on or after 28 October 1929, I have played it safe and included in the survey all films released on or after 1 January 1929. At the other end of the period, I have drawn an equally arbitrary line at 31 December 1941. In a study of this kind, some arbitrariness is inevitable. On the other hand, I have done my best not to be arbitrary in selecting the films on which I have chosen to concentrate.

In deciding which films to look at more closely, I have used the twin criteria of subject matter and popularity. The remaining chapters deal with the two most significant categories of Warners' output – I am avoiding the word 'genre', although the categories do contain elements of accepted genre classification – during the 1930s. They are intentionally loose categories, and attempt to combine story content and studio practice, the latter involving such considerations as how much money was spent on a film, which director it was allocated to and what market group it seemed mainly to be aimed at.[1] The first category, which tends to give precedence to studio practice over subject matter, consists of biographies, costume dramas and prestige productions. It includes all those films which provide an account, however fictionalised, of the lives of prominent individuals, those films in which the characters wear costumes sufficiently out of date (as opposed to merely exotic) for this to be an important element in the audience's response, and those films, like *Show of Shows* (1929) and *A Midsummer Night's Dream* (1935), which fall outside all the other categories and seem to amount more than anything else to a show of studio pride in its resources or its cultural respectability. This first category is the smallest – only 67 films overall – but it accounts for a disproportionate number of long first-runs. The reasons for this should be obvious: as with *Anthony Adverse*, the extra expense of large-scale costume biographies and costume dramas in general meant that the films were given high priority, top casts and correspondingly heavy promotion.

The second category, dealt with in Part II of this book, consists of social dramas, crime movies and newspaper pictures. The dominant characteristic here, I suppose, is seriousness and to a lesser extent realism, although realism tended to disappear from the crime movies once a style had been established, and was never a feature of such early potboiler whodunnits as *In the Next Room* and *Murder Will Out* (both 1930). This category is probably the one for which Warners is best remembered during the 1930s. It includes all the 'social conscience' pictures, many of which used racketeering and gang warfare as a background. Not all the crime pictures, of course, had a social conscience, but I have included them all in this category since the (projected) audience appeal of *The Public Enemy* and *I Am a Fugitive from a Chain Gang* lay in their status as crime pictures – in the excitement of their contemporary action-based narratives rather than in the fact that they tackled social problems. Newspaper pictures were likewise a form of film in which Warners specialised, particularly during the first half of the decade. They had a style of their own – fast-talking, cynical and remarkably articulate on certain issues – and I have included all of them here, whether they deal with serious issues, like *Five Star Final* (1931), or whether, like *Blessed Event* (1932) and *Hi, Nellie!* (1934), they do not.

These two categories provide a vital cross-section of Warners in the

1930s, though between them they account for less than half the films produced by the studio. The other two categories are not dealt with in detail in this book, though frequent reference is made to them, and I shall merely give a rough indication of their general outlines. The third is by far the biggest – 315 films, or over 40 per cent of the studio's entire output – but, unlike the first category, is comparatively little represented in the list of long first runs, other than in the exceptional year of 1933. It consists of musicals, comedies, service and college pictures, action dramas and horror movies. It is clearly a catch-all category and at first sight overlaps with the second category. Many of the films included in the second category, for instance, are action dramas. But those 'relegated' to the third category are no more than this. In *On the Border* (1930), Rin Tin Tin may be involved in an illegal alien-smuggling operation, but that does not make the film one with a marked social conscience. A similar point can be made about comedies. Several of the crime movies are undoubtedly funny – *Smart Money* (1931), for example, *Taxi!* (1932) or *Brother Orchid* (1940) – and it is rare for any Warners script from the period to be entirely devoid of humour. But I think a useful distinction can be made between realistic films with comic situations, and films whose aim is simply to be amusing, like the Joe E. Brown comedies, or *Three Men on a Horse* (1936) and *The Bride Came C.O.D.* (1941). Musicals are fairly easy to define, as are horror movies (although the studio made only a handful of these, and only three – *The Mystery of the Wax Museum* (1933), *The Walking Dead* (1936) and *The Return of Dr. X* (1939) – of any real interest). The term 'action dramas' includes the B-feature Westerns and adventure stories that remained a studio staple throughout the decade, as well as a number of much higher budget pictures in which major stars such as Edward G. Robinson, James Cagney and Errol Flynn grappled with and overcame the dangers of the natural world (*Tiger Shark*, 1932) or twentieth-century machinery (*The Crowd Roars*, 1932; *Ceiling Zero* and *China Clipper*, 1936; and *Dive Bomber*, 1941).

The final category is, like the first, comparatively small (132 films), and it includes a number of movies which one would associate more readily with MGM or Paramount. It consists of sentimental dramas – films in which the chief motivating force is emotional growth or emotional crisis, films which hinge on the beginning or end of a love affair. Most of Bette Davis' most memorable films come in this category, but it also includes the more usual definition of 'sentimental' – Al Jolson's early tear-jerkers *Say it with Songs*, *Sonny Boy* (both 1929) and *Mammy* (1930), and the rather improbable George Arliss vehicle of 1932, *The Man Who Played God*. In many ways, I would like to have given the same kind of detailed consideration to films from these last two categories as to those from the first two. But I am convinced that in this instance more would have meant less. Closer examination of these films would have doubled the length of the book without adding much to its argument. Between them, the biopics, costume dramas, prestige productions and socially realistic films provide a full cross-section of the kind of films and the kind of values Warners was involved with during the 1930s. The comedies, musicals and sentimental dramas were made in the same way and reflected the same kind of world – the same 'New Deal in Entertainment'.

Of the films from the first two categories, I have concentrated on the most successful ones. 'Successful', however, is not the easiest word to define when it comes to commercially produced works of art. One criterion which suggests itself is box office returns. But a satisfactorily complete record does not appear to exist for the period as a whole, or if it does I have not been able to find it. My selection is based on a criterion which takes box office into account but which is, I hope, more flexible. I have, with the aid of the *New York Times* and the *Los Angeles Times*, logged the programmes of the main Warners theatres in both cities throughout the period, also taking into account as many of the company's features as possible, and certainly all the major features, which opened in first-run theatres owned by other chains, and concentrated on those features which had combined lengthy first-runs in both cities. This has a number of advantages in producing a representative list of films (the list itself is given in full in Appendix II). In the first place, since the films would not have been held over for a second or further weeks if they had not been doing good business, it provides a fairly accurate indication of box office response. Secondly, it indicates two fairly distinct audience responses: that of the relatively sophisticated Broadway moviegoer, and that of the traditionally rather different Los Angeles viewer. Ideally, I would like to have included a third or even a fourth city in the survey – Chicago and perhaps a Southern or mid-Western city – but the practical problems defeated me. Thirdly, the concentration on first-run theatres indicates those films which the studio itself was most concerned to promote, either because it thought they would be particularly successful commercially or because, by showcasing them in that way, it ensured that they were. Of the 751 features produced by Warners between 1929 and 1941, just over 270 had a run of at least two weeks in New York or Los Angeles or both – the criterion for inclusion in Appendix II. Of these, I have seen 120 in the course of researching this book, and it is on these 120 films – just over 15 per cent of Warners' total output – that my conclusions are based.

PART TWO

Visions of the Thirties

5 Crime Thrillers and Newspaper Pictures

The established image of Warner Brothers during the 1930s is of a studio with a strong social conscience. 'The general impression,' says Hal Wallis, 'was that we were very liberal in our selection of material.'[1] Like most established images, this view is both true and exaggerated. Certainly, no other major studio produced pictures like *I Am a Fugitive from a Chain Gang* (1932), *Black Fury* (1935), *Black Legion* (1937) and *Confessions of a Nazi Spy* (1939) – films which dealt with difficult and potentially controversial social issues almost entirely avoided by the other four majors. But such films were not really typical of Warners' overall production. Although films dealing more or less seriously with contemporary American society account for just under a third of the studio's output – some 240 out of 751 films – the vast majority of them bear little or no immediate social message. Just because a Warners film was about contemporary America, that did not mean it was a 'socially conscious' film.

Even the most apparently uncompromising of the socially conscious films such as *I Am a Fugitive* and *Black Legion* are, in the end, reassuring about the ability of America's institutions to protect its citizens. James Allen in the former is the victim of an injustice in one morally isolated (Southern) state, while a Constitution-quoting judge ends the latter by stamping out the Black Legion. Reassurance – to be more precise, resolution – is part of a narrative structure common to almost all the contemporary dramas. And it is more than anything else the basic energy of the crime movie model which accounts for the harsh indictment of conditions in the 'social conscience' film. 'When we got a subject like that,' says Wallis of *I Am a Fugitive,* 'we were considered a hard-hitting type of picture maker: *G-Men* and that sort of thing.'[2] The juxtaposition is significant. *G-Men* (1935) is a film unequivocally committed to the idea that the FBI should be given wider powers to fight crime – a law and order film. It could easily be re-released in 1949 to commemorate the 25th anniversary of the FBI, at a time when the Bureau was heavily involved in activities that were anything but liberal.[3] *I Am a Fugitive from a Chain Gang* and *G-Men* were, from the studio's point of view, the same kind of film: hard-hitting and up-to-the-minute.

But there can be no denying that the choice of subject matter did place the studio on the liberal side of Hollywood. The danger of seeing Warners as too radical should not be over-compensated for by seeing it as just another reactionary production company. Its choice of realistic contemporary subjects, for the reasons discussed in an earlier chapter, inevitably led it to tackle the symptoms of Depression America early in the decade, and to deal with the threat of fascism, native or imported, later in the 1930s. It was also inevitable that, in tackling the symptoms, Warners should tackle some of the causes of those phenomena. But as the Depression receded, the studio's style settled. Like most of its styles of film, the early, almost experimental efforts at terse, violent and economical narrative – *Doorway to Hell* (1930), *Little Caesar*, *The Public Enemy* (both 1931) and *Taxi!* (1932) – soon developed into a formula which became the unadventurous mainstream of studio production: its pioneering efforts were diverted elsewhere, to meet different needs. While at the height of the Depression – 1931 and 1932 – Warners' realistic crime movies were regularly promoted in such a way as to put them among the year's most successful films, by 1936 *Bullets or Ballots* is the only one of the year's crime movies and contemporary dramas to have a significant box office career. If crime movies declined in importance, however, realistic films about contemporary society continued to be made right up to Pearl Harbor.

The feature which links the films discussed in the next four chapters is that they all, in different ways, deal with contemporary subjects in which the individual character or characters are in conflict with forces that are primarily social. Emotional considerations – romance; what *Variety* called the 'femme interest' – are secondary. The distinction can be clearly seen by comparing the murder trial in *They Won't Forget* (1937) with that in *We Are Not Alone* (1939). In the former, the traditional prejudices which govern North-South relations are the mainspring of the plot; in the latter, prejudice is merely a contributory element in a doomed and tragic love affair. The former is a social drama about 1930s America; the latter is set in an English never-never land, with Paul Muni adding a remarkably convincing English provincial doctor to his list of character roles.

The contemporary dramas also differ fundamentally from the biopics and costume dramas discussed in Part III. In the contemporary films, since the forces which govern the situation are beyond the control of the individual, action becomes problematic. Neither the charismatic gangsters of *Doorway to Hell* (Lew Ayres), *The Public Enemy*, *Angels with Dirty Faces* (1938), *The Roaring Twenties* (1939) – all James Cagney – and *High Sierra* (1941, Humphrey Bogart), nor the crusading if sometimes misguided professionals of *The Star Witness* (Walter Huston, 1931), *G-Men* (Cagney), *Bordertown* (Paul Muni, 1935) and *Bullets or Ballots* (Edward G. Robinson) can operate in the kind of social vacuum offered to the Errol Flynn of the Merrie England pictures. In a realistic setting heroic, single-minded action is limited by social constraints and, more importantly, it no longer guarantees moral superiority. The gangster pictures are, as Robert Warshow has pointed out,[4] the mirror image of a belief in initiative rewarded by economic and social success, while the course of action open to James Cagney in *G-Men* or to Edward G. Robinson in *Bullets or Ballots* is determined by, rather than itself determining, higher morality. As a result, there is a constant tension between the anarchic individualism which has always been one of the strongest characteristics of the modern hero, and a broader sense of social responsibility. The hero must act, but is not entirely free to do so. The respective careers of Johnny Ramirez (Paul Muni), the embittered Mexican American lawyer in *Bordertown*, and Rocky Sullivan (James Cagney), the gangster with a sense of honour in *Angels with Dirty Faces*, are perhaps the clearest examples of this. Both finally have to temper their individualism with more general social considerations.

The contemporary dramas have another unifying factor: their portrayal of women. Since, in the traditional narrative, action is a male prerogative and emotion a female one, women are consistently relegated to passive or negative roles, providing support for the hero as do Sidney Fox in *The Mouthpiece* (1932), Ann Dvorak in *Massacre* (1934), Karen Morley in *Black Fury*, Ann Sheridan in *Angels with Dirty Faces* and Ida Lupino in *High Sierra*; or threatening the hero's career or life like Constance Bennett in *Son of the Gods* (1930), all the women (with the exception of Beryl Mercer, the mother) in *The Public Enemy*, Bette Davis in *Bordertown* and Helen Flint in *Black Legion*. Only very rarely is a woman allowed to do the male thing of balancing personal considerations against a sense of responsibility: Bette Davis in *Special Agent* (1935) and *Marked Woman* (1937) is virtually alone in doing so, if one excepts the rather special case of *Life Begins* (1932), which will be discussed at greater length in Chapter 8. Independent women are generally portrayed as a threat to the hero. Married women do not fare much better. If it is true that the family is the foundation of the American social system, it is striking how few married couples are shown in American realistic movies as having the strength to tackle major issues together. Marriage is not strong enough to protect the partners in *Five Star Final* or *Black Legion*. But it is woman's natural state. Barbara Stanwyck in *Night Nurse* (1931), Bette Davis in *Special Agent* and Gale Page in *Crime School* (1938) are initially independent operators and decision-makers who are rewarded by a resolution of the narrative – marriage – which, by implication, takes that independence away from them. The fact that, in the realistic pictures, marriage (and therefore loss of independence) is seen as the independent woman's reward only serves to reinforce the belief created by Warners' sentimental dramas such as *The Old Maid* (1939): that feminine independence is an unnatural and probably temporary state. Even the forceful secretaries played by Aline MacMahon in *Five Star Final* and *The Mouthpiece* do what they do because they are secretly in love with their bosses – a motive which is never attributed to male protagonists. In this respect, therefore, contemporary America is not that different from Merrie England or the environment of the Great Men of the biopics: it is a man's world. Action may be problematic, but it is still necessary. And action is a man's prerogative.

Despite these similarities, the films with contemporary subjects inevitably changed with the times. The conflict between organised crime (gangs and syndicates as opposed to individual criminals) and the police provides the subject matter for the largest single group of films, from *Doorway to Hell* to *The Roaring Twenties* (which is in many ways a historical piece). In these films, a definite change of tone can be seen as the decade progresses, shifting from a romantic and somewhat sensational depiction of the gangster milieu in the years up to and including that of Roosevelt's election, to a more 'responsible' focus on the efforts of law enforcement agencies to deal with crime and corruption from *G-Men* onwards. The development is less obvious – but still significant – in the films that deal throughout the period with other social issues: with prison and rehabilitation from *Weary River* at the very beginning (1929) to *Each Dawn I Die* ten years later; with the threat of criminality invading the world of children from *Wild Boys of the Road* in 1933 to the Dead End Kids films at the end of the decade; with various forms of racism directed against Chinese Americans (*Son of the Gods*), native Americans (*Massacre*) and Mexican Americans (*Bordertown*); with the rise of fascism in America, both as a result of Nazi fifth column infiltration (*Confessions of a Nazi Spy*, 1939) and through the machinations of more or less sinister homegrown organisations (*Black Legion*; and *Meet John Doe*, 1941). Obviously there is, over the twelve years, a considerable change in both narrative method and the way in which social forces are depicted. *Weary River* and *Son of the Gods*, for example, are sentimental melodramas with serious themes, while *Black Legion* and *Each Dawn I Die* (1939) are far more precise in their depiction of the surrounding environment. But there is also, as there is in the gangster pictures, a clear change of direction in mid-decade. Society continues to contain the individual, but the relationship grows ever more problematic.

In launching its cycle of crime movies with *Doorway to Hell* in November 1930, Warners was scarcely starting a new trend. The American cinema's fascination with organised crime dates back at least to D. W. Griffith's *The Musketeers of Pig Alley* (1912), and there had been a flourishing cycle in 1927-8, of which the most memorable was Paramount's *Underworld*, directed by Josef von Sternberg. Indeed, most reviews of the early Warner gangster films treat them as the tail-end of an old cycle, rather than as the beginning of a new one. Part of the attraction of the genre was its topicality: gang wars and violent crime, though scarcely an everyday part of the average American's experience, remained very much in the news, and many of Warners' crime movies were based on recent headline stories. Most important from the studio's point of view, however, was the fact that crime movies provided a potentially perfect formula for fulfilling its early talkie policy of realistic and at the same time popular entertainment.

Crime stories are twentieth-century realistic drama at its most conventional. The problems of everyday life are not ordinarily considered dramatic, but when those problems bring the individual into conflict with a concrete manifestation of social rules – the law and the police – they can easily be dramatised in a way which fits most of the conventions. A man who is starving is not, according to conventional dramatic wisdom, especially interesting: to refer back to Sheridan Gibney's point about Anthony Adverse, he remains passive. A man who, because he is starving, steals a few dollars from a hamburger joint, is chased by the police, arrested and sentenced to ten years' hard labour on the Georgia chain gang, is a very much more suitable subject for a conventionally realistic movie. The idea of giving a dramatic focus to fairly ordinary problems or aspirations – poverty, unemployment, sexual inadequacy, alienation, ambition, greed – by making them criminal motives is very much a product of modern industrial society, dating back to the late eighteenth and early nineteenth centuries and finding its most typical manifestation in the novels of Balzac and Dickens, where social realism and crime are frequently linked. In the late twentieth century, crime stories have become the dominant form of conventional realism: there are few non-comic television series which do not involve law-breaking.

But the fascination with crime is not simply a matter of dramatic convenience. It has a deeper appeal. Ever since Rousseau redefined society as something more than merely the sum of its members – as an entity which was as often in conflict with the interests of the individual as in keeping with them – anti-social behaviour has been one of the strongest forms of romantic individualism. A line in *Special Agent*, explicitly referring to the attraction of the kind of story the film tells – 'the public's half-baked hero-worship of the tough guy' – makes the paradox clear. Western society is founded on the notion of individual energy and decisive action, making that energy – the hallmark of the 'tough guy' – admirable, but has necessarily to curtail it in its own interests. Such paradoxes are the basis of popular culture in general, and of film genre in particular. In the Western, the rugged individualism which built frontier society conflicts with the restraints on that individualism imposed by the newly established community: the farmer and the cowman should be friends, but rarely are. In horror movies, the danger and excitement of the unknown vie with a more conservative desire for safety and the boredom of the reassuringly everyday. In crime movies, it is the frustrations of urban society which are dramatised, not merely in the fairly narrow sense defined by Robert Warshow – that crime was the negative image of American initiative – but in a much broader, indeed total, sense. When a man comes into conflict with the law, he comes into conflict with society, whether we see that conflict in political terms or in the much vaguer sense of a revolt against 'the system'. Since we are all, to some extent, frustrated by society's restrictions, we all tend to sympathise with the criminal.[5] In terms of narrative structure, James Allen in *I Am a Fugitive from a Chain Gang* and Rico Bandello in *Little Caesar* (1931) are fairly exact equivalents of one another, both finding their aim of 'being somebody' (they use virtually the same phrase) blocked by social forces beyond their control. In terms of the film's basic appeal, it matters comparatively little that Allen is a basically honest man and Bandello a quintessential creep.

Warners' contemporary social pictures cover a wide range of topics, from gang warfare to newspaper ethics. Generally speaking, the forty or so films discussed in the following chapters are representative of that range, though there is a far higher proportion of 'problem' pictures among them than there is among the contemporary films as a whole. The main reason for this is that, as with the biopics, when the studio tackled a major social issue, it did so on a fairly large scale. The problem films were allocated top writers, major stars and comparatively large budgets. They were road-shown in the major theatres with strong promotional campaigns guaranteeing them longer than usual runs; they were important constituents of the studio's corporate image. For convenience, I have broken down the forty-odd films into a number of thematic groupings. It does need to be emphasised again, however, that it is only with the benefit of hindsight that clear thematic patterns can be distinguished in Warners' production programme during the 1930s. The actual decision to make a particular film at a particular time was determined not by any general policy, articulated or otherwise, but by a number of uncontrolled factors, ranging from availability of script material to popularity of actors and actresses. Of the contemporary films, the group from which any clear social comment is most obviously absent is that consisting of more or less straightforward thrillers. And it is with these films – the lowest common denominator of Warners' vision of the 1930s – that I propose to start. From several of them the police and the law are physically absent; in others, they are little more than the conventional agents of narrative resolution. But in all the films with the exception of *The Hatchet Man* (1932), where codes of behaviour are defined by reference to traditional Chinese customs, it is the law which establishes the norms to which the characters must refer. The individual remains at odds with society. *Night Nurse* and *The Hatchet Man* may be little more than thrillers, but they are clearly related, structurally and thematically, to the social conscience films.

Night Nurse is a strange little film, whose convoluted plot came in for a good deal of criticism from contemporary reviewers. The *New York Times* called it 'a pot-pourri of various things', Philip K. Scheuer of the *Los Angeles Times* referred to it as 'a neat little shambles', and *Variety* described it as 'a chaotic subject'. It has a certain interest for collectors of trivia in being one of only two films the young Clark Gable made at Warners: he plays a psychopathic chauffeur called Nick – a part originally allocated to James Cagney. The film tells the story of a young nurse, Lora Hart (Barbara Stanwyck), who, after fighting to gain admission to the profession and struggling through training, finds herself in a private home looking after two children who are being allowed to die of malnutrition so that their drunken mother (Charlotte Merriam) can collect what the *New York Times* called 'the inevitable trust fund'. Lora saves the children, exposes the corrupt doctor (Ralf Harolde) who had abetted the children's mother, and wins the love of the heart-of-gold bootlegger, Mortie (Ben Lyon), whom she had earlier protected at the hospital and who helps her defeat the vicious chauffeur, Nick.

Like *Life Begins* the following year, *Night Nurse* has a relatively realistic hospital setting and seems, for the first half-hour or so, to be concerned with portraying the vicissitudes of a nursing career. There are a number of everyday hospital scenes, such as a father-to-be nervously pacing the corridor and an assertive mother demanding that her son has a screen round his bed like 'that man over there' ('He's dying,' replies a nurse). Lora's first days in the hospital follow the *Dr Kildare* model. The severe woman in charge of new nurses (Vera Lewis) enforces strict discipline, and the young interns toss a coin for 'the new probationer'. Lora's friend Maloney (Joan Blondell) describes the interns as being 'like cancer: the disease is known, but not the cure'. The vicarious attitude towards nurses which the viewer is assumed to share with the interns is titillated by an unusually explicit scene in which Blondell and Stanwyck undress for bed, the former making a joke about the striptease: 'Oh, it's O.K.: I guess everyone round here has seen more than I've got.' But only one scene, in which a man dies on the operating table in the course of a dramatic operation filmed with close-ups of the anaesthetist's machinery and 'realistic' medical sound effects, actually attempts to dramatise medical activities as such.

The major dramatic weight of the film is carried by Lora's conflict with the criminal milieu, exemplified by the sinister Dr Ranger and the dissolute Mrs Richey ('I'm a dypsomaniac and proud of it!'). The more or less constant party which seems to go on in the Richey household, with its jazz, drunken couples and Mrs Richey herself slumped against the bar, is an imposing image of moral dissolution, not without echoes of the bourgeois party in Eisenstein's *Strike*. Her conflict with this inhuman world enables Lora's principles as a nurse to be given dramatic expression, in a way in which they could not be in the hospital. 'Oh, ethics, ethics, ethics!' she exclaims to the friendly doctor (Charles Winninger) who tells her she should not question Dr Ranger's orders. 'That's all I've heard since I came into this business. Isn't there any humanity in it?' For a while, therefore, Lora has to act against her professional ethics – to rebel. And the status quo has to be restored by extra-legal means. At the end, Mortie tells her that he has been talking to 'a couple of guys'. 'I happened to mention,' he adds, 'that I didn't like Nick too well.' We cut to a shot in an ambulance like the one that opened the film. 'Emergency?' asks the driver. 'No, morgue,' replies his assistant. 'Who is it? A bootlegger?' 'No,' says the assistant, 'some guy wearing a chauffeur's uniform.' And we cut back to Lora and Mortie smiling happily in the latter's car. In *Night Nurse*, it is not so much the general problems of everyday life which are dramatised through an exciting brush with crime, as the more specific vicissitudes of the nursing profession and of medical ethics: the word, as Lora implies, is a recurrent one in the screenplay. And while Lora's humanity is plain for all to see, it can only be rendered active by the brush with crime and by the help of a man acting criminally.

The Hatchet Man which, like *Night Nurse*, was directed by William Wellman, is an equally curious movie, in which the central character's basic criminality – he is an executioner for the San Francisco tong – is treated simply as a profession, without apparent moral condemnation: the focal point of the plot is his destructive love for a much younger woman. In that sense, *The Hatchet Man* is almost a sentimental drama, but the presence of Ralph Ince as an East Coast hood and Wellman's enthusiastically violent handling of the action scenes ensured that the film was seen, at any rate by *Variety*, as 'gang stuff' (albeit 'mild gang stuff').

Edward G. Robinson plays Wong Low Get, hatchet man of the Lem Sing Tong, who is instructed to execute his best friend, Sun Yet Ming (J. Carrol Naish), who came over on the same boat. 'Such a thing is impossible – to kill one's best friend,' he remonstrates. 'Your oath before the tong is an oath before your sacred ancestors,' comes the reply. His old friend Sun calmly submits to his fate and even bequeaths his daughter Toya (played in adulthood by Loretta Young) to Wong. Wong falls in love with her as she grows up, and proposes marriage. She accepts: 'American ways haven't made me forget my duty to my father.' 'Duty isn't consent,' replies Wong, but the marriage takes place none the less. Inevitably, it encounters problems. Toya becomes infatuated with a young bodyguard, Harry En Hai (Leslie Fenton), and Wong, who had sworn a sacred oath to her father to give her 'nothing but happiness', agrees to let her go. The decision, witnessed by a leader of the tong (Dudley Digges), proves fatal to him. He is stripped of his position and his business is boycotted. 'Greetings, O former brother,'

Edward G. Robinson in *The Hatchet Man*, with Loretta Young, Leslie Fenton

declares a note delivered to him in an empty coffin. 'Only a coward could look upon the unfilled coffin of his wife's lover. May it serve to bury the dead honour of your house.'

Wong sinks into poverty, but some years later receives a desperate letter from Toya in Shanghai, where Harry has become an opium addict, and her life has turned into a 'living death'. Wong sets off for China with his hatchets and tracks Harry down to No. 7, Street of the Red Lanterns. His rescue of Toya and his execution of Harry is a Wellman touch that makes even the ending of *The Public Enemy* seem relatively mild. Harry is sitting in a side room of the opium den, slumped against the wall (an earlier scene had shown him writhing feverishly on his bed, muttering 'The hatchet! The hatchet!'). Wong mounts the stairs to rescue Toya from the prostitution (not, of course, explicitly defined as such) into which Harry has sold her. As he comes down the stairs with her, he is accosted by the Madam of the house (Blanche Frederici). 'A woman is the property of a husband under ancient Chinese law,' he tells her and, to prove that he is indeed an 'honourable hatchet man', throws one of his weapons into the eye of a painted dragon on the far wall. He leaves, and Madame Si-Si tells a minion to pull the hatchet out of the wall. She then goes into a side room to remonstrate with Harry for selling a woman who was not his. As she berates him, he remains slumped against the wall, nodding disconsolately. It is only when Wellman cuts

81

to the servant attempting to work the hatchet out of the dragon's eye that we realise that the wall with the dragon is the other side of the partition against which Harry is slumped, that Harry has in fact been killed by the hatchet, and that the nodding of his head is caused by the servant attempting to prise the hatchet loose from the other side. As it is pulled out, Harry slumps forward.

It is macabre details of this kind – earlier in the film, one of Wong's clerks is tossed into a dock, wide-eyed, dead and trussed like Cagney at the end of *The Public Enemy* – that stamp the film as a crime movie, together with the presence in it of a group of six instantly recognisable 'arbitrators' from the East who arrive to settle the tong war in Sacramento. For *Variety*, the gang element was not strong enough: 'Dynamic action or high voltage drama now connected with the scowling Robinson, and implied by the film's title, is missing.' But the presence of a criminal framework is significant. It enables Wong to confront the potentially abstract issues of loyalty and love in a dramatic way. *The Hatchet Man*, however, remains an oddity: it is not really a contemporary realistic drama since, although it is set more or less in the present day, the film is suffused with oriental 'colour' and the trappings of mysticism. It ends with a sound flashback to Wong warning Harry, when the latter had sworn on oath to make Toya happy, that 'the Great Lord Buddha will find you no matter where you are on this earth.'

With *The Hatchet Man*, the studio was still exploiting the various possibilities of the crime movie cycle which had been so successful the previous year. The film was only moderately successful – and even that success was almost certainly due to Robinson, who had, in addition to *Little Caesar*, appeared the previous year in two similarly successful roles (*Five Star Final* and *Smart Money*). The cycle gradually settled down, over the next couple of years, into the familiar fast-talking, realistic and often socially outspoken format. By 1934, however, any foregrounding of social issues in the crime movies had largely disappeared, and they were generally seen as what the *Los Angeles Times*, reviewing *Fog Over Frisco*, referred to as 'mystery melodramas'. But *Fog Over Frisco* was a melodrama that was unusually successful – one of only ten movies produced by the studio that year to achieve a two-week first run at the New York Strand. This may have had something to do with the fact that the film was Bette Davis' first starring role at Warners after her loan-out to RKO: although her name appears below the title, she gets top billing (in a not particularly strong cast). In retrospect, Davis' role seems almost a trial run for some of her later, darker starring roles, most notably in *Jezebel* (1938). She plays the step-daughter of a banker (Arthur Byron) who becomes involved in an immensely complicated – indeed largely indecipherable – securities scandal, apparently connected with an unfortunate love affair. She ends up dead in the rumble seat of her roadster two-thirds of the way through the film (which lasts a mere 68 minutes), and the rest of the movie is taken up with a protracted chase through real San Francisco locations, and with the uncovering of the murderer, thanks largely to the banker's butler, Thorne (Robert Barrat), who turns out to be a secret service operative working undercover. The other characters in the movie are wholly conventional: a nightclub owner, called Jake Bello (Irving Pichel); a sweet young step-sister with the improbable name of Valkyr (Margaret Lindsay); a crusading newspaper reporter (Donald Woods), characterised as 'old stuff by now' by *Variety*; and a little comic relief from Hugh Herbert as Izzy, the press photographer constantly in search of 'the futuristic look' (which seems to involve standing on chairs, from which he repeatedly falls off). William Dieterle's direction has its usual verve. Mordaunt Hall in the *New York Times* felt that the overall lack of credibility was partly atoned for by the 'breathless pace and its abundance of action'.

The film's main source of interest remains Bette Davis as Arlene Bradford, first introduced from behind a bunch of balloons in a nightclub. With a merry cry of 'Bang! Bang!' she bursts them and is revealed. Like subsequent Davis characterisations, Arlene is far from innocent (and her demise is, therefore, all but inevitable). 'The trouble with you is you have too many of your mother's qualities,' her stepfather tells her: 'Bad blood, a rotten inheritance.' Her involvement in crime, from which her evident wealth removes any financial motivation, is entirely pathological. 'You can't imagine the terrible thrill,' she tells her hapless fiancé (Lyle Talbot) as she sits provocatively on his desk, 'wandering around with hundreds of thousands of dollars right under the nose of the police.' She blows him a kiss: 'Big boy! Now write me out a cheque for $50,000!' There is, in the film (as in the Davis persona in general), a tacit equation between female independence and such pathological behaviour. But as in all the crime movies, it is the fact that such behaviour manifests itself criminally that makes it dramatically exploitable.

Another successful crime film to deal seriously but superficially with the world of crime prior to the *films noirs* of the early 1940s is an out-and-out Edward G. Robinson vehicle, *The Amazing Dr Clitterhouse* (1938). It is almost, like the later *Brother Orchid* (1940), a comedy – almost, but not quite. Based on a stage play by Barré Lyndon which had been very successful in London and less so in New York, and in which the title role had been played by Cedric Hardwicke, the film is the somewhat bizarre story of an eminent doctor who sets out to study the pathological effects of crime by involving himself with a gang. This provides the opportunity for comic scenes, in which Clitterhouse's brilliance wins the crooks' respect, and dramatic ones of carefully executed heists and hair's-breadth escapes. In the end, Clitterhouse is arrested but, in the course of a semi-comic trial, he is pronounced insane because of his attempts to argue the sanity of his original experiment. The crime scenes rely on the by now well established depiction of the gangster world, with Claire Trevor as the brash blonde fence Jo Keller; Humphrey Bogart as the manic hood, Rocks Valentine; and Allen Jenkins and the former light heavyweight World Champion 'Slapsie' Maxie Rosenbloom as a couple of bumbling mobsters. There is even a vestige of the older, socially conscious model of crime movies in a scene where Clitterhouse asks Jo why she does what she does if she knows it is wrong. 'Would you ask the same question of one of those stock promoters who fleeces old women,' she retorts, 'or some swell society dame who owns a string of tenements?'

There are, as there were in *The Public Enemy* and other classic crime movies produced by the studio, two kinds of crime: individual and organised; a crime born of disadvantage and revolt, and a crime modelled on big business methods. It is on the individual variety that Warners' crime movies invariably concentrated, with organised crime always introduced in an unfavourable light. The model of the little man versus the world is as central to the studio's crime pictures as it is to its social conscience movies. But by mid-1938 – the date of *The Amazing Dr Clitterhouse* – the focus of Warners' socially realistic features had moved away from the almost self-parodying role that Robinson was increasingly coming to play. In most respects, *The Amazing Dr Clitterhouse* is cousin to the overtly comic *A Slight Case of Murder* (1938) and *Brother Orchid*. The studio's key crime movies were moving towards the far more intense, doomed gangsters played by James Cagney in *Angels with Dirty Faces*, *Each Dawn I Die* and *The Roaring Twenties*.

And indeed, the last two major crime thrillers of the period without a strongly depicted social background are outright *films noirs*: *High Sierra* and *The Maltese Falcon*, containing the first two roles with which Humphrey Bogart is inextricably linked in the public memory. Both scripted by John Huston, the former in conjunction with the novelist W. R. Burnett, the latter marking Huston's widely praised directorial debut, *High Sierra* and *The Maltese Falcon* are turning points in the history of the crime movie. Interestingly, however, both were seen at the time as somewhat old-fashioned reminiscences of earlier film-making styles. *Variety* described *High Sierra* as 'something of a throwback to the gangster pictures of the prohibition era', while Mordaunt Hall in the *New York Times* found in *The Maltese Falcon* 'something of the old thrill we got from Alfred Hitchcock's brilliant melodramas or from *The Thin Man* before he died of hunger'. In fact, both films mark a definite turning away from the old style of crime movies. *High Sierra* is not about gangs at all, but about the tragic failure of a doomed misfit, while *The Maltese Falcon* established almost single-handed the stylised, distinctly unrealistic tenor of the private eye movies of the 1940s. Mordaunt Hall may have underestimated the innovation of *The Maltese Falcon*, but he clearly recognised the tone of *High Sierra*. 'We wouldn't know for certain whether the twilight of the American gangster is here,' he wrote. 'But the Warner Brothers, who should know if anyone does, have apparently taken it for granted and, in solemn Wagnerian mood, are giving that titanic figure a send-off befitting a first-string god.'

Roy Earle (Humphrey Bogart), the hero of *High Sierra*, is a man out of his time. 'Remember what Johnny Dillinger said about guys like you and him,' muses old Doc Banton (Henry Hull); 'he said you're just rushing towards death – that's it, you're rushing towards death.' From the moment Earle is paroled at the start of the film and wanders into a park 'just to make sure the grass is still green and the trees are still there', to the ending in the Californian Sierras where he 'crashes out' to freedom in death, the entire film is structured like an elegiac farewell. Earle visits his old family farm. 'This used to be the Earle place,' a freckle-faced kid tells him, just pointedly enough for a more significant notion than mere change of ownership to be communicated. En route to the West Coast he meets up with a family of uprooted farmers, falls in love with their young daughter Velma (Joan Leslie), and pays for an operation on her club foot. But Velma is not the sweet young thing of Earle's essentially romantic outlook. Once cured, she abandons him for a younger lover, announcing 'I'm not crippled any more, and from now on I'm going to have fun'. Such a statement would be perfectly normal from a gangster's moll. But Earle does not see Velma as a gangster's moll; nor, given her impeccable suburban aspirations, does she. Earle sees her as he first saw her on the road – as innocence itself. And he is deeply hurt when she rejects him with the words 'You're just jealous and mean because I don't want you and I never wanted you'.

Earle also acquires two more fitting companions: Pard, a 'death-bringing' dog (Doc Banton's statement about Dillinger 'rushing towards death' cuts immediately to a shot of Pard rushing to meet Earle); and Ida Lupino's Marie, a loser just like him. The job he has been sprung from jail to do involves working with two incompetent, almost psychopathic kids (Alan Curtis and Arthur Kennedy). 'Small timers,' comments Earle contemptuously when they crash their getaway car. Old Doc, the man he has crossed the country to see, dies of a heart attack during his visit, and Earle is forced to kill a crooked cop called Kranmer (Barton MacLane) in Doc's apartment. In the end, Earle is recognised by an auto court attendant because of Pard and, having put Marie on the bus at a dusty desert truckstop, is pursued up to a pass in the Sierras. Surrounded by sardonic newspapermen and fast-talking reporters, he is cut down by a police marksman. 'Big shot Earle,' sneers a newsman. 'Look at him lying there. Don't amount to much now.' The line, similar to those at the end of both *Little Caesar* and *The Roaring Twenties*, is ironical. Earle's progress through the film is not, like that of Rico Bandello or Eddie Bartlett, a rise and fall: it is all fall.

High Sierra is the swansong of the 1930s gangster, as *The Wild Bunch* (1969) is the swansong of the traditional Western hero. While it may be going too far to equate the change in Hollywood production methods during the decade which was already a year old by the time *High Sierra* was released with the marked confusion of the American social climate some ten months before Pearl Harbor, there are clear parallels. The flat-out growth of the Hollywood studios during the 1930s to economic and stylistic maturity was not maintained during the 1940s (the war years were initially problematic and the post-war years little short of disastrous), nor was the essential optimism which had sustained America in the wake of the Depression and under Roosevelt's New Deal any longer dominant. With the end of American isolationism came an end to the belief in a country able to solve its own problems in its own way, or at any rate the introduction of a problematic into that belief with which in some ways the United States has still to come to terms. The 1940s marks the start of America's continuing involvement in foreign policy and world-scale *realpolitik*, with a consequent retrenchment in optimism and even a growth of paranoia back home. *High Sierra*, for all its excitement and elegiac tone, is a paranoid movie *par excellence*: it shows a world where values have slipped and nothing can any longer be relied on.

The Maltese Falcon, released nine months later, is a further retreat from the real world of the 1930s crime movies, however conventionalised that portrayal of the real world may have been. The plot of *The Maltese Falcon* is probably well enough known in its broad outlines not to need summarising here. And in any case, it is not the plot that is important: the story itself is based on a Dashiell Hammett novel already filmed by Warners under the same title in 1931 and, as *Satan Met a Lady*, in 1936. What is significant is the tone established by Huston with his low angles, frequently mobile camera and use of shots which break the studio's rule of narrative condensation in favour of a sense of foreboding, like the pan up to the flapping curtains beyond which Wilmer Cook (Elisha Cook, Jr) is just visible standing in a doorway on the far side of the street when Spade first makes to kiss Brigid O'Shaughnessy (Mary Astor). The dominant tone is a sense of world-weariness which Humphrey Bogart transfers from his playing of Roy Earle to his portrayal of Sam Spade. But Spade is not a doomed criminal: he is a reasonably successful private eye. His world-weariness comes from realising that he is essentially alone in a narrow world full of people like the epicene Joel Cairo (Peter Lorre), the affably vicious Gutman (Sidney Greenstreet), the almost psychotic Brigid O'Shaughnessy and the immoral kid Wilmer Cook.

Spade's partner Miles, whose death launches the plot, is not someone for whom he has much respect. 'Miles must have had his good points too, I guess,' remarks the cop (Ward Bond) at the scene of Miles' murder. 'I guess so,' replies Spade with clear lack of conviction. Spade's pursuit of the Falcon thus becomes a kind of private quest with no very clear motive ('When a man's partner's killed, he's supposed to do something about it,' he says offhandedly to Brigid at the end). Perhaps the most significant thing of all is the entirely secondary role played by the cops in this and subsequent private eye movies. The energetic restructuring of institutions which was a characteristic of the New Deal and which was celebrated in films like *G-Men* and *Special Agent* had long since lost its power to reassure: the tension between the individual and society was by now almost an existential thing, a one-way struggle with an opponent from which the individual could (or should) expect nothing positive in return. The cynicism about the spread of government agencies which caused Roosevelt's second administration so many problems and which swept Roosevelt's self-styled successor, Ronald Reagan, to power in 1980 is very much at the root of early *films noirs* like *High Sierra* and *The Maltese Falcon*. Where the emphasis in the early realistic films of the decade is on what society has taken away from its individual members (a job, happiness, security, even freedom), with a tacit or explicit statement that society owes it to its members to return those things, the emphasis in Warners' movies at the beginning of the 1940s is almost exactly reversed: the individual need expect nothing from society. More than that: in *Knute Rockne – All American, Sergeant York* and the anti-Nazi movies, the message is that the individual owes society a complete commitment to ensuring that it can continue on its established course. War movies enabled that commitment to be presented in terms of positive physical action – the sort of rampant Americanism that characterises *Sergeant York* (1941). But positive physical action was otherwise short-circuited. If the 1950s was the age of conformism, the 1940s was the decade of heroic conservatism and quiet despair.

In his serious roles at Warner Brothers, Edward G. Robinson was an actor who belonged firmly in the movies of the early part of the decade; the change in his screen image during the 1940s, with films like *Double Indemnity* (1943) and *Woman in the Window* (1944), took place at other studios. Of all the studio's small string of major stars during the decade, Robinson least avoided type-casting. After his huge success as *Little Caesar*, the studio was unwilling to chance him in a wider range of roles (*I Loved a Woman*, 1933, is something of an exception) and equally unwilling to allow his screen persona to develop. Public expectations did not help much: as late as 1938, reviewers were still using his portrayal of Rico as a yardstick. Throughout the decade, he continued to play tough gangsters, tough cops, tough newspapermen and, as a variant, mock-tough gangsters. And it is Robinson who is the star of Warners' occasional forays into gangster farces – in *Smart Money, A Slight Case of Murder* and *Brother Orchid*. Indeed, this last film was made as part of a deal with the studio: if they allowed him to play Dr Ehrlich (1940), he would do just one more gangster picture for them. The interesting thing about his two comic gangster roles, *Smart Money* and *Brother Orchid*, which came at opposite ends of the decade, is just how similar they are.

Nick the Barber (*Smart Money*) and Little John Sarto (*Brother Orchid*) are both tough-talking hoods with a strong sentimental streak. Like Rico Bandello, they have somewhat ridiculous aspirations towards sophistication; unlike Rico, their criminal activities – including, in both movies, murder – are not shown as being sufficiently immoral to alienate audience sympathy. Perhaps the most significant thing about *Smart Money* and *Brother Orchid* is that they show how, even with a comic emphasis, the specifics of Warners crime movies remain essentially the same. Nick Venezelos, the Greek barber in *Smart Money*, is an inveterate gambler from a small-town immigrant background. Indeed, the one thing that marks the earlier movie off from *Brother Orchid* is that, made in the middle of the Depression, it sketches in a genuine social background. For his first disastrous trip to 'The City', Nick raises his gambling stake from other immigrants and the local poor. A fellow Greek gives him $1,000 which he had been going to use to send for his wife ('Maybe I'm better off,' he quips); a black parts with a $5 bill. Nick is thus firmly established from the outset as a man of the people, unlike the other gamblers and crooks (on both sides of the law) he meets later. But the immigrant background, once sketched in, is largely ignored, and *Smart Money* charts Nick's success as a gambler and later as owner of a plush club, the Canary Cottage, which is openly patronised by the local Chief of Police. Part scripted by Kubec Glasmon and John Bright, authors of the source novel for *The Public Enemy*, *Smart Money* is a vehicle for Robinson after *Little Caesar* and for Cagney after *The Public Enemy* (he plays a strictly supporting role as a loyal henchman who dies during a police raid on the Canary Cottage). The relationship between Cagney and Robinson is the nearest thing the film has to a love affair: when Nick takes a (faked) suicide candidate, Irene (Evalyn Knapp), under his wing, he reassures Jack (Cagney) that it is a short-term thing. 'In a couple of days she'll be gone and you can be my sweetheart again.'

In fact, *Smart Money* is one of the most misogynist of all Warners crime movies and shows up that feature of the cycle every bit as clearly as the famous grapefruit scene in *The Public Enemy*. On his first trip to the big city, Nick is suckered by a cigar girl, Marie (Noel Francis), who refuses to return the $100 bill he had entrusted to her as insurance money. 'It's the big city, Hiram,' she sneers when he asks for the money back. 'Scram!' Blondes are Nick's weakness, as the D.A. (Morgan Wallace) realises in setting a trap for him. 'He's nuts for blondes,' he tells Sleepy Sam (Ralf Harolde). 'Send your wife round, he'll go for any old bag.' As John Scott observed in the *Los Angeles Times*,[6] 'All the women in the production are blonde, except, perhaps, a few used as atmosphere'. Even Nick's pet canary is called Blondie. And a climactic moment in the film is that at which Nick exacts his revenge on the blonde sent along by the D.A. by appearing to play along with her, then booting her in the behind as she leaves. 'She had District Attorney written right across her kisser. And before I got through with her, she had Nick the Barber written right across her ... something else.' The scene, according to *Variety*, 'drew a full minute of laughter and almost as much twice thereafter when referred to ... At the Winter Garden they howled, as they're likely to anywhere.' At a time of economic crisis, basic attitudes are likely to surface with greater force than usual, and the role allocated to women in *Smart Money* – as well, to a lesser extent, as in other crime movies – makes it fairly clear that, when the chips are down, it is the men who are expected to take the necessary action. Women are a liability. They pose a threat to Nick the Barber: unreliable, deceitful and likely to get in the way. Even the winsome Irene turns out to be part of the D.A.'s trap. Nick is more magnanimous to her: 'It's all right, Irene,' he reassures her. 'I've always been a sucker for women.' But the point remains the same: women are more likely to sucker than to succour men.

'*Smart Money* will have no trouble upholding its title at the box office,' predicted *Variety* with some accuracy. The film had a 49-day run at the Winter Garden – the second longest of the year – and was one of only seven to be held over for a second week in the Warners Los Angeles theatres during 1931. 'It possesses too much of what currently represents the popular appeal to miss or wobble, and it has a lot of entertainment quality to recommend it.' The popular appeal and the entertainment value, in so far as a distinction can be made between the two, lay in the depiction of a conventionally realistic modern setting in which a man, with a sense of humour and considerable determination, manages to overcome the drawbacks of the Depression. The fact that he does it illegally is offset by the fact that he does it with verve. But women are his downfall: they blunt his perception of the most efficient way of achieving success.

A characteristic that Nick the Barber shares with Little John Sarto is a desperation to appear culturally sophisticated – something which was, of course, a strong element in the make-up of Rico Bandello. After his first win, Nick turns to his black manservant. 'Suntan!' he calls out, 'my hat, my gloves, my cane!' Then he turns to his card partners, admitting: 'I heard that in a play one time' (though the fact that he refers to a play, not a movie, introduces an extra dimension to the comment). 'Have a cigar, boys,' he says during his ownership of the Canary Cottage, offering round a humidor of cheap stogies. 'Fellow in Havana makes them up for me' – a phrase he has heard from a big-time gambler earlier in the film. But while Nick appears to be aware that his sophistication is a veneer, Little John's delusions of grandeur are more real and become a major factor in his downfall. At the start of *Brother Orchid*, he is forced to leave the States for a year, fatally entrusting his crime empire to his second-in-command, Jack Buck (Humphrey Bogart). In London, during his European tour, he is sold a huge diamond which turns out to be a door knob. In Paris, he buys a broken-down racehorse for 150,000 francs and is forced to sell it for 150. In Rome, he buys a magnificent Renaissance bed which turns out to have 'Made in Grand Rapids, Michigan' stamped on the base. By the time he gets to Monte Carlo, he is broke.

There is, of course, a Jamesian element in Little John's disastrous European trip. An essentially sympathetic man with lots of New World energy, he falls easy prey to a string of European tricksters whose sophisticated veneer hides a basic decadent dishonesty. But the final point is a lot simpler: aspirations to sophistication are as much a part of a gangster's downfall as dames. He is, and should remain, a man of the people. In this context, Europeans are simply a worse version of American wealth and high society. And in *Brother Orchid*, which is in many ways the comic variant on *Little Caesar* that would have been unthinkable at the beginning of the decade, it is ordinary people – true Americans – who bring about Little John's rehabilitation. On his return to New York, he is kicked out and shot by Jack Buck and is then rescued by a plain-speaking Montana cowboy, Clarence Fletcher (Ralph Bellamy), who chauffeurs him out of New York at the start and helps him bust Buck's racket at the end. His real rescue, however, is at the hands of a group of monks. Initially Little John, who has lost touch with his origins, is cynically dismissive of these simple folk. Fletcher, for instance, does bird impersonations – something which renders him ludicrous in Sarto's eyes. 'Would you like to have him imitate a robin?' asks Flo (Ann Sothern), who is responsible for their introduction. 'What'll he do,' snaps Sarto, 'eat a worm?' The monks he quite simply cannot understand, though he is impressed when, on waking in the monastery garden, he sees two monks bending over him, apparently with haloes round their heads. But what Little John cannot accept is that there is no percentage in the monks' lives beyond a sense of satisfaction. He plays along happily enough, however, becoming a model monk by unfair means. He produces a record milk yield by spiking the milk with water; and he pays a local kid to hoe the prize zinnias so that he can retire beneath a bench to read a thriller hidden in a flower book. When his deceptions are discovered, he tearfully confesses. The Brother Superior (Donald Crisp) admits that, as a young man, he too paid a local kid to hoe the zinnias – though he gave him 25 cents an hour, not 50. Even as a con artist, Sarto is outclassed.

Gradually, Little John is drawn into the world of the monastery, helping with the flower business – hence the movie's title – and calling on old underworld connections when Buck's mobsters threaten to put it out of operation. He had gone halfway round the world looking for class, he confides to Fletcher, but 'this – this is the real class'. By 1940,

Brother Orchid, like the previous year's *The Roaring Twenties*, is a period piece. The gangster background is strictly conventional, with Robinson parodying earlier roles and Bogart doing his by now strictly conventional late 1930s act as a shifty, murderous henchman out to take control of the racket not by main force but by underhand action. By the end of the decade, the centre of the gangster movie – very much a product of the Depression – had collapsed, leaving only stylistic conventions open to parody (as in *Brother Orchid*) or to exploitation in a kind of vacuum, as in the two *films noirs* discussed above.

Newspaper pictures, another form of contemporary drama which shared many elements with the gangster movies and the social conscience pictures, were a feature of the first half of the decade – of the Depression years and their immediate aftermath, rather than of the more complicated social climate of Roosevelt's second term. In theory, one would expect them to have been prime vehicles for the exploration of social problems and conflicts, since journalism, together with the police and other investigative government agencies, provides an opportunity for the professional investigation of major contemporary issues. But although newspaper headlines are a standard feature in the montages which punctuate the social conscience pictures and crusading reporters do appear from time to time, the newspaper pictures themselves seem to have been little more than a minor stylistic variant of the straightforward crime movies discussed above. They have the same brash energy, the same fast-talking characters, often operating on the fringes of the underworld, and the same linchpin of determined action within a socially specific context. But they do not take that style into new areas of exploration. Of the three particularly successful newspaper pictures made between 1931 and 1934, two are in fact comic in tone; and, as in most comedies, the social background is presented as a largely inflexible reality, about which cynical remarks may be made, but which is not liable to be changed in any real way. There is one fairly clear – although not necessarily decisive – reason for this: as is clear from some of the furore created by the only emphatically non-comic film of the three, *Five Star Final*, Hollywood needed the press and could not afford to alienate newspaper owners by implying that they were doing their job wrongly or inadequately. Good relations with the press represented a fairly crucial element in the studio system's back-up industry. Newspapers, therefore, tend to be presented with some affection: as hives of activity in which disabused professionals go about their business in an exciting and entertaining way.

One other general point is worth making. Journalism is the only major profession in which women operated on a more or less equal footing to men during the 1930s, and the possibility of an active role being played by a woman on the screen was far more realistic. Although Loretta

Young became the family breadwinner in *Weekend Marriage* (1932), Kay Francis played a doctor in *Mary Stevens, MD* (1933), Margaret Lindsay a lawyer in *The Law in Her Hands* (1936) and Jane Wyman a shamus in *Private Detective* (1939), it is the highly conventionalised image of the 'girl reporter' which seems to have been the most successful embodiment of the non-passive female professional. The conventional aspect of the image is perhaps the most important: the ability to be attractive, flirt and talk fast were the characteristics most frequently stressed. All three of the newspaper pictures considered here feature women reporters who are (almost) a match for their male colleagues: Ona Munson as Kitty Carmody in *Five Star Final*, Mary Brian as Gladys Price in *Blessed Event* (1932) and Glenda Farrell as Gerry Krayle in *Hi, Nellie!* (1934). Indeed, Farrell's career was all but centred on the role. She played it in *The Mystery of the Wax Museum* (1933), where she is a welcome foil to the screaming victim played by Fay Wray, and went on, starting with *Smart Blonde* in 1937, to her own series of programmers in which she played ace reporter Torchy Blane.

Neither *Blessed Event* nor *Hi, Nellie!* are particularly memorable films, despite the presence of Paul Muni in the latter. *Blessed Event*, adapted from a successful stage play by Manuel Seff and Forrest Wilson, features a gossip columnist with the New York *Daily Express*, loosely based on Walter Winchell, and played in the film by Lee Tracy, who had gained stardom in 1930 as Hildy Johnson in the Broadway production of *The Front Page*, the play that gave birth to the newspaper picture. 'It gives a thoroughly intimate slant upon that new journalistic institution, the gossiping [sic] columnist,' wrote *Variety*, 'and puts him through a fascinating series of episodes, often wearing a halo of glamor, but often pictured from the mildly cynical side.' Alvin Roberts (Tracy) finds his niche in the newspaper world by getting advance knowledge of forthcoming births – 'blessed events' – from a friend who works in the maternity hospital. Needless to say, not all the births are legitimate, but all the parents are famous. The column is an enormous success, netting Roberts $90,000 a year from the newspaper, syndication rights and a radio show. Roberts is venal in the extreme. When the rival *Star* offers him a job, he holds out for $1,000 a week from his original employer. 'But how can I meet that?' asks the *Express*' editor, Louis Miller (Walter Walker). 'With money,' replies Roberts. His column eventually gets him into difficulties with the underworld when he publishes news of a forthcoming blessed event 'without benefit of clergy', for Dorothy Lane (Isabel Jewell), mistress of a hood called Sam Goebel (Edwin Maxwell). Narrowly escaping being shot by one of Goebel's underlings, Roberts devotes his attention to spilling all the dirt he can get on Goebel, who is shot by Dorothy.

What *Blessed Event* portrays, like other early newspaper pictures, is the immoral world of yellow journalism which, like the Broadway of the

1933 musicals, becomes a fairly accurate metaphor for Depression America. Though the film is for most of the time content merely to present this world, moral considerations do occasionally surface. Fellow reporter Gladys Price (Mary Brian) tells Roberts that his new column, 'Spilling the Dirt', is 'in about the same class as collecting garbage'. But although she leaves him repeatedly in the course of the film, they end up together, and Roberts' success is celebrated: 'What did I ever amount to before?' he asks. 'It's great, it's mine, I made it' – a clear statement of the benefits of initiative. Cynicism is the keynote of *Blessed Event*. When the wife of an unemployed man calls the paper under the mistaken impression that Roberts handles the birth announcements, he inserts an item which ends with the words 'Her husband, Mr Moskowitz, said "What do you mean, unemployment?"' Roberts' mother (Emma Dunn), a dotty lady who is supremely unaware of her son's style of journalism, describes her late husband as 'one of nature's gentlemen: even when he was drinking the most, he never forgot my birthday'. Perhaps more importantly, the public is shown as being avid for Roberts' gossip. The opening sequence has an irate investor calling the *Express* to complain about the column's 'filth' while his wife, daughter and maid rush to read it. The fact that Roberts' near comeuppance is at the hands of a vicious hood effectively diverts any serious moral consideration of his brand of journalism – he becomes a variant on the crusading reporter threatened for his honesty – and he is allowed the final moral luxury of promising Dorothy Lane that he will get Clarence Darrow to conduct her defence.

The predominantly comic tone of the film diverts moral considerations. The irrepressible Ned Sparks, for example, plays George Moxley, a journalist who is demoted to Pets Editor as a result of Roberts' success. 'There are millions of people with pets,' the Editor reassures him. 'There are millions of people with bald heads, too,' rejoins Moxley. 'Couldn't I be dandruff editor?' Even the underworld has its comic side, with Allen Jenkins' bumbling gunman Frankie Wells, constantly dropping his gun in embarrassing places and at one stage left to spend a cosy evening with Roberts' mother. The final comic element in the film marks the debut of a former emcee at Warners' Pittsburgh theatre, Dick Powell, who plays the crooner Bunny Harmon in a way that is a precise parody of his later starring roles. Harmon is star of The Shapiro Shoe Hour, crooning the company's commercial: 'You'll be a hero, If you wear Shapiro Shoes. Ten baby fingers, Can do what they choose; But the baby toes, All demand Shapiro Shoes.' Roberts' mother is a fan of Harmon and asks her son to 'make it up with him'. 'He can make up all he wants to,' Roberts snaps back. 'I'm going to stick to the he-man stuff.' *Blessed Event* is a necessary corrective to the belief that all Warners' forays into the contemporary scene were marked with a strong liberal streak.

Hi, Nellie! is a good deal less cynical than *Blessed Event*, but it is also less precise in its depiction of a social background. Like the earlier film, it introduces a gangster element to break the deadlock of a plot which might otherwise have remained within the limits of journalism. 'It always seems as if a newspaper picture must also have a mystery element,' remarked Edwin Schallert in the *Los Angeles Times*.[7] Paul Muni plays Samuel N. Bradshaw – Brad – managing editor of the *Times-Star* who comes into conflict with the paper's owner (Berton Churchill) over his apparent misjudgment of a story about a scandal in the banking world. Unconvinced of the banker's guilt, Brad refuses to imply that he has absconded with the funds, even though all the evidence points in that direction. The *Times-Star*'s owner tries to sack him, but Brad points out a clause in his contract which protects him against dismissal. 'I'll be sueing you,' he trills over his shoulder as he leaves the owner's office. He is placed in charge of the lonelyhearts column, supposedly run by a Nellie Nelson. Brad bridles at the demotion but makes a success of his new job, and 'Nellie's column is the talk of the town', as a newspaper insert declares. In the course of researching an item, he stumbles on the truth about the disappeared banker, who has been rubbed out by a mobster called Beau Brownell (Robert Barrat). Brad's earlier editorial decision is thus vindicated, and his investigation, which takes him to an extraordinary futuristic nightspot called The Merry-Go-Round Club, with a revolving bar in the centre of the floor, and to a near shoot-out in a cemetery, leads to his reinstatement as editor and to the allocation of the Nellie Nelson column to the office toadie.

'The *Times-Star* editorial room,' wrote Mordaunt Hall in the *New York Times*, 'is another of those strangely ruled places for which Hollywood evinces a great fondness in its search for realism.' But the realism of *Hi, Nellie!* is strictly conventional, featuring Paul Muni as a brash, hard-drinking newsman, hat on the back of his head, feet on the desk, phone cradled on his shoulder, bawling out young reporters and making snap decisions about stories. Most of the film's comedy centres on his being teased about his demotion; the title phrase is chorused at him every time he appears in the newsroom. Glenda Farrell is on hand as the smart girl reporter, and Ned Sparks does another cameo as the wisecracking newsman, Shammy. *Hi, Nellie!*, though rather better than *Variety*'s dismissal of it as 'never more than casually amusing or exciting', is a strictly formulary exercise, with the newspaper world substituted for gangland or the cynical backstage world of the Warners musical. Indeed, its interest lies in the way in which it reproduces the ideology of those worlds. Brad is a man of the people who puts his principles, where necessary, into dramatic action, while the owner of the paper is a fatuous idiot with little professional skill and inversely proportional aspirations to social respectability. As the crisis approaches its peak, he turns up at the *Times-Star* offices in an absurd naval uniform he has been wearing to a society ceremony, and is simply pushed aside by Brad. Even in the conventionalised world of *Hi, Nellie!*, the simple virtues of plain-spokenness, professional skill and a propensity for action are those which are set above money and power. The world of the *Times-Star* is a world in which opportunity still exists and where dynamism is still rewarded.

Five Star Final, on the other hand, is much less conventional and manages, with its combination of social conscience, narrative economy and genuine emotional impact, to be one of the most surprising omissions from the list of frequently revived Warners classics. In it, Robinson follows hard on the heels of Rico and Nick the Barber with his playing of Randall, editor of the *New York Evening Gazette*. Initially somewhat conservative – he is characterised as a man who won't print filth – he is pressured by his editor, Hinchecliffe (Oscar Apfel) and the two advertising managers (Robert Elliott and Purnell Pratt) into running a circulation-building sequel to a twenty-year-old murder case in which a Nancy Vorhees is alleged to have murdered a man who betrayed her. The *Gazette* tracks down Nancy (Frances Starr), now married to Michael Townsend (H. B. Warner), just as their daughter Jenny (Marian Marsh) is about to marry. The revival of the scandal drives Nancy and her husband to commit suicide, and brings the grief-stricken Jenny gunning for Randall. The latter berates the paper's management and resigns in disgust. The film, based on a successful stage play by Louis Weitzenkorn, which had had runs in New York, Boston, Philadelphia and Chicago, is strongly editorialising – a fact which Warners played for all it was worth in the film's publicity. The press book quotes 'a prominent California justice' as claiming, in an address to the Academy, that 'the strongest editorials in the country are not in the newspapers, but in talking pictures'.

Yellow journalism may not have been a major social evil of the early 1930s, but it was clearly a contributory one, and Warners attack it with the same verve they brought to the early crime pictures. *Five Star Final* is an unmistakable studio product. It opens with a montage sequence of busy newspaper activity, normal and not so normal: a pre-title insert of the *Gazette*'s front page; presses running behind the main credits; shots of the newspaper's switchboard; a brief scene of thugs breaking up a newsstand because the proprietor does not have the *Gazette* displayed on top. And the film's final shots make the message quite clear. *Five Star Final* ends with a close-up of the *Gazette* lying in the gutter; a gob of dirt splatters down on to it, and a broom sweeps it down the gutter along with the other garbage. But the film's main interest lies in the oppositions it sets up, which are basically those of the gangster movies and the social conscience pictures. Randall is a man who prints the filth reluctantly – there are repeated 'symbolic' inserts of him washing his hands – at the bidding of the business interests who control the paper.

Washing off the filth: Edward G. Robinson as the editor, with Aline MacMahon, in.
Five Star Final

When he decides to drop the Townsend story and resign, the advertising manager attacks him: 'For two cents, I'd smash your face in!' 'For two cents,' snarls Randall, 'you'd do anything.'

The central opposition of principled editor versus unprincipled publisher is backed up by a secondary one between a happy family, the Townsends, and the rag that destroys their happiness. To get the filth on the Townsends, Randall uses T. Vernon Isopod (Boris Karloff, in his last role before *Frankenstein*), a failed divinity student with a taste for booze and lechery. 'I rode uptown in a cab with him,' says reporter Kitty Carmody (Ona Munson), 'and I've hardly got any skin left on my knees.' The Townsends, on the other hand, are one of the studio's rare serious portrayals of a happy family, evincing the kind of calm contentment that, as in Fritz Lang's *The Big Heat* twenty years later, is set up only to be destroyed. We first see them through the window of their Bronx apartment, happily playing cards. Inside, joy and togetherness reign; outside, Kitty Carmody predatorily paces the sidewalk.

The later suicide sequence firmly establishes the hunter/hunted relationship and its consequences. Nancy Townsend calls Hinchecliffe to beg him not to run the story. A split-screen technique – much touted by the studio in its advance publicity – sets Hinchecliffe against Nancy, then Nancy against Randall as Hinchecliffe passes the buck, then all three of them together before Randall finally hangs up on Nancy. She is left alone in the central section of the triptych. Then, in a full-screen shot, she walks into the bathroom, is seen in silhouette opening the medicine cabinet, then closes the door with a bottle in her hand. There is a strangled cry of 'Oh God!' and a crash. We cut to a priest promising her husband to get in touch with the *Gazette* and to do everything possible 'for you and your wife'. Townsend returns home to tell Nancy the good news. As he opens the bathroom door we cut to a low angle long shot – a piece of visual rhetoric frequently used by Mervyn LeRoy to signify threat – of his daughter and future son-in-law Philip (Anthony Bushell) getting out of a cab. Townsend is forced to pretend that everything is all right, even to the extent of making a fake phone call to Nancy when the kids ask about her absence: in close shot, tears in his eyes, he chats cheerfully to the dial tone. The radio plays jaunty jazz. The kids go out. Townsend walks into the bedroom. There is a cough and a crash, and we dissolve to the radio playing away. The door buzzer goes. Not getting any reply, Carmody and a photographer climb in through a window and find the bodies. She tells him to take pictures. Cut to Randall looking thoughtfully at the phone, then to a newsvendor shouting 'Read about the big suicide!' An insert of the full-page picture pulls back to reveal Philip's parents telling Jennie the marriage is off. It is a sequence which perfectly represents the Warners style, not just in the contemporary pictures but in the biopics as well: a dramatic series of shots which simultaneously advances the plot and expresses the conflict, not so much personalising a general issue as generalising a personal one.

One of the more interesting elements in *Five Star Final* is that, like *Blessed Event* the following year, it makes the *Gazette*'s readers as responsible for the paper's muckraking policy as the publishers. One could not exist without the other. 'Editors have a tendency to put themselves on a little pedestal above the readers,' Hinchecliffe remarks to Randall. 'If I sat on a cigar box,' replies Randall, 'I'd be above ours.' The fact that the *Gazette*'s readers were also the film's audience is something that *Variety* commented on, although it shied away from drawing any conclusions: 'Story is a hard rap at the readers of such tabs ... and while these readers will make up a large part of the audience, they won't mind.' The whole impact of the studio's social conscience pictures is summed up in that phrase: the films were critical, but well within the conventions of entertainment. If the readers didn't mind, though, there is some evidence that the tabs did. An article on the front page of the *Los Angeles Times* by Harry Carr, a respected California newsman, defends the film fiercely and notes: 'So great was the storm of indignation roused in New York against the tabloids that one of the worst of the reeking journalistic gutter rats made a sensational flop and clambered wildly out of the muck, after the picture's New York showing.'

Made for a comparatively modest $290,000 (including $35,000 for Robinson and $19,250 for LeRoy), the film is an impressively direct attack on the gutter press. As Philip K. Scheuer remarked in the *Los Angeles Times*, '*Five Star Final* asks no quarter and gives none. If there is another side to the case, it finds no utterance here'.[8] The film's bias is, of course, a weakness, not because it is unfair to yellow journalism (an area in which fairness is an irrelevant commodity), but because the issues of right and wrong in the Townsend case are so clearly established that it is difficult to see it as much more than a piece of single-instance pleading. But the opposition between morality and money interests (either greed or business sense, depending on one's position) remains significant in terms of the studio's stance during the early 1930s. A memo in the film's production file emphasises that significance. Writing to Wolfgang Reinhardt in August 1945, Alvah Bessie, one of the most radical of the Hollywood Ten, suggested a remake, but adapted to the post-war situation. '*Five Star Final* could,' he suggested,

> if the studio were interested in the idea, be adapted to the topical scene along these lines: an isolationist newspaper could, for instance, dig up some 'dirt' on a nationally-prominent progressive figure, and thereby ruin not only his personal reputation and his family's happiness, but distort what he stands for and malign his worthy cause.
>
> It is a question of whether the studio would be interested in making such a pioneering picture or not. It would mean tackling the real issues of the day – national and international unity vs. the interests of a rapacious minority.

The studio was not interested. Times had changed in the post-war world, and with them the kind of film being made by Warner Brothers. In the light of subsequent events in Hollywood, Bessie's memo is nothing if not ironical.

6 Gangster Movies

The kind of films the studio definitely *was* interested in making throughout the 1930s were ones with gangster themes and settings. They were relatively cheap to make, since they used contemporary dress, minimal sets (seedy restaurants, backroom offices and hotel rooms) and exteriors that rarely if ever called for anything other than the standing sets of the backlot. Additionally, once the formula was perfected – as early, basically, as 1931 – the scripting and pre-production process was ideally suited to Warners' streamlined studio methods. If the plots are all quite similar, the production process was more or less invariable. One of the staples of Warners' output, the films were, of course, extremely popular – more so than the figures in Appendix II imply, since they were rarely prestige productions but could rather be counted on to do solid business in the small-town and neighbourhood theatres, regularly giving a large return for a comparatively small investment. They clearly captured the public imagination; but this is an effect rather than the cause of their success. The cause necessarily lies in the way in which they responded to and reflected contemporary concerns.

Gangster movies were both exciting and topical – a useful combination. But there are other, more fundamental elements in their structure which may go some way towards accounting for their popularity. To start with, they showed characters responding actively and often with a strong sense of personal honour to social circumstances which, in real life, seemed to condemn their audiences to inactive frustration in the face of a 'system' which often appeared *dis*honourable. Naturally, the character of this response varied during the decade; gangster movies were not just a phenomenon of the early Depression years. *Doorway to Hell* in 1930 has the strongly hectoring tone of a silent melodrama: it portrays a rise and fall whose moral rather than social implications are explicitly drawn. The same explicit moral occurs in later gangster films, but increasingly appears to have been added as a corrective to the rather glamorous image of the gangster which the emphasis on action tended to create. As contemporary critics of the genre pointed out, the moral caption which precedes *The Public Enemy* (1931) is largely cancelled out by the impact of the movie itself. But that impact is not in itself immoral or even anti-social. While the activities of the gangster are beyond the law, his behaviour is characterised by a strong sense of small-scale social responsibilities, of group loyalty, to which the law remains oblivious. This point is emphasised by the essential structural similarities between those films in which the central characters are on the side of law and order, and those in which they are not.

Loyalty to the group is a theme which recurs throughout the 1930s. Whether the films are concerned with gangs (*Doorway to Hell*; *Little Caesar*, 1931; *The Public Enemy*; *The Roaring Twenties*, 1939), with law enforcement agencies (*G-Men* and *Special Agent*, 1935; *Bullets or Ballots*, 1936) or with those caught in between (*The Star Witness*, 1931; *Marked Woman*, 1937), the emphasis is always on some form of loyalty to a group in the face of pressures from outside, no matter where those pressures come from. The central characters die because their ambition has alienated them from family or gang more often than just because they are criminals: their downfall is at the hands of their peers rather than the police. In *Taxi!* (1932) and *Marked Woman*, where the central characters survive and even prosper (at any rate morally), it is because they recognise that their interests are those of the community, not those of a narrowly defined individual survival. James Cagney in *G-Men* and Bette Davis in *Special Agent* achieve their personal goals (revenge in the case of the former, happiness in the case of the latter) by siding with the community, now represented – as it could not have been in the declining years of the Hoover Administration – by a Federal Agency.

There are three films which do not quite fit into this pattern: in *Doorway to Hell*, *The Star Witness* and *The Roaring Twenties* the values of the community are less readily identifiable. But the values of all three are strongly determined by the contemporary social climate. *Doorway to Hell* and *The Roaring Twenties* are both picaresque moral tales of a hoodlum's decline; but the first, premiered almost exactly a year after the Wall Street Crash, is romantic, while the second, released shortly after the outbreak of war in Europe, is elegiac. Though the two films are set in almost exactly the same period, their view of the world is radically different, reflecting their date of production rather than the date at which they are set. And *The Star Witness* encapsulates more perfectly than either *Little Caesar* or *The Public Enemy* the conflicts of 1931 – between a sense of social responsibility and a society which is both insensitive to the problems involved in that responsibility and unable, other than by a piece of enormous good fortune, to protect its members.

Despite their similarities, then, Warners' gangster movies evolve during the decade. This can be seen by comparing films which, at different times, deal with the same theme, and by looking at the large shift in the personality of the studio's major male star, James Cagney, which came with *G-Men* in 1935. To begin with a comparison: *Doorway to Hell* and *The Roaring Twenties* bookend both the decade and the cycle. The former looks back as much to crime melodramas such as *Underworld* as on to *Little Caesar* and *The Public Enemy*. *The Roaring Twenties*, on the other hand, anticipates the *films noirs* of the early 1940s as much as it looks back, with explicit nostalgia, to the heyday of prohibition and prohibition movies: 'This film is a memory,' declares the prologue, 'and I am grateful for it.' Both films are based on fact. *Doorway to Hell* is, at any rate in part, a loosely disguised biography of Al Capone. Its hero, Louie Ricarno (Lew Ayres), sets about organising the mobs into an effective business operation, then attempts to retire to Florida. At this point, however, the similarity to Capone ends. Louie is forced out of retirement when a rival gang kills his kid brother; he returns to Chicago, wipes out the opposition and is arrested. The cops, realising they will never be able to pin anything on him, allow his rivals to spring him from jail and execute him. *The Roaring Twenties*, based on a story by Mark Hellinger, draws on Hellinger's direct experience of the New York rackets, and models its central characters even more explicitly on racketeer Larry Fay and singer Texas Guinan, 'Queen of the Night Clubs' (who appeared as herself in a 1929 Warners film of the same title). Eddie Bartlett (James Cagney) returns from the war to temporary unemployment, a stint as a taxi driver and a successful career as a bootlegger. He teams up with a former army buddy, George Hally (Humphrey Bogart) and nightclub star Panama Smith (Gladys George). Ruined by the Crash and what he describes to Hally as 'a new kind of set-up you don't understand', Eddie dies, like Larry Fay, on the steps of a church. 'What was his business?' asks a bystander. 'He used to be a big shot,' comes the reply – the same line used to sum up Roy Earle's career in *High Sierra*, with Raoul Walsh's direction further emphasising the similarity between the two movies.

Doorway to Hell, however, is a straight contemporary gangster picture, while *The Roaring Twenties* is a record, with documentary-style inserts, of a bygone era. Contemporary reviews make this difference abundantly clear. While there is the suggestion that both films are reworkings of a familiar theme, the comments on the use of that theme are very different. '*Doorway to Hell*,' wrote Edwin Schallert in the *Los Angeles Times*,[1]

> will engross the mind, as does some well-written news story of racketeering battles. It contains no flub-dub or hokum. It is a sincere and unornamented presenting of its subject. Whether it is entertainment in the fullest sense at the same time is an entirely different question. The audiences that attend it, and there seemed evidence that they will be large, will find the ultimate reaction of the picture one of peculiar hopelessness and futility. So definitely has the creed of gangland been adopted by the members thereof that nought but the entire wiping out of the ranks would appear to bring the cessation of the guerilla conflicts.

For Frank S. Nugent, writing about *The Roaring Twenties* in the *New York Times* nearly a decade later, Warners did not so much avoid the moral implications of the gangster movie as overplay them,

> with the self-conscious air of an antiquarian preparing to translate a cuneiform record of a lost civilisation. With a grandiloquent and egregiously sentimental foreword by Mark Hellinger ... [and] a commentator's voice interpolating ultra-dramatic commonplaces as the film unreels, their melodrama has taken on an annoying pretentiousness which neither the theme nor the treatment can justify. The dirty decade has served too many quickie quatrains to rate an epic handling now.

Leaving aside the obvious flaw in Nugent's logic – it is surely precisely because there have been so many 'quickie' gangster movies that a deeper treatment can be justified – it is clear that the concerns of the crime movie are no longer directly relevant to the contemporary viewer in 1939, while the attempt to use the form for a quasi-historical character study still seems too novel.

Two features stamp *Doorway to Hell* and *The Roaring Twenties* as belonging nevertheless to the same cycle of movies. First, in both films social problems are shown as being at the root of crime. Before leaving Chicago for Florida, Louie Ricarno pays a nostalgic visit to his birthplace. Eyeing a streetcorner shack with hatred, he remembers that his family used to buy their milk there, and that his brother died of typhoid; it is from this world, it is implied, that his career of crime was designed to remove him. *The Roaring Twenties* makes the same point more tendentiously, with a dramatic 'newsreel' of soldiers' unemployment, and a scene in which a cop comes into a speakeasy, not to raid it, but to bawl out a man with a Vermont licence plate for parking alongside a fire hydrant. Society is going to hell, and its agents are corrupt. Secondly, in both films money is seen as the only way to a better life, albeit in an ironic way. Louie dismisses worries about his being bored when he retires with the words 'I've got enough money to buy something to replace it. Money can buy anything.' In *The Roaring Twenties*, a similar dialogue takes place around a radio being inspected for quality: 'Is it any good?' – 'Ought to be. Cost a lot of dough.' – 'That should make it good. It makes everything good.'

But the differences are more marked and more significant than the similarities. Louie Ricarno, like Rico Bandello, is a hood with a Napoleon complex. He sends his kid brother (Leon Janney) to military academy because 'war is a grand racket' and because, if he himself had been born a couple of hundred years earlier, he 'might have been as big a man as Napoleon'. His final hideout is decorated with a painting of 'Napoleon in Exile'. Eddie Bartlett, on the other hand, has no such aspirations. His partnership with George Hally is governed by a healthy mistrust: 'I don't trust you, George.' 'You could do with a little watching yourself,' replies Hally. 'That sounds like the basis of a partnership,' quips Bartlett. Driven by different urges, the two characters' downfalls are equally distinct. Louie Ricarno, set up for execution, goes out in a blaze of romantic glory. A waiter brings in a meal supplied by his rivals. 'They told me to tell you this was your last supper and it's all paid for.' 'Tell them I'm sorry,' says Ricarno, 'but I'm dining out tonight.' He takes his gun, throws it on the bed, spruces himself up, looks at the Napoleon painting, and walks out of the door. The shot is held on the doorway, and the sound of continuous machine-gun fire accompanies the final caption. Eddie Bartlett's demise is much more downbeat. He sees his former girlfriend Jean (Priscilla Lane) with her boyfriend Lloyd Hart (Jeffrey Lynn). He goes up, pushes Jean away and hits Lloyd. 'What are you trying to prove?' asks Jean. There is a pause, while Cagney looks his most dog-eared. 'Nothing,' he mumbles. He turns, and walks away to his death.

And, in the two films, the explicit message is radically different. *Doorway to Hell* makes no more general point than a final rhetorical warning about the perils of crime. As Louie disappears through the door, a caption appears on the screen:

> The Doorway to Hell is a one-way door. There is no retribution – no plea for further clemency. The little boy walked through it with his head up and a smile on his lips. They gave him a funeral – a swell funeral that stopped traffic – and then they forgot him before the roses had a chance to wilt.

The warning carried by *The Roaring Twenties* is less explicit but more closely related to a wider social concern: an opening montage takes the viewer back from contemporary 1939 to April 1918, when 'almost a million young Americans were engaged in a struggle which they have been told will make the world safe for democracy.' *The Roaring Twenties*, made as Europe entered World War II, starts its narrative with America involved in World War I. While the focus of *Doorway to Hell* is America's domestic problems, that of *The Roaring Twenties* is, at any rate indirectly, America's foreign responsibilities. As a moral tale, it charts a disillusioned response to the Depression. But now that the internal strife has been overcome, the time is ripe for America to make the world safe for democracy again. The ideals must be rediscovered.

Doorway to Hell and *The Roaring Twenties* are just outside the mainstream of Warners' gangster movies. If there was an archetype of the form, it would be an amalgam of *Little Caesar* and *The Public Enemy*, because of their theme and the playing of their central roles. Edward G. Robinson and James Cagney remained the studio's top hoods. Robinson continued to be strongly associated with gangster roles for ten years; while Cagney, having played Lew Ayres' sidekick in *Doorway to Hell* and having started the shooting of *The Public Enemy* in the secondary role (he swapped with Edward Woods after a few days),[2] was the studio's main star in contemporary roles throughout the decade. Although the two films were shot virtually simultaneously, with Hal Wallis supervising *Little Caesar* at Burbank and Darryl Zanuck supervising *The Public Enemy* at the Sunset studio, and were premiered within just over three months of one another, they seem to sit on either side of a stylistic watershed. The former movie, under Mervyn LeRoy's direction and with a screenplay by experimental playwright Francis Edwards Faragoh, still retains the morality-tale air of silent melodrama, with its heavily pointed dialogue, its expressionistic lighting of the streets in which Otero (George E. Stone) and later Rico himself are shot down, and its dubbing of the mastermind behind the Chicago mobs simply as 'The Big Boy'. The latter film, thanks to a more precisely located social background in Kubec Glasmon's and John Bright's original story (adapted by Harvey Thew), to James Cagney's extremely modern portrayal of Tom Powers by contrast with Robinson's rather stagey and consciously larger than life acting as Rico, and finally to the violent energy of William Wellman's direction, sets the tone for the crime movies produced at Warners over the next four or five years.

It would be possible, I suppose, to disregard the social background and to divide the decade's crime movies up into those which, like *Doorway to Hell*, *Little Caesar* and *The Roaring Twenties*, took the gangster milieu at face value and used it for an essentially moral parable of rise and fall; and those which, like *The Public Enemy*, *Taxi!*, *Bullets or Ballots* and *Angels with Dirty Faces*, showed crime in its social setting. But social background cannot be disregarded, least of all with films that draw on contemporary reality and rely in large part for their success on reflecting contemporary concerns and fears. And the difference between *Little Caesar* and *The Public Enemy* is best accounted for, not in moral terms, but by seeing the two films as separate attempts by the studio to find a style and an approach suited to reflecting and reflecting upon that social background. That it should be *The Public Enemy* rather than *Little Caesar* which ended up as the model for the first half of the decade has less to do with its initially slightly greater success (it ran a week longer in New York) than with two factors which indicate the close but problematic relationship between studio production methods and ideology. *The Public Enemy*, with its flatter, more economical style, provided a more suitable model than *Little Caesar*: it could more easily be adapted into a formula than the earlier film, which remains something of a one-off. And Cagney's performance is better adapted to the production formula, requiring less showcasing and remaining subordinate to the needs of the narrative – a feature which was essential to the studio's realistic contemporary films. The kind of film which resulted from this formula was best suited to the needs of the Depression audience. It showed them recognisably everyday figures operating within a situation that was at worst a dramatic exaggeration, at best (in, for example, the home scenes of *The Public Enemy*) a precise description of everyday reality. The basis of Cagney's star persona throughout the decade was his ordinariness – better able to handle himself than many of his contemporaries perhaps, and consistently funnier, but distinctly recognisable. To be able to win a fight and be funnier than the next guy was – and remains – an essential element in the popular self-image of the American (urban) male. Robinson, on the other hand, is almost always *extra*ordinary – larger than life, like Errol Flynn or Bette Davis. He may be more dramatic, but he is less recognisable.

Rico Bandello in *Little Caesar* is, as the title implies, a hood with delusions of grandeur, obsessed with the need to 'be somebody'. He is fascinated both by power, a fascination which leads him to the ruthless control of a section of the Chicago rackets, and by the trappings of power, cultural respectability. Here, however, he is out of his depth. His attempts to ape the Big Boy (Sidney Blackmer) are regarded with some amusement, best expressed in his remark on a painting he has been told cost $15,000: 'Gee, those gold frames sure cost a lot!' He is without family ties: as Gerald Peary suggests,[3] Ma Magdalena (Lucille La Verne), the old harridan who shelters him for $9,850 (his ten grand minus the $150 she allows him for expenses), is a 'surrogate, nightmare version of maternity'. He has no relationships with women. Indeed, as in *Smart Money*, there is a strong hint of homosexuality – the anti-social perversion *par excellence* in popular American culture – in his friendships with Joe Massara (Douglas Fairbanks Jr) and with Otero, the toady who worships him. He climbs alone to power and falls from it alone, dying beneath a billboard advertising the joint success of a couple, Joe and his sweetheart Olga (Glenda Farrell), mouthing the now classic phrase, 'Mother of Mercy, is this the end of Rico?'

Tom Powers in *The Public Enemy*, on the other hand, is a far from isolated individual. An ordinary slum kid, he drifts into crime through poverty. A montage of stock shots sketches in the social background of his Chicago childhood in 1909, and a dramatic scene suggests that a beating by his father (Purnell Pratt), a brutal cop, may also have been a decisive influence. His successful career as a bootlegger is controlled more by a sense of loyalty to his own gang than by a quest for power. His criminal activities cause problems within his family, but these are caused less by Tom than by the attitude of his brother Mike (Donald Cook), whom he despises for his belief in the work ethic ('Ah, that sucker! He's too busy going to school. He's learning how to be poor.'). But Tom is never entirely alienated from his family: his mother (Beryl Mercer) remains devoted to him and is all set, at the end of the film, to welcome him home from hospital when his corpse is delivered at the front door. Indeed, the fact that Tom's body is delivered to his own home, while Rico's is left lying on the street, signals a major difference between the two films. It also stresses the point that, whatever his motives, Tom's behaviour has ultimately violated the sacred unit of the family.

Tom has close relationships with his buddies and associates, notably with Matt Doyle (Edward Woods) and local bar owner Paddy Ryan (Robert Emmett O'Connor), but this does not mean he cannot have relationships with women, even if the two shown in the film – with Mae Clarke (of grapefruit fame) and Jean Harlow – are not especially successful. In choosing an Irish background for Tom Powers at a time when the rackets were clearly dominated by Italians, Glasmon and Bright enabled Warners to stress the warm extended family which became a focus of many later Cagney vehicles, most notably *The Irish in Us* (1935). In the end, *The Public Enemy* is about an ordinary man from an ordinary background whose life of crime, however motivated, violates the sanctity of family life: there is a conflict, not so much between man and society, as between various ways of coping with poverty. The conflict with society is an unquestioned fact, and family and gang are the two possible bases for waging such a conflict. Tom Powers' methods may be illegal, but he never really steps outside society. Rico Bandello, on the other hand, never really steps into it. The only family shown in *Little Caesar* is that of Rico's driver, Tony Passa (William Collier Jr), whose mother reminisces about how he used to sing in church as a little boy before he sets off to see Father McNeil and is shot down on the steps of the church. Rico himself is an extra-social figure, who becomes, as Mordaunt Hall wrote in the *New York Times*, 'a figure out of Greek epic tragedy, a cold, ignorant, merciless figure, driven on and on by an insatiable lust for power, the plaything of a force that is greater than himself'. It was precisely the ordinariness of *The Public Enemy* that led Hall to dismiss the later film as 'just another gangster film ... weaker than most in its story, stronger than most in its acting'. But it was the ordinariness and the acting that made it the model: here, a life of crime becomes, not a Greek tragedy, but a reflection of and on the problems of Depression America.

The formula continued to be ground out over the next three or four years in the form of programmers, occasionally with variants like those discussed above in *Fog Over Frisco*, but with no film achieving the prominence of the two 1931 pictures, or even of *Doorway to Hell*. In the year of Roosevelt's campaign and in the first two years of his Presidency, America's social problems were explicitly recognised and the studio dealt with them more directly. But 1935 saw a marked change in the focus of Warners' major crime movies. In the first place, the Hays Office's new Production Code explicitly forbade the glorification of criminal figures. In the second place, the nation's financial position, along with that of the studio, was improving. A new cycle of films begins with *G-Men* in March 1935 and all, like certain of the early gangster films, are thinly disguised versions of recent headline stories. The difference is that the heroes are cops and government agents. With the stabilisation of the economy and, therefore, of society, the kind of romantic pessimism which characterised the early gangster films is no longer apposite. Crime is no longer the prerogative of lone individuals but of organised syndicates with all the external respectability of legitimate business operations. Alexander Carston (Ricardo Cortez) in *Special Agent* operates with relative impunity from a plush office with accountants and telephones, protected by a battery of lawyers and a public image which stresses his 'anonymous' funding of an orphanage. Al Kruger (Barton MacLane) and Bugs Fenner (Humphrey Bogart) in *Bullets or Ballots* run their rackets from behind the huge pillars and ornate porticoes of the Oceanic Trust and Banking Company or the ironically named cover of the Metropolitan Business Improvement Association. The heroic lone operators putting their lives on the line are now the cops, often undercover (George Brent in *Special Agent* and Edward G. Robinson in *Bullets or Ballots*) and always in danger. Otherwise, not very much changes: the plots are still resolved in shoot-outs, and the women still provide passive moral support.

G-Men, Special Agent and *Bullets or Ballots*, released between April 1935 and May 1936, all dramatise recent events in the 'war against crime'. *G-Men* crams in the most contemporary references – scarcely veiled dramatisations of the Kansas City train depot massacre, the careers of Dillinger and Baby Face Nelson and the Wisconsin resort siege and round-up. *Special Agent* is less specific, but the mainspring of its plot, the trapping of gangster Alexander Carston on tax evasion charges, can obviously be related to the technique finally used to bring Al Capone and a number of other mobsters to justice. And the characters of Johnny Blake and Al Kruger in *Bullets or Ballots* are closely modelled on Johnny Broderick and Dutch Schultz. *G-Men*, wrote *Variety*, 'is the first of the new cycle of gangster pictures, coming in with what is called a new twist'. Almost all reviews of the film refer back to *The Public Enemy* and *Little Caesar*, noting that the 'new cycle' shifts the active hero on to the right side of the law.

This is not without its problems. Backed up by the full panoply of law enforcement, the cop's actions are less heroic: he can hardly lose. In the short run, he may be at threat, and two of the movies introduce an element of undercover work as a way of intensifying that threat. But in the long run he has society behind him. He lacks the element of romantic revolt often associated with the gangster. Characterisation likewise remained a problem in the new cycle: the heroes, being morally impeccable, were also less likely to be interesting. '*Little Caesar, Scarface* and *The Public Enemy*,' wrote *Variety*, 'were more than portrayals of gangster tactics; they were biographies of curious mentalities. They were photographic and realistic analyses of mentality and character (or lack of it). But in the new idea of glorifying the government gunners who wipe out the killers there is no chance for that kind of character development and build-up.' The *Variety* review of *Special Agent* returns to the point: 'Lack of characterisation plus stilted repetitious dialogue robs the melodrama of any chance to grip.' But the format of the old gangster movie still provided the impetus in the new cycle. The shift from gangster to cop is often barely noticeable amid all the generic elements.

In fact, the screenplays of all three movies indicate attempts to overcome this problem. Brick Davis (James Cagney) in *G-Men* is a convert to the FBI from the wrong side of the law, as is Julie Gardner (Bette Davis) in *Special Agent*. Their characters are to a certain extent defined by the switch they make, as much for personal as for principled reasons. Brick Davis wants to avenge the death of a G-man pal, while Julie Gardner falls in love with a government investigator masquerading as a reporter. This decision to change sides not only gives the films a central moral choice on which to focus; it also means that the new converts to respectability carry with them some of the old glamour of illegality. With these preliminary adjustments made, however, the films can get down to business. *G-Men* is a piece of almost outright propaganda for the arming of the FBI. 'See Uncle Sam draw his guns to halt the March of Crime,' trumpeted a studio ad. 'Uncle Sam's fighting agents crash the screen in a Blaze of Gunfire and Glory' was a suggested alternative. Brick Davis is a young lawyer who has been put through college by a gangster called McKay (William Harrigan), apparently with no strings attached. His allegiance shifts to the FBI when his best friend from college, Danny Leggett (Edward Pawley), is shot down outside his office. He goes through a period of rigorous training, becomes a fully-fledged Fed, and is instrumental in a major piece of racket-busting. There is very little more to the plot than that.

But it is the details in *G-Men* which are the most significant element. In the first place, it is the vehicle for some fairly explicit pleading on the part of the FBI, voiced by the Bureau's head Bruce J. Gregory, played by Addison Richards, a stock player specialising in judges and prison governors, who is an obvious fictional equivalent of J. Edgar Hoover. The film is concerned with making three main points on the Bureau's behalf: that it is a highly organised, scientifically run organisation; that it needs well-educated agents; and that it needs to be armed. The first two points are a simple matter of demonstration. We are treated to a display of the FBI's scientific approach – ballistics tests, fingerprint classification, communications equipment, training methods – presided over by former silent star Monte Blue in a white coat. And the recruitment of Brick Davis provides the opportunity for Gregory to tell Jeff McCord (Robert Armstrong), the suspicious professional cop, that the Bureau 'needs these kids with their Doctorates in Law and Philosophy and their Phi Beta Kappas'.

The need for the FBI to be armed, on the other hand, has to be 'proved', and this becomes the mainspring of the plot. The crooks who kill Brick's friend Danny mutter about having 'to get across the State line' to freedom and, before shooting him, comment contemptuously, 'Why, those government agents don't even carry rods!' The central propagandist passage of the movie involves the 'historic' decision to change all this. A montage of headlines (along the lines of 'Crime Wave Sweeps the Mid-West!') and cars speeding away from bank robberies gives way to a final headline, 'Department of Justice Seeks Laws to Fight Crime Wave'. There then follow two establishing shots of Capitol Hill, cutting to Gregory's speech to a Senate Committee: 'Give us national laws ... Make bank-robbery and kidnapping a Federal crime ... Make it a Federal crime to kill a Government agent and to flee across State lines to avoid arrest ...' At a personal level, the film has already 'proved' that gangsters kill Federal agents and then flee across State lines. Something needs to be done. Brick Davis is already doing it, but he needs help. Gregory's main point in his speech is that the FBI must be armed, 'not just with revolvers but with machine-guns, shotguns, teargas, everything else. This is war!' A further series of headlines about the Committee's decisions dissolves to a close-up of a hand writing 'Killed in the line of duty' across the bottom of an agent's record card – further 'proof', should any still be needed, of the need for the new laws. A final sequence 'proves' the popularity of the decision. A delighted Chicago florist (Joseph DeStefani) gives an agent information and, when told to keep his mouth shut, replies with a broad grin: 'You bet! I don't want to get tangled up with you G-guys!'

As always in a Hollywood narrative, however, the real proof is provided by the story of the central individual, Brick Davis. In the FBI, his friend Danny tells him just before being murdered, Brick would be free from corruption: 'No fat-face politician telling you what to do.' This follows hard on a scene in which a certain Joseph Kratz (Edwin Maxwell), a fat-face politician if ever there was one, has tried to pressure Brick into defending one of his hoods on a murder charge. Immediately afterwards, Danny is shot, and Brick's choice is crudely signalled: lying next to the newspaper reporting Danny's death is an FBI application form. Cagney's tough-guy screen personality also influences the choice. 'You sure look funny sitting behind a desk,' Danny had told him. Indeed, the film opens with an even clearer indication to the viewer that all is not well for our boy. In close-up and in a posh accent, Cagney makes a legal speech straight to the camera and to what a slow dolly back reveals to be an empty office. This is not Cagney's style at all. He breaks off the speech with a far more recognisable 'Ah, phooey!' and slings his pen, dart-like, into the back of the door. As a G-man, Cagney can get out from behind the desk and into action. As always, the shift to action signals the correct behaviour. Argument may define issues, but action resolves them.

The final facet of the film's triptych of proof involves the female roles. Brick is torn between two women. One, Jean Morgan (Ann Dvorak), is a dancer involved with chief mobster Brad Collins (Barton MacLane), but harbouring a strong emotional attachment to Brick. She belongs to the world he has left, however, and can only joke about her role in the one he has just entered: 'I could always knit you a bullet-proof vest for Christmas,' she offers. In the end, though, it is her catch phrase which becomes crucial. 'There's no reason a G-man can't kiss an old friend goodbye,' she says to him when he leaves for training in Washington and later, as she dies in his arms after a shoot-out in a diner. Kay McCord, played by Margaret Lindsay, the permanent nice girl of Warners' contemporary movies, is his superior officer's sister and is initially extremely resistant to Cagney's brand of aggressive charm. Only respect for his work as an agent wins her round, but it does so decisively. Brick's choice between the two women is another aspect of his choice between the two worlds, crudely signalled in a scene in which Jean and Kay meet across Brick's hospital bed, Jean clad in black, Kay in white.

Special Agent, made in the same year, goes to nothing like the same lengths to prove that the modern hero should be working for the government. Renewing the successful teaming of George Brent and Bette Davis in *Front Page Woman* (and repeated several more times, in *Jezebel*, 1938; *The Old Maid*, 1939; and *The Great Lie*, 1941), the film starts with the hero already working for the government and the heroine gradually won over to his cause by being won over to him. While in *G-Men* Cagney's choice of action was given an objective correlative by Kay's love, in *Special Agent* it is Bette Davis's gradually growing love for George Brent that decides her to make the switch. 'You'll have to tell me what to do,' she says romantically to Brent in a scene in his car beside a river. In a parallel situation, the man acts on principle, while the woman is motivated by her emotions. Repeating her *Fog Over Frisco* casting as a bad girl, Davis plays Julie Gardner, a book-keeper working for the racketeer Carston (Ricardo Cortez). Brent plays Bill Bradford, an undercover agent for the Treasury – a T-man – posing as a newspaper reporter and out to trap Carston. Gardner helps him do so; Carston abducts her; Bill rescues her; and Carston is brought to justice.

With the model firmly established by *G-Men*, *Special Agent* is at best a cheaply made sequel, making extensive use of inexpensive interiors (offices, nightclubs, hotel rooms). Bette Davis is, as Philip K. Scheuer wrote in the *Los Angeles Times*,[1] 'repressed to the point of demureness'. But the film is recognisably part of the cycle. It opens with a shot of the

Stars and Stripes, then pans down on to the Senate building. We hear a speech about the Federal government taking steps to 'rid the country of the gambler, the business racketeer and the illicit profiteers who are operating in and above the law'. We cut to a group of tax inspectors being briefed, Bill among them. 'Go after them,' they are told. 'Get their books and statements ... You're through observing: raid if necessary!' Their job is to implement 'the will of the American people'. The film features the same patriotic, crime-busting rhetoric as *G-Men*. 'I think you've kicked Joe Public in the pants once too often,' Bill tells Carston. Carston puts himself firmly at odds with the mood of the picture by describing the public contemptuously as either 'live cowards or dead heroes'. And the choice of the individual becomes, once again, a surrogate for a broader choice. 'I can't stand much more of Carston,' Julie tells Bill. 'You *can't*,' he replies, 'and I have a hunch that an uncle of ours in striped pants and a beard *won't*.' The action climax rather misfires, despite a documentary-style dramatisation of modern police methods, with a central control room broadcasting radio messages ('Attention Cars 167 and 168! Green sedan heading your way!'). But it is supplemented by a surprise climax in the courtroom into which Carston, more afraid of jail than death, has managed to smuggle a gun. He raises it to shoot Julie as she testifies. Bill shoots him in the hand. 'I think I'm going to be a sissy,' Julie tells Bill, and faints. A headline announces 'Guilty!' As the judge sums up, bars appear across the shot of Carston. Bill and Julie announce their wedding plans.

All in all, *Special Agent* is a rather jolly little film, taking its issues more or less for granted. *Bullets or Ballots* is equally recognisable as part of the cycle, but far from jolly. Like the two previous movies, it is directed by William Keighley, with a screenplay by Seton I. Miller who had co-scripted *G-Men*, and an original story by Martin Mooney who had provided the basis for *Special Agent*. It is a much darker film than the other two, able to admit, now that the cycle is established, that the war against crime is perhaps not going to be entirely plain sailing. *Special Agent*, as noted in the previous chapter, has an element of self-criticism on the studio's part in its reference to 'the one thing we've never been able to lick: the public's half-baked hero worship of the tough guy'. *Bullets or Ballots* is equally self-referential, beginning with the two chief hoods, Al Kruger and Bugs Fenner, arriving at a movie theatre in their limo to see 'the crime picture'. What they in fact see is a documentary about racketeers, with dramatic music and a hectoring commentary, in which they are both mentioned. The film shows Al being found not guilty, and the judge lecturing the jury – as an upstate New York judge had done in a case in which Dutch Schultz had been set free – on their abnegation of public responsibility. The documentary ends with a newspaper owner, Bryant (Henry O'Neill), promising that he will continue to expose the racketeers: 'They rule by the fear of their bullets.

They must be smashed by the power of your ballots.' We leave the film within a film for a headline announcing Bryant's death, and the camera pans up to introduce Johnny Blake (Edward G. Robinson) ordering a drink.

The entire sequence is significant. Kruger is a hood who is more or less immune because of the extent and the apparent legitimacy of his business operations. Blake, on the other hand, is a tough cop whose 'flying squad' has been disbanded as part of a liberalising initiative: 'Nowadays we're supposed to kiss them and tuck them in.' Very much the tough guy, Blake is also an old friend of Kruger's; once again, the hero's role as a cop is given a rebellious tinge as a result of his former underworld connections. To break the racket, Blake goes underground again. A carefully staged punch-up with the Police Commissioner at Madison Square Garden results in his being supposedly thrown off the force, and he is thus able to infiltrate Kruger's operation, which is in fact run by three respectable financiers with cultured voices and huge houses. In the end, Blake busts the racket but is shot by Bugs before shooting him in return. He staggers out into the corridor, drags himself along the hallway and falls out into the street, thereby triggering off the raid. 'Keep kicking 'em into line, Mac,' he gasps to his old precinct captain (Joseph King). 'I like to think that when those mugs pass a policeman they'll continue to raise their hat.' He dies: the individual has sacrificed himself for society while still remaining somehow on its fringes.

Part of the tone of *Bullets or Ballots* may be accounted for by the casting of Robinson, whose final film this was under his exclusive contract with Warners. But what the film does do is get the crime movie back into its familiar version of contemporary reality: the little man versus the system. The individual cop, even without the manacles of liberal legislation, is no match for the organised mob. And the mob itself is curtailing the activities of the small – and, by implication, honourable – criminal. Nellie (Louise Beavers), the black woman who collects the numbers money in Harlem, and Lee Morgan (Joan Blondell), the nightclub owner who is Blake's closest friend, and who also resorts to petty crime (numbers) in order to survive, are both opponents of Kruger's mob. If Hollywood's portrayal of the criminal was often ambiguous, its portrayal of organised crime syndicates was always hostile. Although the tone of Warners crime movies changes quite decisively with *G-Men* and the advent of the Production Code, and from 1935 onwards the focus is squarely on the conflict between cops and hoods rather than simply on the hoods, it did not take long for the central ideological pivot of the studio's contemporary dramas – the individual versus the cynically powerful system – to reassert itself.

Of all the crime movies, the ones which should have been the most realistic were those which showed ordinary citizens whose lives were

112

touched by crime, trapped between threatening criminals and a police force unable or unwilling to protect them. In fact, those films are no less conventional: where there are no generic patterns to rely on, the depiction of contemporary reality tends to be conventionalised in other ways. Hollywood realism needs some kind of barrier between its audience and the reflections of them on the screen. Between 1931 and 1937, Warners were successful with four films in which ordinary citizens were caught between gangsters and the law. Like the studio's other crime movies, they reflect the changing times. *The Star Witness* (1931) shows a grimly poised balance of power between cops and mobsters; *Taxi!* (1932) and *The St Louis Kid* (1934) submerge social reality beneath the brash witticisms of a Cagney vehicle; and *Marked Woman* (1937) is a dark personal triumph for Bette Davis in the first of her clearly recognisable star roles, ending with her walking off nobly (though not alone) into the fog.

The Star Witness, another early crime movie to bear William Wellman's unmistakable stamp in its action scenes, features an all-American family as archetypal as any to appear on the screen prior to MGM's Hardy Family. It consists, in descending order of age, of Gramps, a feisty Civil War veteran played in what one might best describe as irrepressible style by Charles 'Chic' Sale; a very ordinary Pa and Ma, played by Grant Mitchell and Frances Starr, he an accountant who boasts rather pathetically about the 'importance' of his job, she much given to baking and cheerful commonsense; an out-of-work son (Edward J. Nugent) who spends his life hanging round the pool halls; a sensible daughter (Sally Blane) with a job in a department store who delays family dinner by smooching in her boyfriend's car; and two younger boys (Dickie Moore and George Ernest) obsessed with baseball and fond of exclaiming, 'Oh boy! Chocolate *cake*!'

An opening title stresses the ordinariness of the setting: 'A neighborhood of plain people – in an American city of today.' The Leeds kids, Donny and Ned, are talking about battles with other kids on the block. 'My Grandpa fought at Bull Run!' boasts Donny. Then he sniffs chocolate cake and they run inside. We move straight into an ordinary if somewhat sentimental dinner scene. The two youngest kids are licking the cake spoon, Jackie (Nugent) is celebrating the fact that dinner is pork and beans, and Sue (Blane) is holding things up as usual with her courting. The sentimentality is briefly interrupted by an argument between Pa and Jackie about the latter's unemployment. 'Is it my fault I can't find a job?' asks Jackie belligerently. 'No,' replies Pa, 'but I don't see you busting a leg to get one.' Pa is just about to send Jackie from the table when the row is interrupted – and sentimentality restored – by the sound of Gramps' tin flute playing 'Yankee Doodle'. 'Merciful Heavens!' exclaims Ma. 'Drunk again!' Gramps arrives and Sue is sent down to the cellar for some blackberry jam.

It is important to stress the sentimental ordinariness of this opening, since it becomes a kind of foundation for the movie, and is, at this point, decisively interrupted by the sound of a car chase and machine-gun fire in the street. We cut outside for a brief violent punctuating shot – a man (who later turns out to be an undercover cop) runs into the camera as he is shot down. Then the two worlds, family life and crime, finally meet as Maxey Campo (Ralph Ince, one of the most sinister-looking of the studio's character actors) bursts into the living room, clubs down Gramps, and threatens the rest of the family that he will 'smear the wallpaper wiv you' if they raise the alarm. We cut back to the cop's body lying in the street to show that Campo is quite capable of doing so.

Most of the rest of the movie – based on a recent Harlem gang shooting, thus preserving the actuality of Warners' early crime cycle – is concerned with the attempts by District Attorney Whitlock (Walter Huston) to get the Leeds family to identify Campo, and the counter-efforts of Campo's gang to 'dissuade' them from doing so. The dissuasion takes two forms. The first is vintage Wellman. Pa is picked up outside his office by two men claiming to come from the D.A.'s office, taken to a warehouse and made an offer ('How would you like to take your family and go on a vacation: sunshine, flowers, avocados, you know?') which he rejects. As a result, he is picked up by the ankles and, in a scene that is painfully violent even to a modern audience, is swung repeatedly against the wall until the plaster starts to crack and crumble away. The second method of intimidation is more closely related to the film's theme of crime as a threat to family life. Donny is taken hostage by the gang, the only evidence of his abduction being his baseball bat, cap and mitt left lying in the alley behind the house.

Since Pa has already been beaten senseless for preferring his duty to a $500 bribe, it is left to Jackie to confront the D.A.'s rhetoric. 'This is the fight of every decent man,' intones Whitlock. 'We're not only fighting Campo, we're fighting the whole rotten gang system ... I'll send Maxey Campo to the chair or die trying.' 'Maybe it won't be you who does the dying,' retorts Jackie. Whitlock's assistant, Thorpe (Russell Hopton), also has a go at persuading Jackie. 'Did you ever hear the word duty?' he asks. But he does no better. 'Yes,' sneers Jackie. 'I also heard the word baloney.' The very real dilemma facing the Leeds family is indicated not merely by the things that happen to them, but by the cavalier way in which Whitlock dismisses it, describing Gramps and his descendants as 'a doddering old fool who's half-drunk and a family too weak-kneed to say black is black'. Not only does Lucien Hubbard's screenplay portray the gangsters, in the year of *Little Caesar* and *The Public Enemy*, as 'just so much scum' *(Variety)*; it also portrays the cops as powerless to protect and callous in their attitudes. Whitlock's aim is, at any cost, to send a gangster to the chair – something that the county has so far been unable to do.

114

In the end, it is Gramps, doddering old half-drunk fool though he may be, who saves the day. He tracks down Donny by scouring the city playing 'Yankee Doodle', on his tin whistle until the child manages to signal his presence. And he resolves the conflict between fear and duty by an appeal to basic Americanism. 'I *am* thinking of Donny,' he had told the family in the D.A.'s office. 'And I'm thinking of something else you folks are forgetting: what it means to be an American ... Of course I love Donny. But I don't want him to grow up in a country run by a lot of foreign murderers.' His speech to the court, after he has triumphantly entered in mid-trial hand-in-hand with Donny, returns to the same somewhat chauvinistic theme in relation to the (Italian) gangsters. 'Trouble with us, we're too weak-kneed with them. What would the founders of our country have done with scum like them?' he asks the judge rhetorically. 'A damn dirty furriner can crowd an American so far, just so far.' To applause from the public gallery he turns, punches Campo, kicks his legs from under him, and mutters: 'Now, where's that witness stand?' 'Make it snappy, Gramps,' Ned calls to him. 'We've got beans for supper!' And we cut to a headline: 'Maxey Campo executed!'

What is interesting about *The Star Witness*, apart from the surprisingly modern style William Wellman brings to his first assignment after *The Public Enemy*, is not so much that it appeals to prejudice as a way of encouraging the fight against crime, as that it shares with Wellman's

Plain people: the American family in *The Star Witness*

previous film the same latent optimism about the strength of American society, specifically the family, in the very midst of the Depression, and that it stresses once again the importance of group cohesion – backed up, of course, by principles – in the midst of adversity. What binds the Leeds family together is essentially what relates Tom Powers to his mother and to Matt Doyle, and what Rico Bandello never had: a sense of group identity. Maxey Campo is beaten, not by the D.A., but by American family life. By the time we get to *Marked Woman* near the end of 1937, that group identity has been severely compromised. The interests of the individual are nowhere near so readily identifiable with the interests of society, and the career of Mary Dwight (Bette Davis) is, before a carefully engineered narrative situation endows her with a sense of duty, driven by a twisted version of the same individualism that characterises Louis Pasteur, Emile Zola and the parts played by Errol Flynn around the same period. In a realistic contemporary American setting, that individualism has difficulty in finding a 'useful' outlet.

Like *The Star Witness*, *Marked Woman* is taken from fact, bowdlerising Lucky Luciano's Dannemora 87 brothel into a slightly less explicit clip joint, the Club Intime, in which Mary works. Her reasons for doing so are economic. 'We've all tried this twelve-and-a-half a week work,' she tells the Club's new owner, the Luciano surrogate Johnny Vanning (Eduardo Ciannelli). 'We've had enough of it.' She and the other girls are cynically aware of the nature of their work. 'That's the sugar that makes the flies come round,' drawls Emmy Lou (Isabell Jewell), as she holds up a slinky new dress. Mary's work at the club is endowed with a slightly nobler motive, in that she is using her earnings to put her kid sister Betty (Jane Bryan) through college. The inevitable happens: Betty finds out where the money is coming from, and storms out on Mary, calling her immoral. But then Betty gets drawn into Vanning's world, ends up dead, and Mary vows vengeance. 'I'll get even with you,' she says, 'even if I have to crawl back from my grave to do it.' She nearly has to. Vanning has her badly beaten up, and it takes (of course) the help of a man, city prosecutor David Graham (Humphrey Bogart, in one of his few 1930s roles on the right side of the law), before she can bring Vanning to justice. Again, Graham is more interested in smashing Vanning's racket than in helping Mary, but it is Vanning's treatment of Mary that persuades the other girls – Emmy Lou, Gabby (Lola Lane), Florrie (Rosalind Marquis) and Estelle (Mayo Methot) – to take the stand. They appear in court, demurely clad in black, and Graham waxes lyrical about their courage, lambasting the 'supine city' and the 'men of righteousness' who would not testify.

But *Marked Woman*, for all the triumph of law and order that it portrays, cannot, in the screenplay by established contract writer Abem Finkel and newcomer Robert Rossen, manage anything like the affirmation of Americanism that concludes *The Star Witness*. As the press gather round Graham on the foggy courthouse steps, the five girls walk off into the night, only marginally a group since each is shown separately in close-up as she walks. 'When the fog swallows them up, there is no after-glow from their halos,' wrote Frank S. Nugent in the *New York Times*. 'Count that a point for realism on the screen.' It is, of course, less a matter of realism than a change of attitude (which is a strong determining feature in any definition of 'realism'). After the brief flurry of cop-centred crime movies in the middle of the decade, the studio's forays into the genre became almost uniformly dark, showing at best the individual provided with the opportunity to do the right thing at considerable cost (like Humphrey Bogart in *Black Legion*, 1937), at worst the individual as an alienated victim of an uncaring society, forming, along with the moral individualism of Errol Flynn in the historical epics,[5] the other half of a romantic diptych.

Taxi!, released in January 1932, and *The St Louis Kid*, released in October 1934, are straight Cagney vehicles, included here because they were both surprisingly successful (*Taxi!* was, along with another Cagney vehicle, *The Crowd Roars*, among the studio's five most successful films in the rather bleak year of 1932), and also because they both leave their hero to deal with the anti-group activities of a gang with very little help from the police. In addition to stressing the need for group coherence, they share a great many features, not only in terms of characterisation (in both, the Cagney character is what the *New York Times*[6] called 'the terrier of the screen': brash, belligerent, misogynist, with an essential selfishness only partly channelled into more socially conscious behaviour at the end), but also in terms of narrative structure. Both start in comic vein, introduce a more serious note, revert to comedy for their central sections, resolve the serious theme through fairly violent action, and end on the traditional Cagney wink. It is, in this context, particularly interesting to note what *Variety* had to say about the Cagney role in *Taxi!*

As a deese, does and dem, chip-on-the-shoulder, on-the-make example of young America, the character knows no better interpretation on the screen than that which Cagney gives it. The populace, at least that portion attending the Strand, are now expectant of this player socking all and sundry including all the women in the cast. There's even a distinct tremor of disappointment through the house when no wallop is forthcoming. They start to laugh in pure anticipation of the expected and desired finish.

And Cagney probably has no more partial gathering than the mob which gathers at the Strand whenever they hang out his name. The boys start to gather early and a peek at 12.30 noon will reveal a good-sized assemblage of 90% male. That element which delays deliveries to see a big picture, and drops over from Eighth Avenue and west, goes in a big way for the manner in which James handles his film women. They also enjoy the way he scraps, as Cagney so closely approaches the way the average citizen in moments of everyday stress would like to act that it seems to be one of the strongest bonds between the actor and the witnessing men.

Cagney, in other words, is a kind of wish-fulfilment figure for the low-paid or unemployed male working class, representing a response to the Depression no less real but far less socially conscious than that in other contemporary gangster films.

In *Taxi!*, Cagney plays Matt Nolan, a driver caught up in a war between rival cab companies. This leads him into conflict with a hood called Buck Gerard (David Landau), after Gerard causes the death of Nolan's kid brother Danny (Ray Cooke). He tracks down Gerard and is only saved from killing him by the latter's (apparent) suicide. Nolan thus avoids a criminal act and is reconciled with his girlfriend, Sue Reilly (Loretta Young). In *The St Louis Kid*, Cagney plays Eddie Kennedy, a belligerent St Louis trucker who, together with his sidekick Buck Willets (Allen Jenkins), gets caught up in the then current fight between the mid-Western milk farmers and a Chicago-based combine. Kennedy's involvement in the fight is strictly marginal – at one stage he makes an impassioned defence of the farmers, but only to win over a local judge (Arthur Aylesworth) and escape a sentence for brawling – until the combine kidnaps his girlfriend, Ann Reid (Patricia Ellis). Then, with the help of Buck and the other truckers, Kennedy rescues Ann and beats up the hoods in a semi-comic action finale, the high spot of which comes when Buck, an inept fighter, finally connects with an opponent's chin and bruises his hand.

The story is the same as in *Taxi!*, the major difference being that in *The St Louis Kid* the Cagney persona is well enough established for any pretence at serious treatment of the social background to be abandoned and for the tone to be almost entirely comic. In both cases, the hero is Irish. In *Taxi!*, a joke is made about it when Nolan talks to a bystander in Yiddish, and the attendant cop calls out, 'Hey, Nolan! What part of Ireland do *you* come from?' And in both cases, the Cagney character has an initial contempt for the dames. 'Ah, go back to slinging hash where you belong,' he snarls at Sue Reilly in *Taxi!* when she argues with him at a meeting of taxi-drivers trying to decide what to do about the attack on her father, Pop Reilly (Guy Kibbee). In *The St Louis Kid*, Ann Reid is also a 'hash slapper' (actually, she owns the restaurant), and Kennedy orders four portions of ham and eggs, remarking to Buck: 'I don't think this sweet young thing could remember more than one order at a time!' For a modern viewer, it is generally difficult to appreciate what it is that wins both women over in the end. Presumably the assumption is that the anarchic ebullience diagnosed by *Variety* is irresistible to them.

An 'on-the-make example of young America': James Cagney, with Loretta Young, in *Taxi!*

Taxi! and *The St Louis Kid* show Warners' populism at its most basic. In both cases, the little guy is at risk from big business – the Consolidated Cab company in the former, which is trying to muscle in on the tendentiously named Independent Garage; and the State Wide Company from Chicago in the latter film, which also toys with the theme of the small farming community of Ostopolis, with its folksy sheriff (Spencer Charters), versus the big cities of St Louis and Chicago. In both cases, the New Deal goes into action and, with the tacit but largely invisible support of social agencies, the little guy bands together with other little guys to meet the threat. Indeed, this is how the New Deal was consistently interpreted in Warners' contemporary films: as a fresh encouragement to individual initiative, rather than the introduction of external aid. 'We're living in the United States,' Nolan tells the assembled taxi-drivers. 'We're free and equal, or so they tell us. We have a right to a living, and we're going to go out and take it ... We've got to stick together. Stick together: remember that!' Just over a year later, Roosevelt summed up a year of campaigning – which may have begun after the film's release but whose roots go back much further – with words that echo Nolan's, though suitably transposed into the rhetoric of an Inaugural Address: 'If I read the temper of our people correctly, we now realise as we have never before, our interdependence on each other; that we cannot merely take, but we must give as well; that if we

119

are to go forward we must move as a trained and loyal army ...'[7] The balance of Roosevelt's Address, of course, is concerned with measures of government intervention. But that is not the lesson which was popularly drawn. Speaker after speaker in the Warners' musicals of 1933 calls upon the chorus line to work together, stick together, pull together. And in *Taxi!* (pre-Roosevelt) and *The St Louis Kid* (post-Roosevelt) 'working together' means meeting a threat through direct physical action, not waiting for the intervention of some agency of social justice.

Cagney is the first major star of the 1930s to be 'discovered' by Warners.[8] He achieved prominence in a series of gangster roles, and brought to his non-gangster parts the same action-based individualism. *Taxi!* and *The St Louis Kid* are not message pictures, but they are ideologically identical to the more overtly socially conscious crime movies of the same period: self-reliance without frills is what the situation calls for. It is probably the fact that the films portray this reaction crudely and energetically which accounted for their popularity. And the fact that they do so in a variant of the crime movie formula indicates that it is the production formula, rather than the individual story, which is Warners' major intervention in the field of contemporary realistic drama. Made in a certain way, along certain factory-style lines, with a certain narrative style (characterised by the opening sequence of *Taxi!*, with its scenes of cabbies being intimidated and newspaper headlines announcing a cab 'war'), the films all reflected a similar attitude and a similar response to a troubled social situation. As always, style, studio system and social reality were closely linked.

7 Rehabilitation

Warners made two cycles of prison films. The first, during the Depression years, includes *Weary River* (1929), *Numbered Men* (1930) and *I Am a Fugitive from a Chain Gang*, *20,000 Years in Sing Sing* and *The Mayor of Hell* (all 1933). The second cycle, coinciding with the more individualistic crime movies discussed in the previous two chapters, covers the last three or four years of the decade, and includes *Alcatraz Island* and *San Quentin* (1937), *Crime School* and *Girls on Probation* (1938), *Each Dawn I Die* (1939), *Devil's Island* (1939, but not released until 1940 because of opposition from the French government) and *Castle on the Hudson* (1940), a remake of *20,000 Years in Sing Sing*. All deal with rehabilitation. A society built on the success ethic – an ethic to which the United States clung with great tenacity throughout the Depression and which began to be triumphantly reinstated in the latter half of the decade – necessarily has an ambivalent attitude towards those sentenced to jail. A criminal is one of society's failures, and a captured criminal is a failed failure. Jail thus becomes a place in which the lessons of failure are learned and in which, ideally, the prison system, by putting the criminal through a process of painful correction, burns away the criminality and forges a newly socialised individual. Prison is the ultimate ideological safety net, enabling society's values to be reasserted positively rather than reinforced negatively, as they are when the cop guns down the gangster.

Although the theme of rehabilitation remains constant through both cycles, there is of course a considerable difference of tone on either side of the crucial dividing line of 1935, the year in which the Production Code was rigidified, Roosevelt began to think about his campaign for a second term of office, and Warner Brothers declared their first profit since 1930. The concordance of events is obviously significant, but it did not result, as one might have expected, in a simple shift from despondency to optimism in the prison films, any more than it did in the realistic movies in general. It is, once more, a question of studio production methods and the general ideological climate dovetailing into one another. In the post-1935 movies, the general social background does not need to be blocked in anywhere near as thoroughly: the Depression can no longer provide an explanation for the incarceration of the hero. John Litel in *Alcatraz Island*, Humphrey Bogart in *San Quentin* and James Cagney in *Each Dawn I Die* do not have the 'excuse' with which Paul Muni is supplied in *I Am a Fugitive from a Chain Gang*. And, in the second half of the decade, the streamlined production methods set up for reasons of economy between 1930 and 1934 are sufficiently well established and operating with enough autonomy to allow for greater stylistic and thematic flexibility (although here, as we shall see when we come to *Angels with Dirty Faces*, problems were beginning to arise). In terms of theme, however, individual motivation becomes the keynote in the second cycle of prison films, as it does in the biopics and the Merrie England pictures. Society becomes the background rather than the conditioning factor.

Weary River, released in early 1929, is really a pre-Depression movie and has comparatively little in common with the other prison films, although the plot climax of the hero being released on parole to 'test' his rehabilitation reappears in almost identical form in *20,000 Years in Sing Sing* and again in modified form in *San Quentin*: how else, other than by a dramatic test, is the success of the rehabilitation process to be dramatically demonstrated? But in all other respects, *Weary River* is a quintessential early talkie (it was released in both sound and silent versions), borrowing the structure of a silent melodrama and making its main concession to sound in the title song, sung no less than four times by Richard Barthelmess in the course of the film. Jerry Larrabee (Barthelmess) is a playboy gambler and urbane criminal who ends up in jail as a result of being betrayed. No attempt is made to criticise his chosen form of money-making. In jail, Jerry is lectured by the benevolent warden (William Holden) on the ways of the world. Life, the warden tells him, is 'like a river. Some rivers run in wild, destructive torrents, others through peaceful, pleasant meadows. But even the weariest river finds its way to the sea.' Encouraged by the idea (though it is hard to see why), Jerry finds 'the outlet his soul desired'. He writes a song about a 'Weary River', sings it before a chamber orchestra in the prison chapel, and has it broadcast on radio. Offered the chance of a parole and deciding that 'I'm through with the old crowd, *all* of them,' Jerry becomes the Master of Melody (with apparently only one song in his repertoire), but flees from the stage at his first concert when he hears someone in the audience whispering that he is a jailbird. 'I've decided that as a respectable citizen, I'm a wash-out,' he announces rather peremptorily, and goes into hiding. The warden comes after him in time to prevent him wiping out Spadoni (Louis Natheaux), the hood who had set him up, and engineers a reconciliation with the girl (Betty Compson) who has waited for him throughout.

Despite some details of prison life – notably Jerry's induction, where he is fingerprinted, photographed, issued with prison clothes, and made to strip and bathe in a communal bathroom whose other tub is occupied by a cheerful negro (the final degradation?) – *Weary River* is less about

Jerry's rehabilitation at the hands of the U.S. Department of Correction than it is about an individual finding himself. It has, as one would expect from a film shot at the very beginning of the period, virtually nothing to do with social problems. As *Variety* noted, 'the advantage of *Weary River* considered from the cold cash attitude is that it is artistic without being hard to "get". Its problem is definite, simple; its telling intelligently aimed at those old heartstrings and that sentimental barometer, the adam's apple.' The film's combination of morality and romance would, *Variety* concluded, 'hit Americans where they bruise easiest'.

The problem in *I Am a Fugitive from a Chain Gang* is anything but 'definite' and 'simple' and, if one is to apply *Variety*'s criterion as a way of accounting for its success, the points at which America bruised easiest had shifted somewhat in the four years since the release of *Weary River*. The film is based on Robert E. Burns' autobiography, *I Am a Fugitive from a Georgia Chain Gang*, and some of its more improbable elements – notably the strident newspaper campaign against the hero being sent back to jail – are taken from fact. Moreover, as John E. O'Connor points out in his excellent introduction to the published screenplay,[1] Burns himself was still at large when the film was made, and took considerable risks to promote it, one of which finally led to his recapture. *I Am a Fugitive* registers as Warners' most unequivocally pessimistic picture of life in Depression America, though it is worth remembering that much of it is in fact set during the growth period of the 1920s. James Allen (Paul Muni) returns from the war to a dead-end job in his hometown factory. But he has ambitions to become an engineer, fuelled by his experience in the army, and is soon dissatisfied. 'I've learned that life is more important than a medal on my chest and a stupid, insignificant job,' he tells his uncomprehending family. He goes on the road looking for work, fails to find any, and ends up broke in a Georgia flophouse. He becomes the innocent accomplice of a fellow down-and-out (Preston S. Foster) in a hold-up in a hamburger restaurant, and is sentenced to ten years' hard labour on the chain gang. Faced with the relentless brutality of the system, he finally breaks out and flees to Chicago where, little by little, he achieves respectability. Finally, through night study and hard daytime work, he becomes an established engineer.

In the meantime his landlady, Marie (Glenda Farrell), discovers his secret and tricks him into marriage. The marriage is a disaster and Allen, now a respected local businessman, strikes up a friendship with Helen (Helen Vinson), the daughter of a local worthy. Jealous, Marie informs the police, and Allen is re-arrested. A newspaper campaign is launched against extradition to Georgia, pointing out that Allen has paid his debt to society and is now a cornerstone of the Chicago business community. 'Is this Civilisation?' ask the editorial headlines. 'What has become of State Rights?' Allen nobly agrees to go back to Georgia on

the promise of a full pardon after 90 days on the chain gang, but the deal
is broken by the vindictive warden (Edward J. McNamara), who argues
that 'crime must be punished' and even goes so far as to claim that Allen
is proof of the system's powers of rehabilitation. After the three months,
Allen's pardon is 'suspended indefinitely'. Faced with a lifetime on the
chain gang, he breaks out again, remains on the run for a year and, in
an ending no less famous than that of *Little Caesar*, presents himself one
night to Helen.

As she parks her car and walks past the darkened entry of a garage,
Allen's voice calls out to her. He draws her back into the shadows.

HELEN (her voice choking): Jim! Jim – why haven't you come before?
ALLEN: I couldn't. I was afraid to.
HELEN: You could have written. It's been almost a year since you
escaped!
ALLEN (with a bitter laugh): I haven't escaped – they're still after me.
They'll always be after me. I've had jobs but I couldn't keep them.
Something happens – someone turns up – I hide in rooms all day and
travel by night – no friends – no rest – no peace –
HELEN (clutching him): Jim!
ALLEN: Keep moving! That's all that's left for me.
HELEN (clinging to him): No – please! I can't let you go like this. It was
all going to be so different ...
ALLEN (with a hollow laugh): I hate everything but you ... I had to take
a chance tonight to see you ... and say goodbye ...
(Helen gazes at him with tears streaming down her face; then she throws
her arms about his neck impulsively and kisses him. They cling together
fiercely. There is the sound of a police siren approaching, then fading
away. Allen is startled, then starts away.)
HELEN (following him): Can't you tell me where you're going? (He
shakes his head.) Will you write? (He shakes his head.) Do you need any
money? (He shakes his head, still backing away.) But you must, Jim!
How do you live?
(A car is heard approaching. Allen backs into the dark shadows of the
alley.)
ALLEN: I steal ...[2]

I have quoted this passage from Sheridan Gibney's screenplay at
length because it is responsible more than any other single sequence for
Warner Brothers' reputation as a socially conscious studio, criticising
the failings of American society in an uncompromising manner. As such,
it calls for some comment. Certainly, *I Am a Fugitive* is an indictment of
several aspects of American society, not just in its overall (factually
based) theme, but in its depiction of the employment problems facing
World War I veterans (which, through the rather later bonus marches

124

and Hoovervilles, were a strong contributory factor to Roosevelt's 1932 landslide), and in its uncompromising portrayal of the horrors of the Georgia chain gang. Much of the impact of the film depends on its semi-documentary scenes involving the single, heavy chain to which all the prisoners are attached while they sleep; the slinging of the same chain in Allen's face when he is slow to wake up on the first morning; the beatings administered by the warden with his tawse; the blows Allen receives for wiping the sweat from his brow without asking permission; the 4.30 a.m. to 8.20 p.m. workday, and so on. What is more, the film reverses most of the usual narrative processes. Allen is dedicated to a job which will be socially useful, 'where you can build, construct, create, do things', and wants above all to build bridges, like the one he could see from his office window in the factory at the beginning. Yet at the end, during his second escape, he is shown grinning with pleasure at having been able to blow up a bridge and stop his pursuers. And while women have their usual secondary role in the film – as a threat to a man's career in Glenda Farrell's vindictive, drunken Marie; or as a reward for self-redemptive effort in Helen Vinson's saint-like Helen – they are unable, as the sequence quoted above indicates, to provide the usual salvation. James Allen, for all his efforts and nobility, is relentlessly ground down into a bitter, twisted, criminal failure.

Yet there are a number of factors which offset this apparently total pessimism. In the first place, all the social agencies outside the state of Georgia – notably the Chicago Chamber of Commerce and the Chicago newspapers – are shown as rooting for Allen. And Georgia, like other states in the deep south (see Chapter Eight for a discussion of *They Won't Forget*), is and always has been a convenient repository for the darker side of the American dream. Hollywood's bigots, perverts and psychopaths had been relegated there long before the plays of Tennessee Williams made it their homeland. The implication of the film is fairly clear: remove the chain gang system and reform the administration of justice in Georgia and all will be well. It is the chain gang which is the target of the film, not American society as a whole. James Allen may come dangerously close to poverty in the first part of the film which, like other Warners social conscience pictures, sketches in a realistic social background before moving on to an individual narrative solution. But his arrest is the result of a mistake: he ends up with Pete's gun in his hand, but he was not responsible for or even really involved in the robbery. And the middle section of the film – Allen's rise to fame as an engineer – illustrates the accepted philosophy of hard work leading to success even during a Depression, before a further stroke of bad luck (Marie's vindictiveness) leads to his downfall. *I Am a Fugitive from a Chain Gang* is thus an exception in two ways: an extreme case in being a harsh indictment of authority, and a unique case in that Allen's imprisonment is not really his *or* society's fault.

Nevertheless, the film is far from reassuring, and does pinpoint fairly exactly some of the tensions in Warners' early social conscience movies. The commitment to subjects of contemporary realism – a commitment born out of both a particular market choice and a desire for economical production methods – involves placing the individual in conflict with social forces so as to achieve a dramatic narrative (and *I Am a Fugitive*, with its escape scenes and terse montage sequences, is a very dramatic movie). At the same time, the studio's ideological commitment to basic American values and to the nascent policies of the New Deal made it necessary for those conflicts to be set within the context of a *fundamentally just* society which offered the individual, even under the most extreme circumstances, the chance to re-establish himself (rarely, if ever, herself) through hard work. In the final analysis, the central section of *I Am a Fugitive* is ideologically crucial, and the film's ending functions as a dire warning of the dangers threatening America if the corrupt and unjust barriers to individual advancement and national recovery are not removed. The closing scene of *I Am a Fugitive*, like the montage of revolution which ended *Voltaire* the following year,[3] is a case of 'there but for the New Deal ...'

20,000 Years in Sing Sing, released less than two months later, has a similar tension and offers a similar warning – the pressures are great, but they can be overcome without major changes. In a sense, the old conservative argument is true here: the guarantee of American democracy is that such films can be made. But it is a guarantee strongly compromised, from a reactionary point of view by the problems the films expose, and from a liberal point of view by the fact that, in making them, the values which occasioned the problems are effortlessly reasserted. Warners' social conscience was nothing if not well-balanced. Like *I Am a Fugitive*, *20,000 Years in Sing Sing* is based on a work of non-fiction, in this case the book of the same title by Warden Lewis E. Lawes of New York's Sing Sing prison. The film, scripted by Wilson Mizner and Brown Holmes (the latter having been responsible for the rejected first draft of *Fugitive*), interlocks two separate stories, which is what accounts for the tension. The first is a quasi-documentary treatment of prison life and of Warden Lawes' 'honour system' of rehabilitating prisoners by giving them a gradually increasing measure of freedom and responsibility. The second is the story of Tommy Connors (Spencer Tracy), who enters Sing Sing brashly confident and insolent, is won over by the Warden – here called Long and played by Arthur Byron – but ends up going to the chair all the same. The strangest thing about Connors, the entirely fictional element in the story, is that his death happens *because* he has been rehabilitated: the film's message is reinforced, not undermined, by the necessary dramatic climax.

The film opens with a close-up of a prison whistle blowing. The camera then tracks along in front of a row of cons with titles superimposed: 45 years, 10 years, 23 years. A montage of numbers appears over shots of the prison decks and yard before the title of the film (which is a total, rather than a single jail sentence!) zooms out of the screen. The credits proceed over aerial shots of Sing Sing: Warners was given full co-operation by Warden Lawes in shooting parts of the film on location there. Tommy's induction into Sing Sing is treated in far greater factual detail than Jerry Larrabee's in *Weary River*, and there are a number of scenes of prison life. Connors' story as such is a much more conventional affair. He arrives on the train, surrounded by admirers, joking that 'If I don't like the joint, I'll leave' and telling the attendant newsmen to send the clippings to his girl, Fay Wilson (Bette Davis), because 'she's keeping a scrapbook'. He is also accompanied by ward boss Joe Finn (Louis Calhern), who is unceremoniously thrown out when he tries to bribe the Warden. 'People outside are supposed to be equal,' snaps Long. 'In here, they are.' Connors is initially resistant to the Warden's approach. 'One day you'll learn that no man has a spot in this world except in relation to the people around him,' says Long. 'You've got to be useful to live.' 'Save that for Sunday, Warden,' grins Connors, 'and let me pass the plate.' But Connors is slowly won round by a mixture of harsh treatment and sound advice. When he finds out that Fay has been critically injured in a car crash, he begs the Warden to let him visit her. 'She's the only thing I have,' he pleads. Warden Long, in a highly fictionalised dramatisation of Lawes' honour system, lets Connors go unaccompanied to Fay's bedside. 'Warden,' says Connors, 'I never broke my word, not even to a rat, let alone to a swell guy.'

Connors discovers that Fay's accident was caused by Finn, and that the latter has given her $5,000 to clear him. He finds a gun and is about to shoot Finn when Fay seizes it and begs him to let her do it. Finn is shot, the cops arrive, and Connors goes on the run. The Warden is subjected to political pressure and a campaign of newspaper abuse, including a cartoon of him holding the prison gates open to usher out a collection of striped-suited cons with angelic wings and the caption 'Run along, children!' He is about to resign when Connors walks into his office. 'I told you I'd come back,' he says, 'even if it meant the chair.' It does. Connors refuses to talk to the prison chaplain and, ever the tough guy, refuses to let Fay marry him before he dies. 'You can't have me because I belong to the State of New York,' he tells her. 'And in a few hours the State of New York is going to take me out and burn me and take out my brains and put them in a jar of alky.' Still refusing comfort, Connors finally turns to the Warden as he is about to go to the chair. 'I tell you what you *can* do for me,' he says. 'Give me a light.' There is a long close-up of him lighting the cigarette and holding the Warden's hand with the match in it. Then we return to the opening montage of numbers, leading up once more to the film's title. The readiness of a tough bird like Connors to accept his fate is a powerfully dramatic vindication of the prison system.

Variety, which had been somewhat confused by *I Am a Fugitive from a Chain Gang*, found *20,000 Years in Sing Sing* to be more concerned with prison conditions than with story. In fact, the story is as essential to the depiction of prison conditions as it was in the earlier film. Connors enters Sing Sing a hardened, arrogant criminal. He goes to the chair still a hard man, but with his own sense of honour (in returning to prison and in shielding Fay) vindicated along with the Warden's honour system. It is interesting to compare the film with *Angels with Dirty Faces* (discussed later in this chapter). In the latter film, Rocky Sullivan similarly sacrifices himself for a principle, dying a coward to dissuade the Dead End Kids from a life of crime. But there are two crucial differences: Rocky has to sacrifice his honour to achieve the desired effect while Tommy Connors goes to the chair a brave and noble man. And in the latter film it is a small group of individuals who benefit, while in *20,000 Years in Sing Sing* it is the entire system of benevolent prison reform. In the earlier film, which is very much a companion piece to *I Am a Fugitive*, showing that the prison system is not everywhere as in Georgia, both the essential justice of the American legal system and the personal honour of the gangster are somehow celebrated. It is a strange but significant combination, illustrating another aspect of the studio's social conscience pictures. The film manages to relate the honour of the romantic anti-social individual to the strengths of a basically sound if temporarily problem-ridden society.

Of the later cycle of prison movies, only two were particularly successful in both New York and Los Angeles: *Alcatraz Island*, which had two-week runs in both cities, and *Each Dawn I Die*, which ran for three weeks at the Strand and two weeks in Los Angeles. This box office success is particularly strange in the case of *Alcatraz Island*, which was a B-feature produced by Bryan Foy's unit – one of the few films of its kind to be included in this survey, since they rarely played more than a week in the flagship theatres. Exceptionally, *Alcatraz Island* was held over for a second week at the Warners Hollywood and Downtown theatres in Los Angeles, breaking the usual double-feature pattern by being paired with a different film in each week. Its hero, Gat Brady (John Litel), is a successful and generally noble big-time criminal. He may feel obliged to tell his daughter Annabel (Mary Maguire) that 'crime doesn't pay', but feels equally obliged to add 'well, not always'. He has, he claims, never killed anybody. He is arrested owing $235,000 in back taxes. The judge refuses to honour a deal with the D.A., and Brady is sentenced to a $50,000 fine and five years in Leavenworth. But he gets into a fight with Red Carroll (Ben Welden), a small-time hood whose brother he had earlier refused to protect (with the words 'Killing isn't part of this racket'). Held responsible for the fight, he is sent to

Alcatraz, where he again encounters Carroll. This time, Carroll is stabbed to death by another con, Dutch (Vladimir Sokoloff), and the weapon palmed off on Brady. Brady is sentenced to death, but thanks to the efforts of Assistant D.A. George Drake (Gordon Oliver), who has fallen in love with Annabel, and above all to the testimony of another con, Harp Santell (Dick Purcell), who turns out to be an undercover FBI agent, Brady gets off and is sent back to Leavenworth for another six months, followed by parole.

Alcatraz Island is a good, tough movie, complete with violent action, headline montages and lurid captions like the one that introduces us to The Rock: 'America's penal fortress, grim and mysterious as its name, where cold steel and rushing tides protect civilisation from its enemies' (when it came to rhetoric, Warners' B-features were no different from Republic's programmers). The film also contains some fairly detailed footage of life in Alcatraz, particularly in the mess hall scenes, where a sign saying 'Clean Your Plate or Go Without This Meal Next Day' is stencilled on the table, tear-gas tanks hang overhead, and the cons move out in silence to a series of alarm-bell cues. The film, like larger-budget crime movies from the same period, has a tension similar to that found in the earlier prison movies. But here the tension is expressed in a different way. On the one hand, Brady is definitely rehabilitated mentally. At the beginning of the film, he tells Annabel's governess that 'there's only one way to get big dough, and that's the way I got it'. But at the end, as he stands on the tracks before returning to Leavenworth, he comments chastely to Annabel and Drake that he 'used to think dough was the greatest thing in the world': now he perceives other values. On the other hand, no real attempt is made to render his criminal activities unsympathetic or even unattractive. And his rehabilitation is strictly a personal affair. Society has had very little influence on it, and the interests of society at large are not what bring it about.

The wider social context is also fairly secondary in *Each Dawn I Die*. Frank Ross (James Cagney) plays a reporter who is framed and sent to jail for exposing a racket. He begins to turn into a hardened criminal. 'Now I'm a convict,' he tells the Warden (George Bancroft). 'I act like a convict. I think and hate like a convict.' This, clearly, is the reverse of rehabilitation. But through his friendship with big-time criminal Hood Stacey (George Raft) he discovers a new kind of honour in the world when, following a bizarre set of circumstances (a breakout in which Stacey's underworld connections betray him), he ends up back on the side of the law and is set free to fulfil Stacey's dying request: to live his life 'as he might have lived it if he'd had the right breaks as a kid'. The Warden hands him a signed photo of Stacey with the inscription 'I found a square guy'.

Each Dawn I Die is *I Am a Fugitive* with a happy ending. Ross ends up in jail as the result of a frame-up, is degraded by the experience, but is rescued from total brutalisation by a rather improbable stroke of luck. But it is, paradoxically, a much bleaker picture than *I Am a Fugitive*. The kind of rehabilitation offered to Allen in the central section of the earlier film is virtually denied to Ross who, in the central section of *Each Dawn I Die*, is shown in considerable detail learning the ways of prison life. When he walks out free at the end, it is into an uncertain future, like Bette Davis in *Marked Woman* – a parallel underlined by the fact that he, like her, is ostensibly on the right side of the law throughout. Warden Armstrong is an exception in the prison system; the other prison staff beat Ross up to make him 'confess'. And the most telling image of the film is of Ross breaking down before the Parole Board: 'Please get me out of here. I can't do any more time.'

Although rehabilitation remains the theme throughout the studio's prison pictures, it is heavily submerged in both *Alcatraz Island* and *Each Dawn I Die*. The stress on individual initiative and prosperity which characterises both the late 1930s in general and the films produced at Warner Brothers in particular left little room for the sympathetic depiction of an institution designed to help those individuals whose initiative had failed them. What is more, the gradually hardening opposition among conservatives to Roosevelt's centralised government agencies and to what, in the aftermath of a number of Supreme Court reversals of his executive decisions, was beginning to be seen as a kind of Washington megalomania, made it much less acceptable to portray government agencies of whatever kind as no-holds-barred fighters for the cause of justice. There is no room for a Warden Lawes in *Alcatraz Island* or *Each Dawn I Die*. Both films end on a truce between two individuals on different sides of the law – Brady and Drake in the former, Ross and the Warden (or Ross and Stacey) in the latter. The world of the *film noir*, where individual alliances transcend and obliterate all social contracts, is not far away.

Kids at risk from social pressures was another topic in which the theme of rehabilitation was embedded. The 1930s, in Hollywood, was the age of the child star. And although Warners did not become involved to anything like the extent of MGM, with its Andy Hardy series and its star vehicles for Judy Garland and Mickey Rooney, it none the less produced a number of movies with and about kids. There was, for example, the series of films based on Booth Tarkington's Penrod.[4] There was imported South African child star Sybil Jason, a would-be answer to Shirley Temple, who starred in *Little Big Shot* and *The Captain's Kid* (both 1936). On a related theme, the studio produced a number of college pictures, from *College Lovers* in 1930, through *Flirtation Walk* in 1934, to *Brother Rat* (1938) and its 1940 sequel, *Brother Rat and a Baby*. In them, adolescents grappled with the problems of romance and group responsibility, the test usually being provided by a sporting encounter. In *Brother Rat*, military cadets Wayne Morris, Eddie Albert and Ronald

Reagan painfully but comically discover their duties to each other, their girls and the institution of which they are members, with the climax centring on a ball game. Even here, the theme of group responsibility remained strong.

But by far the most successful of the studio's kid movies featured the Dead End Kids – Billy Halop, Bobby Jordan, Leo Gorcey, Bernard Punsley, Gabriel Dell and Huntz Hall – whom it acquired from Goldwyn (whose 1937 movie *Dead End* had given them their name), and featured in a number of films, starting with *Crime School* in 1938 and ending with *Dead End Kids on Dress Parade* (set in a military academy) the following year. After that, the Kids transferred studios to Monogram and, minus Halop, became the East End Kids and, later, the Bowery Boys. The first two Dead End Kids movies were by far the most successful, and both focus strongly on the theme of rehabilitation. But the idea of kids at risk was first treated by the studio much earlier in the decade, in *Wild Boys of the Road* (1933). In the early and the later films, a group of kids drifts into petty crime as a result of environmental influences – poverty, slum homes – and is finally rescued by benevolent authority (in *Wild Boys of the Road* and *Crime School*) or by adult example (in *Angels with Dirty Faces*). I propose to deal fairly briefly with the first two films, since they are in almost every sense minor variants on the prison rehabilitation movies, and to look more closely at *Angels with Dirty Faces*, both as a classic example of the kind of contemporary drama Warners was making towards the end of the decade, and as an example of the production process typical to that kind of film.

'Is the youth of the land hitch-hiking to Hell? You can ignore the facts, turn a cold shoulder on the problem. But there it is!' The film which accompanied this theatre lobby catchline, *Wild Boys of the Road*, certainly focuses on the problem of kids – girls as well as boys – driven into a life of drifting round the country on freight trains, in and out of crime and confrontations with the police. The police, as in many crime movies, become the faceless agents of society: they simply serve to dramatise the conflict and are given little chance to appear as anything other than repressive. And, in characteristic fashion, William Wellman stresses the more than moral threats to the kids in a scene in which Tommy (Edwin Phillips) loses his leg on the railroad tracks. But since the kids were never anything but victims, it is not hard for a benevolent judge (Robert Barrat), with kids of his own, to step in at the end and save them from degradation and crime. *Variety*'s comments point to a major problem with the film: 'Every incident, every character ceaselessly brings to mind the most gruesome underside of the hard times. It may be a public service to herald these facts to unwilling ears, but the theatre cannot well hope to prosper materially in such a venture.' Indeed, the film was not particularly successful: Warners gave it a prestige opening at the Hollywood Theatre in New York, but it ran for only two weeks (the average at the Hollywood was five to six weeks) and for only a week in Los Angeles. There are a number of ways of accounting for this: the film had no star names, it was depressing, it sat athwart conventional expectations. In addition, it would seem that, in order to be commercially successful (and therefore effective in any sense), the studio's social conscience pictures needed the traditional entertainment feature of a strong narrative line and a more conventional handling of character and motivation.

The first two Dead End Kids movies, although they may be (at any rate in the case of *Crime School*) a good deal more conventional in their handling of social problems, certainly achieved the requisite balance. In the first, the kids are sent to a reform school where they learn nothing but how to become hardened criminals. They are saved from this fate by the intervention of Mark Braden (Humphrey Bogart), Deputy Commissioner of Correction, who takes over the school and, with the help of the sister of one of the kids (Gale Page), reforms the school and rehabilitates the inmates. At the end, another kindly judge (Charles Trowbridge) declares: 'You boys are all right. I look forward to the day when there'll no longer be any need for reform schools: we are going to do our best to help you.' What makes this piece of rhetoric essentially different from that in the equivalent scene in *Wild Boys of the Road* is that it is not taken entirely seriously. At the end, the Dead End Kids are seen sitting in court, neatly suited, consulting a book entitled *How to Break into Society*. The irony in the title is fully intentional. As Frank S. Nugent remarked in the *New York Times*, they are 'certain to backslide before their next picture comes out. Anyone can see they're natural recidivists'.

The attraction of the kids in *Crime School* lies in the fact that they are never likely to be anything else but petty criminals in and out of trouble with the law, whereas the child outlaws of *Wild Boys of the Road* are mainly victims of circumstance. In Hollywood terms, the criminal is more attractive because he is active; the victim, by definition, is passive. Treating the social problems of children during the Depression, and deprived of the essential free will and action of the crime movie, Hollywood could do nothing but sentimentalise their plight. By the late 1930s, the production formula had evolved into something both more complex and more secure. There is no – or less – need for sentimentality. The re-establishment of basic American values, loudly trumpeted in *Knute Rockne – All American* (1940), involves a corresponding shift towards the individual resolution of social problems, something to which Warners' firmly established narrative and production methods were far better suited. Rehabilitating the Dead End Kids would have meant integrating them into the mainstream of American society, where they would no longer have been the Dead End Kids. *Crime School* simultaneously celebrates and warns against energetic anti-social behaviour. So, to a much greater extent, does *Angels with Dirty Faces*.

Crime School had been a B-feature, produced by Bryan Foy's unit. *Angels with Dirty Faces*, on the other hand, was a major production right from the start. The studio's basic aim can, as always, be summed up quite simply: to make a good, profitable picture. But the choice of subject matter – a contemporary story involving a charismatic criminal and a group of kids bent on following in his tracks – necessarily involved, even without the supervision of the Breen Office, the adoption of a particular moral position. In the end, there is very little point in speculating as to whether, without Breen, the moral tone of the film would have been different. If Breen had not existed, he would have to have been invented (as, indeed, he was). The Breen Office represented a self-regulatory function installed by Hollywood itself, and as such is an inseparable part of the production climate. Nevertheless, the tension between the excitement created by the vivid action scenes inherent in the crime story and the need to adopt a critical distance from the characters who indulge in crime (Cagney, Bogart and the Dead End Kids) is crucial both to the success of *Angels with Dirty Faces* and to its importance as an example of Warners' role in the reflection and reinforcement of contemporary ideology.

The allocation of the film to Michael Curtiz tends to tip the balance in the direction of crime melodrama, involving the same focus on individual morality demonstrated through action as Curtiz's film of the same year, *The Adventures of Robin Hood*.[5] This is not to say that Curtiz was an *auteur* working against the system, merely to identify him as its most skilled practitioner. But the balancing elements introduced by the screenplay and above all by Pat O'Brien's role as the priest, Father Jerry Connolly, are every bit as important as Curtiz's verve. *Angels with Dirty Faces* toys with the same anarchic individualism that characterises *Robin Hood*, but since the picture has a contemporary setting, that individualism must ultimately be curtailed and integrated. Anti-social behaviour provides the energy (and perhaps accounts for the box-office success) of the film, but it is not in the final analysis an anti-social film. During the 1930s Warners remained, for reasons that have as much to do with box office as morality, a socially 'responsible' studio. Uncompromisingly harsh indictments of the American way of life have never played any real part in the American entertainment industry. The tensions of *Angels with Dirty Faces* are the tensions of American ideology in the 1930s, balanced between rugged individualism and social stability. The metaphor of crime provides a framework in which those tensions can be dramatically explored: Rocky Sullivan does what he has to do for himself, but his own sense of what is right is strongly influenced by the social environment, to some extent represented by his priestly alter ego, and dramatically demonstrated by its effect on the kids who idolise him. The conflict, of course, cannot be entirely resolved. As always, the ending of the film is a piece of narrative manipulation which manages, through a particular instance, to reconcile energy with stability and to suggest that such a reconciliation can be generalised. Energy is likewise the keynote of the production process, while in production terms the stability is represented by the market for which the film is made – a market which is attracted by the energy but is not prepared to admit its logical consequences.

The studio, of course, did not see the tensions in these terms. For the production executives it was a question of making an exciting picture which would be acceptable to Breen, the critics and audiences in general. But an awareness of the tensions surfaces repeatedly during the making of *Angels with Dirty Faces*. Two general instances make this clear. When Harry Warner saw the film a week before its official preview at Warners' Hollywood Theatre, he sent the following memo to Hal Wallis:

> Dear Hal,
> I saw the Cagney picture ANGELS WITH DIRTY FACES and that is some production. I only hope that we don't have any censure trouble with it for it's one of the best pictures I've seen in many a day. It teaches a lesson but you know people don't understand just what you're trying to do.[6]

The other instance of tension can be seen by looking at the story of the film, as outlined in the official studio synopsis which went out with the other advertising material. I include it in its entirety because, in addition to making further plot summary unnecessary, it perfectly captures the tone of the film.

> The story opens in the squalid tenement district of a great American city. Two slum boys, Rocky Sullivan (James Cagney) and Jerry Connolly (Pat O'Brien), need money to see 'The Covered Wagon'. To get it, they break into a freight car loaded with fountain pens and stuff their pockets with the pens. They are discovered by police and try to get away. Jerry is successful. Rocky is captured and sent to reform school. Years pass. Rocky is now a big shot gangster being released from federal penitentiary after serving a three year sentence for racketeering. He has taken the rap for his attorney, James Frazier (Humphrey Bogart), on Frazier's promise that Rocky will get $100,000 when he gets out of prison. On his release, Rocky returns to his old haunts and meets Jerry, now a priest. Jerry is fighting to make good citizens out of the boys of the slums. There is still a great bond between the two men.
> Jerry arranges for Rocky to take a room in a tenement, hoping that the latter will meet Laury Ferguson (Ann Sheridan), his childhood

sweetheart, and change his way of living. Rocky and Laury meet and fall in love. As Rocky walks down the old street again he is set upon by six young hoodlums, Soapy (Billy Halop), Swing (Bobby Jordan), Bim (Leo Gorcey), Hunky (Bernard Punsley), Pasty (Gabriel Dell) and Crab (Huntz Hall), who pick his pocket and race to their hideout in the boiler room of a tenement. It is Rocky's old hideout and he goes there and gets his money back and wins the friendship of the boys. When they find out who he is, they idolise him. Rocky learns that Jerry wants the six boys to go to his gymnasium and play basketball and when Rocky asks them to do it, they go.

Rocky then goes to Frazier's office to collect his $100,000. Frazier is now tied up with Mac Keefer (George Bancroft), who controls the city politics. Frazier and Keefer decide to double cross Rocky and send three thugs out to kill him. He is walking home with Laury when he senses the plot and outwits the gangsters. Then he goes to Frazier and forces him to call Keefer and tell Keefer to give Rocky the $100,000. Rocky loots Frazier's safe of records that implicate high city officials in the wholesale racketeering. Rocky goes to Keefer's night club and is given the money. However, when he leaves the club, the police, called by Keefer, who has told them that Rocky kidnapped Frazier, arrest him. Frazier, knowing that Rocky has the damaging records, brings about his immediate release.

At once, Jerry decides to clean up the town even though it means fighting Rocky. His decision is made after Rocky becomes a partner in Keefer's night club and induces Laury to quit her job and become a hostess in the club.

Jerry gets the support of a powerful newspaper and starts his drive against racketeering. On the eve of a grand jury investigation, Frazier and Keefer decide to kill Jerry. Rocky overhears the plot and shoots both men in their office in the club. The gangsters' henchmen and Rocky start to shoot it out and the police come. They trap Rocky in a warehouse and he refuses to come out. Jerry goes in after him and Rocky uses him as a shield in a desperate attempt to escape. But the attempt fails. Rocky is wounded and captured. He is tried for murder, found guilty and sentenced to the electric chair. Now he is the hero of all the slum boys in America. They read of his exploits avidly. When they learn that he will go to the chair unflinching, they cheer him.

Just before Rocky starts down the last mile, Jerry comes to his cell. He asks Rocky to do one thing for him – one last fine gesture – to die yellow. Rocky laughs at him. Jerry points out that it may save thousands of boys from lives of crime but Rocky still refuses. He's going to die like a man.

As he enters the death chamber, Rocky changes his mind. He goes to the chair screaming – almost fainting from fear. And the boys in

Crime prevention: Cagney and the Dead End Kids in *Angels with Dirty Faces*

all the slums of all the great cities despise him because he turned yellow. Only Jerry and Laury know the truth.

There are several comments called for by the above synopsis – the fact that the part played by Ann Sheridan, who shared third billing, appears as little more than a footnote; the regular interpolation of temporary climaxes (the brush with Keefer's gangsters, Rocky's first arrest) to keep the story moving – but the most crucial one is that the final sentence is misleading. It is not just Jerry and Laury who know the truth: the audience knows it as well. Rocky remains, for the audience, the heroic figure he has been throughout – ennobled by the bond between him and the priest, redeemed by the love of Laury, set in principled contrast to the cowardly Frazier and, even more importantly, to the crooked politician Keefer. Equally important is the success of his criminal career. He effortlessly outwits the Kids in the opening scene of the modern story, outwits the gangsters who try to ambush him, and has no trouble eliminating Frazier and Keefer (an action which he carries out to save his old buddy and at the risk of his own life). Contrary to what is implied by the synopsis, it is Rocky who is the moral superior in the film, since he sacrifices his life for his friend and his reputation for the Kids. In contrast to this individual strength, the forces of society are wholly secondary. It is Jerry, not the police, who gets Rocky out of the warehouse. The busting of the racket is brought about by Rocky, not by the Grand Jury investigation. And it is a personal bond, not a social conscience, which results in Rocky 'dying yellow'. Rocky is a gangster because of environmental influences: the opening sequences are unequivocally set against a background of poverty, and the fact that the Kids use Rocky's old hideout stresses the parallels between their lives. The young Rocky's statement of principles to the young Jerry – 'Always remember: don't be a sucker' – is a creed to which the Kids equally subscribe. That such an idol should sacrifice his honour to protect 'the boys in all the slums of all the great cities' from a life of crime is what makes his action all the more noteworthy. It also, of course, makes it highly ambiguous.

Angels with Dirty Faces: Rocky about to 'die yellow'

If they were at times uncertain as to how to handle the subject, Warners showed no such uncertainty when it came to the business of production. The production of *Angels with Dirty Faces* shows the studio system in operation at maximum efficiency on a relatively straightforward contemporary subject. By the time the film went into production, the problems of 'morality' had been ironed out. They crop up from time to time during the actual shooting, but are discussed in operational rather than moral terms: once the project was established, the aim was to maximise its potential. The story, according to Walter MacEwen,[7] originally came from an idea by Mervyn LeRoy (who had negotiated the Dead End Kids deal), but Rowland Brown had dropped it because LeRoy wouldn't pay enough. In the end, Brown got original story credit – something he was later unsuccessfully to query – and writers John Wexley and Warren Duff were set to work on a screenplay on 28 January 1938. One of the problems with Brown's story seems to have been strong reservations from the Breen Office, as a letter to Jack Warner from Breen on 19 January makes clear:

This goes to you in confirmation of my telephone conversation today with Mr MacEwen with regard to the script ANGELS WITH DIRTY FACES, which you submitted for our consideration. As I told Mr MacEwen, while it might be possible to make a picture from the basic story which would meet the requirements of the Production Code, the script, in its present form, is not acceptable on a number of counts. I list these briefly below:

It is important to avoid any flavor of making a hero and sympathetic character of a man who is at the same time shown to be a criminal, a murderer and a kidnapper. In order to achieve this, great care will be needed both in the writing and actual shooting of the picture.

The present portrayal of the three young boys as indulging in criminal activities, shown in detail, is not only a violation of our Code, but enormously dangerous from the standpoint of political censorship everywhere. This should be changed so as to eliminate all criminal details.

The present script also violates the Association's ruling re 'Crime in Motion Pictures' on a number of points, as follows:

The successful kidnapping for ransom.

The gun battle with the police, in the course of which a policeman is shown dying at the hands of the criminal.

The unpunished gangster murder of the man in the telephone booth.

There then follows the usual list of detailed objections, twenty-three in this case

The Duff-Wexley version initially fared no better. MacEwen wrote to Wallis on 4 April:

> At Sam Bischoff's request, I sent Joe Breen a copy of the treatment on ANGELS WITH DIRTY FACES.
>
> Breen has called up very concerned about this treatment, which he regards as the gravest problem that has confronted them in the last couple of years...
>
> I asked Joe not to send out any tough letter on this treatment, but instead to have a conference with Bischoff and the writers, as I was sure none of the difficulties were insuperable. Breen will get together with Sam on Wednesday.

The Breen Office, it should be stressed once more, was not Hollywood's enemy; it was a part of the system. Breen's objections were noted and negotiated on, and a compromise was reached. This was the effect of the meeting between Breen and Bischoff. By 20 May, Breen was giving his general approval, though he was still concerned about the kidnapping, and the final execution scene, which he was sure would be cut in Britain.

Brown's story was clearly only going to use three kids. On 28 April, however, Wallis sent a memo to Bischoff telling him to tell the writers to use *all* the kids: with them, Cagney and O'Brien, the picture was 'sure-fire box office'. The picture's final billing gives a fairly clear indication of how Warners assessed the respective box-office pull of the various elements in the package. The billing in printed advertising approved by Jack Warner on 2 August 1938 is as follows:

100%	James Cagney and Pat O'Brien
	Angels with Dirty Faces
85%	Humphrey Bogart
	The 'Dead End' Kids
50%	Ann Sheridan, George Bancroft
30%	Billy Halop
25%	Warner Bros. Pictures Inc.
	Bobby Jordan, Leo Gorcey, Gabriel Dell, Huntz Hall
	and Bernard Punsley
	Directed by Michael Curtiz
20%	Screenplay by John Wexley and Warren Duff
10%	From a story by Rowland Brown[8]

The title cards on the film itself establish a slightly sharper hierarchy:

1. James Cagney and Pat O'Brien in
2. Angels with Dirty Faces

3. with Humphrey Bogart, Ann Sheridan, George Bancroft and The 'Dead End' Kids
4. Directed by Michael Curtiz. Screenplay by John Wexley and Warren Duff. From a story by Rowland Brown.

When the film was re-released in 1948 (in a double bill with *They Drive by Night*), Bogart's name was moved up above the title.

Angels with Dirty Faces was originally budgeted at $582,000 on 25 June 1938, with the broad divisions as follows:

Story	$12,500
Warren Duff	$13,950
John Wexley	$6,767
Director	$39,000
Associate producer	$14,700
Assistant directors	$4,300
Cameraman and assistants	$5,300
Cagney	$85,667
O'Brien	$24,200
Bogart	$8,800
Halop	$6,500
Gorcey, Punsley, Dell, Hall:	
$2,500 each	$10,000
Jordan	$800
Gale Page[9]	$4,160
Outside talent[10]	$5,033
Extras, bits, etc.	$25,992
Musicians	$10,800
Property labour	$4,712
Construction of sets	$37,400
Other	$80,731
DIRECT COST	$401,312
Studio overhead @ 40%	$160,623
Depreciation @ 5%	$20,065
TOTAL	$582,000

There was a minor revision after release, bringing the studio overhead up to 45% (and the overall budget up to $602,000), but that does not affect what is of interest to us now: the proportions. 8% of the budget went on the story, just under 20% on production staff salaries, just under 30% on sets and plant (with specially constructed sets accounting for under 10%), and 42% on talent, with Cagney's salary accounting for a massive 20% of the direct cost. The budget for *Angels with Dirty Faces* is a fairly exact indication of the financial advantages of a contemporary crime story: $239,656 – nearly 60% of the budget – goes on meeting studio salaries of one kind or another, $80,731 on the use of existing studio facilities, and only $80,925 (a bare 20%) is spent specifically on the film itself. The single most expensive set was the tenement street, budgeted at $22,941 – $12,500 on construction, $4,010 on extras and $2,084 on bits. The shooting schedule was modest. Despite problems with faulty blank cartridges, Curtiz brought the film in in 38 days of actual shooting – 8 days more than originally allocated. Economy, however, was part of the studio's production method, not of its public image in the late 1930s: the official preview programme suggests that the film cost more than $1,000,000 to make and took eight weeks to shoot!

The memos during shooting indicate another conflict – or perhaps it was a productive tension – within the studio. The energetic economy of narrative which paralleled the organisational economy of production was not always compatible with it. Michael Curtiz, the studio's star director of action pictures, could be relied upon to deliver the goods in terms of action, but not always in terms of schedule. On *Angels with Dirty Faces*, production memos to Tenny Wright from the Unit Production Manager, Frank Mattison, grow increasingly desperate as the film gets further behind schedule.

29 July 1938. Company is now four days behind schedule. You can tell from yesterday's report that Mike spent the day adding shots that were not in the script and building the sequence, all of which takes a great deal of time. Mr Curtiz is yelling for iron doors and bars along the prison set for the doors thru which Cagney passes on his way to the chair. Bob Haas[11] is doing the best he can but I am sure you do not want to go outside and build any new iron gates. For your further information, Mr Curtiz has spoken about making an additional scene in a BROADCASTING STATION of Pat O'Brien. We still have no OK on this from BISCHOFF, but I will keep after him and let him get an OK from Mr WALLIS because this set will no doubt have to be built. It is not in our Budget.

From present indications we will finish this picture on SATURDAY, AUGUST 6. This is 5 weeks and 5 days, so you see my estimate of 36 days to shoot the picture is very nearly correct. We are going to run over the Budget but not a very great deal unless Mike goes screwy when we get outside on the New York Street to continue the gun battle.

I think Mike should be ashamed of himself for telling you yesterday he received no co-operation, for if we gave him only what is in the script we should have finished with the WAREHOUSE day before yesterday.

While the shots he has added are no doubt building up the sequence, there is no mind-reader on the lot that can keep ahead of Mike when you turn him loose with machine guns, revolvers, bullets and gas bombs. I think he would rather play cops and robbers than eat. [12]

8 August 1938. I have been going over our costs and budget on this picture and we are going to run over the budget even tho we have $32,000 left on last FRIDAY. This makes another picture on which Mike Curtiz goes over his Budget. We will be 38 days in the shooting of this picture, knowing from the start that Mike would average at least 36 days, and it is not fair to the department or fair to you yourself to knowingly under-budget Mike's pictures. Mike has been in the Studio long enough so all departments know the man and how he works.

Such problems are obviously an inevitable corollary of applying a factory method to the production of art, but it does seem as though they intensified in the late 1930s. Towards the end of the decade, the ebbing of the general economic crisis together with the studio's own gathering ambitions (treated in more detail in Part III) led to some relaxation of the system's rigidity and enabled an assertion of individualism within the system as well as within its product. This was the era of the unionisation of Hollywood, and of Warners' stars like Davis and Cagney taking on the studio management. Obviously, the production system which had dominated Hollywood – and Warners – since the advent of sound was changing. And just possibly the rough edges and ambiguities which, for a modern audience, make Warners' films of the late 1930s far more accessible than those of a mere five years earlier have their origins in this breakdown in hierarchy, itself doubtless related to the change in the national social climate.

The ambiguity of the finished film's message continued to worry the studio, as the very moral slant given to its publicity campaign indicates. The exhibitor's handbook includes specific instructions in this respect:

In selling this picture, it should not be geared down to the gangster level ... No 'killer' type of copy or exploitation will sell the importance of this production ... In order to do the business this picture warrants, it must be sold as a powerful human document ... It opens the door for co-operation from leaders in welfare work, heads of organisations interested in youth uplift work, women's clubs, civic clubs, PTAs, Boy Scouts, Big Brothers and city officials.

Suggested exploitation ideas included: a 'dirty face' contest; a column in church papers; a 'there but for the Grace of God go I' contest; an invitation to local magistrates to sentence juvenile offenders to see the film; an 'Angels with Dirty Faces' club adopting boys who have 'strayed'; and talks with environmental themes by judges, educators and

142

wardens. The actual publicity slogans in the press book hover between sensationalism and uplift:

> Chunk by chunk, they cut out his heart ... in slums, in reformatories, in prisons! Now he returns to the slums to get his vengeance on the world! (This to accompany a portrait of Cagney).
>
> I pledge my life ... that this story shall not be their story ... that his end shall not be their end! (This to accompany pictures of O'Brien and the Kids).

The exhibitor's kit also contained a letter of endorsement, blown up to be used as an ad, from Franklin L. Matthews, Chief Librarian of the Boy Scouts of America.

Angels with Dirty Faces is by no means Warners' last crime movie of the decade, but it is the last to be so explicitly concerned with rehabilitation. As such, it exemplifies the conflicts between the studio's social conscience pictures and their increasing appeal as straightforward action movies. The assumption expressed in the story synopsis – that the slum kids of America will necessarily idolise the violent criminal who goes nobly to the chair – is a revealing one, and it clearly necessitated the attempt to generalise the reaction by the Dead End Kids in the film – contempt for Rocky's cowardice – to slum kids throughout the country. But the increased realism of the screenplay makes the generalisation an afterthought. Father Jerry is prepared to admit that crime indeed does pay, but appeals to Rocky's friendship and sense of honour to persuade the kids otherwise. The fact that Rocky's death is not the death of a coward to the audience – it may be to the Kids in the movie, but it isn't to the kids in the movie theatre – shows that the conflict between a strong individualistic morality and a sense of social responsibility, a conflict that characterises most of the studio's post-1935 crime movies, is no longer entirely reconcilable. The rehabilitation of the Dead End Kids is unconvincing, as it was at the end of *Crime School*. By the end of the decade, contemporary action movies can no longer portray society as an extension of the individual. The anti-social behaviour which is the appeal of the Dead End Kids and the force behind the narrative of all the later crime movies becomes the dominant factor. That the author of the original story for *Angels with Dirty Faces*, Rowland Brown, should also have been the author of *Doorway to Hell* is perhaps significant. No amount of adjustment can obscure the fact that it is a slightly old-fashioned theme in conflict with the realism of its details and the energy of the system that produced it.

8 Racism, Fascism and Other Issues

Racism and fascism are not themes we readily associate with Hollywood. Indeed, for many critics, they are more often hidden features than explicit themes in Hollywood movies. But they are issues to which Warners returned a number of times during the 1930s. In *Confessions of a Nazi Spy* (1939) as well as in the later *All Through the Night* (1942) fascism appeared to be a foreign threat administered by sinister men with heavy accents. But it could also be a homegrown disease, as it was in *Black Legion* (1937) and *Meet John Doe* (1941), which made it a trickier subject to handle, since it was the ideas, not the ideologues, which had to be shown to be alien. All the films with racist themes – *Son of the Gods* (1930), *Massacre* (1934), *Bordertown* (1935) and *They Won't Forget* (1937) – necessarily deal with a homegrown problem, though they strive to present it as a temporary aberration, not an endemic state. Nevertheless, the films were made: reassuring they may have been, but wholly bland they were not.

The reason they were made, of course, often had to do as much with market decisions as with a determination to tackle a social problem (though it could equally be argued that the market could have been supplied with other, less controversial product). All the same, it is relatively easy to 'account' for the making of *Son of the Gods*, *Massacre* and *Bordertown*. They were star vehicles whose theme offered a conflict around which to build a narrative. Within the studio system, which may have been only precariously established when the first of the three films was made at the end of 1929, but which was firmly installed by the time of the last two in 1934 and 1935 respectively, the only real variables were star and story material. Everything else – production planning, scripting, narrative structure, shooting schedules, publicity and marketing – remained fairly constant, with differences being essentially those of scale. More time would be spent planning and shooting, and more effort expended on publicising, an *Anthony Adverse* than an *Alcatraz Island*. But even on a film like *Anthony Adverse*, actors and extras cost more than sets, while in the contemporary subjects, as the budget for *Angels with Dirty Faces* indicates, cast salaries were by far the biggest item. In all the major features, what was marketed was a star in a particular story.

Stars were the major determining factor in a film's success (or at any rate the one which could be predicted with the greatest certainty), and as such stars were a determining factor in its budget. The studio could not hope to recoup – and therefore would not spend – a lot of money on films without 'marquee values'. Similarly, stars were one of Hollywood's major ideological vehicles. The public's image of a star – as *Variety*'s comments on *Taxi!* make clear – was what conditioned its response to the situation in which the star found her- or himself. And that image was, in turn, a product of market demand and a reflection of public values. The closed circle referred to in Chapter One[1] is much more readily seen in the case of star images than anywhere else in the studio system: when it came to stars, the public got what the public wanted because the public wanted what the public got. The first three films to deal with racial prejudice – *Son of the Gods*, *Massacre* and *Bordertown* – were all star vehicles, built round actors strongly associated with the impersonation of minority groups. Richard Barthelmess' most famous silent role had been as a Chinese in *Broken Blossoms* (1919), and he returned to playing a Chinese in *Son of the Gods*. In *Massacre*, he plays a Sioux Indian. In *Seven Faces* (1929) and *Scarface* (1932), Paul Muni had begun a career of impersonation which was to reach its peak with his portrayal of Louis Pasteur, Emile Zola and Benito Juarez. As in the last mentioned case, in *Bordertown* Muni plays a Mexican, though in a contemporary American context. And in that context, whereas the problems of white, preferably Irish Americans, could more easily be explored through the hero's conflict with the law, those of non-white Americans tended to rely on the hero's conflict with society at large.

Son of the Gods is more a sentimental melodrama than a social picture – though it does contain lines which explicitly discuss prejudice. 'Race prejudice has always existed,' Lee Ying (E. Alyn Warren) tells his son Sam Lee (Richard Barthelmess). 'The only weapon we can use to defeat it is tolerance.' But the context in which Sam encounters prejudice in the film is exclusively romantic: the girls he dates reject him when they discover that beneath his all-American playboy exterior he is oriental. Everyone else in the film is horrified by these manifestations of prejudice: 'You know,' Sam's friend Kicker (Frank Albertson) remarks after a particularly nasty feminine outburst, 'I feel like I've just stepped on a baby's finger.' Later, after the film's crucial conflict between Sam and heiress Allana Wagner (Constance Bennett), the latter is taken to task by Sam's friend and mentor (Claude King). 'I think you're the most arrogant, the most ruthless creature I've ever known,' he tells her. 'I'm a Californian,' replies Allana: 'I was raised among Chinamen.' 'Pardon me,' corrects Sam's friend, 'among coolies.

A question of race: Richard Barthelmess and Constance Bennett in *Son of the Gods*

Sam Lee is a gentleman.' That line alone should make it clear that *Son of the Gods* is not a plea for generalised racial tolerance, but for respect for an individual of a certain social standing regardless of – indeed, in spite of – his race. In the end, a twist in the plot – Mordaunt Hall called the film 'violently inconsistent' – reveals that Sam is not Chinese at all, but a foundling from the streets of San Francisco rescued by a friendly Irish cop.

But *Son of the Gods* does not completely dodge the issues of racism. The plot twice repeats the same pattern: Sam is secure and happy, but has this taken away from him by encountering prejudice in a member of the opposite sex and retreats into an anti-white prejudice of his own. On both occasions, the prejudice manifests itself in a dramatically violent way. In the first part of the film, Sam is happily established as a student on the West Coast, with polo ponies and a smart roadster. A trip with a group of society girls ends in disaster when the girls discover his racial background. 'Sam Lee, a Chink!' screams Connie (Geneva Mitchell) hysterically. 'I wouldn't let him *touch* me!' Sam returns to his father in Chinatown (for which scenes the film was originally shown in two-strip Technicolor) and informs him that his 'quest for knowledge is at an end. Conditions become unbearable. The only friends I made were the ones I bought with your money.' He flees to Europe, takes a job on the Côte d'Azur and meets Allana, who silences his indirect

146

attempts to explain that he is not what he seems – i.e. not white – and reassures him that 'there are no prejudices among our class'. When she discovers the truth, however, her reaction is rather different. She strides across the palm court of a smart casino – a set borrowed from the musical *Sally* (1929) – and screams abuse at him: 'You cur! You liar! You cheat! You dirty, rotten Chinaman!' She strikes him again and again across the face with her riding crop. Sam remains impassive as the weals appear and the blood begins to flow: it is, by any standards, a dramatic presentation of racism.

When his father dies Sam returns to New York to take over the business. 'I used to believe in love, brotherhood, charity,' he tells his father's secretary Eileen (Mildred van Dorn), who is also the friendly cop's sister. 'But they're only names, words, lies . . . I am not of your race, Eileen, and I no longer wish to be . . . I am Chinese, and from now on I shall live as one.' He severs all business ties with the white community, and tells his lawyer (George Irving) to extend credit to no more white firms: 'I do not wish to listen to a continual repetition of my offences against white people.' Allana phones to apologise, but Sam will not accept the call. She becomes seriously ill, and her father (Anders Randolf) pleads with Sam to help, promising him every dollar he has. 'I'll give you every dollar *I* have to buy Allana,' replies Sam, adding to the outraged Wagner: 'It hurts, doesn't it?' In the end, however, Allana and Sam are reconciled. 'But darling, you're you,' she promises. 'You're the one I love.'

It is, given the forces which have been unleashed earlier in the film, a very unconvincing ending, not simply because Sam turns out to be white after all – something about which, to be fair, he is less than delighted – but also because Allana's change of heart leaves untouched the racial prejudice which has been the film's linchpin. But within the context of the narrative structure, it is the only possible ending. The problem has been posed at an individual level (Allana's attack) and has to be resolved on the same level (her remorse, atonement – she becomes seriously ill and almost dies – and final adoption of the 'correct' attitude). 'Its plea for racial and religious tolerance will rate with the classes,' wrote Walter R. Green in *Motion Picture News*, 'while the dramatic and sentimental love story will get over with the masses'.[2] Such commercial balance would seem to have been all.

Massacre, in which Barthelmess plays a Sioux Indian called Joe Thunder Horse, is a good deal less evasive and in some ways a genuine oddity, so much so that *Variety* seriously wondered whether the film was 'timely', and Mordaunt Hall in the *New York Times* doubted its 'expediency'. The Barthelmess character is a successful performer in Dawson's 3-Bar Ranch Show, a carnival Wild West show. He makes $400 a week, has an extensive wardrobe, a black servant (Clarence Muse) and a monogrammed roadster. At the beginning of the film, he is starring at the Century of Progress World's Fair in Chicago, when an Indian from the Spotted Eagle reservation comes to tell him that his father is dying. Returning to the reservation for the first time since childhood, Joe finds that his people are being exploited and expropriated by the agent, the gloriously named Elihu P. Quissenbery (Dudley Digges), and his corrupt henchman Doc Turner (Arthur Hohl). When his sister Jennie (Agnes Nascha) is raped by one of Quissenbery's heavies, Shanks (Sidney Toler), Joe buys a rope from a passing cowboy, pursues Shanks in his roadster, lassoes him and drags him from his car. Joe is arrested, given a rigged trial, but escapes. He alerts the Federal Commissioner for Indian Affairs, J.R. Dickinson (Henry O'Neill), to the plight of his people, and the machinery of Federal benevolence begins to roll. When Shanks dies of his injuries, Joe is given a fair trial and found not guilty; Quissenbery and Taylor are removed from office and indicted; and Joe takes a job in Washington 'to help eradicate what Lincoln 70 years ago called an accursed system'. 'This,' he tells Lydia (Ann Dvorak), the reservation girl who helps him and, of course, falls in love with him, 'is a real job, not like shooting at balloons in a carnival.'

The element of violent personal action undertaken to resolve a social evil is clearly crucial to *Massacre*, but Ralph Block and Sheridan Gibney's screenplay shows a surprising awareness of the problems of the native American. At the outset, Joe Thunder Horse is a fake Indian, bedecked in carnival costume and speaking cod-Indian to the crowd. 'Get this junk off me,' he orders (in modern American) as soon as he is back in his dressing room. He dons a white suit and stetson, and goes off to visit a wealthy white girl (Claire Dodd). She flirts with the idea of his Indianness, showing him a room full of 'Indian' art which he barely recognises: 'What's all this?' he asks. 'I wasn't on the reservation since I was a kid. I wouldn't know a medicine man from a bootlegger.' She lies back seductively on the couch, cooing 'Redskin!'. He bends over her. 'Red lips!' he grins.

Once on the reservation, however, Joe begins to feel his racial allegiance. 'Is this the reservation?' asks his black servant, Sam. 'White folks don't give Indians much of a break. Sure is dry!' Joe's father's land is spirited away by the agent, part to himself, part to Doc and part to a 'tribal fund'. 'And old Quiz just dares any Indian to get it out,' he cackles. Joe discovers other abuses: his younger brother has been whipped for 'leaving the reservation without permission'; rights have been sold to a film company to make a commercial for patent medicine with a black actor, dubbed Chief Black Star, playing an Indian. 'They're being fooled into selling their birthright,' he says angrily to Lydia. His first trial (for attacking Shanks) is manifestly crooked. His counsel enters a plea of 'Guilty' without consulting him, and a tame Indian judge sentences him to 90 days, then turns to Quissenbery to ask 'OK?'. Shanks' rape of Jennie is, for a 1930s movie, remarkably explicit, and it is of course this which triggers off – as well as justifies – Joe's violent acts of retribution.

But *Massacre* is very much a New Deal film. Joe's actions would have been powerless without the intervention of Dickinson. Individual action is not in itself decisive. Escaping from the reservation, Joe hops a train, pausing for a moment alongside a boxcar on which the NRA Eagle is clearly visible, and heads for Washington. He finds that

A question of race: Richard Barthelmess as Joe Thunder Horse in *Massacre*

Dickinson's hands are tied. 'Every move I make is blocked by the same organised group that has been fighting the Indians for years,' the Commissioner tells Joe. 'Water power, oil rights, cattle ranges, timber: whatever the Indian happens to own, they get away from him. They control public opinion and they control legislation.' Dickinson's fight is Roosevelt's fight writ small, in favour of the rights of the American people and against entrenched business interests. Joe's case enables Dickinson to go into action. 'Sioux Indian becomes American Dreyfus,' declares a newspaper headline. Joe is invited to address a Senate Investigation, and his speech inevitably becomes an exercise in New Deal rhetoric. 'The Indian as citizen, huh? He hasn't any constitutional rights . . . You used to shoot the Indian down. Now you cheat him and starve him and kill him off by dirt and disease. It's a massacre any way you look at it.' There is applause in the Senate, but the

149

investigation is dramatically interrupted by a policeman arriving to arrest Joe for Shanks' murder. This gives Joe – and the film – just the necessary opportunity to convert from violent political action to a belief in the benevolent power of the Roosevelt Administration. 'We'll never get a square deal by breaking the white man's law,' he tells the Indians who bust him out of jail. And the film's ending proves him right: the white man's law gives him his freedom. *Massacre* is the New Deal film *par excellence*. Joe's faith is justified, and the wrongs of a corrupt administration are righted.

Bordertown, released a year later in the watershed year of 1935, is much less concerned with examining the predicament of a minority group – in this case, Mexican Americans – than it is with charting the painful experience of an individual member of that group. Indeed the ending, in which Johnny Rodriguez (Paul Muni) tells the Padre (Robert Barrat) that he is going 'back where I belong . . . with my own people' is more or less explicitly segregationist. *Bordertown* is the story of Johnny Rodriguez, a Mexican living in Los Angeles. By studying at night school, he qualifies as a lawyer but makes a mess of his first big case and is lectured by the judge: 'You, sir, in not preparing your case properly, have failed in your obligation to your client.' Insulted by the other attorney, Johnny lashes out and is barred from practising. He becomes bitter and decides that money, not principles, is what counts in the world. 'The people who love me are poor, dirt, like I am,' he tells his mother (Soledad Jimenez). 'They can't give me what I need . . . A man's entitled to whatever he can grab. I found that out. And I'm going to grab from now on.'

He hitchhikes south, and ends up as a bouncer in the Silver Slipper Club, a gaudy gambling casino just across the Mexican border (the town is not identified, but the background to the film is clearly Tijuana's fashionable Agua Caliente gambling mecca of the 1930s). He is so successful that the owner, Charlie Roark (Eugene Pallette), makes him a partner. Roark's wife Marie (Bette Davis at her most predatory) falls for him, and kills her husband by leaving him drunkenly asleep in his car in the garage with the motor running. Now boss of the Silver Slipper, Johnny is able to raise the money to open a plush new club, La Rueda, one of whose opening night customers is Dale Elwell (with Margaret Lindsay once again playing the foil to Davis' devil woman), the rich Californian who had been the defendant in Johnny's one court case, and whose lawyer had humiliated him. He falls for her and she toys with him, fondly calling him 'Savage!' and telling a friend that the attraction reveals 'the prehistoric in me'. Johnny visits her in Los Angeles and, despite a frosty reception from her English-accented butler, is given some encouragement by Dale, though there is a clear implication that he was presumptuous to bring south-of-the-border alliances into the Land of the Free. Furiously jealous, Marie accuses him of murdering her husband, but he is freed when she goes berserk on the witness stand. He returns to Dale and proposes marriage. 'Marriage isn't for us, not even to talk about,' she tells him. 'You belong to a different tribe, savage.' It is the nearest the film comes to open discussion of racial prejudice, but it is not a point that is allowed to develop. Johnny tries to kiss her, and Dale, screaming 'Let go of me, you filthy brute!' runs from the car, and is knocked down and killed. It is enough to convince Johnny that he should return to his 'own people', back on Olvera street. He sells La Rueda for $250,000, uses the money to endow a law school, and goes to confession in the church of Nostra Señora la Reina de Los Angeles.

The opening of *Bordertown* is a standard demonstration of local boy making good. There are a number of shots establishing location and local colour – jumping beans in a window; jalapeno peppers in a restaurant display; a sign saying 'English spoken here' – before the camera settles on a plaque declaring 'Pacific Night Law School' in Spanish and English; a tilt down reveals the same sign in French and Chinese. We are clearly in the ghetto. The camera tracks up the steps, and dissolves inside to the Graduation ceremony where the students are singing 'My country, 'tis of thee'. The principal makes a rousing speech about Johnny's achievement: 'He had the courage to lift himself above his environment . . . he solved his own problems, realised his opportunities and duties as an American citizen.' Johnny embraces his 'mamacita', and they all go off to celebrate at a party where 'La Cucuracha' is danced and the Padre proposes a toast. Johnny makes a heavily accented speech. 'I done – I *did*! – like Lincoln and I'm going to keep on doing like Lincoln. It's like the Señor Judge said: This is America, the land of opportunity. A man can lift himself up by his bootstraps, provided he has the strength – and the boots!' The final, ironical comment is significant: everything else in the film is downhill as far as opportunity is concerned, with Johnny only able to achieve financial success in a dubious enterprise, becoming directly involved in two violent deaths, and not able to find happiness until he returns to his starting point.

Bordertown was extremely successful at the box office, reopening the refurbished Broadway Strand with a run of just over two weeks (exceeded that year only by *G-Men, Captain Blood* and *Frisco Kid*). But its success was due, not to its theme, but to the fact that it was a star vehicle. 'Paul Muni in his best screen performance and Bette Davis equalling, if not bettering, her characterisation in *Of Human Bondage*,' wrote *Variety*, adding almost as an afterthought: 'An interesting yarn, fine direction . . .' In the case of *Bordertown*, the exigencies of narrative – basically, that it is an individual (star) destiny, not a general theme, which must be explored – act against any real exploration of the theme of racism, if they do not actually conspire to make the film latently

151

Bordertown: Paul Muni as the Mexican American, with Bette Davis

racist. Johnny's journey to self-knowledge involves the discovery that white women – at any rate high-class white women – are not for him. The treatment of a radical subject did not necessarily mean a socially conscious movie: the basic conservatism of the narrative form and of the studio system which generated that form could as easily tip the balance away from a 'message' as towards one.

They Won't Forget, Warners' last major film of the 1930s to deal with prejudice, is not concerned with racial conflict but with the historical antipathy between North and South. Produced and directed by Mervyn LeRoy shortly before he left the studio for M-G-M, it is, like many of Warner Brothers' contemporary dramas, based on an actual case – the recent Atlanta trial of Leo M. Frank – and taken from Ward Greene's account of it, *Death in the Deep South*. A young girl, Mary Clay (Lana Turner, in her first role of any size), who is a student at a commercial college in the Southern town of Flodden, is murdered on Memorial Day. The police first arrest the black janitor, Tump Redwine (Clinton Rosemond), but District Attorney Andy Griffin (Claude Rains), sensing that there is no political capital to be made out of the trial of a black and anxious to win the nomination for U.S. Senator, is reluctant to prosecute. Further investigation reveals a chain of circumstantial evidence pointing towards Robert Hale (Edward Norris), a Northerner who teaches at the College. Hale is brought to

152

trial amid a gradually mounting tide of prejudice: a New York detective (Granville Bates), brought in by Hale's wife Sybil (Gloria Dickson), is beaten up by a mob; bricks are thrown at the car of defence attorney Mike Gleason (Otto Kruger). Hale is found guilty and condemned to death, but the Governor (Paul Everton), although realising that it will mean the end of his political career, commutes the sentence. Hale is, however, pulled off a train and lynched by a mob headed by Mary's brothers. At the end of the film, Sybil Hale bursts in on Griffin and his friend, reporter Bill Brock (Alyn Joslyn), like Jennie Townsend confronting Randall at the end of *Five Star Final*. 'You're the one who's responsible,' she says to Griffin. 'You stirred up the hatred, for no other reason than to further your ambition. Deep down in your hearts and souls, you know it's the truth.' As she leaves, there is a high-angle shot as Brock and Griffin watch her emerge on to the sidewalk. 'Andy,' says Brock, 'now that it's all over, I wonder if Hale really did it.' 'I wonder,' muses Griffin.

The bare bones of the plot hardly do justice to the movie, which Frank S. Nugent of the *New York Times* compared favourably to both Fritz Lang's *Fury* (1936) and *Black Legion* (1937). It is, along with *Confessions of a Nazi Spy*, Warners' most emphatic social document of the second half of the decade. 'With courage, objectivity and simple eloquence,' wrote Nugent, the film 'creates a brilliant sociological

They Won't Forget: Claude Rains leads for the South

drama and a trenchant film editorial against intolerance and hatred.'
They Won't Forget is both a high-class example of a Warners contemporary social picture, with Robert Rossen and Abem Kandel's screenplay impressive for the accuracy with which it deals with prejudice, and set somewhat apart from normal studio production by the determination with which Mervyn LeRoy, both producing and directing, handles the material.

Opening with a set of monumental credits, hewn like relief mountains from a parched desert, it launches straight into the extended set piece of Memorial Day, with a group of Civil War veterans watching from beneath a statue of General Robert E. Lee that bears the inscription 'All the South has ever desired is that the Union should be preserved'. 'I was jes' dreamin',' says one old-timer, awaking from his snooze, 'about the day we were in Chattynoogy.' 'Only six of us left,' muses another. 'Maybe next year there will only be five or four or three or none. But they won't forget. They won't never forget. If they do, we'll get up out of our graves and remind 'em.' Intercut with the parade is the murder, which is thereby directly linked to the history of the South and the attitudes which are its legacy. Tump, the janitor, sits in his basement cubbyhole reading *Parisian Nights*. He hears the elevator bell ring, but by the time he gets upstairs there is no one to be seen. He hears footsteps going up. 'If yo' leg's walkin' better, it's O.K. with me,' he mutters. Cut to Mary in the classroom. At the sound of the footsteps, she turns. The camera moves into close shot. The door creaks open. A shadow falls into the room: Mary's reaction indicates it is someone she knows. Cut to a volley and the Last Post at the Civil War Memorial.

We never discover who killed Mary. Throughout – and untypically – the theme of prejudice is given greater weight than the answer to such a fundamental narrative question as who did it. The specific and the general – murder and Southern bigotry – remain linked throughout, and the theme of prejudice is constantly made explicit. The announcement of the trial is accompanied by a montage of a map of the U.S. with tickertape instructing editors to sell the 'prejudice angle'. 'The war's started again,' remarks Brock, who remains a cynical observer of events. Further screaming newspaper montages, all pinpointing the same theme, punctuate the trial. As the verdict is awaited, a young juror is passed a note saying 'Vote guilty if you feel like living'. A silent crowd gathers in the street. Since the Production Code forbade the depiction of execution – here it is portrayed by a train rushing past on the track next to the one halted by the mob, with a gallows-like device snatching a mail bag from a gantry – the film is robbed of that climax, and uses the moment instead to restress the basic theme: we cut immediately to a poster proclaiming 'Andy Griffin for U.S. Senator'.

They Won't Forget is outside the normal run of Warners' social conscience pictures, and for that matter of their contemporary dramas. It has no central individual destiny to which its theme can be related. Robert Hale is a comparatively minor character who appears little in the second half of the film; Sybil Hale is in no position to alter anything; and Andy Griffin, declaring in an arm-waving summing up beneath a revolving ceiling fan that 'Ah, who love the South, yield to no man in mah respect for the North', is anything but sympathetic. This may have had something to do with the film's relatively modest impact: there are signs that *They Won't Forget* was, at some stage, expected to do a great deal better than it did, though whether that was before or after completion it is impossible to say. At all events, it does not seem to have been pushed particularly hard, perhaps because of its lack of marquee values and its unusual theme and structure. Like *I Am a Fugitive from a Chain Gang* (also directed by LeRoy), the film rather limits its critique by being set in the South (it would, *Variety* thought, be likely to 'run up against difficulty there'), and there are no general lessons to be drawn from it about American justice. Newspapers are indicted in passing for drumming up hatred, but that is scarcely the film's major point. *They Won't Forget* remains a study of a particular case, closely following Green's original book but, in 1937, no longer able to achieve the resonance or even the indignation of a social conscience picture from the first half of the decade.

Black Legion, on the other hand, the first of three films to deal with right-wing organisations, is firmly in the mainstream of studio production, with bursts of dramatic action, an individual destiny as its centre, and the familiar supporting cast of two women, one lovingly supportive, the other selfishly predatory. It is very much a committed film, exposing the operations of a right-wing terror group similar to one which had functioned in the mid-West in 1935-6, and which had resulted in a headline-grabbing Michigan trial in which a Legion member, Dayton Dean – like Frank Taylor (Humphrey Bogart) in the film – turned State's evidence. Together with *Confessions of a Nazi Spy*, *Black Legion* shows Warners dealing with a major political issue along lines similar to those employed in the social conscience pictures of the Depression years.

But there is one crucial difference, accounted for by the same ideological shift which happened in other realistic contemporary dramas around 1935-6. In the earlier movies, the normal mechanisms of American society have gone awry, and the lives of individual Americans are threatened by forces which can best be dealt with by the enlightened intervention of the Administration – the judge in *Wild Boys of the Road*, the Indian Commissioner in *Massacre*, the D.A.'s assistant in *Cabin in the Cotton* (1932). In the post-1935 movies, the normal mechanisms are shown as being restored and society is at risk from a variety of subversive organisations which briefly seduce Americans away from basic Americanism. For James Allen, Joe Thunder Horse or even Tommy Powers to be anti-social is understandable if ultimately mistaken. For Frank Taylor in *Black Legion* to be anti-social is, though explicable in terms of a particular narrative, fundamentally wrong. Individual anti-social behaviour carries on through the crime movies of the late 1930s, but it has about it the aura of maladjustment, not romantic revolt. That revolt has passed into other, more stylised forms, like the Merrie England pictures. In the later social conscience pictures, large-scale anti-social behaviour is the prerogative of sinister subversive organisations. In the end, the message of *Black Legion* and *Confessions of a Nazi Spy* is the same as that of *Knute Rockne – All American*, a film which is unlikely ever to be regarded as a social conscience picture.[3] They all reaffirm basic American values which have survived the Depression and are presented as the only true guarantee of the freedom of the individual, that phrase which is perhaps the most ideologically dense in the entire repertoire of American political rhetoric.

The three films discussed here which deal with various forms of fascism – *Black Legion*, *Confessions of a Nazi Spy* and *Meet John Doe* – are, then, much less obviously radical than *I Am a Fugitive from a Chain Gang*, since they celebrate an essential social stability rather than analyse the dangers posed by the collapse of that stability. In brief, the early films are New Deal pictures at a time when the New Deal was a radical alternative to the conservatism of Hoover and Coolidge; the later films are New Deal pictures at a time when the New Deal was established, if not entrenched, in a conservatism of its own. But the similarity between the two groups of films none the less remains: both examine social problems in an essentially realistic context. And both use the same narrative method. While in *Bordertown* the destiny of the individual hero decisively pushes the wider social issues into the background, and in *They Won't Forget* the wider issue of North-South animosity is not focused clearly on an individual character, in *Black Legion* the two threads – an individual destiny and a broader social problem – are so closely interwoven that the film becomes a classic example of a socially realistic Warners product of the late 1930s.

In the first place, it is typical of studio production methods. Taken from contemporary history, it is based on a story by A-feature producer Robert Lord turned into a screenplay by contract writers Abem Finkel (*Hi, Nellie!*, *Black Fury*, *Special Agent*) and William Wister Haines (*Alibi Ike*, *Man of Iron*). In the second place, the combination of the story of one individual and the examination of a broader social problem more or less forces the screenplay into a close examination of the immediate social background, making the film a compelling portrait of everyday fascism. The film's dramatic interest – as opposed to its wider implications – stems from its depiction of the problems created within Frank Taylor's family and workplace by his drift into right-wing terrorism. Gangsters could perhaps be shown in a social vacuum; ordinary working people could not.

Black Legion needs to indicate the ordinariness of Frank Taylor for the nature of the threat of the Black Legion to be made clear, and for that reason the film deserves to be looked at in greater detail than any other in this chapter. It starts dramatically enough: the film's titles are superimposed on a striking piece of graphics. A group of people silhouetted against the sky are dominated by a sinister hooded figure, its arm outstretched. From this, however, we cut to a series of very ordinary scenes of men at work and of family life. The film proper opens with close-ups of machinery and of men working. This gives way, in the normal grammar of establishing shot/medium shot/close shot, to Frank joking with his friend Eddie (Dick Foran) about the latter's hangover. At lunchbreak, the first hints of sinister forces within the workplace emerge through the treatment of a fellow worker whose Jewishness, thanks to the Production Code, can only be shown indirectly. Some of Frank's workmates mock 'Huniak' Dumbrowski (Henry Brandon) for his intellectual pretensions (he goes to night school). Frank defends Dumbrowski: 'What's it to you,' he asks, 'if he's always got his nose in a book?' 'Yeah,' sneers Cliff Moore (Joseph Sawyer) with appropriate gestures at his nose, 'and a plenty big one!' Frank is, at this stage, not merely a nice guy; he is also a good worker with prospects of promotion. 'O.K.,' he tells Eddie when he realises there is a good chance of his becoming foreman, 'we'll give 'em a week's work between now and quitting time.'

The next sequence shows Frank and Eddie's home life. Frank's neighbour, Mrs Grogan (Dorothy Vaughan), jokes with her daughter Betty (Ann Sheridan) about how she will have to 'make up Ed's mind for him just like I made up your father's mind for him'. Buddy Taylor (Dickie Jones), Frank's young son, bursts into the family kitchen, all dirty from playing baseball, boasting about how he 'smacked' another kid. As they do the dishes, Frank tells his wife Ruth (Erin O'Brien-Moore) about the vacuum cleaner and new coat he will be able to buy her with his foreman's wage, and Buddy rushes off to listen to Speed Foster on the radio. The only hint of disruption in these happy scenes is provided by a brief scene in which Pearl Danvers (Helen Flint) – a woman whose moral standing is indicated by the fact that she is divorced, lives in a hotel and reclines on the bed with a large stuffed toy beside her as she talks on the telephone – tries to talk Eddie into another date with her. Eddie stalls, but there is a slight sense of unease.

Next morning, Frank goes out to look at a new car. '18 miles to the gallon, strictly airplane dashboard,' boasts the salesman. But at work Frank discovers that Dumbrowski has got the foreman's job. That

157

night, sitting bitterly at home, he retunes the radio to an 'America for Americans' broadcast. 'Do you want our beloved red, white and blue flag replaced by the vile banner of anarchy?' demands a voice. When Buddy wants to listen to Speed Foster, Frank snarls, 'Shut up and listen to this guy: he's making sense.' It is crucial to the film's method that the threat of the Black Legion should first be shown as disrupting home life, with Frank speaking harshly to his kid. In a similar vein, Eddie is pursued by the predatory Mrs Danvers who, although she is not actually connected to the Legion, becomes a key figure in the final trial and is, throughout, presented as a similarly unpleasant contrast and threat to the warmth and stability of family life.

But it is at work that the crisis is actually provoked. Frank has a minor confrontation with Dumbrowski over a broken drill bit. Cliff intervenes. 'How does it feel, being pushed around by a Huniak?' he asks, and whispers in Frank's ear about how he can meet some guys who think the same. The next sequence shows Frank going into a pharmacy and asking for 'the third bottle from the end on the second shelf'. The pharmacist gives him a sharp look, then leads him through the back of the shop and gives a secret knock on the door. Frank goes down the steps into a basement – the furtiveness and the descent are important elements in the scene – and finds a speaker addressing a small meeting about the threat posed by foreigners. 'Like poisonous vipers, they have bided their time while they feed and fatten on the bleeding breast of America . . . With fire and sword we will purge the land of these venomous scum.' Frank is inducted into the Black Legion, an organisation of 'free, white, 100 per cent Americans' at a secret ceremony in the woods, attended by robed and hooded figures. A gun is held to his head while he swears his oath of allegiance against 'the anarchists, the Roman hierarchy and their abetters'. He pauses before his final descent into thuggery – a pledge to mete out violent punishment to the Legion's enemies – but is bullied into continuing. At the end of the ceremony he is given a half bullet as a symbol of trust: 'The other half we will send you the day you betray that trust.' He then has to shell out for his uniform and a revolver.

The escalation of events is important: a minor grievance, capitalised on by Cliff, pushes Frank further and further away from his normal self, deep into the clutches of the organisation. The effects of this are immediately demonstrated. Frank is shown preening with his revolver in front of a full-length mirror, but unable to justify his actions to Ruth when she discovers the revolver. It is to guard the house, he suggests. 'After what you've paid for it,' she retorts, 'there's nothing left in the house to steal.' 'It's worth any sacrifice, isn't it,' he asks her, 'to be able to protect your house and family and . . . and . . . things like that?' Clearly house and family are the things threatened, rather than protected by Frank joining the Black Legion.

158

His first act as a member is to participate in an attack on the Dumbrowski farm – an action which indicates, as *Variety* pointed out, how easily the supposed aims of such an organisation can be diverted into the settling of personal grudges. Old Dumbrowski (Egon Brecher) rushes out to protest, shouting 'We good Americans. We pay taxes'. He is knocked down and his house set on fire. A long shot of the burning building cuts to a shot of Frank laughing uproariously over a mug of beer. 'We don't take no lip from anybody,' he boasts to his fellow legionnaires. The following scenes focus on the Legion's activities, its organisation and the effects it has on Frank. Now the foreman, he is able to buy the new car and is shown driving it home with a baseball bat and a vacuum cleaner on the back seat. To stress the true 'price' of such goods, there follows a montage of speeding cars, a cut-price drug store being wrecked, newspaper headlines and radio reports. This in turn cuts to the Legion's boss listening to the same radio report that ends the montage, then hearing from an aide a report on the profits from sales and membership. 'Don't forget the millions we were going to make on Oil Explorers Incorporated before the District Attorney started sniffing around,' he warns. The Black Legion, like the John Doe Clubs, is cynically run by crooks for profit. Working people are not only being manipulated, they are being cheated as well. 'What this country needs,' declares the boss, further demonstrating his turpitude, 'is more patriots – at so many dollars a head.' To increase the flow of dollars, the order goes out that every member is to recruit two new ones. Frank attempts to recruit a Texan workmate; while he is doing so a machine strips its gears, and he loses his foreman's job for negligence. In a classic example of Warners' compression of dramatic narrative developments into a string of breathlessly brief scenes (the fact that the film was directed by Archie L. Mayo suggests that this was a studio trademark and not, as one might infer from the biopics, a Dieterle trademark), the film reaches its crisis. Frank's neighbour, Mike Grogan (Clifford Soubier), is made foreman. In a sequence made up mainly of angled close-ups and shadows on the ground, he is woken in the middle of the night, leaves his house to investigate, is grabbed, suspended from the branch of a tree and flogged. Cut to a row between Frank and Ruth in their kitchen. She tells him that 'only a bunch of dirty, despicable cowards would do a thing like that'. He slaps her, she leaves, and we cut to a shot of her and Buddy on a bus. The entire sequence lasts little more than a minute.

The next part of the film focuses on Frank's gradually awakening conscience following Ruth's departure, and neatly brings the rather general presentation of the Legion's activities into a sharply personal context. Frank tries to back down, saying he may not be able to give the organisation the time it needs; he is threatened by Cliff. Later, he is picked up in a bar by the reappearing Mrs Danvers, whom he takes home, violating the last vestige of his old identity. They drunkenly sing in the kitchen; the neighbours listen in horror until Eddie comes in and throws Mrs Danvers out. Frank reveals to Eddie – and us – that he has lost his job. He confesses to his Legion membership and the attack on the Dumbrowski place. 'I swore a sacred oath to stick to them,' he tells Eddie, who replies, 'You swore a sacred oath to Ruth, too.' Cliff arrives and arranges to have Eddie dealt with. 'Maybe,' shouts Eddie as he is dragged out, 'they ought to change the name of your outfit from the Black Legion to the Yellow Legion.' Accompanied into the woods by hooded Legion members, Eddie manages to run away, but is shot down. Frank is left standing over the body, a close-up reaction shot showing only his eye through the slit in the hood. Screaming 'Ed! Ed!', he rushes off into the scrub, tearing off his robes as he goes. He staggers into a diner and drinks glass after glass of water. Two cops come in and Eddie's murder is announced on the radio. The cops grab Frank when he reacts in horror to the news.

The departure of Ruth, the affair with Mrs Danvers and the death of Eddie are the 'proof' of the danger of the Legion, and the rest of the film is spent in dramatic demonstration of this and in reassertion of the values from which Frank has strayed. Since Frank's guilt is not in doubt, the trial scenes are mainly an exercise in rhetoric, the first part shown via a dramatic radio programme, 'The News Parade', with pulsing music and a staged version of the cross-examination read into a microphone by a series of announcers.[4] Then there is a cut to Frank in jail. He is brought out to confront Ruth, stands for a moment, then falls to his knees, puts his arms round her waist and weeps. From here until the end title, *Black Legion* portrays Frank's final struggle with his conscience and demonstrates the consequences of his actions. A Legion official visits him in jail. 'If you don't want to be loyal to your friends,' he says threateningly, 'you should consider your wife and child.' He tosses Frank the other half of the bullet from the oath-swearing ceremony, then begins to outline the story Frank will tell on the witness stand. He is to say that Eddie's death was in self-defence during a row about Mrs Danvers, who had abandoned Eddie when she discovered that he drank. As Mrs Danvers gives her evidence – an unconvincingly hesitant performance – there are cutaways to Ruth and Frank, the latter looking more and more wretched. On the stand, he starts the agreed story, but when he hears the defence attorney suggest that his 'gratitude to Mrs Danvers gradually turned to love', he breaks down. 'No! No!' he sobs. 'It's all lies! The Black Legion did it!' He promises to tell the whole story and to identify the members of the Legion, who are all (conveniently) in the court room. 'I don't care what happens to me,' declares Frank, proving his redemption as an individual, 'I got it coming to me.'

The summing up by the judge (Samuel Hinds) is along the lines of that by the judge at the end of *Wild Boys of the Road*. But here it fits better with the rest of the narrative, since the stability of the values which the judge proclaims is no longer in doubt, at any rate officially. If the judge's speech resembles the tone of anything in the studio's 1930s output, it is that of Knute Rockne's speech to the committee investigating sport. 'Your idea of patriotism is hideous to all Americans,' he tells the legionnaires. Invoking Lincoln – the person most often cited as an absolute value in Warners' social conscience pictures – he summarises the Bill of Rights and concludes: 'The American people made their choice long ago . . . Their wisdom built the whole structure of our democratic form of government . . . It is our duty to guard [the principles] jealously if we are to remain a nation of free men.' The broader issue of the threat to American values from right-wing secret organisations is deftly interwoven with an individual destiny as Ruth struggles to reach Frank after he has been condemned to jail for life. The camera tracks in to a close-up of her being held back by the police, and the end title comes up, superimposed on the same graphics as appeared at the start of the film.

In the final analysis, the film's study of fascism cannot be dissociated from its examination of an individual case history: the narrative methods perfected by Warners throughout the decade may blur the finer political distinctions, but they enable the particular and the general to be made more or less interchangeable. *Black Legion* is a very American tragedy. It is undoubtedly an attack on right-wing groups, but an attack combined with reassurance about the basic stability of the system from whose failures those groups necessarily drew their strength. This does not, of course, make it any the less effective as an attack. But it does indicate how perfectly attuned the studio was in the latter half of the decade to American mainstream ideology. If the early social conscience pictures stress that things can be all right once more if everybody works together, those of the late 1930s stress that now they *are* all right they should not be disrupted. Of course, as any social history of America in the 1930s will reveal, the lingering after-effects of the Depression, in terms of poverty and unemployment, lasted right into the war years. But they were no longer officially recognised. And *Black Legion* is a film which admits to, but never truly recognises, a social problem.

The two remaining films of the period to deal with the threat of fascism both stand somewhat outside the normal run of studio production, *Confessions of a Nazi Spy* because of its strongly documentary flavour and its stream of explicitly propagandist statements, *Meet John Doe* because it is not really a Warners production, but a film made on the Warners lot by an independent producer with a largely imported cast and crew. *Meet John Doe*, with its crowded shots of ordinary people looking straight at the camera, its Christmas Eve climax and its abrupt injections of folk wisdom and sentimentality, bears the unmistakable imprint, not of the studio, but of one of the decade's undeniable authorial personalities, that of Frank Capra, its director.

Confessions of a Nazi Spy is taken from a series of newspaper articles on the 1937 spy trials by former G-man Leon Turrou, and has a comparatively slender narrative thread. The top-billed star, Edward G. Robinson in the role of investigator Edward J. Renard, does not appear until halfway through, when he cracks the Nazi spy ring and propaganda machine run throughout the United States by a Dr Kassel (Paul Lukas). As a film, its message is clear: though released well before the outbreak of World War II, it identifies the Nazi Party as a threat to humanity in general and to America in particular. 'Decades from now,' thought *Variety*, 'what's happening may be seen in perspective. And the historians will almost certainly take note of this daringly frank broadside from a picture company.' Duly taking note of it four-and-a-half decades later, one is bound to admit that historical perspective justifies the strident tone of the propaganda against the Nazis. But it is also hard not to be struck by the extent to which the propagandist aim results in the situation being simplified, leading Frank S. Nugent of the *New York Times* to call the film 'childish': 'Membership in the National Socialist party cannot be restricted to the rat-faced, the brute-browed, the sinister. We don't believe that Nazi propaganda Ministers let their mouths twitch evilly whenever they mention our Constitution or our Bill of Rights. We thought that school of villainy had gone out with *The Beast of Berlin* made back in '14.' Indeed, the appeals to the emotions made by *Confessions of a Nazi Spy* are not all that different from the appeals to honest working folk made by the recruiters for the Black Legion.

In addition to its coverage of the spy trials, the film makes three main points: that Hitler's aim is the subversion of American democracy; that his organisation is well established in the United States; and that his methods at home and abroad are crude and unfair. The film is more a series of dramatised scenes of Nazis at work than it is a conventional narrative. A Nazi orator lectures an audience of wildly cheering German Americans that they are Germans first and that 'Germany must save America from the chaos that breeds with democracy and racial equality'. Nazi officers discuss the ease with which they are managing to establish a network in the United States, because 'after all, the Americans are a very simple-minded people'. The Nazis' aim, they assert, is to destroy 'the chain which holds the whole American system together: the Constitution and the Bill of Rights'. As in all propaganda films, almost every scene has the feeling of an invisible presence – that of the ordinary American viewer at whom the dialogue is really aimed. Towards the end, a Nazi leader

A threat to America: George Sanders and friends (Lionel Royce, Henry Victor) in
Confessions of a Nazi Spy

standing against a map lectures his followers that 'all our efforts must now be directed against the strongest remaining democracy, the United States'. The audience is being all but directly warned: the threat is real, and its means of implementation insidious.

The basis of Hitler's American organisation, the film suggests, is the German-American Bunds, described by Renard as consisting of 'half-witted, hysterical crackpots who go Hitler-happy', whereupon the film cuts to Dr Kassel visiting an American Horst Wessel Camp to inspect the boys and girls of the National Socialist Youth. The 'reality' of life in Germany is described by a woman returning to America from a trip back home. The sheep have gone from the heath because of Hitler's stormtroopers, the 'old Pastor' is in a concentration camp, and 'our family speaks in whispers'. The ship's hairdresser promptly reports her to the SS. A dissident German American intellectual who speaks out in a meeting is told that 'the Fatherland doesn't require criticism: it requires obedience', is taken into a back room, beaten up and hustled aboard a ship back to Germany. Clearly, the Nazis are not nice people. Equally clearly, they pose a direct threat to America.

Fictionalised scenes are backed up by a dramatisation of Nazi spy methods: a mail route via Scotland; the young spy Schneider (Francis Lederer) using a secret communication code to acquire a package of blank passports. And there are direct references to organisations in

163

Hitler's pay. 'From now on,' Kassel tells his minions, 'your watchword call will be "America for Americans" ' (as in *Black Legion*, an oblique reference to the 'America First' movement), and their aim will be to promote 'dissent and class hatred'. There is also newsreel footage of Nazi rallies in Germany and of the invasion of Czechoslovakia, with a voice-over remarking 'God knows what peace-loving nation will be next!' There are montages of swastikas zooming out of a globe, presses printing Nazi propaganda, swastikas lining out over the Atlantic then spreading out across the U.S., leaflets being pushed into mail boxes, thrown from aeroplanes and found by a child in his lunch box. A final montage dissolves into a shot of the White House as the D.A. declares, to applause in court, that 'America is not just a remaining democracy, America *is* democracy!' At the end, sitting in a restaurant, Attorney Kellog (Henry O'Neill) declares to his associate: 'I don't think, Renard, we're going to have that sort of trouble here.' The door opens, and ordinary people enter, immediately identifiable by Renard as 'the voice of the people'. 'We'll show 'em!' mutters the voice of the people defiantly. 'America the Beautiful' plays over the final credits.

Meet John Doe is similarly untypical of Warners' production styles and methods, merely using studio facilities and released under the company's banner. Otherwise it is an outside production, scripted by Robert Riskin, Capra's collaborator on *It Happened One Night* (1934) and *Mr Deeds Goes to Town* (1936), using Goldwyn artists Gary Cooper, Walter Brennan and Barbara Stanwyck, bringing in an outside art director, costume designer, composer and montage specialist (the inimitable Slavko Vorkapich). Only the cinematographer George Barnes, the sound man C.A. Riggs and the musical director Leo Forbstein are regular Warners personnel. It is easy, however, to see why Capra should have brought the project to Warners, at any rate in the wake of his disagreement with Harry Cohn at Columbia, and why they should have taken it in. It is a socially conscious film which reinforces the danger of what Renard in *Confessions of a Nazi Spy* had said could not occur: 'it' almost does happen here, and it is the same 'voice of the people' of *Nazi Spy*'s final scene that prevents it.

Briefly, *Meet John Doe* tells of a newspaper campaign to turn an out-of-work ball player, Long John Willoughby (Gary Cooper), into a spokesman for the ordinary American viewpoint. 'John Doe' finally rebels against what he sees as exploitation of him and his followers, but the ordinary people – in an unmistakably Capra-esque scene set in a small town – beg him to stay with them and to encourage the 'John Doe Clubs' they have set up. The Clubs turn out to be financed by a sinister oil millionaire, D.B. Norton (Edward Arnold), who has a private uniformed motorcycle militia and is described as 'a wicked man with a vicious purpose'. The purpose, of course, is to have himself elected President with the support of all the John Does. When

Doe/Willoughby threatens to expose him at a massive John Doe Convention, Norton turns the crowd and Long John once more retreats into obscurity. He emerges one last time, on a snow-swept Christmas Eve, to commit suicide so as to draw the people's attention to corruption in general and Norton in particular. He is dissuaded by the newspaperwoman with whom he has fallen in love (Barbara Stanwyck) and by a crowd of ordinary people who gather round him. 'We need you, Mr Doe. We lost our heads and acted like a mob . . . Please come with us, Mr Doe.' The camera tracks across Norton and his rich friends gathered on the roof. Gary Cooper's brows knit briefly, Beethoven's 'Ode to Joy' fades up on the soundtrack, the hero picks up his girl and, pointing to a typical citizen, turns to Norton and declares: 'There you are, Norton: the people. Try and lick them.'[5]

Meet John Doe is an entertaining and skilfully crafted movie, with the same frequently irresistible tide of sentimentality that characterises Capra's later *It's a Wonderful Life*. But in style, it is no more a Warners picture than it was in production terms. It portrays Willoughby as an Everyman figure rather than as an individual hero, and is shot through with folk wisdom, mostly from the mouth of Walter Brennan. Its depiction of the social background is generalised almost to the point of allegory, and the ordinary people are strictly anonymous. Finally, it allows its hero no moments of decisive physical action with which to test his decision: throughout, Willoughby's decision is, as at the end, *not* to act. By comparison with Warners' other contemporary dramas, *Meet John Doe* seems leisurely and vague, 'more vehement than conclusive', as *Variety* put it, adding: 'the director is more zealot than showman. His exhortations for the liberal sprinkling of the milk of human kindness are more vocal than dramatic.' Showmanship and drama were, throughout the decade, two key elements of Warners' social conscience pictures.

The three remaining contemporary dramas to be discussed in this chapter constitute something of a grab-bag of themes. None really belongs in any of the categories so far discussed, though each overlaps with more than one category. *The Mouthpiece* (1932) deals with crooked lawyers, a recurrent element in both gangster movies and prison pictures; *Life Begins* (1932), like *Night Nurse*, indicates that it is possible for a contemporary conventional narrative to deal with women, if not in a less formulary way, at any rate in a less secondary one; and *Black Fury* (1935), as well as providing the opportunity for Paul Muni to impersonate another minority group, deals, like many of the social conscience pictures, with a story from recent American headlines. In a way, the three films provide a useful summing up to this chapter and for this part of the book, since *The Mouthpiece* is absolutely typical of studio production in its narrative form and its depiction of reality, *Life Begins* fairly untypical on both counts, and *Black Fury* an indication of how, in direct contrast to *Black Legion*, the investigation of a social problem through an individual's experience of it can also result in the specifics of the problem being glossed over and ignored.

Above all, the three films indicate how tenuous is any direct equation between contemporary social history and the movies produced by Hollywood. The studio system was a form of production with its own organisational and economic exigencies. And those exigencies were always, at an explicit level, given precedence over an accurate representation of social reality. This does not mean, of course, that social and economic reality are not represented in the films. They are present in the system as well as impregnating the material on which the system drew. But the deformations of historical reality brought about by the process of representation were many and various: they cannot be accounted for by any one formula, however complex. Certain procedures recur and certain guidelines are possible, but the relationship between Hollywood in the 1930s and America in the 1930s is a dynamic and a dialectical one. With an eye to those procedures and guidelines, each movie needs to be viewed as an entity at once discrete and homogeneous.

The Mouthpiece, supposedly based on the career of an actual New York shyster lawyer, is the first of a trio of legal films to be released in early 1932, with Warners beating Columbia's *For the Defense* and RKO's *State Attorney* by a matter of weeks. Instead of simply being a legal drama, however, Warners' film is also a study of rehabilitation: an exercise in redemption via debasement. Vincent Day (Warren William) is a brilliant young Assistant D.A. who becomes disillusioned with his honest career when he successfully prosecutes an innocent man in a murder trial. This disillusionment is portrayed in typically dramatic fashion, the film opening with Day's summing up of the trial: 'I ask you to go with me to a lonely churchyard and stand beside the grave of that poor innocent girl . . . Would to God we could bring her back into the sunshine. We who are left can only listen to the command of the Great Jehovah: whosoever sheddeth man's blood, by men shall his blood be shed.' Cut to a close-up of the accused, and to an insert of the straps being fitted to his feet. A newspaper headline declares 'Execution at 10 o'clock'. Day sits nervously in the office of D.A. Forbes (Walter Walker), his eyes on the clock. At the last moment a phone call comes through, revealing that someone else has confessed to the murder. Forbes grabs the telephone but takes a while to get through. A man runs to stop the execution. As he gets to the door, there is a humming noise, the lights dim, and there is an insert of a hand throwing a switch. Cut back to Day, who sinks into his chair. 'I'll never prosecute another case as long as I live,' he declares.

Day goes on an extended drunk, until he is finally given the idea for a new legal career by a bartender called Paddy (Guy Kibbee).

'Sensationalism,' he advises, 'Barnum and Bailey. Give them a swell show and they won't even stop to think.' Day rises to prominence and wealth as an unscrupulous defence lawyer who always gets his client off. We are shown a couple of examples of his antics. He cross-examines a boxer, Pondapolis (Stanley Fields), whose crucial piece of evidence is that he cannot be knocked out. Day dismisses him from the box, then suddenly turns and floors him with a surprise punch. Charge dismissed. In another case, he has to demonstrate that the poison his client administered is not, in fact, lethal. In court, he grabs the bottle and swallows its contents then, while no one is watching, discreetly draws a line on his watch 40 minutes ahead. The jury goes out, and members occasionally peer back into the courtroom to check that Day is still alive. In the end, they reluctantly return a verdict of Not Guilty. Day bustles out of the courtroom, across the street and into a nearby office where he lies down on a table and is covered by a sheet. 'Better hurry with that stomach pump, sweetheart,' he growls at a nurse. He later reveals that he had coated his stomach with raw eggs, and that the poison takes 45 minutes to work.

If Day's courtroom antics are effectively demonstrated, so too is his basic dishonesty, in a scene in which he restores money taken by an embezzler, himself openly pocketing 25 per cent ($10,000). When the industrialist whose money it is (Morgan Wallace) objects, Day points out that he has been party to a felony by agreeing to restitution without prosecution. 'The wages of sin and success,' remarks his secretary, Hickey (Aline MacMahon), as she puts the money in the safe. 'Nice business!' Throughout the film, Hickey acts as a kind of wry conscience to Day, much as does Taylor, the secretary role also played by MacMahon in *Five Star Final* the previous year. She looks after him, rescues him from his drunks, perhaps saves his life at the end, and in general humours him without explicitly approving of him.

Day's real rehabilitation, however, is at the hands of Celia, a sweet young thing from Kentucky, played by newcomer Sidney Fox in what appears to have been her only role with the studio. She takes the job with Day to make enough money for her marriage to Johnny (William Janney), and yearns to leave the big city for her home town of Riverport, Kentucky, with its 'clean air, trees, people I've known all my life'. She is initially impressed by Day, but resists his advances and walks out on him when she learns of the poison trick. Day watches her cross the street with Johnny, experiences acute remorse and goes back on the bottle. But Johnny becomes involved inadvertently in a court case which will send him to jail unless Day agrees to reveal the criminal background of his opponent, Joe Garland (Jack La Rue), and his boss, J.C. (Ralph Ince), with whom Day has had dealings. Hickey nurses Day back to sobriety with cold cloths, coffee, a shower and orange juice. Celia tries to thank her. 'Forget it, kid,' quips Hickey. 'It's all in a day's work, as the street-sweeper said to the elephant.'

Day puts the finger on Garland, and then decides to quit, all but repeating Celia's words: 'I'm through. I'm going back to civil practice. I want to get out into the air. I want to breathe. I'm tired of crooked streets and crooked people.' He accepts an invitation to Celia and Johnny's wedding. But the results of his rediscovered conscience are dramatic. As he leaves his office for the ceremony, Hickey looks out of the window and sees a suspicious car on the far side of the street. She runs screaming down the stairs to stop Day. Outside, he buys a newspaper from a stand, the car revs up, there is a close-up of its tail pipe as it appears to backfire, and Day falls against a pillar. The newsvendor turns to hand him his change and sees that the newspaper is riddled with holes. Hickey hustles him into a cab and tells the driver to take them to the emergency hospital. There is a close-up of Hickey and Day in the back of the cab. 'Good old Hickey,' mutters Day. 'You're always around when I need you, aren't you . . . sweetheart.' He slumps on her shoulder. End title.

The Mouthpiece may expose the career of a crooked lawyer, but it does so along established narrative lines: dramatic decline into dishonesty/ rise to wealth, dramatic demonstration of the dishonesty, sentimental rehabilitation ('You've made me ashamed of myself,' Day tells Celia, 'and in doing that you've made me realise I had something I thought I'd succeeded in losing: a conscience') and dramatic retribution, bundled up together in a terse, smart-talking narrative. Its relation to contemporary reality is, at best, indirect. Together with *Taxi!*, released three months earlier, it represents the bedrock of the studio's handling of contemporary reality, using the issue of illegality as a spur to the central character's action: it is the character, not the issues, which controls the narrative. *The Mouthpiece* was remade in 1955 as *Illegal*, starring Edward G. Robinson – who could equally well have played the role in the original.

Of all Warners' contemporary dramas to achieve a degree of success in the early 1930s, *Life Begins* is the most surprising, though its presence in Appendix II may be misleading: it is the kind of film that will almost certainly have done better in the cities than in the sticks. Nevertheless, it was one of only five 1932 films to have a two-week run at the fairly uncosmopolitan Warners Hollywood theatre (along with the comedies *Fireman Save My Child* and *Blessed Event*, and the action movies *The Crowd Roars* and *Tiger Shark*). It is a bizarre mixture of comedy and high drama with semi-documentary footage of life in a maternity hospital (or 'Lying-in Hospital' as an opening insert more discreetly calls it).

The film had its origins in a play by Mary McDougal Axelson presented at Columbia University and transferred to Broadway, where it ran for only a week – an unusual start for a major Warners picture. Its dramatic backbone is the story of Grace Sutton (Loretta Young), a young woman jailed for the murder of a man who, it is implied, has tried to assault her. Already pregnant by (one presumes) her husband Jed (Eric Linden), she is brought from prison to hospital to have her baby. Her physical condition has deteriorated to the extent that doctors have to decide between the baby's life and hers. They consult Jed, who tells them to save his wife, but eventually go with Grace's own decision to save the baby. At the end, the chief nurse, Bowers (Aline MacMahon), hands him the baby. He turns his face to the wall, declaring 'No, I don't want to see it, I don't want to see it!' 'Your wife came to just at the end,' says Bowers, 'and told me to give it to you, to say that she sent it.' The music fades up as Jed walks away with the baby, a little finger reaching up towards him. It is an undoubtedly sentimental scene, and the circumstances of Grace's confinement, and above all the choice between her life or the baby's, are close to melodrama. But *Life Begins* is distinctly unusual for the way in which it dramatises everyday emotions connected neither with crime nor with romance. Equally interesting is the fact that it is Grace's decision, not her husband's, which is heeded by the doctors. And though her death can easily be assimilated to a long, reactionary tradition of maternal self-sacrifice, it is important to note that the film places a woman in a position where it is she who makes the decision and others who must adjust to it. Finally, the film is remarkably matter-of-fact in its portrayal of the minor and major crises of childbirth, a point emphasised by its downbeat ending. As Jed walks away, the phone rings. Bowers answers it. 'Yes,' she says, 'the bed's ready.' Dissolve to a shot of Grace, smiling. The title 'Life begins' appears on the screen, which fades to black; the music comes up and 'The end' appears.

A variety of 'maternal' reactions are depicted in the secondary characters; and although these may be a feature of the film's origins as a 1930s-progressive college drama, they are none the less striking for their lack of conventional elements (other than a comic addition to the original play in the form of Ringer Banks – Frank McHugh – who is as conventionally panic-stricken a father-to-be as ever graced a farce). Apart from McHugh, however, the film contains vignettes only of a number of women who share Grace's ward. A psychopathic woman (Dorothy Peterson) wanders in from another ward, desperate for the baby she cannot have. 'This is where I should be,' she tells Grace. 'I think if I could get away from that ward upstairs I could have it any day . . . They don't believe in my baby. And if they don't believe in it, you see, I can't have it.' When she steals a baby from a crib, Bowers handles her calmly and sympathetically. Another woman stresses to anyone who will listen that she is unmarried and proud of it, and that she intends to follow contemporary progressive orthodoxy by refusing to kiss and cuddle her baby. An Italian woman loses her baby and is comforted by Grace. But the most interesting of the secondary characters is Florette, a good-time girl played in inimitable fashion by Glenda Farrell, who is determined to have her twins adopted. To another woman who tells her that there is nothing on earth like the happiness of having children, Florette exclaims 'Horsefeathers!' She hides gin in her hot water bottle, and is frankly contemptuous of mother love. 'Shall I rock the baby bumpkin?' asks Bowers of the woman in the next bed. 'Oh, my God!' exclaims Florette and rolls over in disgust. But when she hears two society ladies discussing the adoption of her babies – the boy, they decide, is perfect, but the girl is going to have to be put in a State home – she becomes fiercely possessive. 'Scram!' she tells the society ladies, and sings a nightclub song, 'Frankie and Johnny', as a lullaby to one of her babies.

Florette's conversion to motherhood may not exactly be radical, but it is free from most of the conventions of screen motherhood, as is the film as a whole. What is perhaps most striking about *Life Begins* is that it is a film about women who are neither secondary nor involved in romantic entanglements. The doctors are male authority figures, but are very much in the background; the fathers are comic (Bates), overruled (Jed) or absent. And the fact that it is about a number of women together reduces the conventional element even further, since it

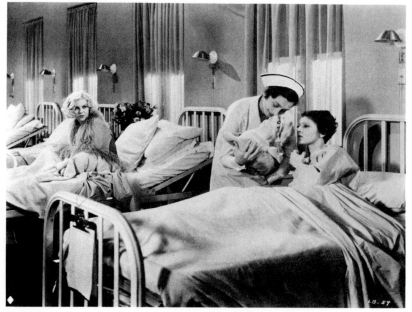

Life Begins: Glenda Farrell (left) with Aline MacMahon as the nurse

makes the usual narrative procedures impossible. 'She's on the same fix as the rest of us,' decide Grace's fellow patients, disregarding her criminal background, 'and we all ought to do what we can to help her.' In the early 1930s, Warners' experiments with contemporary dramatic subjects took the studio into a number of unexpected areas, none more unexpected than *Life Begins*. Sadly but, I suppose, inevitably, it was not an area that was further investigated. Motherhood as it appears elsewhere in the decade is almost always the prerogative of an older woman, and the dramatic focus is on her offspring's problems, not hers. Only in *Four Daughters* (1938), *The Old Maid* (1939) and *The Great Lie* (1941) are a mother's hopes and disappointments examined in any real detail, and there the focus is more on the lost lover that the child represents than on the mother's relationship with her child.

Finally, *Black Fury*, which is the only Warners picture of the decade to deal extensively with the question of unionisation and industrial unrest. It is partly based on the 1929 murder of a coal miner by company police in Imperial, Pennsylvania, with an original story by Judge M.A. Musmanno, who had been involved in the case. The screenplay, part-written by Abem Finkel who later wrote *Black Legion*, centres on a Polish miner, Joe Radek (Paul Muni), who gets caught up in the establishment of a radical alternative to the Federation of Mine-Workers (FMW) and, when one of his friends is killed by a company cop, goes on the rampage. He barricades himself in the mine with the cop and threatens to blow it up if his and the other miners' demands are not met. The company recognises the error of its ways and Joe becomes a modest hero. Surrounded by pressmen and newsreel cameras as he emerges from the mine, he simply comments 'Glad we win. Thank you', before going off with his girl Anna (Karen Morley).

Black Fury is overshadowed by Muni's performance – intense, volatile, with the lines delivered in a heavily accented broken English and peppered with Radek's favourite exclamation of 'You betcha my life!' Initially, Joe is interested only in working hard enough to raise money to buy a farm and marry his sweetheart. He refuses to attend union meetings ('What for I need meeting? I got my Anna!') and expresses his philosophy of life with terse simplicity: 'Work and shut up!' 'Joe Radek,' he adds, 'he like everybody, and everybody like Joe Radek.' His elevation to president of the breakaway union is a matter of pure chance, not to say error. Anna runs off to Chicago with Slim Johnson (William Gargan), and Joe goes off to get drunk, then bursts in on a meeting at which the FMW man, Farrell (Joe Crehan), is trying to tell the miners of Coaltown that they've got it pretty good. A low murmur of 'Good big strike!' fills the hall, and there are dark mutterings that the FMW is 'living off the fat of the land'. Joe butts in, drunkenly shouting 'Joe Radek not afraid to fight . . . Everybody . . .

fight!' If Joe's presidency of the new union is a mistake, so too is the union itself. The whole situation has been engineered by the sinister Henry B. Jenkins (Purnell Pratt) of Industrial Detective Services Incorporated to break the power of the FMW and drum up work for his own thugs and blacklegs. After Joe's speech, an agitator calls Jenkins to tell him that 'I've got a dumb Huniak named Radek lined up to do the dirty work for us'.

Joe's rise to political militancy is, then, ascribed to his state of mind after Anna leaves him – not the sort of thing he would normally do – and his passage to direct action is as a result of an equally personal (i.e. non-political) event. His best friend Mike Kumansky (John T. Qualen), with whom he lodges, is an FMW official who subsequently turns him out of the house and shuns him on the street. Later, Mike is cornered and killed by one of Jenkins' heavies, McGee (Barton MacLane), while Joe looks on. It is this which prompts Joe's final stand: 'It my fault, I got fix it for Mike. They no go back. They got to win.' Thanks to the investigation triggered by his threat to blow up the mine, Washington discovers that the strike has been deliberately provoked by Jenkins and his mob connections. The whole thing, therefore, becomes a minor dramatic hiccough in an otherwise peaceful industrial situation. None the less, the film uses the language and imagery of industrial conflict. Placard-bearing strikers march down the main street of Coaltown and kids in the schoolyard shout 'Dirty scabs!' as replacement workers are brought in. Similarly, the depiction of the Pinkerton surrogates, the industrial police, is uniformly negative: no outfit headed by Barton MacLane could ever be anything other than rotten, and his militia is made up of thugs and criminals ('First time I ever been on this side of a copper's uniform,' mutters one of them as he dresses for action). By contrast, the workers are noble representatives of the 'little man', gathering in groups to observe events and falling back before McGee's mounted police in a scene where the location of good and evil can scarcely be in doubt. 'Them hunkies sure got a healthy respect for a cop on a horse,' remarks McGee. 'Something they brought from the old country.'

If brief indications of the cause of unrest are inevitable – the early scenes do sketch in a realistic background of exploitation: there must, after all, have been something for Jenkins' agitator to agitate – any development of this into a fuller examination of industrial conditions and relations is buried by the rest of the film's emphasis on a personally motivated vendetta carried out against a criminal organisation. The breaking of Jenkins' organisation is on an exact par with the removal of Quissenbery and Doc Turner at the end of *Massacre*: an abuse is removed, and the situation reverts to the normality from which it should never have been allowed to deviate. An interesting point of comparison between *Black Fury* and *Black Legion*, both scripted by

Polish miner Paul Muni at a union meeting in *Black Fury*

Finkel, is that in both films the cause of the trouble is a corrupt manipulator with underworld connections. In *Black Legion*, the destruction of the Legion returns the characters to the starting point. In *Black Fury*, the exposure of Jenkins does the same for the miners, but with their earlier grievances untouched. It is not a film about industrial relations, but about a heroic individual who stands up for the rights of his fellow workers. He does it because his girl leaves him, and he gets his girl back by doing it.

Warner Brothers was not and, within the context of its development and its industrial base, could not have been a forum for radical social criticism. Its depiction of contemporary reality in the first half of the decade (as well as, in a slightly different way, the second half) is of an economy hit by a Depression brought on by greed and economic mismanagement – by an abandonment of the basic principles of Americanism to which Roosevelt appeals in his Inaugural Address – and redeemable through the cooperative policies of the early New Deal. To portray this, the studio needed both a basic position and a dramatic structure – things which, in popular culture, tend to be related. Two contemporary comments on *Black Fury* could well stand as comments on all the studio's social conscience movies. According to Andre Sennwald in the *New York Times*, 'the most accurate commentary on the picture's social viewpoint occurs accidentally at the Washington arbitration conference near the end of the film: "There was never any real issue in this controversy".'

Variety's editor Abel Greene develops the point more strongly and more explicitly, and his comments are unusually revealing:

> *Black Fury* is basic box office. It has intrinsic celluloid values and a star, Paul Muni, who is no mean marquee equation. But more, this sociological cinematic exposition, by the very nature of its theme, is packed with promotional potentialities. Provocative and attuned to a day and age where the administrative 'new deal' lends added significance to the story, *Black Fury* is something which the exploitive boys can go to town about. Only the locale will limit the nature of the ballyhoo.
>
> Disturbing chiefly by inference, possibly left-wing radical by innuendo, canny Burbanking evidences studio wisdom in pruning, motivating and editing in just the right degrees. The labor struggle if, perhaps, in one or two spots, a bit too drab and cruel in its exposition, is kept clear of dangerous shoals. Enough basic melodramatics for straight theatre values are there, plus, of course, the superlative histrionism [with] which Muni usually endows any flicker . . .
>
> Dialogicians Abem Finkel and Carl Ericksen and director Mike Curtiz evidence nice restraint without sacrificing the basic element of strife. By emphasising the disgruntled labor vs. strike-breaking syndicates, they've steered clear of the general embarrassment that usually attends any labor vs. capital theme. If anything, intelligent capitalism management is given a subtle boost.

A 'new deal in entertainment', or the Burbanking of 1930s America.

PART THREE

Visions of History

9 Foreign Biopics

Although Warners' reputation during the 1930s was as a studio that specialised in contemporary subjects – a reputation won as the result of a specific policy choice on the part of the company – not all its films were contemporary. Throughout the decade, there is a definite and, in commercial terms, highly visible strain of costume dramas and prestige productions of one kind or another. Warners' big-budget productions, however, do not begin to take on a distinctive character until about halfway through the decade, with the opening in New York, early in February 1936, of *The Story of Louis Pasteur*. The dense, almost breathless economy of Sheridan Gibney and Pierre Collings' screenplay and the verve of William Dieterle's direction set a model for the kind of biopic the studio would produce for the rest of the 1930s: a narrative of considerable dramatic excitement built round serious issues and with an idiosyncratic central character who is obstinate and admirable rather than simply likeable.

In the wake of Louis Pasteur came Florence Nightingale (*White Angel*, 1936), Emile Zola (*The Life of Emile Zola*, 1937), David Garrick (*The Great Garrick*, 1937), Benito Juarez (*Juarez*, 1939), Knute Rockne (*Knute Rockne – All American*, 1940), Paul Ehrlich (*The Story of Dr Ehrlich's Magic Bullet*, 1940) and Julius Reuter (*A Dispatch from Reuters*, 1940), all battling entrenched prejudices of one kind or another with an unshakeable conviction in the rightness of their cause and an obstinacy which was as much a product of their own obsessive strength of character as it was a commitment to the important principles for which, in different fields, they fought. The real-life heroes were supreme individuals, proving what could be achieved by a steadfast adherence to truth, justice and knowledge. If the social conscience pictures were the product of the early Roosevelt years in their direct but essentially optimistic treatment of social problems, the biopics were the mirror of the middle Roosevelt years in their liberal adherence to the power of the humanist individual who was a basic guarantee – or perhaps watchdog – of the principles of democracy.

At a more directly commercial level, most of Warners' prestige productions during the 1930s can be seen as examples of the Hollywood vehicle. The early biographies provided suitable roles for George Arliss who, along with John Barrymore, was the studio's major recruit from the legitimate stage during the changeover from silent to sound films. The later biopics were also vehicles, often selected and fought for by the stars themselves, for Paul Muni (Pasteur, Zola and Juarez) and Edward G. Robinson (Reuter and Ehrlich). In the same way, the rash of Merrie England pictures[1] in the second half of the decade, from *The Charge of the Light Brigade* (1936) to *The Sea Hawk* (1940), were basically Errol Flynn movies. The notion of vehicle can also be applied to two other major prestige productions, *Show of Shows* and *A Midsummer Night's Dream*, the former (in 1929) existing exclusively as a showcase for the entire roster of studio talent, the latter making a bid – and a successful bid in the light of the films that came after its release in 1935 – to move the studio away from its exclusive image as producer of popular realist films: it was a vehicle for the studio's pretensions and, in that sense at least, no different from *Show of Shows*.

The various American biographies made by Warners, from *Alexander Hamilton* in 1931 to the highly partial portrayals of John Brown in *Santa Fe Trail* (1940) and George Armstrong Custer in that film and in *They Died With Their Boots On* (1941), are less easy to see in terms of a single development. The first is undoubtedly an Arliss vehicle – perhaps the least successful that the studio made – while the latter two, although they both star Flynn, seem at first sight to be an instance of rather odd casting and to give a singularly confused picture of American history. The American biopics will be discussed in the next chapter, but the general change in prestige productions between 1929 and 1941 is instructive in a number of ways. Although the major part of the studio's output at the beginning of the sound era was comparatively lightweight – musicals, romances and flapper comedies – Warners' attempts to appeal to the upper end of the market still followed the traditions of the silent cinema in offering an element of fantasy and exotic extravagance as a leavening to the more realistic fare. Respectability, however, was still an idea firmly equated with the legitimate stage. Like the other studios, Warners had limited success in this field. *Disraeli* was an enormous hit, at any rate with critics and New York audiences. It ran longer in first-run theatres than any other Warners film in the period covered by this book: 60 consecutive days in the Warner Theatre at Broadway and 52nd Street, followed by a further 16 weeks in the slightly smaller Central, after which it could still manage a two-week run 'at popular prices' at the Strand – a total of 190 days in a seven-month period. The press book for the 1933 re-release boasts that it ran for 1,697 consecutive days in theatres round the globe, had been shown in more than 29,000 separate motion picture houses and had been 'seen and cheered by more than 170 million persons speaking 24 different languages'. Even allowing for publicity department hyperbole – all these figures, with the possible exception of 1,697, can probably be reduced by a third – it is still an impressive achievement. But for every expensive stage-based success, there was any number of equally expensive costume films that never really made it: films like *Dancing Vienna* (1929), *Bride of the Regiment*, *Song of the Flame*, *Sweet Kitty Bellairs* (all 1930) and *Kismet* (1931).

When the total number of pictures in production was cut back after 1930, it was the stagey extravaganzas and the silent-style epics which tended to disappear: the 1931-3 period saw very few prestige costume pictures. After a brief attempt to emulate M-G-M's *Grand Hotel* formula with *Union Depot* in 1932, Warners settled for smaller-scale productions. The studio had little choice: the financial crisis of those years did not enable it to make big-budget pictures whose success was uncertain, and it seemed unable to find a formula in which big spending would be rewarded by big returns. The studio's 'epics' – *The World Changes* (1933), *Babbitt* and *Madame Dubarry* (1934) and *Oil for the Lamps of China* (1935) – were only moderately successful. The first and last alone make it in the long-run list, thanks mainly to extended New York bookings: *The World Changes* managed only a week in the Los Angeles theatres, as against the twelve weeks notched up that year by *Gold Diggers of 1933*. It is not until 1936, with *The Story of Louis Pasteur*, *Anthony Adverse* and *The Charge of the Light Brigade*, that the studio seemed to get the formula right. Thereafter the pattern was set for the rest of the decade. Energies were concentrated on one major prestige production per year, which almost invariably turned out to be Warners' most successful movie – *The Life of Emile Zola* (177 days, three Oscars and first place in the *Film Daily* poll) in 1937, *The Adventures of Robin Hood* (42 days, three Oscars, 7th in the *Film Daily* poll) in 1938, *Juarez* (69 days, one Oscar and 8th place) in 1939, and *Sergeant York* (163 days, one Oscar and 2nd place in the *Film Daily* poll) in 1941. The last two years of the survey indicate a certain growth of confidence in the formula: there were six films that could be described as prestige productions in 1940 and three in 1941.[2] But the fact that the beginning and the end of the decade show certain similarities in the pattern of production should not be allowed to obscure the very real change in the studio's strategies. Apart from anything else, the early prestige productions owe a good deal to Broadway or to the reputation of Broadway; the later ones are all Hollywood.

Disraeli is Warners' first biographical talkie about an eminent foreigner, and the only one until *Juarez* to be directly concerned with a politician. It is, however, only very marginally a 'political' film. 'By classification,' wrote *Variety*, '*Disraeli* belongs with those older stage pieces known and best described as a "starring vehicle". To think of *Disraeli* without Arliss is to shudder. This is the first instance since dialog pictures of such a piece being done. There will never be many of the same kind for obvious reasons.' George Arliss had played the part of Disraeli on the stage when the play opened in Montreal in 1911; at a revival at the Knickerbocker Theatre in 1917; in a number of other productions in America and abroad; and in a silent movie version in 1921. By choosing Arliss in *Disraeli* as its first prestige talkie, Warners were scarcely gambling on an unknown quantity. The film was nevertheless a gamble in the sense that it was designed to prove that Warners could turn out highbrow films, and more generally that the talking picture could offer audiences throughout America the chance to see a serious Broadway play performed by its original cast – an area first exploited by Jesse Lasky and Lewis J. Selznick in the silent period.

Whether American audiences wanted this chance was another matter. 'While it is possibly true,' wrote *Variety*, 'that some of the peasants won't get the smartness or appreciate the subtle shades of the Arliss technique, it seems certain that the de luxe audiences will take to *Disraeli* in a big way.' They did. *Film Daily* likewise heralded the success of Warners' gamble: 'Warners, with this and other pictures, have demonstrated their ability to turn out Grade A product.'[3] Given this evident intention on the part of the studio and the extent to which the intention was fulfilled, it is possible that, without the financial crisis which the Depression inevitably brought to Hollywood, the history of Warner Brothers in the 1930s might have been different. It is not a question that can be taken much further, though the attention lavished on *Disraeli* does indicate that, at the start of the sound period, Warners had taken no single, clear production policy decisions. And what is absolutely clear is that the films made there during the decade were, perhaps more than with any other studio, a response to changing social circumstances and thus changing audience tastes.

Disraeli deals with the Conservative politician's efforts to purchase the Suez Canal and thereby realise his dream of making 'my Sovereign Empress of India'. He encounters opposition in the form of an anti-Semitic Governor of the Bank of England, Lord Probert (David Torrence), and the schemings of the Russians, whose cause is served by a beautiful spy, Mrs Travers (Doris Lloyd). Abetted by a pompous young man, Lord Deeford (Anthony Bushell), who is in love with Disraeli's devoted admirer, Lady Clarissa Pevensy (Joan Bennett), the Prime Minister wins the day, thanks to a mixture of inspired deviousness and bluster. George Arliss – or 'Mr George Arliss', as he is billed – with his English accent, his almost quizzical delivery of the rhetorical dialogue, head set slightly on one side, and his impeccable timing, gives exactly the kind of studied performance the play calls for and the studio expected. It is his first talkie, and every effort is made to preserve the theatrical flavour of the piece.

The director, Alfred E. Green, a senior studio director at the turn of

Disraeli: George Arliss at the despatch box

the decade, simply gives Arliss his head. A recurrent feature in the film
are long, silent shots, either at the beginning or at the end of a scene,
designed to establish Arliss' presence or to emphasise his dominance of
the scene – an exact equivalent of the big stage 'entry' or the
well-pitched curtain line. The film prepares us for Disraeli's first
appearance through a scene at Speaker's Corner, where a speaker asks
the crowd whether they want England 'to be ruled by an outsider, a
Jew, whose grandfather was a Hytalian', and a brief scene in the
Liberal Club where the Prime Minister is described as a 'dangerous
visionary' who is no match for Gladstone. The next scene, set in the
House of Commons, shows Disraeli to be very much of a match for
Gladstone, and it does so mainly through the introduction of the star: a
shot of a figure dozing under a top hat as Gladstone drones on; then the
hat is removed to reveal Arliss' disdainful smile; he stands slowly,
bows, looks round and starts to speak. From that moment on, the film
is his – as, of course, it was intended to be. But stagey does not
necessarily mean excessively verbal: dependent on an eloquent use of
political rhetoric and a relatively complicated plot, the film is none the
less striking for the way in which it signals its key points visually. When
Disraeli encounters difficulties in raising the money for the Suez Canal
purchase, he is left sitting disconsolately in his library. 'Something may
happen, something shall happen,' he intones. 'What . . . God knows!'

A long silence follows in which Disraeli merely sits there. As in the silent cinema, the importance of the moment is still registered by the holding of a shot.

One interesting point about *Disraeli* is the way in which it stresses the Jewishness of the central character and of the banker, Myers (Ivan Simpson), who finally raises the money for him, as contrasted to a marked strain of anti-semitism in several of the other characters. This is clearly designed to evoke sympathy for Disraeli, and is interesting in view of the fact that, eight years later, the word 'Jew' is not allowed even to be spoken with reference to Captain Dreyfus in *The Life of Emile Zola* or, three years later again, about Paul Ehrlich. Otherwise, the only small point of direct contemporary reference that could perhaps be drawn from the portrayal of Disraeli is that he is a distinctly commonsense politician, combating the Victorian charity-consciousness of Deeford ('I have plans for building model cottages . . .') with a terse 'The working man wants bread, not bricks'. But it is not a point which should be overemphasised in what is essentially a period film.

If *Disraeli* seems elegantly old-fashioned, *Voltaire* (1933), which also starred Arliss, appears to exist in some eighteenth-century never-never land. *Variety* saw the later movie as 'an effort to recapture the charm of *Disraeli* but making more of a bid for popular favor'. The screenplay, by college professor Paul Green and playwright Maude T. Howell, focuses on the Calas case – that of a wealthy merchant wrongly executed by Louis XV, which became an eighteenth-century *cause célèbre* – but otherwise wreaks havoc with history. Voltaire is portrayed as a royalist who has access to the King through his friendship with Mme de Pompadour (Doris Kenyon). It is, supposedly, not the King who is at fault, but the scheming Count de Sarnac (Alan Mowbray), who is in league with Frederick the Great. Louis himself (Reginald Owen) is a gentle, bumbling individual ready to redress grievances once they are pointed out to him. In the film, Voltaire's major coup in drawing Louis' attention to the Calas case is to stage a play at Versailles with Nanette Calas (Margaret Lindsay) in the title role, in which the events of the case are simply transposed to an Oriental court. It takes Sarnac to point this out to Louis.

Arliss gives his usual larger-than-life performance but the film, as directed by Warners veteran John G. Adolfi whose last movie it turned out to be, repeatedly reduces the events to a kind of pantomime. The opening sequence sets the tone of noble sentiments in a simplistic framework. An introductory title explains who the hero was. 'One man dared to speak out for the rights of an oppressed people . . . He educated the masses to think and act . . . This man – a hundred years ahead of his time – was Voltaire . . . The great humanitarian of the 18th century.' We cut to a map of France, then track in over a series of model rooftops (the same miniature used in *Svengali* in 1931) to a mob reading a Voltaire pamphlet. The mob smashes the windows of a bakery and carries off the food. Cut to an elegant gambling salon, with Louis and Pompadour. 'He's teaching the people to think,' says Louis, reiterating the point of the opening title. 'Every day it gets more difficult to collect my taxes.' Cut to Sarnac saying 'Voltaire!' in disgust and to a close-up of his foot grinding a pamphlet. Cut finally to a close-up of a hand with a quill, writing. Enter Arliss.

As if to offset the fact that a far from appalling state of affairs appears to exist in and around the French court (the mob makes only one further appearance, shouting 'Vive Voltaire!' at the gates of Versailles), the screenplay gives Voltaire a number of bursts of humanitarian rhetoric to punctuate scenes in which he plays the courtier or sits scribbling late into the night. Told that he is making himself ill through overwork, he exclaims, 'I'll never die. I haven't the time to die while there are thousands of people oppressed, starving, tortured, who need every ounce of my strength.' Learning that the King has signed Calas' death warrant, he rouses his servant with a cry of 'My torch!' 'Your torch, master?' asks the puzzled man. 'Fresh pens and ink,' explains the great man. But it is his threatened arrest which provokes Voltaire to his greatest rhetorical heights. 'You may burn my body,' he announces, 'but you can never destroy my soul. It is in the hands of the people of France. When de Sarnac comes to arrest me, he will have to batter down the doors. And the echo of those blows shall awake the people of Paris.'

Voltaire, of course, is not arrested; nor are we shown much evidence of oppression and less still of torture. Even Nanette Calas' description of her father's case to Mme de Pompadour is discreetly elided by means of a dissolve. The reason for this has to do with the film's irresolvable dilemma: to show a mistaken ruler rather than a fundamentally flawed system and, in relation to the contemporary situation in America, to show that the wrongs can be righted without a revolution. In this respect, the film's final scene – a montage of running feet, rushing carriages, pamphlets, rioting crowds, fighting, the 'Marseillaise' being sung and the Tricolor fluttering (remarkably similar to the 'Marseillaise' sequence in Gance's *Napoleon*) while the flaming words 'Justice – Truth – Liberty' zoom out of the screen – is rather puzzling. Set in the context of Voltaire's dire warning to his monarch that a revolution will occur if he does not introduce reforms, it is less difficult to understand: the sequence acts as a warning of what will happen without reform. It shows, to stretch a point, how Louis failed where Roosevelt must not.

Voltaire is Warners' last foray into old-fashioned biography, and one of Arliss' last pictures for the studio.[4] If *Disraeli* and *Voltaire* are remnants of an archaic style of film-making at Warners, simplifying the

183

issues and relying more on a glamorous and elegantly phrased narrative than on discussion, the studio's next major biopic after a gap of three years, *The Story of Louis Pasteur*, seems to herald the beginning of a new age. It is the first of three major screen biographies starring – and, in production terms, dominated by – Paul Muni. Muni, possibly the most neglected (but also the most dated) major star of the 1930s, became, for the years in which he essentially took over from George Arliss as Warners' chief prestige actor, a kind of thinking man's Lon Chaney, impersonating the great men of history in a series of thoughtful and intense performances aided by extensive make-up jobs. Speaking of Muni, Hal Wallis uses a quite different tone from the one he uses about Cagney (with whom he never got on), Davis (with whom he had problems) and Bogart (whom he regarded as one of his major discoveries). His tone indicates the respect and perhaps apprehension with which Muni was viewed by the studio during the late 1930s.[5]

The actor inaugurated projects, refused others, had a unique degree of script control and left his mark on the films in which he appeared way beyond the simple fact of starring in them. In the pre-production stages, there seems to have been a constant flow of executives and studio cars between Burbank and Muni's home in Palos Verdes bearing draft versions of the screenplays of *Zola* and *Juarez*. He attended final script conferences to an extent and with an influence apparently denied – or at any rate not aspired to by – other contract stars. He would, says Wallis, not agree to films which he felt did not make some significant point: from *I Am a Fugitive from a Chain Gang* in 1933 to *Juarez* in 1939, he is Warners' social conscience actor *par excellence*. The studio's only other major star who appears to have exercised an influence of this kind – that is to say, based on the overall content and tendency of the film rather than on the potential of the starring role itself – is Edward G. Robinson. But Robinson remained a contract star, often playing heavyweight parts in lightweight films like *Brother Orchid*. With the possible exception of *Hi, Nellie!*, Muni never appeared in a film which did not have 'significance', at any rate as defined by 1930s movie criteria. He became synonymous, in studio publicity and public image, with the company's prestige products.

The Story of Louis Pasteur marks his definitive ascent to a privileged position within the studio. 'Muni is dominating,' wrote Edwin Schallert in the *Los Angeles Times*.[6] 'One cannot question in any respect the authenticity that he lends his portrayal. It is a fine mental portrait.' One can find almost identical phrases in all subsequent reviews of Muni's biographical performances. *Louis Pasteur* itself is likewise a model in narrative terms for the biopics that follow: *The Life of Emile Zola* may be more complex and more far-reaching, and *Juarez* may be more politically adventurous, but it is *Pasteur* which establishes the structure. The screenplay's aim is to make the impact of the hero's discoveries accessible to audiences who know little and care less about preventive medicine in particular and scientific discoveries in general. What is more, it achieves this aim without any basic falsification of the material – a claim which cannot really be made about *Disraeli* and certainly cannot be made about *Voltaire*. Whereas the latter film relies quite heavily on a sentimental sub-plot to carry certain of its points, *Pasteur* rarely uses romance to strengthen its arguments. In that respect, it is something of a breakthrough, operating on the assumption that Pasteur's work is more important than Pasteur 'the man' – a fact emphasised by the minimal opportunities offered in the final script to Josephine Hutchinson as Marie Pasteur, despite second billing. Only once is outright sentimentality used to heighten a scientific dilemma, and that is when Pasteur's friend Pfeiffer (Frank Reicher) arrives with a boy (played by the angelic Dickie Moore) who has been bitten by a rabid dog. Pasteur, gazing at the suffering child, has to decide whether to risk prosecution by treating the child without a medical practitioner's licence. Naturally, he does so.

The basic method of the screenplay – and the film as a whole – can best be indicated by two sequences in which a scientific problem is dramatically defined through a rapid succession of brief scenes. The first comes right at the start. The film opens with a title: '1864. A Doctor's Office in Paris.' A doctor is hurriedly preparing to leave, drops his instruments on the floor, picks them up and puts them back in his bag! A man steps from behind a curtain and shoots him. Cut to a courtroom, where the murderer is claiming that the doctor killed his wife by treating her with dirty hands. He hands a pamphlet to the President of the court. 'Doctors! Surgeons!' it reads. 'Wash your hands! Boil your instruments! Microbes can cause disease and death to your patients!' It is, of course, signed by Louis Pasteur. Cut to a doctor describing Pasteur as a 'menace to France' and to Charbonnet (Fritz Leiber), President of the Academy of Medicine, passing on the news to Napoleon (Walter Kingsford). 'Most people who go to hospitals are carried out dead,' comments the Empress Eugénie (Iphigenie Castiglione). 'Why?' 'Yes, why, Charbonnet?' asks the Emperor. We cut to a microscope shot of microbes and to the voice of Pasteur dictating a pamphlet. The technique of introducing the Muni character first through his voice and his writings is one that becomes standard practice in the biopics. The next shot is the first time we actually see the actor, bent over a microscope, muttering 'Nothing definite. Try again!' 'Again?' asks his fellow researcher. 'Yes, again!' replies Pasteur. 'And again! And again!' The opening sequence has certain similarities to the openings of both *Disraeli* and *Voltaire*, but it presents the arguments so much more dramatically and, above all, so much more succinctly that comparison is not really useful.

The second key sequence – a biopic archetype – involves Pasteur's anthrax vaccine. He has, by now, been forced to leave Paris. The Franco-Prussian War has been and gone, via a title declaring 'Pasteur was fighting microbes, the real enemy of France'. A change of government is indicated by a brief shot of Napoleon's portrait being replaced by that of Thiers (Herbert Corthell). A newspaper headline tells us that all of France is suffering from an outbreak of anthrax. The only exception is the village of Artois which is, of course, where Pasteur is conducting his immunological experiments. A trial is proposed: fifty sheep will be injected with anthrax-contaminated blood. Twenty-five of them will have been injected previously with Pasteur's vaccine, twenty-five of them will not. The day arrives when the results of the experiment will be known. A carnival atmosphere prevails in Artois: bands play, press photographers are everywhere, and customers at the village inn pour scorn on Pasteur's claims. Lister (Halliwell Hobbes) arrives from England, and he and Pasteur join the huge crowd heading for the sheep pens. The crowd arrives first at the uninoculated sheep: they are dead. It rushes on to Pasteur's sheep: they are equally motionless. Pasteur and Lister react with puzzled gloom; they had been sure that inoculation was the answer. Just then a dog barks and the sheep, which had merely been dozing, jump to their feet. The vaccine has been shown to work and Pasteur is vindicated, but the film hardly pauses to register the triumph: it is a feature of Warners' biopics that mid-film climaxes act as a lead into the next part of the film rather than as a summation of the preceding one. Here, Pasteur's young assistant, Martel (Donald Woods), takes the opportunity to propose to Annette Pasteur (Anita Louise). Then, almost immediately, the celebrations of the success of the immunisation experiment are interrupted by a cry of 'Mad dogs! Mad dogs!'. As Pasteur and Lister watch the superstitious treatment of the bite victim, they muse on a possible cure for hydrophobia, and the film moves swiftly and relentlessly into its second major topic. The next we see of Pasteur, it is a year later. Annette is pregnant, and Pasteur himself has greying hair. He receives a letter from Lister congratulating him on making childbirth safe in London, Brussels and Prague because of his insistence on the sterilisation of maternity equipment. Pasteur's reading of the letter is interrupted by a howl from downstairs, and he rushes away to take a blood sample from a rabid dog.

The breathlessness of the narrative in *The Story of Louis Pasteur* becomes almost comic at times: there is little pause for reflection and scientific discovery seems always to be equated with a dramatic action. *The Life of Emile Zola* the following year is much less breathless, but it makes use of the same basic structure of dramatisation to highlight problems which are not in themselves dramatic. The film was clearly conceived of as a sequel to *Pasteur*. 'In bringing Emile Zola to the screen,' declares a studio press release, 'Warner Bros. has kept the

186

same combination of talents that made possible *The Story of Louis Pasteur* – Paul Muni, William Dieterle, the director, and Tony Gaudio, also a 1937 Academy winner, the cinematographer.' But the similarities caused the studio some concern. Henry Blanke warned Wallis against casting the original first choice, Josephine Hutchinson, as Mme Zola because she had played opposite Muni in *Pasteur*: there were, he claimed, already quite enough similarities – the French setting, Muni's beard, etc.[7] Care was taken with the make-up to 'let the audience see it is Muni'.[8] But the studio was not so much concerned with reproducing *Pasteur* as with capitalising on and surpassing it. Blanke wrote to Ebenstein in New York when the script was almost complete that 'I consider it nearly ten times as strong as *Louis Pasteur*.' He went on to make a bizarre suggestion which gives some indication of the kind of impact and respectability for which Warners were aiming. 'At the end of the picture, we show Zola being buried at the Pantheon with the most famous speech by Anatole France delivered at the grave. My idea would be to have this person played by a very famous man in America such as Chief Justice Hughes, Cordoza, or a Nobel Prize winner such as Eugene O'Neill or Sinclair Lewis (who, by the way, I have heard is not such a good talker).'[9]

Sadly, nothing seems to have come of the idea: France was played by a newcomer to the screen, Morris Carnovsky, with a Broadway career behind him. But there are other pointers to the very special status accorded from the start to *The Life of Emile Zola*. Delicate negotiations were carried out with Dreyfus' widow, Lucie, who was still alive when the film was made, to ensure that she would find it acceptable (and, of course, not take legal action against it). The head of the Paris office, Robert Schless, even went so far as to make a direct approach to the French government for their reaction to the project. The reported response of Léon Blum is indicative of another intention which seems to have played some part in the studio's thinking. Blum expressed the opinion, according to Schless, 'that such a picture might cause a great deal of commotion here in view of the tense political feeling and party hatred. Consequently, the release in France at this time of such a picture would be regarded by the Government as an additional unnecessary cause for trouble, and consequently desiring to avoid any such incidents, they could not offer any protection.'[10] *Zola*, with its theme of anti-semitism in the French army, judiciary and executive, touched on a topic which had clear contemporary parallels. The government, through the Minister of War (Gilbert Emory), is clearly implicated in the affair: when Colonel Picquart (Henry O'Neill) discovers the real culprit, the Minister refuses to intervene and release Dreyfus. 'It must not be,' he says. 'We owe it to the Army.' 'But you can't close the tomb over a living man!' exclaims Picquart. 'Can't we?' asks the Minister blandly.

Some attempts were made in the screenplay to defuse the situation, though these can be ascribed to the Production Code rather than to Warners. The word 'Jew', for instance, is never spoken. The only time it appears in the film is when a high-ranking officer, seeking the source of the leak of military information to the Prussian Embassy, runs his finger down Dreyfus' military record. His finger stops opposite 'Religion: Jew'. 'I wonder how he ever got to be on the General Staff,' muses the officer. 'That's our man.' But the relevance of the Dreyfus case to developments in Europe and to the rise of fascism in the United States as dealt with in *Black Legion* in the same year was clearly present in the mind of Heinz Herald – who, like producer Henry Blanke and director William Dieterle, was German – when he sent the studio the first synopsis of the story he had written with Geza Herczeg in July 1936. It was accompanied by an emotional, misspelled letter in rather erratic English. 'The film,' stated Herald, 'is not an ordinary biography, it contains far more: the eternal, ceaseless fight for freedom and right. The right, basis of all human society, represents the equilibrium of the world. If this equilibrium is ever put out of balance, it shakes the entire globe. It is immaterial whether it happens in Germany or France or in Turkey, but the whole world trembles whenever the foundation of society, the right, happens to be infringed. We think that it had never been more timely than today to know this, see it and hear it.'[11]

Such parallels are only implicit in the completed screenplay, as they are in that of *Juarez* two years later. But the film's slant is undeniably anti-militarist and the preaching of tolerance has a much greater edge here than in *Voltaire*. *The Life of Emile Zola* does indeed seem to be fired with the same kind of commitment that characterised the social conscience pictures earlier in the decade, but a commitment which implied the need for America to take a position in world affairs in addition to setting its own house in order. The film is far more accurate than *Pasteur*, making only minor adjustments to history, all of which were carefully considered in advance by Wallis, Blanke and Dieterle.[12] *Nana* is predated to 1871, making it Zola's first successful novel and placing it before the Franco-Prussian War; Mme Dreyfus (Gale Sondergaard) is shown visiting Zola to make a direct appeal; and Dreyfus' rehabilitation is brought forward so that it occurs before Zola's death. But certain of the pre-production decisions do indicate that the studio began to get cold feet about the political implications of its story: the rejected titles of *Justice, Injustice, Truth, Truth is on the March, The Light of Reason, Truth Conquers, Conscience of Man, The Man with a Conscience* all imply a considerably more general point than the one finally adopted (changed from *The Story of Emile Zola* because it was too similar to *The Story of Louis Pasteur*). And by the time the provisional script was submitted to Breen, there was only one political reference that caused offence – the inclusion of the word 'revolutionary'. The rest of Breen's objections follow a more familiar track: concerns about Nana's profession ('The showing of prostitutes to many people, is highly offensive') and other moral matters ('We suggest that you do not definitely refer to the books Madam Bovary and The Confessions of Claude. Please have in mind that these books are looked upon, by many people throughout the world, as "pornographic" literature.').[13]

By the time the film was finally released, Warners were satisfied that offence would not be caused and that they had a non-inflammatory prestige production on their hands. The premiere was to be a night of solemn pomp: Jack Warner issued instructions that only an overture was to be played before the screening and that on no account was a cartoon to be shown. The film's release seems to have been treated with something approaching reverence. On 12 August, publicity director Charles Einfeld cabled Jack Warner about the reception the film had received in New York:

> MAJOR BERNHARD SEARS SCHNEIDER MYSELF STOOD VIRTUALLY CHOKING BACK TEARS OF PRIDE AND MINGLED EMOTIONS AS ZOLA RECEIVED TRIBUTE AND OVATION LAST NIGHT BEFORE MOST BRILLIANT AUDIENCE EVER ASSEMBLED UNDER ONE ROOF WHO CAME IN SPITE WORST RAIN AND ELECTRIC STORM WHICH LASTED ALL EVENING KILLING SIX AND RAISING HAVOC STOP ALL THOUGHT OF THE COMMERCIAL SIDE OF ZOLA WAS FORGOTTEN AS AUDIENCE AND REVIEWERS LIFTED PICTURE INTO REALM OF THE GREATEST CULTURAL CONTRIBUTION TO HUMANITY

Frank S. Nugent of the *New York Times* echoed the rapture: 'Rich, dignified, honest and strong, it is at once the finest historical film ever made and the greatest screen biography, greater even than *The Story of Louis Pasteur* with which the Warners squared their conscience last year.' And a special editorial by Red Kann in *Film Daily* makes it clear that it was not just Warners' conscience that was being squared by the film. 'It is our ambition for *Zola*, as it must of necessity be for anyone in the business who recognises that merit deserves its reward, that it slays, wows and panics 'em up and down the land. Firstly, since it rates, and secondly, for the potential significance which it points up.'[14]

With *The Life of Emile Zola*, Warners achieved the status that *Anthony Adverse* had set them on the road towards the previous year; and they did so with a film that, while it may not exactly be radical, is far from escapist. The plot is more complex than that of *Pasteur* because the issues are more general. Zola achieves fame and fortune as a chronicler of poverty in *Nana*, but loses some of his original fire as he grows fat and prosperous – so much so that his old friend Cézanne (Vladimir Sokoloff) abandons him. Drawn into the Dreyfus case almost against his will, his triumph is much slower in coming than was Pasteur's, at

189

any rate in film time: he loses his court case, the mob turns against him, and he must flee, penniless, to England before his final rehabilitation and eulogy in the Pantheon. Since the screenplay deals with a political situation, the forces that oppose Zola are better organised and more powerful than was the medical establishment which blocked Pasteur.

Zola's decision to involve himself in the Dreyfus case is portrayed with the same economy and features the same highlighting of choice as the sequences from *Pasteur* discussed above. For example, the arrival of Mme Dreyfus to plead with Zola coincides with his receipt of a letter about his candidacy for the Académie Française – his final elevation to a position of comfort and respectability. Lucie Dreyfus is pessimistic about her chances, especially since the court martial of the real culprit, Esterhazy (Robert Barrat), has been stage-managed by the army to avoid a scandal. 'There's nothing to be done,' she says, 'unless some fool . . .' Zola cuts her short: 'My life is lived, Madame.' After she has gone, he finds she has left her papers behind. He runs after her, but she has already left the house. Returning to his room, Zola picks up the letter from the Académie, and the camera tracks in on the words 'You need not fear their decision' which are picked out by a mask. Zola looks up at the portrait of Cézanne, smiles and tears up the letter. He picks up Mme Dreyfus' papers and starts to read. We cut to the offices of *L'Aurore* as he reads 'J'Accuse' to the editor. The reading of the article is the first of Muni's big set speeches in the film (the second is during his own trial, and both were released on a special record). And it is followed by the sort of montage that was becoming a regular feature of Warners biopics, replacing the action montages of the gangster films with something designed to dramatise the taking of a position. The newspaper workers gather at the glass partitions of the office to listen; the presses churn out the article; people buy newspapers; the front window of *L'Aurore* is smashed by a brick; Zola's books are burned in the street; effigies of the author are burned; Zola himself flees a mob in his carriage. And we cut to the beginning of the trial. As in *Pasteur*, no effort is spared to make the issues exciting; and no time is wasted once the climax has been reached. Indeed, the most striking thing about the biopics is their double rhythm: slow and pompous in their background, fast and frenzied in their moments of climax.

Juarez was made by very much the same team that made *Zola*: Blanke as Associate Producer, Dieterle as director, Muni as star, Gaudio as cameraman, Warren Low as editor. It is both a less successful and more ambitious film, with a screenplay (by Wolfgang Reinhardt, Aeneas Mackenzie and John Huston) that hovers between the economy of the earlier biopics and a stab at a more poetic approach (for which Huston appears to have been responsible). The film's subject matter is also potentially more inflammatory. *Juarez* deals with

190

the setting up by Napoleon III of a puppet regime in Mexico headed by Maximilian von Hapsburg, and with the overthrow of that regime by Benito Pablo Juarez and the execution of Maximilian. The original intention had apparently been to produce a rather more romantic film of the doomed love of Maximilian and Carlotta, his bride, based on Bertita Harding's bestseller, *The Phantom Crown*. But when Muni agreed to take the role of Juarez, the balance shifted. Much of *The Phantom Crown* remains, however. Napoleon III, played in fine demonic form by Claude Rains, is the villain of the piece. In an opening scene, we see him hoping for a Confederate win in the Civil War so that 'America would be too weak to impose the Monroe Doctrine'. Any lingering doubts as to his villainy are dispelled when, shortly afterwards, he describes democracy as 'the rule of the cattle, by the cattle, for the cattle'. In a later scene, where he talks to US Ambassador John Bigelow (Hugh Sothern), he becomes a figure of ridicule, absurdly perched on a wooden horse for a heroic portrait.

Maximilian (Brian Aherne), on the other hand, is presented as he was in Harding's novel: as an honest man who has been duped by Napoleon. 'I did not come here to conquer but to rule peaceably,' he says wistfully. He refuses to go along with the conservative landowners, who expect the return of the land taken from them by Juarez's government: 'We will permit no one to infringe on the interest of the great majority of our subjects,' he says. Juarez himself (Paul Muni) is presented as a principled and noble patriot. Abraham Lincoln is a constant guarantee: we first see Juarez reading a letter from the American President; he carries a portrait round with him under the most difficult of circumstances; and there is a carefully staged scene of emotion when he hears of Lincoln's assassination. The film's final scene stresses Juarez's grief at having had to execute the 'honest' Maximilian. It begins with a long shot of a cathedral suffused with dusty light in which Maximilian lies in state. Juarez walks forward. There is a close shot of him looking down at the coffin. 'Forgive me,' he murmurs. Then the camera tracks back in front of him as he leaves, with the altar and its candles in the background. The intention is plainly to absolve Juarez of the responsibility for Maximilian's death, and to place the blame, if not on history, at any rate on Napoleon. The latter, however, is a secondary character who appears little in the second part of the film, and some of the strangeness of *Juarez* can be accounted for by a tension between the desire to present a historical confrontation between two individuals, neither of whom is villainous, and a structure – that of the biopic – which tends to rely on being able to place its central character in confrontation with a clearly unjust system or individual.

The film plays very heavily on the Muni personality, particularly in the way in which the actor is introduced. A man is shot crying 'Viva

Juarez: Paul Muni as the Mexican leader

Juarez!' We cut to close-up of the letter from Lincoln, addressed to Juarez, held by two unidentified hands. The camera looks over the letter reader's shoulder as a group of men enter. Muni's voice reads a proclamation, and there is a close-up of his hand signing it. Only then do we get the first shots of Muni's face and the effect is, as it was intended to be, startling. Muni's features resemble those of the real-life character he is playing more completely than in any previous film, while remaining unmistakably those of Muni.

The film's efforts at symbolism represent its most interesting failure – a clash, perhaps, between the studio's determination to produce another prestige biopic, and Huston's desire to do something different. *Juarez* is punctuated by a number of chorus-like scenes in which groups of straw-hatted Mexican peasants react to the various political events. Maximilian's arrival in Mexico also has a distinctly eerie feel, as he walks down the gangplank at Vera Cruz to a magnificent official welcome from which anyone other than officials is notably absent. Future developments are hinted at by a vulture perched on top of one of the triumphal crowns. The most ambitious sequence of all concerns Carlotta's return to Europe and her ensuing madness. Maximilian is in a prison cell, pacing up and down to the sound of a clock ticking. Intercut with this is a similar shot of Juarez, pacing to the same ticking. We cut to a wave breaking into the camera, then to the far side of the

Atlantic where Carlotta (Bette Davis) sits slumped in a dustily lit room. She reaches out, calling 'Max!' Cut back to Maximilian's cell, as he walks towards the camera. Carlotta's voice screams 'Max!' as the soldiers come to take him to his execution. As he is shot, a white dove – the symbol of Maximilian and Carlotta's love, through her favourite song, 'La Paloma' – takes off from a nearby cactus.

The origins of *Juarez* suggest a project which was to have been much more in line with the earlier biopics, both stylistically and politically. The abandoning of the plan to film *The Phantom Crown* with Edward G. Robinson in the secondary role of Juarez provoked a flood of complaints: from Harding's publishers ('Juarez, to ninety-nine Americans out of a hundred, means nothing – a hard-to-pronounce Spanish name with no associations. Phantom Crown conjures up all sorts of images of splendour and romance, gallantry and tragedy'); from Harding's agent ('People today associate the name of Juarez with the Mexican town and will think this is a modern "border-town" story'); and from a horde of ordinary Americans from Pennsylvania to Texas.[15] Harding's novel had attracted attention, and Warners appear to have been not the only studio interested in filming it: a discreet enquiry at the Hays Office revealed that MGM, Columbia and 'another studio' were working on it.[16] So, too, was Mexican director Miguel C. Torres, who completed his film and brought an action against Warners for plagiarism. Warners resolved the situation by distributing Torres' film with all the promotional enthusiasm one would expect from a major handling a competitor's work, thereby ensuring its oblivion.[17]

Once the change in emphasis had taken place, Warners followed their normal practice on biopics, certainly in the wake of *Zola*, of engaging in painstaking research. They commissioned *Notes on the Life of Benito Juarez* from Jesse John Dossick of New York University's School of Education – an enormously detailed, 123-page biography with 10 pages of notes, 27 pages of quotations, and a 10-page bibliography. Transcripts and translations of Juarez's diary, proclamations and speeches were collected. Herman Lissauer, head of the Research Department, answered a query from the Publicity Department by saying that a full bibliography of the books used in researching *Juarez* would run to over 500 volumes. At one stage, Henry Blanke even asked to view the 167,000 feet of film shot by Eisenstein for *Que Viva Mexico!*, 'parts of which I can use marvellously for montages, etc.' The completed picture was expensive, even by prestige biopic standards. The final budget was $1,251,000 despite 'terrific efforts' on the part of Anton Grot to cut down on set costs.[18] *Zola* had cost a mere $700,000. And *Juarez* was the first film to use the new Eastman Super XX high-speed stock.

As with *Zola* and the French government, efforts were made to ensure that the film would be acceptable in the cinemas of the country in which it was set. J.G. Mullen of the Warners office in Mexico City warned that 'it would be very dangerous to have a picture that does not conform to historical fact' and discreet enquiries were made as to the acceptability of the treatment. The efforts were successful. On 7 July 1938, Blanke received a letter from a Colonel Velarde stating that 'the National Palace and the Mexican Congress are 100% with you'. President Cardenas sent Jack Warner a telegram wishing him luck with the premiere.[19] But more interesting than the Mexican response are the parallels between Napoleon III's annexation of Mexico and Hitler's territorial ambitions in Europe – parallels which were drawn both during pre-production and after the film's release, but which Wallis strenuously denies: there was, he says, 'nothing like that' in the studio's intentions.[20] Perhaps there wasn't, at any rate officially. But the choice of a historical subject which related to the current situation in Europe is very much in line with the trend in studio production in the late 1930s, and this is frequently corroborated by the studio files.

The most interesting surviving memos in the studio archive are dated 2 November and 24 November 1937 (that is to say, early in the scripting process), from Wolfgang Reinhardt to Henry Blanke. They are written in German, which would have restricted the number of studio personnel who could have read them: in the case of *Juarez*, Blanke and Dieterle. The first concerns modifications to the draft outline by the director and the star. Dieterle had, in a way which Reinhardt claims was typical of him, modified the well-balanced rhythms, mood and small details of the outline to give it his usual 'D-Zugtempo' (express train tempo). The result was that an interesting and unusual script threatened to become a formula. Muni's interventions were even more harmful: they had transformed Huston's wonderful ideas 'in Scheisse' (into shit). What did they think they were doing? Even Thalberg would not change scripts in this way.

The memo gives a rare glimpse into some of the conflicts that could take place at Warners during the preparation of a Muni picture. It would never have been written if Reinhardt had not been angry, and the reasons for his anger are instructive. In the first place, the usual smooth functioning of the studio system seems to have been interrupted by the sorts of 'creative conflicts' it was, by and large, designed to suppress. Secondly, Reinhardt saw the danger of a film which could make an important political statement being transformed into a neutral biopic, and transformed by the actor responsible more than any other for the studio's reputation as a socially committed organisation. The second of Reinhardt's memos complains that Aeneas Mackenzie, who had done much of the preliminary research on *Juarez*, was 'no motion picture writer' and was, above all, not capable of handling the 'political and ideological' implications of the story. 'Every child must recognise,' argued Reinhardt, 'that Napoleon in his intervention in Mexico is no one other than Mussolini plus Hitler in their adventure in Spain.'

It would be quite possible, given the attitudes of Muni and Dieterle and the innate cautiousness of the studio machine, that the casual observer, let alone 'every child', would have missed the parallel. But this does not seem to have been the case. Certainly, the studio was cautious, as a memo from Walter MacEwen to Henry Blanke on 11 May 1938 makes clear:

> As soon as you get your first script on JUAREZ I think you should send a copy of it to Jeff Sherlock of the Breen Office. Breen has called to say that we may face considerable trouble abroad with this picture, in view of a growing tendency to ban all pictures containing anything of a revolutionary nature.

Nor was it just foreign reactionaries who could create problems for a sympathetic portrayal of Juarez's national liberation struggle. In September 1938, Warners received a letter from Father P.J. Dooley of the Holy Redeemer Rectory in Webster Groves, Missouri. Though the tone of the letter suggests a crank, the opinions for which Father Dooley claims to speak were not ones that the studio could afford totally to ignore. Referring to an article in his local paper, Father Dooley declares:

> If it is your intention to merely present the tragic story of Maximilian and Queen Carlotta, eliminating the sinister machinations of Benito Juarez, well and good. This should offer very splendid movie material.
>
> However, if, as the article intimates, you have in mind anything tending towards a glorification of Benito Juarez, permit me to give you a word of friendly warning. To the Catholic mind Benito Juarez is one of the arch-villains of history. Any picture that will tend to glorify him would undoubtedly arouse Catholic indignation far more than that to which 'Blockade' is now being subjected.
>
> However, it is safe to predict that such a picture would meet with opposition by non-Catholics as well. By this time nearly everyone has been brought to realise that the present set-up in Mexico is absolutely Communistic and the work of Calles and Cardenas is purely an enactment of the program begun by Juarez.
>
> For an accurate understanding of the real facts connected with this subject, permit me to suggest that you read 'Blood Drenched Altars' by Francis Clement Kelley, who is universally recognized as an authority on Mexican affairs.

That Warners should, under these circumstances, have set out to make a film which not only *did* unequivocally glorify Juarez, but also made clear the parallels with the situation in Europe, is surely worthy of note. In pre-production, unit manager Al Alborn wrote to Lee Anthony of the cutting department asking him to provide 'some long shots of masses of people presumably listening to a speech made by a dictator, such as shown in newsreels of Mussolini or Hitler talking, that we could use for the Dieterle picture for the scene where Maximilian comes out on the balcony with a child that he and his wife had adopted.'[21] The recognition, if not necessarily the intention to stress, that there is a parallel is surely clear. The same recognition, this time backed up by an intention to stress it, can be seen in the special *Film Guide to the Warner Bros. Picture Juarez* prepared by Harold Turney, head of the Drama Department at Los Angeles City College. Under the heading 'Then and Now', Turney writes – in a way that, given the origins of the booklet, must surely have been sanctioned by the studio – that

> seventy-five years of world progress have made little difference in the ideals and ambitions of men and nations. In this year, 1939, there are leaders whose principles are those of authority, whose selfish interests demand conquests . . . Thus in the selection of the story of Juarez, we find the reflections of a series of present day events, each with its own modification, but the same fundamental ideas as the basis. The theme of the picture, *that democracy can make no condescensions to the most benevolent authoritarianism*, is significant to the present day world.[22]

The political implications of the picture are confirmed by a plan, never actually put into effect, to dedicate it to Roosevelt, and by the fact that all reviewers – even in the trade press – mention them. *Juarez* was, wrote *Variety*, a 'story that points up the parallels of conflicting political thought of today and three-quarters of a century ago'. Frank S. Nugent in the *New York Times* was much more explicit: Warners had 'not sidestepped the responsibilities imposed by the theme's political parallelism. With pardonable opportunism, they have written between the lines of Benito Juarez's defy [sic] the text of a liberal's scorn for fascism and nazism.' It is doubtless worth noting that the *New York Times* is the only place in which the *specific* parallel is pointed out.

Juarez seems to have taken the non-American biopic about as far as it could go in reflecting and reflecting on a contemporary situation, as well as straining the form's conventions to – or beyond – their limit. At all events, the two remaining foreign biopics of the decade are considerably less interesting. *The Story of Dr Ehrlich's Magic Bullet* and *A Dispatch from Reuters*, both starring Edward G. Robinson, indicate that the form had become a formula. *Dr Ehrlich's Magic Bullet* is the more interesting – and was the better received – of the two, since it tackles a subject which had been taboo on the screen for many years: syphilis. In many respects, it is a remake of *The Story of Louis Pasteur*. Robinson's Paul Ehrlich pursues scientific knowledge with the same missionary zeal as Muni's Louis Pasteur, bent over a test tube in an unheated laboratory, coughing tubercularly and finally collapsing from over-work. He encounters the same ingrained professional conservatism. 'I am not interested in your ideas and experiments,' he is told by the Prussian-accented Geheimrat of the Hospital (Montagu Love). 'I am only interested in your behaviour as a member of this hospital. You must leave, Ehrlich: it's conform or suffer.' And he is supported by the same discreet and loving wife, played this time by Ruth Gordon. The film also toys with the by now familiar issue of anti-semitism. 'I have nothing against Dr Ehrlich professionally,' says a leading doctor at the hospital, 'although I must confess to a certain feeling about persons of his faith in our profession.'

Above all, *The Story of Dr Ehrlich's Magic Bullet* uses the same narrative methods to dramatise Ehrlich's research as did the earlier film. There are montages of hard work, of the search for the syphilis serum (numerically labelled test tubes succeed one another, and are in turn succeeded by Gothic numerals – 30, 200, 300, 417, 542 – zooming out of the screen, until the successful formula, 606, is reached). And the dilemmas of scientific progress are dramatically heightened in a familiar way. To prove the efficacy of his diptheria serum, Ehrlich must carry out an experiment almost identical to Pasteur's on the sheep: inoculate twenty of the sufferers with his serum, and leave a control group of twenty uninoculated. The difference here is that the sufferers are children. The problem is set in context by an argument between Ehrlich and his friend Emil von Behring (Otto Kruger). It is developed through a montage of progress charts, surgical instruments, low-angle shots of the doctors leaning over the sickbeds, and through a track along the beds showing feverish children. This sequence ends with a number of close-ups of suffering children, forcing a choice on Ehrlich. He decides to inject the control group as well. The Geheimrat tries to stop him, and the climax is reached in a close shot of a black-coated arm attempting to restrain a white-sleeved one from injecting an angelic, feverish toddler. Ehrlich wins and, after a brief interlude when it appears that he and von Behring are to be fired, the sequence is completed by the Minister of Health (Donald Crisp) leading Ehrlich to the bedside of his grandson saved by the 'magic bullet' of Ehrlich's injection.

A Dispatch from Reuters, made later the same year, has a less emotional subject – the development of the world's first news agency – and is a much more low-key affair. By late 1940, Warners' biopics were, perhaps, a little too familiar. *Variety* felt that the film 'aims to catch attention from audiences interested in historical subjects, and as such will do nominal business in the regular runs'. Nor did it do well in the first runs: it opened at a non-Warners theatre, the Globe, and did less than average business. The pattern of the film is, once again, familiar. Reuter pursues his idea, first of pigeon post, then of taking a franchise on telegraph and cable services, against the opposition of the establishment, and with all the usual setbacks. The key conflict is the final one. Reuter manages to beat all the other agencies to the news of Lincoln's assassination by a margin of twenty-four hours. No one believes him, thinking he has invented the news to gain notoriety. There is a national scandal, angry crowds mill in the street – why, it is not entirely clear – and questions are asked in the House. Finally, the news is confirmed, and Reuter achieves his apotheosis by being allowed to make a little speech in Parliament: 'A free press is the symbol of a great people: truth is freedom.' This is not the only example of the film's impeccably liberal credentials. 'I want to use my invention to serve *people*,' Reuter tells a group of bankers who plan to take advantage of it to make a Rothschild-like stock market killing.

A Dispatch from Reuters is the swansong of the Warners biopic. The studio's main interests had by now moved elsewhere – to other prestige productions, to affirmations of Americanism through its American biographies, and to a more indirect comment on the social situation through its melodramas and *films noirs*. But there can be no denying that, during the half-decade in which foreign biopics were Warners' flagship, they provided an excellent example of how contemporary issues could be transmuted into a narrative formula. Pasteur, Zola, Juarez and, in pale shadow, Ehrlich and Reuter were second-generation New Dealers before their time.

10 American History

Warners' forays into American history during the 1930s, other than in the strictly conventional form of 'B' Westerns, are extremely limited. As a studio, they seem to have preferred their history to be foreign, perhaps because foreign biographies carried with them virtually no audience preconceptions, and were thus more easily adjusted to contemporary values. Other than disguised biographies of American gangsters, Warners in the 1930s produced few major American biographies. Of those they did produce, one, *Alexander Hamilton* (1931), was a George Arliss vehicle. Two deal with twentieth-century figures who are relevant to the problems of the years in which they were made: *Knute Rockne – All American* (1940), because its hero was a symbol of basic American values at a time when the country faced the challenge of involvement or non-involvement in the war in Europe; *Sergeant York* (1941), because Alvin York's down-home heroism in World War I pointed clear lessons for World War II. Only *They Died With Their Boots On* (1941) deals with the life of a major American hero from the past, and a very ambiguous one at that: George Armstrong Custer. *Santa Fe Trail* (1940) looks at America on the verge of the Civil War, but its message, like the film itself, is very confused, and the only major historical figure to appear in it,[1] the abolitionist John Brown, plays a curious secondary role in Raymond Massey's demonic performance. Finally, there are two James Cagney vehicles, *Frisco Kid* in 1935 and *Oklahoma Kid* in 1939, which place the star in situations very similar to those he faces in contemporary roles, having to choose between selfishness and social commitment. The second does not seem to have captured the public imagination and I have not included it – though with some regret, since it is a curious film (any film that casts Cagney and Bogart in a Western could scarcely be otherwise) and has the same ambiguous attitude towards the frontier days of the nineteenth century as do *Frisco Kid*, *Santa Fe Trail* and *They Died With Their Boots On*.

None the less, the American costume dramas and biographies do act as a distinct complement to the foreign biopics, though they overlap with them very little in terms of production policy: four out of the six successful ones were made at the very end of the period, in 1940 and 1941, at a time when the foreign biopics were all but finished. The big American history pictures take over. And where the foreign biopics

199

stress specific values such as truth and tolerance, which are certainly necessary in the particular narrative contexts but little more than reaffirmations of the American way of life (note, for instance, the use of Lincoln as an unquestionable guarantee in *Juarez*), the American pictures offer a passionate but much less clear affirmation of Americanism. This, indeed, seems to be their point: to remind audiences (or perhaps to celebrate with audiences) the things which had made and should still be making the country great. The films have much of the tone of an advertisement that was placed in the *New York Times* in 1940 by 'Fight for Freedom Inc.' and which attacked the non-interventionist 'America First' movement. It drew explicit parallels between American values and the need to combat Hitler. The war had 'something to do with the defence of Democracy and human decency – with the defence of human freedom against the onslaught of lawless lust for power . . . This is the fight for freedom – our fight against Nazi Germany's attempt at world conquest.' By reaffirming American values at this time, Warners were adapting the policy of earlier years in the decade to the eve of war. Other films of the period – *Confessions of a Nazi Spy* (1939), *The Sea Hawk* (1940) and *All Through the Night* (1942) – are more explicit in their call for intervention or at any rate commitment. But the American historical and biographical films clearly belong to the same general trend.

One other general point about the films is worth noting. While the foreign biographies show a clear development in the career of Paul Muni, with the actor's impersonation at least as important to the audience as the character he is impersonating, neither of the two American biopics at the end of the decade uses an established studio star. Pat O'Brien as Knute Rockne is, like all the actor's roles, solid rather than charismatic, stressing the very ordinariness of the football coach. And ordinariness, elevated to the status of folk myth, is the quality most obviously associated with Gary Cooper's Alvin York.[2] Both Rockne and York are ordinary Americans who rise to greatness because of their Americanness. Unlike Pasteur, Zola and Ehrlich, they are not brilliant men; unlike Disraeli and Juarez, they are not politicians.

The subject of Warners' first American biography of the decade, however, *was* a politician, though in a period which makes the term 'patriot' more suitable. *Alexander Hamilton* deals with a scandal in the years following the War of Independence. Unfortunately, the eighteenth century seems to have been the one least suited to Warners' production methods, and while Arliss frequently achieves the requisite – or conventional – note of eloquent elegance, the rest of the film, under the uninspired direction of John G. Adolfi, does not. It tells the story of the first Secretary of the Treasury in Washington's administration, and of his key role in two vital Bills: the Assumption Bill, under which the United States, rather than the individual states, would assume responsibility for America's post-war debt, thus consolidating the new Federal government; and the Residence Bill, which established the nation's capital at Washington, in the hope of balancing the claims of North and South.

Playing a statesman, Arliss repeats his *Disraeli* performance, standing intense and moved (and apparently wearing lipstick) as he listens to Washington's farewell to the Navy at Rocky Hill in November 1783; or easily pacifying a riotous crowd outside Independence Hall with his eloquence and steady stare. But Hamilton's honour is most clearly established through a potentially sordid episode from his private life. Based on a play written by Arliss himself in association with Mary Hamlin in which he had had considerable success on the stage, the film focuses on a ploy by the wicked Senator Roberts (Dudley Digges) to discredit Hamilton and undermine his plans for national unity. Roberts' plan involves Hamilton's seduction by an adventuress, Mrs Reynolds (June Collyer), during his wife's absence in England. Threatened with exposure and personal ruin if he does not withdraw his Bills, Hamilton remains steadfast. 'I'll sacrifice my name, I'll sacrifice my house,' he tells his wife (Doris Kenyon), 'but by God, Betsy, I can't sell my country.' The scandal breaks, Betsy does not leave him (a sentimental little scene in which he picks her some flowers as she packs her bag ensures that), and the Bills are carried. At the film's darkest moment there is a sudden fanfare and George Washington (Alan Mowbray) enters the room to tell Hamilton that he has 'upheld the honour of the Secretary of the Treasury at the expense of the honour of Alexander Hamilton'. 'The defeat of Alexander Hamilton,' rejoins Arliss, 'is of small value by comparison with the triumph of this great nation.'

Alexander Hamilton is a studiedly patriotic film. It opens and closes with shots of War of Independence soldiers marching to the strains of 'Yankee Doodle', national flags flutter, and all in all it is very much a prestige product. In addition to capitalising on Arliss' stage success in much the same way as *Disraeli*, it was used for the gala opening of Warners' newest and plushest West Coast theatre, the Western, at Wilshire and Western in Los Angeles (later rechristened the Wiltern). But, like most Arliss vehicles, it is distinctly old-fashioned. *Variety* described it as 'an ancient song sung in a jazz age'. 'Trouble is,' the review continued, 'the whole thing is timid theatrical make believe, framed by an actor for audiences of a day when Little Lord Fauntleroy was a juvenile hero instead of comedy relief, and youngsters hissed heavies instead of cheering them.' The strategy of *Disraeli* was obviously not to be repeated; but Warners could not afford to have the picture consigned to respectable oblivion, and their press campaign tried to establish a contemporary relevance. One suggested story in the publicity kit quotes a recent speech by President Hoover at Valley Forge, claiming that his own appeal for firm and far-sighted action struck 'the keynote of Alexander Hamilton'. A billboard campaign drew an even more explicit parallel: 'What,' it asked, 'did George Washington do when America's prosperity wasn't worth ten cents on the dollar? He sent for Alexander Hamilton!' In fact, the film does have two rather prophetic parallels with the current situation in the United States: the country's unsettled debt to its soldiers, and the presentation of Hamilton as an unequivocal and justified supporter of centralised government, as Roosevelt would be a year or so later. But it is difficult to see such specific parallels as other than fortuitous.

It is difficult, too, to find direct relevance in *Frisco Kid*, although clearly the film's portrayal of Cagney's realisation that the true outlet for his energetic individualism is in service to the community, echoing his conversion in *G-Men* earlier in the year, is not without ideological significance. 'San Francisco, 1854,' declares an opening title. 'A seven-hilled metropolis on whose north shore flourished the infamous Barbary Coast.' The Barbary Coast was quite a favourite with Hollywood in the mid-1930s, providing a kind of urbanised equivalent to the frontier, as well as a nineteenth-century parallel to Chicago gangsterism. United Artists had released *Barbary Coast* a few months earlier, and MGM would do a slightly updated version of the theme in *San Francisco* the following year. Warners' *Frisco Kid* centres on Bat Morgan (James Cagney), who arrives penniless in a waterfront bar and is promptly shanghaied. He escapes and, after killing the notorious Shanghai Duck (Fred Kohler), half joins forces with the good guys. Charles Ford (Donald Woods), editor of the *Tribune* and the film's chief spokesman for decency, approaches him after the fight: 'Mr Morgan,' he says, 'you've done San Francisco a service.' Morgan cleans up the Coast through a protection racket and attempts to cut down the lawlessness. But a riot at the opening of the San Francisco Grand Opera results in the murder of a judge and the shooting of Ford. A vigilante committee tries Morgan along with the Coast's other bar owners and heavies. He is saved by the love of Jean Barat (Margaret Lindsay), owner of the *Tribune*, whose father had been killed trying to fight the Coast. She agrees to be a kind of parole officer to him.

Frisco Kid is an efficient action movie, as is indicated by the fact that the 'service' Morgan does San Francisco is to kill someone. The action is expertly handled by one of Warners' most underrated directors of the period, Lloyd Bacon. The fight with Shanghai Duck, a huge man with a hook instead of a hand, is spectacularly well staged, and the lynching scene is typical of the best moments in a Warners' action movie. Morra, the gentleman gambler (Ricardo Cortez), is urbanely resigned:

'Gentlemen,' he says, 'you win: I pass.' Daley, the corrupt politician (Joseph King), on the other hand, is reduced to a blubbering, pleading wreck. There is a high-angle shot of the crowd outside as a man crawls out along a gallows arm to fix the ropes. The nooses drop into shot. Morra and Daley are pushed out of the window, and we cut to the ropes snapping taut.

The most interesting aspect of *Frisco Kid*, however, is the adjustment made to the Cagney persona as the country moves out of crisis into a period of normalisation. In the classic tradition of the Hollywood narrative, the change takes place on both a personal and a philosophical level. On the personal level, the brash man of the people encounters and overcomes class. 'I love you,' Jean Barat tells him, 'but you can never mean anything to me. There's a world of difference between us.' But privately she senses 'something good in him', and in the end, to the dismay of the *New York Times'* Andre Sennwald, who found it 'embarrassing', the two are united: old world, moneyed liberalism going off hand in hand with the rugged individualism of the new world. It is worth noting that the context is historical and both the protagonists of European descent. Earlier that year, the same actress had not been able to overcome similar barriers in a modern setting between herself and a Mexican in *Bordertown*. But here, Morgan's rugged individualism is the key factor. 'Well, dog eat dog,' he muses after exacting revenge on his shanghaiers. When his best friend (George E. Stone) is killed for trying to intervene on the side of good, Morgan tells Barat, 'The only thing you get for trying to help others is a kick in the face'. Finding himself condemned to death by the vigilante committee, he declares bitterly that he has 'walked into a hanging party by trying to do things her way'. The fact that he is saved by an individual is also significant: the America of the mid-1930s has to rely on its own resources rather than on the intervention of a paternalistic government. Interestingly, both United Artists' *Barbary Coast* and Warners' *Frisco Kid* cast women in this actively redemptive role, Miriam Hopkins in the former, Margaret Lindsay in the latter.

Women revert to their usual roles of passive support in the four remaining American history pictures: determined mothers (*Sergeant York*), quietly supportive wives (*Knute Rockne – All American*) and nobly grieving loved ones (*Santa Fe Trail* and *They Died With Their Boots On*, where the part is played both times by Olivia De Havilland, the studio's specialist in the role). The period of normalisation has given way to an impending crisis that seems to call for the traditional 'masculine' qualities of bravery and active dedication to principles. *Knute Rockne – All American* is the nearest Warners came during the 1930s to doing a major contemporary biography. Rockne, football coach at the university of Notre Dame and the father of modern American college football, had been killed in a plane crash in 1931, and the film, premiered at South Bend, Indiana, home of Notre Dame, was released to coincide with a round of Rockne celebrations and the opening of a Knute Rockne Memorial Building at the college. The film has, of late, achieved something of the status of a camp classic, since it has Ronald Reagan as the young football hero, George Gipp, whose brilliant career is prematurely ended by his death from pneumonia. On his deathbed, he pulls coach Rockne down towards him and croaks, 'Some day, when things are tough, maybe you can ask the boys to go in there and win just once for the Gipper'. The phrase, immortalised in Gary Trudeau's *Doonesbury* comic strip, is scarcely typical of the film, which is often folksy but rarely sentimental. In fact, the Gipper's death is its only real descent into outright sentimentality. For the rest of the time, the epithet best suited to *Knute Rockne – All American* is 'rousing'.

The film is given the same treatment as the foreign biopics. Bosley Crowther in the *New York Times* refers to its 'reverential respect and intimations of immortality'. But it resembles the biopics in other ways, too. Lloyd Bacon, who replaced William K. Howard as director because of the latter's drinking problems,[3] has adopted the Dieterle style of breathless compression, linking scenes which dramatise decisions with montages of training sessions, quarterbacks running, the Notre Dame band playing and scoreboards recording victories. The film neatly dovetails three classic American themes: the immigrant's rise to prominence in the new land; the birth of an American tradition – here, sport – and the determination to keep it pure and uncorrupted; and the more general morale-boosting theme of basic Americanism.

Knute Rockne opens in Voss, Norway, in 1892. Lars Rockne (John Qualen) tells his children about the land of opportunity: 'It's big enough for anything or anybody; that's why we're going there.' A montage of hopeful immigrants arriving to the strains of 'America the Beautiful' cuts to a dinner table in Chicago. Young Knute (John Sheffield) comes in and is shouted at for being late. Asked where he has been, he replies, 'Outside, playing the most wonderful game in the world: it's called football'. When his father remonstrates in Norwegian, young Knute corrects him. 'Poppa, don't talk Norwegian, talk American. We're all Americans now, especially me: I'm left end.' A further montage of Knute, now played by Pat O'Brien, shows him working as a postal clerk. Postmarks pass across the screen, bringing the year up to 1910. There is a conversation about going to college, a montage of shots of Notre Dame, ending with Rockne arriving with a suitcase. 'It took me six years of hard work to make enough money to get here,' he tells his room-mate Gus Dorais (Owen Davis Jr.). 'I didn't come here to play football, Dorais, but I might find a little time for it.' He does, of course, and shines both as an academic student and

The coach (Pat O'Brien) and his 'boys' in *Knute Rockne – All American*

as a football star. At the end of his freshman year, the President of the College surveys his achievements: 'Honour man in your class. Next year you'll be Captain of Football. That's a rare combination.'

Rockne's success closes the immigrant part of the story; his foreignness is never referred to again, nor do we see his family after he has entered Notre Dame. The film is now free to move on to the football. Football movies were no innovation for Warners; they had been producing them on low budgets on and off since *The Forward Pass* in 1929. Indeed, sports movies remained a staple of studio production throughout the decade, from the baseball films like *Elmer the Great* (1933) starring Joe E. Brown (a one-time professional ball-player) to medium-budget films like *Kid Galahad* (1937). But *Knute Rockne – All American* concentrates on sport to a far greater extent than do most of the other films. It documents Rockne's innovation with the forward pass with which Notre Dame (at any rate according to the film) came back to win against Army in 1913. And, in a typical sequence, it shows Rockne, now coach, developing the number-calling plays which have become a staple of American football. At the end of one season, he takes his 'boys' to a vaudeville house as a treat. While the students cheer the girls, Rockne looks thoughtful and begins to jot something on the back of an envelope. At home, he tries out his idea of signals-by-choreography with his wife, Bonnie (Gale Page), and two elderly professors, who are obliged to call out the sequence of numbers. Cut to a gym: footballers are moving resentfully to a piano accompaniment. The new routine is tried out to devastating effect on the field, to the sound of the sportscaster's voice-over ecstatically describing it as 'a symphony'.

Knute Rockne – All American is clearly determined to deliver the goods to football fans, but it aims to do more than that. Part of Rockne's dedication to the game has to do with its untarnished image. He angrily throws out a man who tries to place a bet on the outcome of a game with the words 'You've done your best to ruin baseball and horse-racing. This is one game that's clean and it's going to stay clean.' And he stresses the game's character-building potential. The game, he tells his boys, 'consists of teamwork: football is a place for clear minds'. And, in a passionate speech to a Washington committee investigating allegations of grade-fiddling for football stars, he enunciates the film's basic message. 'Games such as football are an absolute necessity to the nation's best interests,' he declares. 'Every red-blooded young man in any country is filled with the natural spirit of combat.' In Europe, this has led to war, but in the United States 'we've replaced it with football'. 'We're living in the twentieth century,' he warns. 'To limit a college education to books and laboratories is to give too narrow a meaning to education . . . The most dangerous thing in American life is that we're getting soft, inside and out.' Pat O'Brien's delivery of the speech, rising to the kind of belligerent zeal that was the actor's speciality, is a little piece of Americana in its own right.

It would be wrong, I think, to see the film as indicating a shift towards the right on the part of Warners at the end of the decade. It reaffirms the same belief in individual self-reliance and concern for fellow-Americans that characterised or at any rate underpinned the social conscience pictures of the early 1930s. But it does so, of course, in a very different social context. America, it suggests, is being threatened by the same cynicism (viz. the scene with the gambler, which reprises a number of 'crooked politician' scenes from the gangster movies) and the same indifference that had characterised the final Hoover years. Lest the more general lessons should be lost on the audience, the film is sandwiched between a Foreword and a funeral eulogy which point the necessary attitudes. 'The life of Knute Rockne,' declares the Foreword, 'is its own dedication to the Youth of America, and to the finest ideals of courage, character and sportsmanship for all the world. Knute Rockne was a vital force in moulding the spirit of modern America through the millions of young men and boys who loved and respected him, and who today are living by the high standards that he taught.' At the end, Notre Dame's Father Callahan (Donald Crisp) delivers a sermon from the cathedral pulpit, outlining Rockne's achievements and the influence he has had on generations of students. 'They're teaching his standards of clean living and sportsmanship to hundreds of thousands of American youths.' The film ends with a montage of teams and college pennants, and a shot of a ghostly Rockne superimposed on the Notre Dame field. The lessons were welcomed by the trade press – *Variety* described the film as 'an inspirational reminder of what this country stands for. And decidedly timely' – and apparently responded to by the audience. With this film Warners decisively entered a new phase, in which the lessons of Americanism had to be stressed if the country was not to fall prey to demagogy or indifference. One practical implication of these lessons was that America should enter the war in Europe.

A major element in the appeals to Americanism that characterise Warners' historical movies from *Knute Rockne* to *They Died With Their Boots On* is that they should be apolitical. This seems to have been a concomitant of the use of national history. Foreigners could become involved in political conflicts with their government or with prejudice. Americans who did so were likely to divide the audience, and this was to be avoided at all costs. Nowhere is this desire to be apolitical more striking – and more harmful – than in *Santa Fe Trail*. In terms of narrative, let alone political significance, it is hard to be quite sure what it is about. It is certainly not about building a railroad from Leavenworth to Santa Fe. The film tells a highly fictionalised story of two real West Point graduates, J.E.B. – 'Jeb' – Stuart (Errol Flynn) and George Custer (Ronald Reagan), on the eve of the Civil War. They are assigned to 'Bloody Kansas' where John Brown and his abolitionists are wreaking havoc. Brown, portrayed by Raymond Massey as a murderous fanatic with an almost permanently curled lip and a selection of the Bible's more vindictive phrases, is driven from Kansas and finally defeated at Harper's Ferry, Virginia. He dies prophesying war. Stuart gets the girl (Olivia De Havilland) and Custer gets the Secretary for War's daughter (Suzanne Carnahan).

In many respects, as *Variety* noted, the film looks like a formula action picture, but 'once it's established this isn't just another Injun yarn, *Santa Fe Trail* looks headed for top grosses and holdovers, with romantic angles further helping for the femme trade'. As a commercial gamble – if, indeed, there was any element of gambling in it – it seems to have paid off: *Santa Fe Trail* was one of the studio's top five films for 1940. It also represents a fairly clear attempt, as does *They Died With Their Boots On* the following year, to find roles for Errol Flynn outside the Merrie England pictures which had been his stock in trade since he first came to Warners. Attempts to star him in contemporary stories like *Green Light* and *Another Dawn* in 1937 had not been successful, and the American nineteenth century seems to have provided a useful staging point, enabling him to ride horses and confront principles, simplify issues and win the girl, much as he had done in the costume pictures. And this is very much how Michael Curtiz treats the material in *Santa Fe Trail*. Punished for being rebellious students (though, of course, first-class soldiers), Stuart and Custer receive the most dangerous first assignment possible – Kansas. We cut away to their smiles of pleasure: now the action can begin. And the two big action set pieces – the capture of one of Brown's wagon trains, in which rifles are hidden in cases marked 'Bibles'; and the rescue of Stuart from the town of Palmyra, 'cancer of Kansas' – are in the best Warners/Curtiz style. The former, with its stunt work around a runaway wagon, is particularly impressive.

Nevertheless, the issues which Stuart/Flynn smilingly confronts are difficult historical ones – slavery and the origins of the Civil War – which were still relevant to America in the 1930s, and no amount of evasion on the part of the screenplay can dispel a certain unease about their treatment. 'For anyone who has the slightest regard for the spirit – not to mention the facts – of American history,' wrote Bosley Crowther, 'it will prove exceedingly annoying.'[4] Even *Variety* conceded that 'some historians may find fault' with the film. To work as a Flynn vehicle, *Santa Fe Trail* needs a villain – a Sheriff of Nottingham figure. And John Brown is thus portrayed as a crazed fanatic, shot virtually throughout in harshly lit, low-angle close-ups, and ready to sacrifice his son at the drop of a Bible. Although some of the hatred is deflected on to Brown's sidekick, Rader (Van Heflin), a murderous psychopath who does things like adjusting his horse's bit so tightly that it bleeds at the mouth, Brown's ideas are never allowed to register as anything other than the extreme ranting of a demagogue. Discussion of them is forestalled by Stuart's gentlemanly assertion that 'the South will settle its own affairs, without loss of pride and without being forced into it by a bunch of fanatics'. After he has halted the runaway wagon, Custer is given a brief opportunity to question Stuart's confident position. 'Jeb, there's a purpose behind that madness,' he points out not unreasonably, 'one that can't easily be dismissed.' Stuart dismisses it: 'It isn't our job to decide who's right and who's wrong,' he retorts, 'any more than it is John Brown's.' 'I'm sorry, Jeb,' Custer concedes, 'you're right.'

It is not the only time that view is expressed. 'The traffic in political ideas is not the job of the United States Army,' General Robert E. Lee (Moroni Olsen) lectures the West Point students early in the film. But the philosophy of discipline without involvement or personal responsibility is hard to reconcile with either Stuart's own ideological certainty or the much more committed line found in other Warners films of the period. Released less than a year before America entered the war and replete with the usual appeals to Americanism – 'We are not yet a wealthy nation, except in spirit,' the cadets are told on graduation by Secretary of War Jefferson Davis (Erville Anderson) –

Santa Fe Trail is none the less one of the studio's most reactionary films of the decade. In this context, the interesting thing is that, even here, the studio was unable to avoid a certain commitment to social history. Robert Buckner's original screenplay, shaped by the studio in the usual way, did not have to put Stuart and Custer in quite such direct conflict with Brown. It could have opted for the more generalised conflicts of *Jezebel* (1938) or *The Old Maid* (1939), both of which have similar settings – or even of *Gone with the Wind* (1939), whose success may well have had something to do with the choice of period. But *Jezebel* and *The Old Maid* were both Davis vehicles. As a Flynn vehicle, *Santa Fe Trail* required an external issue rather than an inner conflict around which to create the possibilities for its male hero to engage in action. The dynamics of casting also had their ideology.

Sergeant York, which was in an advanced state of pre-production before *Santa Fe Trail* was released, could not be more of a contrast. It is the most directly interventionist film produced by Warners in the whole period between the outbreak of war in Europe and Pearl Harbor. Although it followed in the tradition of the studio's biopics – and was clearly seen as doing so by reviewers and public – it is, in other respects, not wholly typical of Warners' production methods. The package was brought to the studio by a veteran independent, Jesse L. Lasky, with a draft screenplay already completed; it was directed by a non-contract director, Howard Hawks, whose name appears on a card of its own immediately after the main title with the indication 'A Howard Hawks Production'; as with *Meet John Doe*, the top-billed stars, Gary Cooper and Walter Brennan, were both borrowed for the production; finally, the screenplay ironically anticipates modern-day credits at a time when the classic studio system was beginning to be replaced by a looser production framework.[5] *Sergeant York* is credited to no less than four writers: Harry Chandlee, who had done the preliminary investigation work with Lasky in Tennessee, including interviews with York himself; Abem Finkel, who had helped Chandlee and Lasky produce a draft screenplay from Chandlee's treatment; and studio writers Howard Koch and John Huston, who had 'polished up' the result.[6] Cooper was borrowed, after protracted negotiations, from Goldwyn for $150,000 in return for an option allowing Goldwyn to borrow Bette Davis for *The Little Foxes* for the same amount.

Neither of these arrangements – the deal with Lasky or the loan-outs – was problem-free, indicating the difficulties the studio had when it stepped outside its normal area of operation. Lasky's status at the studio and his continued involvement in the screenplay meant that the production sometimes came dangerously close to a hand-to-mouth situation. Two-and-a-half weeks into shooting, Unit Manager Eric Stacey sent Tenny Wright a despairing report. 'I have repeatedly been up to Mr Lasky asking for more script,' he complained, 'but don't seem to be getting anywhere. It is a very serious situation on a picture of this size that we are waiting for a script, or nearly so.'[7] Both Cooper and Hawks seem to have deviated from efficient studio practice in a way that confused the resident production staff. On the first day's shooting, Stacey reported to Wright, 'Mr Cooper reported a half-hour late, which is nothing unusual for Cooper, I can assure you'.[8] Hawks' determination to work at his own pace and under his own conditions did not much please Stacey either. 'Mr Hawks has been in the habit of providing tea and cake for his staff every day,' he reported, again after the first day's shooting. 'This was done today and much appreciated,' he adds defensively, 'and I can honestly say that no time was lost by so doing.' Hawks' hand was also detected in the script delays: Lasky and the writers did not, thought Stacey, want to send up pages of script because 'they want Hawks to look it over and are afraid to send it out without his approval since he will change it all anyway'.[9] Hawks was very quick and efficient on the dialogue scenes, but slowed down disastrously on the action, frequently changing angles and set-ups. Stacey sent Wright a whole catalogue of such changes on 24 March with the note: 'I am only listing these things on paper to show how difficult it is to get anything accomplished on this picture.' When weather put the production behind schedule, Hawks simply left to go to the Kentucky Derby, and the last day's shooting was directed by Vincent Sherman.[10]

All these problems, however, did not prevent *Sergeant York* from being the studio's main prestige production of 1941. It had a magnificent gala opening at the Astor Theatre in New York which 'the Sergeant' himself attended. The film was kept as a roadshow picture for almost as long as *A Midsummer Night's Dream* and fiercely protected from other forms of exploitation. An all-purpose memo from Jack Warner, dated 14 July 1941 (ten days after the premiere), declares, in Warnerese, 'So there will be no misunderstanding this note is to specifically inform all concerned that we will not permit the broadcasting of SERGEANT YORK in any form, shape or manner until I personally okay it, at a very later date'. The results of this special promotion seem to have paid off: *Sergeant York* was Warners' most successful picture of the year by far, winning an Oscar for Cooper – the studio's first Best Actor award since 1937 – and coming second in the *Film Daily* Poll, behind *Gone with the Wind*, of course, but by a surprisingly small margin of votes. By March 1942, it had grossed $3,999,215.

The story of *Sergeant York* is a piece of American folk history. Alvin York, a Tennessee farm boy who gave up hell-raising for fundamentalist religion, overcomes his pacifist principles to become America's most decorated soldier in World War I, single-handedly wiping out a machine-gun post and capturing 132 German prisoners. Coming home to a hero's welcome, he shuns the limelight and returns to a farm in the valley of the Three Forks of the Wolf near Jamestown, Tennessee, where he still lived when the film was made. Like *Knute Rockne – All American*, the film combines a slice of basic Americana with an up-to-the-minute appeal to the American conscience. Unlike *Rockne*, it does so in the explicit context of the war in Europe. Described in the official studio synopsis as 'a sturdy survivor of the pioneer age', York is portrayed in the first part of the film as a Good Old Boy, resisting the exhortations of Pastor Pile (Walter Brennan) to 'shake Satan off your shirt tail' with an even folksier refutation of the Pastor's already folksy argument. 'I ain't no bird, I ain't no squirrel,' he points out, 'and I sure ain't no bee.' He is a natural dead shot with a rifle, as demonstrated in a turkey shoot early in the film, and as explained to a dumbfounded sergeant on an army rifle range who assumes that all conscientious objectors are gun-shy weaklings. 'I never learned,' York tells him. 'Folks down home said I could shoot a rifle before I was weaned. Course, they was exaggerating some.' A direct parallel is drawn between down-home values and over-there heroism. York gets a bead on the German machine-gunners by making the same gobbling noise which made the turkeys break cover in the turkey shoot; after each shot, he calmly licks his gunsight, and mutters 'Just like a flock of turkeys' as he picks off the six Germans who charge him. An essential part of his heroism is his modest refusal to let his fame change him. He turns down offers from Hollywood, Ziegfeld and a breakfast food company with the words 'Things like that ain't for buying and selling'. Muttering 'I'm a-goin' home', he does just that, to an idyllic farm, arm-in-arm with his childhood sweetheart (Joan Leslie). By 1940, the Sergeant seemed more ready to buy and sell his exploits: his deal with Lasky and Warners gave him a $25,000 advance, $25,000 on release, and 4% of any gross over $3,000,000; 5% over $4,000,000; 6% over $6,000,000; and 8% over $9,000,000.

York's awareness of his own status is, of course, explicitly excluded from the studio's treatment of his life. In addition to celebrating his Americanism, the screenplay emphasises York's Christian principles and the way in which he overcame them to fight for his country. The conversion is a fine piece of country melodrama. When he is cheated out of a piece of land on which he has set his heart, York sets off through the rain on a vendetta against the man who has cheated him. A sudden bolt of lightning cleaves a tree beside him, kills his mule and splits his rifle in two. Heavenly music plays. York picks himself up and studies his mutilated gun, then heads for Pastor Pile's church, whose lighted windows shine through the rain. He walks up the aisle to the sound of the congregation singing 'Ole Time Religion' and is welcomed into the flock by Pile. We cut to him teaching a Sunday School class. Just as he reads the words 'Thou shalt not kill' to the children, a voice

Conversion to the cause: Sergeant York (Gary Cooper) seeks inspiration.
Opposite: the scene as shot in Burbank's Tennessee

is heard announcing that America has entered the war. Warners had lost none of their skill in making conflicts of ideas instantly – indeed crudely – legible.

Drafted into the Army because Pastor Pile's church is not registered as a sect opposed to the war, York argues the point with his commanding officer (Stanley Ridges), swapping Bible quotation for Bible quotation in a scene which preserves the first part of the film's style of affectionately sincere comedy. The commanding officer ends the argument by handing York a history of the United States, calling it 'a whole people's struggle for freedom'. York is given leave to go home to Tennessee and figure it out (not an approach to conscientious objectors for which the Army was noted). Sitting silhouetted against the sky in his favourite spot beneath Daniel Boone's tree, York spends the night thinking. A sound montage reprises his discussion with his commanding officer, with isolated words like 'country' and 'good' lending a spiritual quality to his moment of choice. When the light of dawn comes up, York has decided that it is his duty to 'render unto Caesar . . .'. There is no more directly inspirational moment in any Warners film of the period, not even the openly religious *Green Light*, and it is a measure of Hawks' success in establishing the character and tone of the film that the sequence appears striking rather than embarrassing.

212

The contemporary relevance of the story can have been lost on no one. Bosley Crowther, for instance, devoted the whole first paragraph of his *New York Times* review to it.

> At this time, when a great many people are thinking deep and sober thoughts about the possible involvement of our country in another deadly war, Warner Brothers and a bewildering multiplicity of collaborative producers and writers have reflected propitiously upon the motives and influences which inspired America's No. 1 hero in the last war. And in *Sergeant York*, which opened last night at the Astor, they have brought forth a simple and dignified screen biography of that famous Tennessee mountaineer who put aside his religious scruples against killing for what he felt was the better good of his country and the lasting benefit of mankind.

The promotional campaign stressed contemporary relevance to the virtual exclusion of all other angles. The Sergeant – almost everyone appears to have referred to him as such, 23 years after the end of the war – went on a special speaking tour. To an audience at Arlington on 30 May 1941, he declared: 'Liberty is not merely something the veterans inherited. Liberty is something they fought to keep.' He vigorously attacked right-wingers and non-interventionists like Lindbergh and Senator Wheeler. 'The Senator,' he said, 'ought to know

you can't protect yourself against bullets with an umbrella. We must give all our aid to England.' A studio promotional pamphlet, *The Private Lives of a Motion Picture* by Bill Rice, is equally explicit: 'That it comes to the screen at all is the result of World War Two's menacing threat to Democracy . . .' And the film's press book included a directly inspirational story about a young Brooklyn usher at the Astor, one Abe Hases, who had had his mind changed by the film even more than by what 'the big guys in Washington' had said. 'I talked to Sergeant York in the flesh,' he is quoted as saying, 'and you know he's just the kind of a guy who'd go straight to hell for what he thinks is right. So you begin to think quick that you might be under those bombs or at the other end of the bayonet. You say to yourself: "Sitting on your rear is kind of stupid with two-thirds of the world on fire and the edge of the flames beginning to lap at you."' Abe Hases undoubtedly existed, and his words were equally undoubtedly ghosted by a studio publicity writer. *Sergeant York* may not have been directly instrumental in getting many young Americans off their rears, but everything about the film – its timing, its tone and its promotion – indicate that that was what it was intended to help do. That, and make money.

They Died With Their Boots On, Warners' last historical sortie of the period, has none of *Sergeant York*'s explicit commitment. It is very much a companion piece to *Santa Fe Trail*, which it closely resembles in a number of respects. It picks up the character of Custer after the Civil War, transfers the role to Flynn, and splits the Reagan role of buddy between Arthur Kennedy and George P. Huntly Jr. There is the same wooing of an initially unattainable Olivia De Havilland; once won, she quickly falls into place as the same dutiful wife with the same premonitions of disaster. Charley Grapewin merges the comic relief roles played in *Santa Fe Trail* by Guinn 'Big Boy' Williams and Alan Hale. Though few of them are discussed here, the Flynn Westerns, after *Dodge City* (1939), *Virginia City* (1940) and *Santa Fe Trail*, had by now an established formula every bit as solid as the biopics and the Merrie England movies. Above all, *They Died With Their Boots On* shares with *Santa Fe Trail* a disregard for the facts of history and an emphasis on the importance of heroic action. As *Variety* put it, in a less philosophical variant of the arguments advanced justifying *The Story of Louis Pasteur*, 'the test of the yarn is not its accuracy but its speed and excitement'.[11]

Under Raoul Walsh's direction, the movie has more coherence than *Santa Fe Trail*. It takes Custer through West Point and the Civil War to his command of the Seventh Cavalry and it ends with Little Big Horn. The West Point scenes echo not only those of *Santa Fe Trail*, but also a string of service pictures made by Warners throughout the decade.[12] Custer rides into the Academy accompanied by a black servant and a pack of dogs, wearing an elaborate uniform modelled on that of Murat.

214

He is casual with his superior officers, who none the less admire him ('I kind of like that man,' remarks one after a particularly striking piece of insolence on Custer's part). 'If you ask me,' says the Commanding Officer, 'he'll have the worst record of any cadet at West Point since Ulysses S. Grant.' Inevitably, someone muses 'I wonder what happened to Grant'.

Ironies of that sort are fairly typical of the first half of the film. The news that Lee is advancing on Gettysburg is greeted with the remark, 'Now where in hell is Gettysburg?' The ironies are significant: to a far greater extent than *Santa Fe Trail*, the Custer biography in this film plays on the established values of American history, as *Juarez* had played on the established value of the name of Lincoln. In portraying Custer as a hero who understands the problems of the Indians and sacrifices his regiment at Little Big Horn to protect General Terry, it casts in the role of villains not the Indians – Custer 'respects' the honour and above all the horsemanship of Crazy Horse (Anthony Quinn) – but a more familiar demon from the early social conscience pictures: unscrupulous big business interests. As in Columbia's 1939 *Jesse James*, the real villains are the railroad companies. When Crazy Horse accuses the white men of breaking treaties, we cut to an insert of the treaty, and then to 'the Company' hatching its devilish plan to start a war by spreading rumours of gold in the Black Hills. This will produce a gold rush, violating Indian territory, provoking Indian attacks and thus necessitating the intervention of the Cavalry; the Indians will then be wiped out or moved on, and the Company can get the land it needs for the railroad. Custer can thus be absolved of all moral blame by being made a victim of economic progress, like the Indians who kill him. A title midway through the film prepares us for this: 'And so was born the 7th Cavalry, which cleared the plains for the ruthless advance of a civilisation that was the mortal enemy of the red race.'

Such considerations apart – and they are little more than a gloss on the main action of the film – *They Died With Their Boots On* is an action movie using known history as a patriotic emblem. The emphasis throughout is on a rousing depiction of American militarism. Even John Ford does not use the song 'We Shall Gather at the River' as consistently as Warners use 'Garryowen' here. It is first heard over the title announcing the formation of the 7th Cavalry; it plays as ghostly background when Custer is deprived of his command as a result of some 'legal skulduggery' by the Company; it plays over the film's best scene, as the 7th rides out to Little Big Horn in the half-light of dawn ('Where's the Regiment riding?' asks Arthur Kennedy. 'To hell, Sharp,' replies Custer. 'Or to glory: it depends on your point of view'); and it plays over the end title, as a ghostly Custer is superimposed on a shot of the 7th after Beth Custer (Olivia De Havilland) has succeeded in winning her husband's 'dearest wish': protection for the Indians. All Flynn's movies present an uncomplicated kind of individual heroism, in which both elements are important: the character's rugged individualism is the source of his unproblematic heroism. And the latter is typified here by the way Custer sets glory above money. 'There's one thing you can say about glory,' he declares at one of the film's low moments. 'You can take it with you when it's time to go.' Premiered six days after Pearl Harbor, the film follows in the wake of the American biographies of the decade's end, arguing for American honour and individualism to be allowed to find its true expression, away from the pressures of government and business corruption. Its details may be very different, but it is ideologically identical to *Knute Rockne – All American* and *Sergeant York*.

11 Epics and Other Prestige Productions

The small group of epic sagas and novel adaptations that Warners made in the 1930s was their least successful strain, both as films and (perhaps accordingly) from a commercial point of view. There were comparatively few of them. The six discussed in this chapter more or less constitute the list, the only other ones being *So Big* and *Scarlet Dawn* in 1932, *Babbitt* in 1934 and *Tovarich* in 1937. Their comparative failure reinforces the point that it was a combination of star vehicle and a narrative structure suited to studio production methods which accounted for the success of Paul Muni in the biopics and of Errol Flynn in the Merrie England pictures. Indeed, of the epics and novel adaptations, it seems to have been those which can be seen as vehicles – George Arliss in *Old English* (1930) and John Barrymore in *Moby Dick* (1930); to a lesser extent, Edward G. Robinson in *The Sea Wolf* (1941) – which were reasonably successful. The point, however, needs some qualification. Certainly, the most ambitious and least successful of the group, Pat O'Brien in *Oil for the Lamps of China* in 1935, seems to have been hampered by what *Variety* called its 'ordinary cast name strength' (i.e. absence of stars) and the studio's failure to get the script sorted out before shooting began: very untypically for Warners, thirty minutes were cut from the film after a preview.

The World Changes (1933), on the other hand, was a star vehicle of a kind: the central character is played from the age of eighteen to nearly eighty by Paul Muni. But it is the Muni of his early Warners years – of *Black Fury* and *Hi, Nellie!* – rather than the Muni who found his place in the biopics. If the frequently used distinction between an actor-impersonator and actor-star has any validity (the former changes with each part, the latter remains the same in all parts), then Muni was an impersonator. And it was not until the studio found a formula in which the entire weight of the film could be made to hinge on the impersonation that they were able to realise the actor's star potential. In *The World Changes*, this does not really happen. The other novel adaptation, *Anthony Adverse*, is something of a special case. It has already been looked at closely in a preceding chapter; and although its success may have had something to do with the policy of costume pictures which came in its wake, it is surely significant that none of them takes the same approach or draws on the same kind of material, either in source or in period. When Warners imported a non-contract star for a central role, it was almost always a sign that they were stepping outside their normal area – something further indicated by the fact that, in most such cases (*20,000 Years in Sing Sing*, *Meet John Doe*, *Sergeant York*), there was an element of outside production control or finance involved in the film.

The first two major novel adaptations of the decade opened within a week of one another in 1930, *Moby Dick* on 14 August at the Hollywood Theatre in New York, *Old English* on 21 August a few blocks away at the Warner. *Moby Dick* was one of five films that John Barrymore made for the studio. No prints seem to have survived of the first two, *General Crack* (1929) and *The Man from Blankleys* (1930), so I cannot really comment on them, other than to say that they were well received by both critics and public.[1] The remaining three films – *Moby Dick* (1930), *Svengali* and *The Mad Genius* (both 1931) – all provided ample opportunity for a bravura Barrymore performance (the latter two are extraordinarily similar) of the kind which did not really fit the studio's style and production methods. They have the rather leisurely structure of silent movies, not the economy of Warners' most typical and innovative films of the early 1930s. Like most studios, Warners inherited a number of stars from the silent period, or else acquired them as a result of the First National takeover. Very few of these actors survived the first three years of the new decade, either fading from view or transferring to other studios. The failure rate seems to have been much higher among actresses: Corinne Griffiths, Dorothy Mackaill, Billie Dove, Winnie Lightner, Constance Bennett and Marilyn Miller were all groomed for a stardom that never quite happened. Indeed, it is true to say that not until the middle of the decade, with Bette Davis and Olivia De Havilland, did Warners come up with a female star who really 'represented' the studio. Perhaps this was because the films they were making did not provide much opportunity for actresses; or perhaps they did not make that kind of film because they did not have the actresses. Bette Davis' early career, particularly her roles in *The Man Who Played God* and *Cabin in the Cotton* (both 1932), suggests a combination of the two explanations: they did not make the kinds of films best suited to the actresses they had.

But it was not only actresses who failed to make the transition from silent to sound film. Jack Mulhall, Alexander Gray and Douglas Fairbanks Jr are, along with Barrymore and Arliss, lead actors who disappear from starring roles at Warners after the early 1930s. The studio's two major stars of the first half of the decade, James Cagney and Edward G. Robinson, both achieved stardom in, and only in,

Warners talkies (though the latter had a reputable career on the stage). The Barrymore vehicles exploit both the actor's fondness for large-scale dramatic gestures and his ambition to be a kind of Douglas Fairbanks Sr – athletic, glamorous and irresistible to women. *Moby Dick* has elements of both these personae; it also has something of the silent feature about it, which is not all that surprising since Warners made a silent version of the story, *The Sea Beast*, also with Barrymore, in 1926. The screenplay takes predictable liberties with Melville's novel, focusing as much on the romantic relationship between Ahab and Faith Mapple (Joan Bennett) as on the quest for the whale. There is nothing metaphysical about Ahab's determination to kill Moby Dick; it is more a twisted vendetta occasioned by Faith's apparent rejection of him because of his peg leg. Having killed the white whale, he can return to the white girl: the two climaxes follow hard on one another's heels. From a shot of Ahab standing on the whale's back leaning on a harpoon as blood spurts up round him, we cut to a shot of Moby Dick being cut up by a group of singing sailors, then to a revived, clean-shaven, smartly dressed Ahab. Returned home, Ahab hobbles past the tavern, definitively rejecting the demon drink. There are close-ups of his stump preceding along the streets of the town as he approaches Faith's house. As always, she is sitting under a tree. The dog runs up to greet him. Faith cries out 'Ahab! Ahab!' and the film ends on a romantic two-shot and a sentimental exchange. 'Why, Ahab Creely, you're crying!' says Faith. 'So are you,' he retorts.

The extent to which *Moby Dick* was a vehicle for Barrymore can be seen from the opening sequences. As the ship docks, he is doing show-off acrobatics at the masthead for the benefit of the girls on the quayside. Then he throws his harpoon fair and square into the centre of a bucket on the deck, slides down a rope and swings ashore on another. He chucks one girl under the chin. 'How old are you?' he asks. 'I'll be eighteen next Tuesday,' she simpers. 'See you Wednesday,' grins Ahab. His wooing of Faith is similarly rambunctious. His first response to meeting her is to sing a little ditty: 'I like 'em white / I like 'em black / I like 'em pink or green./ That's the cutest little. . ./ That I have ever seen.' He follows her into church, taking a newly acquired canine friend with him. He sits next to a prim lady who has to sniff flowers to banish the smell of drink. There is a subjective shot of the pages of a hymn book going out of focus. At the end of the service, Ahab makes the dog hold up its paw to Faith – which, of course, wins her over. But the twisted, one-legged Ahab is very much a Barrymore role, too, standing wild-eyed on the bridge screaming, 'I'm still the Captain! Ha! Lucifer, star of the morning, be my skipper now!'

The film's other major selling point was its action sequences and special effects, the former projected on to a specially enlarged screen at the New York premiere. Although the whale allegedly cost the studio

$120,000, it is about as convincing as the dilapidated Jaws that assaults tourists on the Universal Studios Tour. In the first encounter, it tugs a model boat along like a water-skier; at the kill, Ahab is able to clamber on to its back and drive in his harpoon as though claiming it for the United States. What remains impressive, however – and what, according to Mordaunt Hall in the *New York Times*, 'caused more than one woman to cover her eyes with her program' at the premiere – is the handling of the gory details: the blood that fills the water as the whale mangles Ahab's leg, or that spurts up around Ahab in fountains as he finally kills it. And the amputation scene, complete with a shot of Barrymore screaming in agony as half-chewed food dribbles from his mouth, remains powerful even by modern standards of violent overkill.

Old English is devoid of violence, though no less morbid. Based on Galsworthy's novel *The Stoic*, it tells the story of old Sylvanus Heythorp (George Arliss), an octogenarian roué who commits suicide (on screen) by eating an over-rich meal so as to protect his illegitimate grand-daughter from ruin. The details of why this should be necessary involve the kind of business deal in which Galsworthy delighted. But what is interesting is that the film should deal in a straightforward, even light-hearted way with issues like suicide and illegitimacy (in the same context, it is worth noting that whores figure quite openly in *Moby Dick*, and the word 'brothel' is spoken by Ahab). The basic respectability of *Old English* appears to have been guaranteed by Arliss' presence in it (as, perhaps, was that of *Moby Dick* by Barrymore's). The film was a prestige production for up-market audiences, and the comments of *Variety* are interesting in this respect. Noting that the film would probably do more business at $2 than at 50¢ a ticket (i.e. as a roadshow rather than on release), the review goes on:

> Warner Brothers may take a loss on Arliss, with *Disraeli* or *English* or both, or as they probably did with *Green Goddess*,[2] but meanwhile the film industry immeasurably profits. That comes through Arliss. He's a greater uplift to the screen than he has been to the stage, for the stage is centuries old and has held some great actors. But none greater than George Arliss. As those stage personators have come down through posterity and legend, so will the name of Arliss live in the theatre of all time . . . and maybe Warners will make money with this picture. They deserve to.

Warners' promotion of George Arliss is a corrective to our tendency to view the studio in the early 1930s as a producer of realist, socially conscious pictures. They were also concerned with establishing them-selves as a major on the wider market, and the Arliss vehicles were an important part of that strategy. *Old English* is very much an Arliss vehicle. Directed, like *Disraeli*, by Alfred E. Green, its primary – if not exclusive – aim is to showcase the actor. His introduction carries the same build-up as in *Disraeli* and *Voltaire*; there are the same long, silent 'curtain-line' shots,[3] and there is any number of opportunities for extended Arliss business. The screenplay provides him with ample occasion for stagey delivery. Reprimanded by his elderly, hatchet-faced daughter (Ethel Griffies) for his adolescent behaviour with the line 'Anyone would think you were 40 instead of over 80', Heythorp retorts, 'Not if they saw you!' He reminisces about Jenny Lind, Edmund Kean and the days of his youth with a wistfully melodramatic, 'Great days, all gone!' It is the death scene, however, which provides the vintage Arliss moment – a twelve-minute sequence of glorious ham. He consumes his magnificent meal, but has his brandy taken away from him by his daughter. He staggers to his feet – the only time he does so unaided in the entire film – muttering 'Last night to call me soul me own', then totters over to the bottle. When he tries to pick it up, he finds that the feeling has gone from his hands. He bangs them on the table, claps them, still feels nothing, then staggers back to his easy chair with the bottle balanced on them. He manages to pour himself a drink, downs it, then mutters, 'What's this? Red?' He passes his hands in front of his eyes, and realises he can no longer see. 'Oh, red,' he remarks calmly. 'Tomorrow, tomorrow . . .' He sinks into immobility and there is a slow fade. It is a scene on a level with Barrymore's suicide in *Grand Hotel* (1932), down to the pool of light round Heythorp's chair which isolates it from the rest of the room.

The only other real example of a bravura performance by a star in a novel adaptation among Warners' movies of the period is that by Edward G. Robinson as Wolf Larsen in *The Sea Wolf* ten years later. The two films book-end the decade, their differences perhaps less important than their similarities, the most important being the bid for literary respectability which remained a feature of studio production policy. *The Sea Wolf* was not an enormous success, probably because of the unsuitability of Jack London's tale for the Warners method and of Robert Rossen's inflated screenplay. The film seems to be the outcome of a determination to find a prestige vehicle for Edward G. Robinson, an actor whose style only really accorded with that of the studio when he was playing the fast-talking, aggressive modern roles – in *Little Caesar* and *Five Star Final* – which he had come to detest. His performance in *The Sea Wolf* is impressive and fascinating without being particularly satisfying. Indeed, both the *Variety* and the *New York Times* reviewers accuse him of overacting. The problem with *The Sea Wolf* is that it is almost two distinct films: a Michael Curtiz action movie with shipwrecks, violent fights and a sadistic, larger-than-life central character; and an attempt, in Rossen's screenplay, to portray the complexity of Larsen's character, making him his own victim in the same way that others are victims of his actions. Robinson plays a man

221

who is both a sadist and an emotional cripple, but the screenplay does not really reconcile the two roles. In effect, the film splits into two casts, with Robinson commuting between them. He persecutes the drunken Dr Louie (Gene Lockhart), who finally commits suicide by throwing himself from the mast; makes use of the one-dimensionally villainous Cookie (Barry Fitzgerald); and confronts the rebellious Leach (John Garfield). Then, in long, analytical and rather literary dialogue scenes, he argues metaphysics with the shanghaied novelist Humphrey Van Weyden (Alexander Knox).

Michael Curtiz is very much at home with the action sequences. The sinking of the ferryboat in San Francisco harbour which results in Ruth Webster (Ida Lupino) and Van Weyden becoming passengers aboard Larsen's *Ghost* is impressive, even if Bosley Crowther did find fault with the rather too obvious use of the studio tank. But Curtiz is less at home with the dialogue scenes. *The Sea Wolf* in its 1941 version (there had been two previous movie adaptations, one in 1914 and one in 1931) is very much a product of its age: it tries to introduce the moral despair of the *film noir* into a novel to which it was reasonably suited, but into a genre of film into which it fitted much less happily. The presence of John Garfield as George Leach particularly emphasises the problem. He opens and closes the film, entering a San Francisco bar at the start and telling a man who tries to pick his pocket, 'If you find anything in there, I'll share it with you', and escaping the shipwreck with Ruth in the final shot. His rebelliousness, which leads to an abortive mutiny attempt, seems strangely anachronistic – all Garfield moodiness and pre-Method intensity – as does his fatalist acceptance that he will die in the locked cabin as *The Ghost* goes down ('O.K., I'll drown. My number was up the moment I came on board. I knew it').

The doomed loser – as played by Bogart in *High Sierra* or Garfield himself in *Four Daughters* (1938) – seems out of place on the high seas in 1900. Larsen's own fatalism – a copy of *Paradise Lost* pulled from his bookshelf by Van Weyden has underlined the passage 'Better to reign in Hell than serve in Heaven' – belongs to a different age. Barrymore's Ahab could be redeemed by love, at any rate on the screen; such redemption is explicitly denied *High Sierra's* Roy Earl, and that of George Leach in *The Sea Wolf* is far from convincing. Robinson's Larsen, however, sits between the two – a philosophical tyrant ('I had it all figured out,' he howls as his plans fail: 'I *can't* be wrong!'), and a pathetic figure, wanting to be understood by at least one man (Van Weyden). Throughout the decade, Warners had perfected a style – of scripting, production and even performance – which enabled them to deal with complex issues through a kind of narrative shorthand: the crises of Pasteur, the dilemmas of Juarez, the commitment finally made by Cagney in *Frisco Kid* or *Angels with Dirty Faces*. But when, in *The Sea Wolf*, it became necessary for the issues to be spelled out, as they are in the long scenes in which Van Weyden reads Larsen his 'description' of the Captain, there is a sense of uneasiness. Van Weyden's language is too literary – it is, after all, basically that of London the novelist, whom he represents – and the points being made are not always clear. By 1941, Warners' prestige productions could no longer operate in the kind of ideological vacuum which characterised *Old English* and *Moby Dick*. The trends of the past four or five years, in which contemporary issues had found their way even into the Merrie England pictures, and in which narrative method had been perfected, leave *The Sea Wolf* strangely bereft of impact, either as an action drama or as a psychological study.[4]

Some of the problems with the film are anticipated in the three epic sagas of the middle of the decade, *The World Changes*, *Oil for the Lamps of China* and *Anthony Adverse*, all of which show the studio's style and production methods at variance with intractable material. Warners' problems with *Anthony Adverse* have already been discussed at length in an earlier chapter, but most of them seem to have stemmed from the fact that the studio was dealing with the kind of project that was not part of its normal output, but towards which it was trying to move in the second half of the decade.

Anthony Adverse has many of the hallmarks of a Warners movie of the 1930s, especially a compression of narrative details into a series of instantly legible shots. At the start, for instance, Don Luis tells Maria that he is to have treatment for his impotence – though the word itself is never used – 'in order that you may have a husband who is a husband, not just an invalid'. Maria looks wistfully at a painting of the Madonna and Child. After Don Luis has gone, the camera tracks into a close-up of Maria praying in front of the candlelit shrine. 'Denis, dear Denis,' she exclaims. 'Oh, merciful Mother, help me to forget him.' The shot ends on a luminous profile of Anita Louise; cut to a shot of Denis standing moodily in a window, with matching lighting. Later, as they plan to elope, we cut immediately to a low angle of Don Luis prancing round the hall, declaiming 'Your husband is complete again!' There are the usual montage sequences, like the rows of business ledgers in Bonnyfeather's office, with the dates on their spines indicating the passage of time. And there is the eloquent fluidity of Mervyn LeRoy's camera in the ending, as Anthony and his son set sail for the New World in search of 'peace of mind', the camera taking off in a long, circular crane movement round the poop deck of the ship, ending on a shot framing Anthony, his son and the Stars and Stripes. But the film also has its moments of leaden pretentiousness, earnestly signposting its literary origins. There is the recurrent image of the Madonna, which so worried Joseph I. Breen; there are trick shots like the reflection of Don Luis in Denis' wine glass which heralds the duel; there are the Hervey Allen-style intertitles such as 'He dealt in slaves, and became a slave to his own power' and 'Sick in mind and body, Anthony found no comfort from the growing torment within him'; and there is Pedro de Cordoba's ethereal Brother François, who acts as Anthony's conscience during his African 'season in hell'.

One thing *Anthony Adverse* emphatically does not have, however, is direct relevance to its contemporary audience. It is a costume drama whose ideological significance lies in its narrative structure (the hero as cipher to the world) and in its emphatic statement that life's problems are to be solved on a personal and spiritual level. The foundling child navigates a strictly personal course through life's reefs, abandoning the slave trade for personal reasons rather than attempting to abolish it, and refusing to involve himself in the issues of Napoleon's empire. His exchange with the dying Brother François, an active campaigner against slavery, exemplifies the movie. 'You are dying,' Anthony tells him. 'No, Anthony,' replies Brother François, 'it is you who are dying, not I.' The death of the spirit, in other words, particularly the hero's spirit, is a worse death than that of the body (compare Custer's words about money and glory in *They Died With Their Boots On*[5]). By Warners' standards, *Anthony Adverse* is a somewhat reactionary movie – an MGM picture in more than just style.

The same is not true of the other two sagas of mid-decade, both of which attempt to engage with complex issues of personal and social responsibility, but both of which run into structural problems. *The World Changes* is not actually drawn from a novel – it is based on an original story by studio writer Sheridan Gibney with the inspirational title *America Kneels*, turned into a screenplay by another contract writer, Edward Chodorov – but it has all the scope and ambition of an Edna Ferber epic. Like *Knute Rockne – All American*, it is an attempt to encapsulate the American experience, but on a much grander scale. It tells the story of Orin Nordholm Jr (Paul Muni). Born on a wagon train in the Dakota Territory in 1856, Orin grows up on a frontier farm, but seeks wider horizons. With advice from Buffalo Bill Cody (Douglass Dumbrille), he opens up the Chisholm Trail from Texas to Abilene and goes into partnership with a Chicago meat tycoon, James Claflin (Guy Kibbee). Orin marries Claflin's daughter, Virginia (Mary Astor), takes over the business when Claflin dies and becomes a multi-millionaire.

The second section of the story concentrates on Nordholm's family life, which is little short of disastrous. Virginia is an inflexible snob who despises the meat business and, with it, Orin. She attempts to keep her sons away from it, to bring them up as cultured young gentlemen, and to arrange socially prestigious marriages for them. Under the pressures of conflict between Orin and her ambitions, she collapses and dies, for which Orin's sons (Donald Cook and Gordon Westcott) blame him. They go on to become the sons their mother had hoped for, growing prosperous as stockbrokers while Orin subsides into retirement. The sons, however, are ruined by the 1929 Crash, and Orin devotes his fortune to restoring the name of Nordholm. His mother Anna (Aline MacMahon), now over ninety, arrives from the Dakotas and takes Orin III (William Janney) back, along with Selma Petersen II (Jean Muir), granddaughter of Orin's childhood sweetheart. Orin himself dies after discovering that his son has committed suicide and that his daughter-in-law is planning to run off with her lover.

The closing scenes of the film – the Crash, Anna's trip to New York (as she drives from the station, we hear newsboys in the street announcing the stock market collapse); the marriage between Orin's granddaughter Natalie (Patricia Ellis) and a ludicrous English baron (Alan Mowbray) interested only in her money who runs off when he hears of the family's ruin – tip dangerously close to melodrama, but the film as a whole is an ambitious and interesting attempt to trace seventy years of American history and to reaffirm certain of the basic values which appear to have been undermined in the modern world. Indeed, *The World Changes* was, until quite recently, regularly shown in American high school history classes, more or less as a documentary.[6] Seventy years of history, taking in the frontier, the growth of American capitalism, its collapse and the possibilities of a rebirth (an affirmation of faith rather than a statement of fact for a film released just after Roosevelt's election) are too much to handle in 90 minutes; and the earnest tone of the movie denied it major box-office success. 'It's a film that won't appeal to the hotsy-totsy type of fan,' wrote *Variety*, 'but the parents will bring the youngsters, which should sort of balance things.' The terseness of narrative style which had been evolved in the crime pictures and which would be perfected in the biopics goes some way towards holding the whole thing together. It is unmistakably a Warners picture, linked by montages which fill the gaps in the narrative: a spinning globe (which also appears behind the credits) and shots of a town street, Indians riding, a telegraph key and a railroad train (1867 to 1877); the globe, a train, a hot air balloon, paddle steamers and cars (1893 to 1904); globe, cars, planes, racing cars at Indianapolis and a modern liner (up to 1929). The opening sequence is also pure Warners. A title, 'Dakota Territory, 1856'. Long shot of a plain. Medium shot of Orin Sr (Henry O'Neill) leading a covered wagon, with chickens on the side and a cow trailing along behind. Cut to a medium shot of Anna, tossing and turning in the wagon. She calls, 'Orin! Orin!' He stops the wagon and helps her from it. She kneels on the ground, hugely pregnant, claws at the dirt, feels it and shows it approvingly to Orin Sr. 'Praise God,' she says. 'Here may we live and prosper and may our baby be strong!' Then she turns towards her husband, begging, 'Hold me, Orin!' The second time she calls out his name it turns into a cry. The camera tilts up to the sky and then down again to the sound of hammering. Orin Jr is now a year old, Anna is chopping wood and their farm-house is almost built.

The almost mystical tone of the relationship between people and land is one that the remainder of the movie will attempt to preserve. But its major focus – a surprisingly complex one – is the conflict between the simple pioneer spirit of the Nordholms, and Orin's development of it into the world of business. Essentially, his drive destroys his home life, helps him build the country, is perverted by greed on the part of his sons, and is finally reconciled with the honour and simplicity of the pioneers in the closing sequences: business is not essentially good, but it *is* essential. Anna's early reproach – 'Money! That's all you ever dream of!' – is too simple, but it seems borne out by Orin's disastrous marriage to Virginia, entered into more out of ambition than love. Virginia's collapse into madness is dealt with in a typical scene of overlapping crisis. Orin has just returned from the stock market where, by the skin of his teeth, he has saved his empire. He collapses, exhausted, on to his bed. The door opens, and in comes a wild-eyed, wild-haired, spectral Virginia. 'Butcher! Butcher!' she screams, raises her arms above her head, collapses and dies.

But Gibney's story and Chodorov's screenplay are at pains to establish Orin as a man of honest vision, not a scheming businessman. He knows his trade better than his workers: he wanders the stock yard dispensing advice, telling a man not to wear a black hat in summer, another how to cut a rib, another to wash the floor daily with ammonia, and wades up to his thighs into a pool of overflow water, pointing out the flecks of fat which indicate that part of the animal is still being wasted. His pioneering efforts with refrigeration cars – like Adam Trask with his lettuce in *East of Eden* – are contrasted with the narrow conservatism of the bankers. 'It's an ingenious idea,' one sneers, 'but just a little bit nebulous.' His near ruin is brought about by a combine of businessmen whose motives are selfish, not economic: 'He's coming ahead too fast,' they decide; 'he's got to be stopped.' To the banker (Arthur Hohl) who refuses him finance for the refrigeration cars, he says: 'If I only had a heart like yours, Patten, I'd use it to freeze meat with.'

Orin is portrayed throughout as a simple American, whose rugged individualism is channelled into capitalism. He is contemptuous of his son's Oxford education (as we are encouraged to be when the boy comes out with 'I say, mater, let me have a few pounds'). Orin finally rounds on Virginia for her 'foolishness and waste and stupid, petty snobbery'. His simple American values are reasserted near the end when he meets Natalie's betrothed, one Sir Philip Ivor, Bart. The marriage, it is revealed, has been arranged by Orin's son John in return for a fishing lodge in Scotland. Sir Philip breezes into Orin's club and confidently introduces himself. 'Natalie is one of the choicest feminine bits I've seen,' he confides, 'and I've been everywhere.' Orin response is curt and immediate: 'Go away!'

The World Changes appeals, not always subtly, to a whole string of basic American beliefs – the value of hard work, the superiority of the United States over the effete Old World, the threat to capitalism from its unacceptable face of corruption and greed – in preparation for the affirmation of the end. Old Anna arrives in New York and finds herself surrounded by descendants she has never seen. 'What do you do?' she asks one. 'Well, let me see . . .' he begins uncomfortably. 'Nothing,' Orin replies for him. Anna turns to Sir Philip with the same question. He leaves, muttering 'You'll forgive me, but . . .' 'Leeches! Liars! Fools! Thieves!' bursts out Orin, and LeRoy gives us a similarly rhythmic close-up of each member of the younger generation to emphasise the point. When the stock market collapses, Anna's belief in the value of real work is reaffirmed: 'I knew this was wrong: it had to be. There's no pride in it, no satisfaction.' When the wedding ceremony is disrupted by the absence of the groom (he has fled) and the bride's father (he has committed suicide beneath the double blow of his financial ruin and his wife's infidelity – personal crisis again being linked to history), Orin goes upstairs and discovers his son's body. As he looks down at it, the body changes into that of Virginia and back again. He staggers down the hallway towards the stairhead,

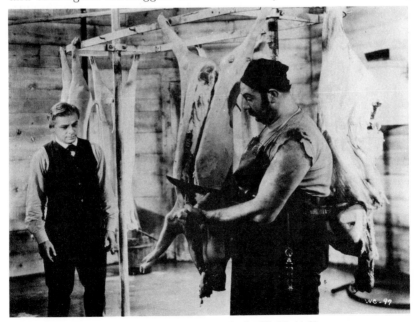

Learning his trade: Paul Muni as Orin Nordholm in *The World Changes*

227

while the film flashes back to the Dakota scenes, to Orin as a baby and to his encounter as a young man with Cody. Finally, it flashes back to Virginia. Orin has negotiated the stairs, but collapses and dies on the bottom step. The film ends with old Anna, Orin III and Selma II repeating the prayer she had said with Orin Sr at the opening. Anna looks out to the town of Orinville, and recalls the prairie as it was when she first arrived: empty. She smiles. End title. More fully than any other Warners movie, *The World Changes* offers a metaphor for the American experience of the Depression, showing its roots in the perversion of business practice into speculation, and its solution in the honest business principles of Orin, who tells Orin III that he will 'buy back the name of Nordholm for you, and give it to you free and clear'. Like the crime movies, the film has a strong element of metaphor, above all in Orin's family. But its shortcoming is dramatic: it is too sprawling for the metaphor to have the same impact as in the crime movies.

The only other time Warners were to try this kind of business saga was two years later, in *Oil for the Lamps of China*. Again directed by Mervyn LeRoy, the film is based on a best-selling novel by Alice Tisdale Hobart – a fact signalled by the time-honoured device of pages turning behind the credits, and occasional inserts of the printed page in place of the montages of *The World Changes*. But where the original novel was a violent indictment of the paternalist attitude of the Atlantis Oil Company, both towards its employees and towards the people of China, the film is hampered by the need to assert the basic honesty of American business methods and of American imperialism in general. Stephen Chase (Pat O'Brien) is sent to China 'to dispel the darkness of centuries and instil the light of a new era'. Also to make profits for Atlantis. 'I want you to remember,' he is told, 'that the Company always takes care of its own.' Stephen's experience is rather different. He has the patent for an oil lamp he has designed stolen from him by someone at head office; his wife loses her child because company business obliges him to be away while she is in labour; and when he rescues company funds from a band of marauding Communists, his only reward is to be demoted. In the end, the Company comes through. A telephone call from New York ensures that Stephen is restored to his proper position and the film, unlike the book, ends happily.

No film demonstrates the ideological contradictions of Warners in the 1930s – and, for that matter, of the New Deal – more clearly than does *Oil for the Lamps of China*. Rather than show the Company itself as being heartless, uncaring and profit-dominated, Laird Doyle's screenplay finds its villains in individual executives. An opening disclaimer denies all possibility of an attack on the oil industry, declaring 'The oil business was chosen because light has always been symbolic of progress'. Chase is persecuted by his new boss, McCargar (Donald

Crisp), who sends him to the desolate storage outpost of Kin Nang, airily dismissing his wife's pregnancy: 'Your wife's not the company's problem, the tanks are. I'm not offering you the post, I'm ordering you.' At a later posting, Chase is confronted with Communism, portrayed as a bunch of Oriental gangsters who drive round in fast cars overturning the donkey carts of innocent peasants. He manages to smuggle out the company's funds to Shanghai and becomes a hero, but his promised promotion is blocked by another corrupt executive, Hartford (Henry O'Neill), who demotes him to a clerk's job in the hope that he will resign and thereby save the Company from having to pay him a pension. Chase is saved after a dramatic insert in which Shanghai telephone operators are shown putting through a call to New York. ('It's so obvious,' Hartford's boss tells him angrily. 'I can't understand why you didn't give it to him before.') It is as though FDR himself had stepped out of the garage shadows at the end of *I Am a Fugitive from a Chain Gang* and restored Paul Muni to his rightful position in society.

As though to compensate for its compromise on the question of business ethics, *Oil for the Lamps of China* deals with the question of married relationships more fully than any other film of the decade. Chase's marriage to his wife Hester (Josephine Hutchinson) is a contract, freely entered into by both of them when Chase's fiancée fails to turn up on the boat that brings Hester. She is alone, her father having died en route. 'What I'm proposing,' suggests Chase, 'is a partnership. You contribute a home, I'll protect it.' 'I think I can be useful and happy with you,' Hester finally decides. The very ordinary nature of their arrangement – extraordinary only in the sense that it is articulated – is profoundly modified when Hester loses her baby because 'you have a brass plaque on your soul belonging to the Company'.[7] She finally agrees to remain with him on her own terms. 'I've found something that will keep me yours always,' she tells him. 'I'm part of you, but you aren't part of me. That's marriage.' 'I don't understand,' says Chase. 'No man would,' replies Hester.

Oil for the Lamps of China is an interesting oddity for three basic reasons. First because, even after the disastrous preview, the film still managed to do good enough business to put it in the studio's top ten films of the year and was promoted in such a way as to win a place on *Film Daily*'s Honor Roll with a respectable 64 votes, ahead of Warners' own *Black Fury* and Fox's *The Little Colonel*. A movie on which time and effort had been expended could, within the studio system, recoup its costs even if the studio was unhappy with it. Secondly, the problems Warners experienced with the screenplay were very similar to those encountered on *Anthony Adverse* the following year: the different structures and complexity of a best-selling novel were less suited to the streamlined production set-up at Warners than they were, perhaps, to other studios, and adaptations of major novels or stage successes constitute a comparatively small proportion of the studio's output during the 1930s. Finally, the studio's ideological position, reflecting and contained within the ideology of the New Deal itself, made it necessary for contemporary social problems to be treated by means of a suitably indirect metaphor. For a variety of reasons, the studio's economic and organisational history predisposed it towards an acceptance rather than any fundamental falsification of the reality of America in the 1930s. But the element of metaphor was essential: the use of a gangster setting as a metaphor for the corruption of American ideals; the use of the foreign biopics as a metaphor for the American spirit and dedication to ideals of progress through individual initiative. The direct confrontation of the problems of the business world, however, even in the comparatively metaphorical setting of China, posed more problems than the system or its narrative practices could satisfactorily resolve.

The three remaining films to be dealt with in this chapter are of less interest from the point of view of this book, since each is a prestige production designed to achieve a specific market objective. *Show of Shows*, premiered at the Winter Garden in New York on 20 November 1929 (where, according to the *New York Times*, mounted police controlled the crowd 'in none-too-polite tones'), is nothing more or less than a stage review of the kind produced by most major studios to herald the advent of sound.[8] Warners' effort comes complete with a vaudeville master of ceremonies (Frank Fay), addressing an imaginary audience and apparently ad-libbing on camera. To a modern viewer, the experience seems interminable: the film runs well over two hours, consisting of sixteen separate numbers (one of which, with Nick Lucas and Myrna Loy, was cut at an early stage and is missing from surviving prints), most of which are in Technicolor (though, again, surviving prints are monochrome). The entire roster of studio stars, with the notable exception of George Arliss, puts in an appearance, from John Barrymore (whose voice is heard here for the first time on film) doing a Shakespeare soliloquy, to Rin Tin Tin who barks a message to the moviegoer.

There are, perhaps, a couple of things worth noting about *Show of Shows*. The first is the presence of Georges Carpentier, the boxer (who appeared in one other picture for the studio[9]). Here, he sings a song made up entirely of boxing metaphors ('I used to lick a man who was nearly twice my size,/ But I have no defence at all against a pair of beautiful eyes'), and dances an 'Elimination Contest for the Champion of Love' with Alice White and Patsy Ruth Miller. The second is the extraordinarily geometrical drill-routine choreography of Larry Ceballos and Jack Haskell, from which Busby Berkeley was soon to rescue the studio. The film, which cost $800,000 (most of which it is tempting to imagine being spent on staircases for the dance numbers), was not particularly successful, and was roundly condemned in *Variety*: 'Reason for the reckless use of footage appears to be the studio's disinclination to hold the chorus numbers down. Practically all are way overboard on time, finale of the picture being the worst offender in running at least 1,000 feet and appearing endless. Result is that the numbers build to a point and then linger to taper off.' 'It's like a fast backfield with a weak front line,' *Variety* concluded, 'or a big stage benefit with too much show.'

In 1929, Warners' chief aim was to establish themselves as a major studio, not as a major studio producing a particular kind of film. Over the next five years, they recorded a profit only once (in 1930), and between 1931 and 1934 ran up recorded losses of over $30,000,000 (though this was, of course, offset by massive assets), before creeping back into profit in 1935 with a surplus of $764,158. Under these conditions, it is inevitable that they should have concentrated on economical 'realist' movies (though the simple equation between financial difficulties and style of film-making is not one that can be taken too far: there were other reasons, which have already been discussed). But by 1935, the social climate was changing and, with it, the studio's financial position and its production philosophy. Though the change did not really reach the mainstream of Warners production until the following year (with *Anthony Adverse* and the beginning of the biopics), the 1935 production of *A Midsummer Night's Dream* can clearly be seen as a flagship for the change, while the following year's *Green Pastures* is a less spectacular reaffirmation of their determination to hold on to their share of the 'respectable' market.

A Midsummer Night's Dream was a lavish re-creation of an already lavish production of Shakespeare's play performed at the Hollywood Bowl under the direction of Max Reinhardt in the summer of 1934. The two major hits of the Bowl production – Olivia De Havilland, a newcomer, as Hermia and Mickey Rooney as Puck – were brought in for the movie, which was nominally directed by Reinhardt, although his credited co-director (and former pupil) William Dieterle apparently did most of the actual work on set. The fact that much of the studio's publicity for the film deals in statistics is significant. As well as being a prestige production, the *Dream* was also extremely expensive and, since this went outside the normal run of studio practice, it was inevitable that the fact should be used for all it was worth. The statistics themselves are impressive: a 70-day shooting schedule; three sound stages used simultaneously, with a ramp built out of one of them to extend the playing area over the props and costume workshops; 85 miles of exposed film.

The results, almost inevitably, were striking rather than truly successful. The Nijinska ballets do have a magical quality about them,

231

particularly the one early on where the mist gradually solidifies into dancing figures, but they are rarely less than a (35mm) reel – ten or eleven minutes – in length. The performances of the mechanicals are a matter of taste. To Andre Sennwald of the *New York Times*, Joe E. Brown was superb as Flute while James Cagney tended to overact as Bottom; I would put it exactly the other way round, though I might modify the epithet 'superb'. There is a lack of consistency between the young male leads (Dick Powell and Ross Alexander) and the young female leads (Jean Muir and Olivia De Havilland), the former relentlessly jolly, the latter frequently adopting a kind of sing-song delivery. And Mickey Rooney as Puck is alternately engaging because of the young star's permanent combination of freshness and profess-ionalism, and irritating because the camera seems to linger interminably on his animal noises and grimaces.

None of this, however, matters much in the final analysis. *A Midsummer Night's Dream* was designed to be an epoch-making event and, by the time it was finally released – simultaneously in New York and London on 9 October 1935; a day later in Paris, Vienna and Sydney; and with a gala opening at the Warners Theatre in Beverly Hills the following week – there was little chance that it would be anything else. A poem penned by the Publicity Department but not, apparently, used suggests the sort of approach Warners *might* have made to marketing the movie:

In Elizabethan times,
Though they were well equipped with rimes,
They didn't have the fine art
Of staging scenes, bizarre, immense,
Of Warners' sheer magnificence,
Directed by a Reinhardt.

But the studio in fact adopted a very discreet campaign, stressing Reinhardt's reputation, the authenticity of the research done for the film, the fidelity to the text and the commitment of all concerned to Shakespearian culture. And it was in those terms that the film was received. 'If this is no masterpiece,' wrote Andre Sennwald, 'it is a brave, beautiful and interesting effort to subdue the most difficult of Shakespeare's works . . . It is a credit to Warner Brothers and to the motion picture industry.'[10]

A Midsummer Night's Dream was not merely Warners' bid for respectability: it was released at a time when the industry as a whole was straining for respectability shortly after the introduction of the Production Code. In this context, it may well be that reactions from that fringe area between the industry and the general public are the most accurate gauge of the project's success. 'DEAR JACK', said a cable received after a studio preview, 'MY CONGRATULATIONS TO YOU MIDSUMMER NIGHTS DREAM IS THE MOST BEAUTIFUL PICTURE I HAVE EVER SEEN IT COMES THE NEAREST TO PERFECTION OF ANY MOTION PICTURE YET PRODUCED THANK YOU FOR LETTING ME SEE IT I AM SO HAPPY FOR YOU THAT THE FIRST SUCCESSFUL SHAKES-PERIAN PICTURE SHOULD BE PRODUCED BY WARNER BROTHERS MY BEST REGARDS LOUELLA O PARSONS.' Even more significant is a letter written by the head of the MPPDA himself, Will Hays, in reply to an enthusiastic letter from the President of the Shakespeare Association of America:

> I note with thanks your letter of September 17th. I believe, as you do, that the production of 'A Midsummer Night's Dream' marks an outstanding achievement in the progress of the screen and, may I add, a new epoch in the popular and universal appreciation of Shakespeare.
> ... the event is a challenge to that public opinion which has demanded the greatest possible entertainment, the best possible literature, and the highest artistry from the motion picture screen. The production of 'A Midsummer Night's Dream' is an event of major importance not only to the motion picture industry but to all those who have cooperated and are now helping in the better picture movement in the United States.[11]

A Midsummer Night's Dream did not, of course, spark off a Shakespeare cycle of any kind, at Warners or anywhere else. Reinhardt was at one stage supposed to do a second picture for Warner Brothers but nothing came of the plan: the company's respectability established, the impetus of prestige production moved elsewhere. The nearest thing to a sequel produced at Warners was the adaptation of Marc Connelly's stage hit, *The Green Pastures*, the following year. Here, according to Thomas Cripps,[12] the original commitment to a lavish production was considerably scaled down and the film ends up, as *Variety* put it, 'not big in the spec sense – it's impressive on its secular, homely appeal without being religious in the Sunday-school sense'. Like *A Midsummer Night's Dream*, *The Green Pastures* is an interesting example of a studio experiment without any real follow-up. It did moderately well, though managing only a two-week run in each of its first-run locations. It was the studio's last real attempt to re-create a Broadway success – unless one counts the very different *Tovarich* (1937) – and in retrospect the fact that the play had an all-black cast and is set in an all-black heaven seems almost irrelevant. *The Green Pastures* was already a stage success, and the $800,000 budget was the result of that success, not the play's subject. Like most studios in the 1930s, Warners produced a number of films like those discussed in this chapter, in which the established criteria of artistic respectability were imported into the movies to prove that Hollywood, too, could be respectable. Inevitably, the films bear the Warners stamp. But it is often obscured by a rather deadening effort to be culturally proper. The studio's real innovations in the large-scale feature lay elsewhere – in the biopics and in the Merrie England films.

12 Merrie England

Along with the gangster movies, the social conscience pictures and the Busby Berkeley musicals – a heterogeneous bunch – the Merrie England films are probably Warners' most recognisable product from the 1930s. There were not, however, all that many of them. Even if one includes *The Prince and the Pauper* (1937), where the usual elements of romance and action are reduced to a minimum, there were only six films in this category, from *Captain Blood* in 1935, which looks in retrospect to be a kind of pilot, to *The Sea Hawk* in 1940. After that, Errol Flynn spent the next five years appearing almost exclusively in war movies, and his only return to anything like the Merrie England format was to a sad aftershock, *The Adventures of Don Juan* in 1949. Nor are the six films devoted to a single historical period. *The Adventures of Robin Hood* is set in a romanticised version of the reign of Richard the Lionheart as perceived from 1938; *The Prince and the Pauper* is set at the end of the reign of Henry VIII; *The Private Lives of Elizabeth and Essex* (1939) and *The Sea Hawk* in the reign of Elizabeth; *Captain Blood* in the Civil War period and *The Charge of the Light Brigade* (1936) in the middle of the nineteenth century.

But the films do have many features in common and, in the wake of *Captain Blood*, are clearly part of a similar market strategy. They all star Errol Flynn; and, in four of the six, Olivia De Havilland is his co-star (though in *Elizabeth and Essex* her name is relegated to below the title). Flynn, who was Australian, was publicised by the studio as being Irish and, in the six films, was able to use his distinctly unAmerican accent to advantage. Five of the films were directed by Michael Curtiz, *The Prince and the Pauper* being the work of William Keighley, whom Curtiz replaced on *The Adventures of Robin Hood*. It is in theme, however, that the greatest similarities between the six films are to be found. In all six, Flynn plays the kind of character already discussed in relation to *Santa Fe Trail* and *They Died With Their Boots On* (which, of course, postdate the Merrie England cycle): a man for whom moral and political decisions are unambiguous, and who is provided with the chance to put these decisions into practice through direct physical action. Only once – in *The Private Lives of Elizabeth and Essex*, by far the most complex and ambitious film of the cycle – is this course of action unsuccessful: Essex is beheaded. The way in which the Flynn character evolves from

Captain Blood to *The Sea Hawk* is significant, as is the fact that the studio failed to find any other successful showcase for his talents over the same period. Flynn becomes the least problematic embodiment of Warners' philosophy of individual morality, reflected more ambiguously in Paul Muni's biographical impersonations and James Cagney's contemporary struggles between selfishness and social conscience. Both the individualism and the morality of the Flynn character are important: the guarantee of the former lies in the fact that he is unquestionably doing the 'right thing'. Flynn's Merrie England roles shade easily into his wartime roles, up to and including *Objective Burma* (1945), where a similar attempt is made to establish the heroic acts of an individual as both the core of the narrative and the bearer of the film's ideology.

The second thematic link between the six films arises directly out of this first point, and is, if anything, more significant. In all the films, Flynn becomes the more or less persecuted and isolated defender of a legitimate, benevolent authority which is threatened with usurpation or subversion.[1] In *Captain Blood* and *The Sea Hawk*, he is a gentleman pirate devoted to the interests of the King/Queen, whose power is threatened by scheming courtiers. In *The Prince and the Pauper* and *The Private Lives of Elizabeth and Essex*, he exposes plots to undermine the monarchy by self-seeking noblemen and restores legitimate authority, if not to its true course, at any rate to an awareness of what that course should be; to do so, he has to go outside the law. In *The Adventures of Robin Hood*, he becomes an outlaw in defence of the true monarch, while in *The Charge of the Light Brigade* he disobeys orders and, as a result of the Charge, restores the honour of his regiment and 'changes the course of the war'. The model is not all that different from the one found in some of the early crime movies, where the gangster hero observes a code of honour lacking both in his gangland rivals and in the social system which has forced him into crime in the first place by denying him the possibility of advancement elsewhere. It is above all significant that, in every one of the Merrie England movies, the character played by Errol Flynn ends up on the wrong side of the law, fighting his countrymen in the form of corrupt politicians and their sadistic henchmen – the same perverted forms of authority that feature in the social conscience films. He is restored to legitimacy at the end of the film (even if posthumously, as in *The Charge of the Light Brigade*; or in the eyes of the movie audience alone, as in *The Private Lives of Elizabeth and Essex*). More importantly, it is the legitimate authority, not the Flynn character, which gains most from the restoration. Errol Flynn is the conscience of the Merrie England pictures, the embodiment of an action-based morality which is that of the frontier adapted metaphorically to the political context of Roosevelt's second term.

Captain Blood, premiered at the New York Strand on Christmas Day

1935, is a part of the shift towards more prestigious projects by the studio in the middle of the decade, but is in other respects a somewhat tentative film. It is a large-budget picture, but without the extravagant action scenes or the sumptuous sets which are a staple of later films in the cycle. The major expenditure was on the final sea battle, and many of the opening scenes bear unmistakable signs of economy. The marquee values – stars – are slight. Errol Flynn had appeared in only two films – as a corpse in *The Case of the Curious Bride* and in two brief scenes in *Don't Bet on Blondes*, both in 1935 – while Olivia De Havilland, imported from the stage production of *A Midsummer Night's Dream*, was, with two co-starring roles,[2] scarcely better established. But Warners do not seem to have regarded the picture, once completed, as a gamble: their opening of it in the middle of the holiday period – Christmas Day in New York, New Year's Day elsewhere in the country – proves that. The film's hero, Peter Blood, is a victim of misunderstanding and corruption after the quelling of Monmouth's rebellion and is trans- ported to the West Indies. There he is brutally treated by a vindictive Governor (Lionel Atwill), but saved from worse punishment by the intervention of the Governor's high-spirited niece (Olivia De Havil- land). Blood leads a slaves' revolt and saves Port Royal from destruction by capturing the Spanish galleon which is attacking the town. With his crew of freed slaves, he lives the life of a noble pirate aboard the captured galleon until, in recognition of his services, he and his crew are sworn into the King's navy by a duly enlightened King James.

The opening of the film is desperately slow: Warners have yet to adapt the economy of the contemporary films to the costume pictures. And, barring the odd sado-masochistic insert of treadmills, branding and whipping carried out by the dastardly 'other side', it is not until the climactic and rightly famous sea battle – all explosions, stunts, falling spars and flashing swords – that the style of the cycle is definitively established. Another weakness in *Captain Blood* which is ironed out in subsequent movies is the way in which the resolution – Blood's restoration – appears something of a tacked-on coda: rather 'ten-twent-thirt' (i.e. better suited to the grind houses), thought *Variety*. Nevertheless, *Captain Blood* has all the features of later films in the cycle, perhaps best represented in the scene of the slaves' revolt, where Blood's first act is to save the town from attack rather than, as one might have expected, to join in: once again, the outlaw is the true upholder of law. A society which expels a Blood (or a Robin Hood or a Sea Hawk) is a society which has temporarily lost sight of its true values.

The Charge of the Light Brigade is on a much grander scale. It is, wrote *Variety*, 'an elaborate, nicely geared thrill picture that is calculated for the big box office where properly ballyhooed'. More than properly ballyhooed, the film was indeed big box office, and did much to consolidate Warners' commitment to Errol Flynn costume epics. It is not a film that concerns itself greatly with issues: the villainous Surat Khan (C. Henry Gordon) is so black (in both senses of the word), massacring women and children and plotting nefariously with the Russians, that the question of moral right hardly arises. But the film does stress once again the equation between an impulsive, action-based individual viewpoint – what the film repeatedly identifies as a question of honour – and the correct course of action in a given historical context. Mere political (and even strategic) considerations are clearly secondary.

Despite its title, *The Charge of the Light Brigade* spends a good two-thirds of its running time in India, only moving to the Crimea for the dramatic resolution of both action and theme. Captain – later Major – Geoffrey Vickers (Errol Flynn), while serving in India with the 27th Cavalry (the 'Light Brigade'), saves the life of Surat Khan of Suristan during a leopard hunt. The potentate vows a debt of gratitude; later, when in league with the Russians, Surat Khan spares Vickers during an attack on the garrison at Chukhoti, while most of the rest of the troops are wiped out. Vickers determines to have his revenge, and the famous charge at Balaclava enables him to exact it. Surat Khan is watching from what he foolishly imagines to be the safety of the Russian lines, and Vickers is able to reach and kill him. In Michael Jacoby and Rowland Leigh's screenplay, the Charge of the Light Brigade becomes a personal vendetta. Flynn's eyes light up when the General tells him that Surat Khan is with the Russians at Sebastopol; before leading the Charge, he exhorts his men with an emotional speech, ending with the words 'Men of the 27th, our objective is Surat Khan! Forward!'

The major thematic link between *The Charge of the Light Brigade* and the other Merrie England pictures is that Vickers has to falsify military orders for the Charge to take place. The idea of a charge is rejected by the generals in command: 'Your plan is admirably daring, but it's too wild.' Vickers is given an order for the Light Brigade to retreat, which he is to deliver personally. He sits and stares at the map, on to which his discovery of the Chukhoti massacre is superimposed; then he forges a new order. In the best Warners tradition, his decision turns out to be the correct one. In a kind of coda, there is a final valedictory superimposition of Tennyson's poem over a tattered Union Jack fluttering in the breeze, together with a headline assuring us that 'Charge turns tide of war'. Sir Charles Macefield (Henry Stephenson) looks at the letter sent by Vickers, accepting sole responsibility for the Charge, then burns it and raises his glass to propose a toast 'for conspicuous gallantry'.

Faced with the absence of any real emotional opposition to Vickers' position, the screenplay has to introduce the character of his brother, Captain Perry Vickers (Patric Knowles), who is both his rival for the hand of Olivia De Havilland and the representative of a policy of appeasement. Appeasement is given very little chance, with the same line of dialogue – 'You're not with the diplomatic service now: you're with my regiment at the front. You'll obey my orders' – repeated almost verbatim on two occasions: by Colonel Campbell (Donald Crisp) to Perry when he suggests negotiations with Surat Khan, and by Geoffrey to his brother when the latter argues against the Charge. This dual function for the character of Perry, romantic and political, while fairly irresistible dramatically, is not without problems when it comes to motivation. It is sometimes hard to see why Olivia De Havilland should initially prefer the diplomat to the hero. But she undergoes a kind of conversion, which parallels that expected of the audience: 'Tell Perry,' she says archly to Geoffrey in their final encounter, 'that I think his brother is the finest man I've ever known.' A track into close-up emphasises the point, as it had her true allegiance – to honour (Geoffrey) above romantic infatuation (Perry) – earlier in the film.

It is probably a little too early, in 1936, to see this round condemnation of appeasement as having any wider political significance in the context of events in Europe. But what seems beyond doubt is that the commitment to an action movie has, as in the later Flynn epics, a broader ideological significance: men following their instinctive sense of honour are more likely to take the right decision than men demeaning themselves in political intrigue ('Take your dirty intrigue out of here,' Geoffrey tells Perry early in the movie). Action is right, intrigue is wrong – a Hollywood philosophy intrinsic to the kind of narrative produced by the studio system at its peak. And *The Charge of the Light Brigade* is very much an action movie. It capitalises on the buddy-buddy relationship between Flynn and David Niven, best exploited in the 1938 *Dawn Patrol*. Sent off on a dangerous mission from Chukhoti which will result in his death, Niven hands his watch to Flynn so that it can be passed on to his family 'just in case'. 'Looks a pretty cheap one,' remarks Flynn, playing down the emotion but intensifying the camaraderie; 'does it go?' 'If you wind it,' replies Niven, and rides off to his death. In the action sequences, notably the attack on Chukhoti, Olivia De Havilland plays the same nobly supportive role that will be hers in *Santa Fe Trail* and *They Died With Their Boots On*: while Vickers organises the defences, she marshals the women, children and natives. And any doubts about right and wrong are buried, as they are intended to be, beneath the bravura of the ten-minute charge scene, a wonderfully orchestrated combination of superimposed Tennyson, extreme long shots of the valley, long shots of the front rank, close-ups of the principals, tracking shots in front of and beside charging horses, high angles of the carnage created by the

Russian artillery, and stunt shots of men falling from their horses and rolling straight into the camera. One is inevitably reminded of Joan Blondell's remark about Michael Curtiz: 'a cruel man with actors and animals'[3] (though he shared responsibility for the charge with 2nd unit director B. Reeves – 'Breezy' – Eason). Even more so, one comes out of it all convinced that Hollywood elaborated its ideological statements through action far more than through discussion and dialogue.

The Prince and the Pauper, released eight months later in June 1937, is more a romp than an action movie, but it places Flynn in his by now familiar position of upholder of true values against the entrenched positions of intrigue. The story, of course, is based on a tale by Mark Twain, one of the most sophisticated early spokesmen for straightforward Americanism, and the screen adaptation is fairly accurate, with one crucial change: in keeping with the theme of honour versus intrigue, the misunderstanding which leads to the substitution of the pauper Tom Canty for Prince Edward is complicated by having the Earl of Hartford (Claude Rains) privy to the fact and bent on exploiting it for his own selfish ends. But theme alone is not enough: *The Prince and the Pauper* was the least successful of the Merrie England films. The reasons are, perhaps, those outlined by *Variety* with its usual vigour:

> Produced with sincerity and lavishness, the film is a long gamble because it is a costume picture minus any romance whatsoever. The commercial aspect seems wholly concerned in the timeliness of a Coronation sequence and the name of Errol Flynn. It is not enough . . . Production values, photography and sound are up to standard, but it doesn't seem that William Keighley, in his direction, has captured sufficient sympathy for the two youngsters to compensate for the romantic loss in having no fiancee for Flynn. The fragile plot scarcely holds together a full length screen play. Audiences will likely want to believe it could happen, but the actuality of the screen turns fancy into reality. For some reason the bigger the scenes and the more elaborate the composition photography, the less convincing it becomes.

Despite Frank S. Nugent's lukewarm praise – he found the film 'likeable', 'affectionate' and 'gently humorous'[4] – *The Prince and the Pauper* seems to have been more designed to exploit potential audience interest in the Coronation of Edward VIII than to respond to any other market force. Flynn, as the soldier of fortune Miles Hendon, makes his entrance thirty-five minutes into the film and is secondary to the plot, though instantly recognisable as the Errol Flynn of the Merrie England pictures. At the end, he turns down an offer of the Captainship of the Royal Guard because 'my trade is soldiering'. Elsewhere, the confusion engendered by the mistaken identity – much enhanced by the casting of the Mauch Twins in their only major starring roles – is played basically for laughs. Prince Edward is mockingly crowned with a bucket in Offal Court, while Tom Canty causes consternation by using the Great Seal to crack nuts and by drinking the bowl of washing water brought to him by a string of elderly lords in waiting. Once or twice the populism that Warners shared with Twain breaks through. Tom refuses to sign a proclamation for a window tax – 'Why, that's taxing sunshine!' – and Edward, restored to the throne, abolishes a number of bad laws with the words 'My Dad – that is, the late King – told me to use the Great Seal sparingly in making laws'. All things considered, however, *The Prince and the Pauper* – which fades out with the two twins together, Edward remarking to Tom that the Great Seal '*is* good for cracking nuts, isn't it?' – may reinforce the formula for Warners costume dramas but does little to develop it.

If *The Prince and the Pauper* marked time, Warners' next Merrie England picture, *The Adventures of Robin Hood*, was a triumph – critically, at the box-office and as the definitive movie of the cycle. It is virtually the studio's only feature from the 1930s to retain its power over a general, as opposed to a specialised, modern audience. It is, as Rudy Behlmer points out in his introduction to the Wisconsin screenplay,[5] very much a product of its time: it is hard to imagine just how it might have been if it had been made, as originally planned, with James Cagney in the title role or even, as it would have been if he had not got badly behind schedule, when directed by William Keighley. As it is, *Robin Hood* is the peak of achievement for both Errol Flynn and Michael Curtiz. Although much of what has been said here about Warners' production methods has played down the importance of the individual director, there is little point in denying Curtiz's stamp on *The Adventures of Robin Hood*. 'I consider him at the very top of directors,' says Hal Wallis.[6] 'I think he was way ahead of his time. When I see the camera work and what he added to a picture, it was worth any problems in so far as schedules and budget were concerned. He would elaborate; he would contribute something.' Admittedly, this was said some forty years after the event, and there is a good deal of contemporary evidence that budget and schedule problems were a major source of conflict between Curtiz and production executives.[7]

Perhaps the crucial thing about *The Adventures of Robin Hood* is that, because it shows the system operating at maximum efficiency, both in the sense of exactly capturing audience requirements and in the sense of providing the perfect framework for the skills of producer (Wallis), director (Curtiz), writers (Raine and Miller), art director (Weyl), composer (Korngold) and star (Flynn), the film seems effortless. Clearly it was not effortless, but the fact that it seems so is the result of a production system on which all the apprenticeships had been served.

Weyl's monumental sets are validated by Curtiz and Polito's awesomely smooth crane shots and tracks, and by the combination of great sweeps of orchestrated movement with sudden stasis – Robin swinging on a creeper to confront Sir Guy (Basil Rathbone), the Sheriff (Melville Cooper) and Marian (Olivia De Havilland); the choreography of the final fight. Elsewhere, Curtiz's fondness for expressionistic lighting and composition give the film its key moments. In the trial of Marian, the misleadingly messy composition – a crowded long shot – is suddenly given focus as the camera cranes down on her in her silver dress amidst the sombre surroundings of the castle. And the final revelation of King Richard (Ian Hunter) is a similar moment of bravura: the drab monk's robe is suddenly flung back to reveal the magnificent, lion-emblazoned costume.

Warners' early use of Technicolor on *Robin Hood* obviously enhances its visual quality, and if I have emphasised that quality more strongly than in other films so far discussed, it is because the film's impact relies more on its sumptuousness than on its action, however finely choreographed that action may be. If in *The Charge of the Light Brigade* the action is the vehicle for the morality, in *The Adventures of Robin Hood* the spectacle is the guarantee of the vaguely populist message. One fact pointed out by Behlmer is particularly significant here: the early draft of the screenplay by Rowland Leigh (who had co-scripted *The Charge of the Light Brigade*) made Robin a yeoman rather than a nobleman, presumably because the film was at that stage a Cagney project.[8] The shift to Robin the noble outlaw (and, of course, to Flynn) is a clear indication of the move towards a greater conservatism on the part of Warners in the second half of the decade: though right and wrong remain the same, the hero replaces the little man in fighting for right. In *The Adventures of Robin Hood*, the Merry Men, once each has been introduced in a vignette scene, become anonymous aides to the central heroic individual, and the peasants, once they have been used to teach Marian a lesson in social responsibility, become rubber-stamp guarantees for the same individual, reduced to crying 'God bless you, Sir Robin!' The reference in *Variety* – presumably ironical – to 'Robin Hood and his Sherwood Forest gangsters' only makes the shift more obvious.

The shift from action to spectacle between *Captain Blood* and *The Adventures of Robin Hood* is significant. The heroes portrayed by Errol Flynn may still have to fight for their honour from time to time, but to a considerable extent they are now allowed merely to embody it, as of right. For the first time in Warners' Merrie England pictures, the more disturbing elements of populism – particularly the idea of a quasi-superhuman champion – begin to emerge. If anything, the penultimate film of the cycle, *The Private Lives of Elizabeth and Essex*, intensifies the shift, reducing action to a minimum (a few scenes in darkest Ireland, which resembles a Florida swamp more than a peat bog), increasing the spectacle, and focusing the interest on the conflict between the two stars, Flynn and Bette Davis. But *The Private Lives of Elizabeth and Essex* is not really in the mainstream of the Merrie England pictures. It is, in the first place, far more Bette Davis' film than Errol Flynn's, the outcome of a running battle with the studio for roles which she felt suited her better. It is, at any rate in intent, a major performance, though it did not win her an Oscar nomination (she received one that year anyway, for her less grandiloquent but finer performance in *Dark Victory*).

Davis' Elizabeth is a combination of make-up and mannerisms, held together by the intensity that she managed, in her heyday with the studio, to bring to all her roles. Significantly, she is introduced into the film with the same reverential build-up accorded to Muni in *Juarez*. In her first scene, she is hidden behind a screen, identifiable only by her voice and her shadow on the wall as she prepares to receive Essex (Flynn). The reception begins by showing us Essex, whom we have already seen in procession to the Tower. The visual rhetoric, familiar from *Robin Hood* and to a lesser extent from *The Prince and the Pauper*, is the camera equivalent to the script economy of the biopics, except that here it is designed to slow down – to stress – rather than to speed up, to contribute to the feeling of pomp and spectacle rather than to the breathless dramatisation of issues. The sequence opens on a shot of a heraldic crest (as the film had opened on a mock heraldic version of the Warner Brothers logo), then the camera pans down to a massive door with soldiers on either side. The door opens, and men with their backs to the camera bow and draw aside. As Essex enters, the camera tracks away in front of him, behind him, and alongside him. Only then is Bette Davis introduced, through a camera movement similar to that at the beginning of the scene, which somehow equates the actress with the set: a close-up of a fleur-de-lys on her costume, then a slow tilt upwards to a slight low angle of the Queen.

As in *The Adventures of Robin Hood*, the syntax of shot dominates the film, testifying to a shift from theme to spectacle, indicating that the Merrie England cycle, like the biopics with *The Story of Dr Ehrlich's Magic Bullet* and *A Dispatch from Reuters*, had reached a kind of stagnation. Indeed, the parallel atrophy of the two cycles perhaps indicates that, by the end of the 1930s, Warner Brothers as a whole had settled down to a comfortable output of formula pictures, the reverse image of the achievements of the studio system earlier in the decade, robbed of the social tensions that had produced the most striking films, and to some extent reflecting the complacency of the United States in the middle of Roosevelt's second term.

Norman Reilly Raine and Aeneas MacKenzie's screenplay is based on a 1930 play written for the Theatre Guild by Maxwell Anderson,

243

with Lynn Fontanne and Alfred Lunt in the main roles. Anderson's poetic language has been considerably toned down for the film, but the staginess remains, both in the lack of action and in the corresponding complexity of the relationship between Elizabeth and Essex: character, in other words, replaces action. Elizabeth loves Essex, a man considerably her junior, and is loved by him in return, but suspects that he wants to usurp her throne. Essex, on the other hand, bridles at being commanded by a woman, and is kept in constant uncertainty as to whether he is talking to a lover or a monarch. In the end, they come into political conflict over a disastrous Irish campaign, and Elizabeth has Essex executed, to her own cost but for the good of England. Anderson's language dominates many of the exchanges, as for example when Elizabeth bemoans her lot to Sir Francis Bacon (Donald Crisp): 'Oh, Bacon, I am only a woman! Must I carry the weight and agony of the world alone?'

Beneath the heightened dialogue, however, lurk some familiar Merrie England themes. Where Anderson located the conflict firmly in the principal characters, making their respective roles the prime cause, the movie's screenplay intensifies it through the machinations of two scheming courtiers, Sir Robert Cecil (Henry Daniell) and Sir Walter Raleigh (Vincent Price) – 'Yellow, squeaking rats who only show their teeth when frightened,' as Essex calls them. Essex, as his triumphant return from Cadiz at the film's opening shows, is the true upholder of England – the fighting man of honour – even if he finds himself put in the wrong by the court. To emphasise the point, we cut from his triumphal procession to Cecil and co. plotting: 'Something has to be done to tarnish him, or she'll be sharing England's throne with him.' The rather minor character played by Olivia De Havilland, Lady Penelope Gray, is recruited into the same conflict – in love with Essex, jealous of Elizabeth, and aiding the plotters.

But in the end it is visual rhetoric that dominates, becoming self-sufficient and rather contradicting the established belief that the Hollywood camera is wholly narrative-controlled. Here, the narrative is itself subject to the rhetoric of spectacle – something which, by the end of the Merrie England cycle, carries its own ideological significance. No scene makes this clearer than the final interview between Elizabeth and Essex, before the latter's execution. It takes place in a long, arched room furnished only with a throne at one end, where Elizabeth sits, and lit by a window which looks out over the courtyard where the gallows has been built. The entrance is via a huge trapdoor in the floor, through which Essex leaves at the end of the interview, condemned to death by a reluctant Queen. The scene is primarily legible, not through the dialogue exchanges, but through the visual syntax which covers Essex's execution and Elizabeth's reaction to it. As Essex leaves the room, Elizabeth suddenly gets to her feet.

Merrie England: Bette Davis and Errol Flynn in *The Private Lives of Elizabeth and Essex*

'Robert!' she cries. 'Take my throne, take England! She's yours!' Essex doesn't stop. Elizabeth lowers herself sideways into her seat. Cut to a shot of the courtyard ready for the execution, then back to a long shot of Elizabeth from the left – her left – with the window in the centre of the frame. Cut to a tracking shot of Essex crossing the courtyard, then a high-angle long shot of the courtyard, and a low-angle medium shot of Essex as he turns at the top of the scaffold steps. Cut into a low-angle close shot: Essex looks up, kisses the ring Elizabeth has given him, and says 'I'm ready'. Cut to a long shot of Elizabeth as before, which then tracks in towards her at the sound of a drum roll: Essex has been executed. Cut to the window, pan right and track in fast to a close shot of Elizabeth. Cut to a long shot straight down the room, from the position from which Essex left. End title. The sequence, without any dialogue or, after the very beginning, any eye contact between Elizabeth and Essex, tells us more about the separate worlds they live in, the strong emotional bond of their relationship, and the impossibility of that bond bridging the separation between the two worlds, than any dialogue scene. And it does so, as in the best scenes in *The Adventures of Robin Hood*, through the articulation of space – of setting and decor – rather than through what we more usually understand by the *mise en scène* of performers. The effect is no less 'dramatic' than the narrative shorthand of the biopics, reducing the conflicts and issues of

245

the Merrie England cycle – the relationship between the individualistic hero and the structures of authority – to a kind of stylised confrontation in which words have become redundant.

The final movie in the Merrie England cycle, *The Sea Hawk*, also involves Good Queen Bess – this time played by Flora Robson as a testy old lady – and, like *Captain Blood*, has Errol Flynn in the role of a noble pirate, Francis Thorpe, who plunders the Spaniard for booty to help the English crown, and who is, finally, instrumental in saving his country from the Armada. Released in September 1940, *The Sea Hawk* is almost entirely formulary, and even includes hints of generic self-parody (Thorpe's first audience with his Queen is built up rather like Essex's entry into Elizabeth's court, but it is not Flynn who swaggers through the door: instead, it is his pet monkey who scuttles round it, to general embarrassed merriment). As before, the elements are: an honest monarch who is misled by scheming courtiers; the outlaw and man of action with an unwavering loyalty to Queen and country; the woman (Brenda Marshall) whose allegiance shifts from the plotters to whom she is tied by blood to the man of action whose nobility she recognises; an outside enemy against whom the honourable are united; and a series of action scenes which test the bravery and signal the commitment of the man of action.

The structure of the narrative is also familiar. *The Sea Hawk* opens with scenes of naval action in which Flynn captures a Spanish galleon. Returning home, he is confronted with two problems which require action of different kinds: the British coffers are severely depleted, and the unity of the court is being undermined by Lord Wolfingham (Henry Daniell, the sinister Cecil of *Elizabeth and Essex*). Wolfingham's goal is 'a monarch friendly to the interest of Spain on the English throne'. 'Yourself?' enquires the Spanish Ambassador (Claude Rains – a piece of casting designed to dispel any doubts about the dishonourable intentions of Spain). 'Yes,' replies Wolfingham unequivocally, indicating that naked self-interest overwhelms any genuine political motive. Flynn sets off for Panama on an almost disastrous mission to capture Spanish gold, and Wolfingham persuades the Queen that the Sea Hawks should all be arrested. Flynn returns in time to save England, Elizabeth and the treasury. Thus the structure is action/ problem/ action/ resolution, the action sequences filmed with Curtiz's usual efficiency, the intrigue scenes set in the by now familiar massive sets, where open space becomes a signifier of importance for the issues at stake, while the staging isolates the noble individuals (Thorpe and the Queen) from the knots of scheming courtiers. The relative morality of the two sides is defined through a crude polarisation. The 'hell' of a Spanish galley with its giant of a drummer beating merciless time is contrasted with Thorpe's ship, surging through the water to a romantic Korngold score, with happy sailors chatting and laughing on deck. In the first battle, 'one lone cannonball out of a whole broadside' from the Spaniards passes harmlessly through Thorpe's sail, while the Sea Hawk's return fire is deadly accurate. Later in the film, when Thorpe is taken prisoner, we see him chained to an oar in the galley, with a dead man chained to the oar next to him. When the galley is captured, the same oarsmen – minus, of course, the dead man – set off for England, singing happily. The final guarantee of the superiority of the Sea Hawks is provided by Doña Maria (Brenda Marshall), who discovers that 'I'm at least as much English as Spanish, maybe more', and switches sides.

The Sea Hawk is a good deal more action-centred than *The Private Lives of Elizabeth and Essex*, and makes much less use of the visual rhetoric discussed above, though the open spaces of the English court, the Spanish inquisition and the castle chamber in which Thorpe fights Wolfingham conform to the established practice. *Variety* felt that the intrigue scenes were 'expendable' and 'tiresome' and that this would account for 'a profitable – but not generally socko – voyage through the box office'. But the date of the film is significant. 'Count on the Warners to inject a note of contemporary significance,' remarked Bosley Crowther in the *New York Times*, in the course of a review that is otherwise written almost entirely in pastiche Sabbatini. England threatened by the treacherous might of Spain is a clear parallel to England threatened by the Third Reich, as Elizabeth's closing speech – more to the camera than to the court – makes clear: 'When the ruthless determination of one man threatens to engulf the world, it is the duty of all free men . . .' etc.

There are, I think, three general conclusions to be drawn from the biopics, costume dramas and other prestige productions produced by Warners during the 1930s. In the first place, they represent an effort by the studio to establish itself as a fully-fledged major, initially with one-offs like *Show of Shows* and the George Arliss vehicles at the start of the decade, subsequently as a major company capable of producing the kind of lavish movies generally associated with other studios which its particular history, coupled with the financial problems of the Depression years, had at first prevented it from doing. These prestige productions do not account for more than a tiny proportion of overall output in terms of number, but they do account for a considerable slice of production capital and remain a crucial element in the studio's elaboration of a public image, both for the industry and for the public as a whole. Secondly, until the formula became firmly established as it did with the biopics and the Merrie England pictures from about 1937 onwards, there was a period of more or less painful adjustment during which the studio's previous production methods and resulting narrative practices came into conflict with the new material. This can be seen in films like *The World Changes*, *Oil for the Lamps of China* and *Anthony Adverse*. And, once the conflict was resolved, there was an inevitable tendency for a new set of practices to establish themselves, and for the form to drift inexorably towards a rigid formula. The crisis of the Depression, coinciding with the advent of sound, had a galvanising effect on Hollywood; the ebbing of that crisis had its effect too.

Finally, as can be seen even more clearly in the social conscience pictures and, to a lesser extent, in the main bulk of Warners' output – the 'catch-all' category referred to in Chapter 4 – the greater confidence, indeed the complacency, of Roosevelt's second term during which the Depression no longer dominated American politics and during which the strengths of capitalism could be reaffirmed, is clearly reflected in the spectacular individualism which characterises both the major biopics and the main Merrie England pictures. The economic position of the studio, like that of the nation, was firmly assured, and that fact is necessarily reflected in both the kinds of film being made and the way in which they were made.

CONCLUSION
The Burbanking of America

In the preceding pages I have referred exclusively to Warner Brothers: that, after all, is what the book is about. But I could frequently have substituted 'Hollywood' or 'the American film industry' for 'Warner Brothers'. The conclusions drawn about the studio's production methods, the films it produced and its role in reflecting and shaping American ideology apply as much to the wider context as they do to the limited focus of a single studio. Indeed, there is a paradox at the heart of this book: I have focused on Warner Brothers both because it was typical and because it was unique. But it is a paradox rather than a contradiction. My aim has been to examine the studio system in operation during its heyday. While the choice of Warners was certainly not random, I might equally well have chosen another studio. But it had to be a single studio, since I was determined to argue as much as possible from the specific to the general – from individual films to the framework in which they were produced; and to do that, it was necessary to examine a coherent 'body' of work – the output of a particular studio.

I chose Warner Brothers partly because of the availability of archive material and of prints of the films themselves, but above all as the result of an initial impression of the methods and output of that studio which only a detailed survey could confirm or refute. Fortunately, the survey confirmed the impression, which was of a studio with an unusually strong commitment to contemporary – and, as a result, socially significant – subjects; and the impression was backed up by a belief that Warner Brothers/First National was the studio whose structure most clearly represented that of Hollywood during the 1930s. I believed, and still believe, that the two things are related. The specific development of the company and its role in pioneering talking pictures, together with the background of the Warner brothers themselves in distribution and exhibition, naturally inclined the studio towards a more realistic and more socially conscious kind of film-making.

But the popular critical association of Warner Brothers with 'social conscience' pictures – an association found as much in the contemporary trade papers and newspaper reviews as in subsequent critical histories – is based on a fairly small proportion of the company's overall output. Nor did the other studios avoid contemporary reality in their choice of subject matter. Warners may have made more such films than other studios, but the Depression is, for example, an important element in MGM's *Dinner at Eight* (1933), and the same studio produced its quota of crime movies, notably the *Thin Man* series,[1] which have a tenuous but important connection with the 'real world'. Contemporary reality is similarly a key element in many of the films produced at Columbia, from *It Happened One Night* (1933) to *Mr Deeds Goes to Town* (1936) and *Mr Smith Goes to Washington* (1939). Social, economic and political problems figure in, for example, Goldwyn's *Dead End* and MGM's *Three Comrades* (both 1937), and even RKO's Astaire-Rogers musicals do not exist in a complete vacuum: no film can. What is more, escapist movies are often as important a guide to contemporary values and ideology as those which deal explicitly with the contemporary social situation. 'In each period,' the young Marx wrote in an unfinished article for the *Rheinische Zeitung*,[2] 'reactionaries are as sure indicators of its spiritual condition as dogs are of the weather.' I am not sure how much Marx knew about dogs, and I am absolutely certain he was unaware of the American slang usage of the word to mean a bad movie, but the phrase would work just as well if he *had* been talking about cinematic 'dogs'. There are few clearer indications of the basic, unadmitted attitudes and aspirations of an audience than a movie or a television series geared to exploiting them. *Crossroads* and *The Days of Our Lives* can tell us more about the contemporary climate in Britain and America than *Brideshead Revisited* or *Roots*: it is the gap between a reflection on and a reflection of reality.

Perhaps, then, this book should have looked exclusively at Warners B features and bromides. But an extended discussion of bad movies can be a depressing business,[3] and in the context of American film production during the 1930s it is, perhaps, a less meaningful exercise than an examination of those films in which the studio, for a variety of reasons, was prepared to invest a large proportion of its time, effort and money and which, partly because of that investment, were successful at the box office. Poverty Row companies turned out low-budget programmers throughout the decade, but their profit margin was extremely slender. And in an industry whose prime motivation was commercial, those films which were commercially the most successful become, almost by definition, the most significant. The product was geared to the market. And since the market was an entertainment one, it is the most successful product which can best indicate the relationship between production methods, films produced and audience response – a relationship which, since it is based on assumptions about audience expectations and the extent to which those expectations were fulfilled, is in part if not entirely an ideological one. Warner Brothers, it should be added, produced some extremely fine movies during the 1930s, and those movies deserve to be looked at and understood.

In the preceding pages, therefore, I have looked at the early economic history of Warner Brothers, at the production system which operated at the studio throughout the 1930s (and which, for all its unique features and its extremely streamlined nature, was typical of Hollywood as a whole during the decade), and in some detail at a number of the major films produced there. I have, of course, seen only a fraction of the studio's output for the period in question – slightly less than 20 per cent of the films produced between 1929 and 1941. The 70-odd films discussed in detail in this book represent only half of even that percentage – under 10 per cent of the overall output. Nor does that 10 per cent include all the major box-office successes, as a glance at Appendix II will make clear. I have not, for instance, discussed Warners' monumentally successful string of musicals, from the pre-Busby Berkeley days of *Sally* in 1929, through Berkeley's 1933-4 heyday of *42nd Street*, *Gold Diggers of 1933*, *Footlight Parade*, *Dames* and *Wonder Bar*. Some of those musicals do contain a strong element of contemporary reality, especially the 1933 trio; from others, notably *Wonder Bar*, it is entirely absent. Nor have I discussed the straightforward action movies in which men – Edward G. Robinson in *Tiger Shark* (1932), James Cagney in *The Crowd Roars* (1932) and Wayne Morris in *Kid Galahad* (1937) – face dilemmas of individual and group responsibility similar to those faced by Errol Flynn. I have discussed the sentimentality which surfaces in a good many of the contemporary dramas, but have ignored the Jolson vehicles *Say it with Songs*, *Sonny Boy* (both 1929) and *Mammy* (1930) in which sentimentality is the mainspring. I have discussed comedy thrillers like *Smart Money*, *Brother Orchid* and *The St Louis Kid*, but not the studio's ordinary comedies with equally contemporary settings like *Three Men on a Horse* (1936) and *The Bride Came C.O.D.* (1941). I have looked at films which reflect changes in contemporary society, but not films like *Ceiling Zero* and *China Clipper* (both 1936), which celebrate technological advances by pitting an individual hero against natural rather than social forces. And finally, I have referred repeatedly to the role played by women in a whole range of movies, but have not dealt other than in passing with a series of films, from *The Office Wife* (1930) to, at the end of the decade, *Jezebel* (1938), *Dark Victory* (1939), *All This and Heaven Too* (1940) and *The Great Lie* (1941), in which women – specifically, in the later films, Bette Davis – attempt to come to grips with problems that, while they are explicitly emotional, nevertheless give a clear indication of the options with which a woman could realistically be presented in a 1930s narrative.

Obviously, to have discussed all these films would have made this book impossibly long. But length is not the only reason why I have omitted them. In focusing on the films which I have chosen to include, I have been able to cover what I believe to be a representative cross-section of Warners movies from the 1930s – both the contemporary social dramas of Part II, with their direct reflections of prevailing attitudes, and the prestige productions, biopics and costume dramas of Part III, which reflect the same attitudes more indirectly. The 70-odd films discussed in the body of this book give a more than adequate idea of how, to borrow Abel Greene's phrase, Warner Brothers 'Burbanked' America in the 1930s.

Greene's review of *Black Fury* is a rare if not unique example of an explicit description of the way in which the potentially dangerous implications of a contemporary subject could be removed by a deft manipulation of the narrative and a suitable 'melodramatisation' of motives, turning an examination of a social problem into an affirmation of the values which had produced it. Even the more obviously political *Black Legion* could easily be recuperated into the affirmation of a belief in the basic solidity of American democracy. 'It is not,' wrote Frank S. Nugent in the *New York Times*, 'a pretty picture, certainly not a flattering one. Were we as sensitive about our national prestige as foreign countries are about theirs, it would be summarily withdrawn from circulation.' The word 'exploit' has an intriguingly ambiguous meaning in film industry parlance; and Warner Brothers were able to exploit the problems of 1930s America at the box office. But they did so from a standpoint of unshakeable belief in America – the same belief that lay behind the philosophies and appeal of Roosevelt's New Deal. As the New Deal evolved from an inventively new, if not exactly radical, approach to the problems of an over-extended and under-regulated economy into an orthodoxy of its own, so the tone of the studio's pictures shifted from problem-solving to celebration, with a counter-strain at the end of the decade examining both those personal problems that are brought to the surface in a time of economic stability, and questions of foreign policy which could no longer be ignored.

What remains constant throughout the decade, however, is the way in which the process of 'Burbanking' worked. Like most if not all ideological operations, it was never explicit. The kind of film the studio decided to make – the decisions on what would or would not 'work' at the box office – was determined by a number of assumptions which, when they became explicit, became so only in terms of observed effect, not analysed cause. The Dead End Kids plus Cagney, O'Brien and Bogart would be 'sure-fire box office'.[4] Or, as the press book for *The Fighting 69th* (1940) put it, 'It has everything audiences want – terrific laughs, pathos, drama, biographical fact and six of the screen's favourite stars playing the real-life adventures of the most celebrated heroes of the Rainbow Division'. The publicity campaigns were geared to the accepted commonplaces of box-office wisdom, not concerned with the rationale behind that wisdom. In the same way, studio memos are, it can confidently be said, concerned with *how* to do it, not why. A virtually unique exception is Wolfgang Reinhardt's memo on the political implications of *Juarez*,[5] dismissed with a testy 'nothing like that' by Hal Wallis.[6] To a certain extent, the 'why?' is the province of the critic, but the various contemporary reviews quoted throughout this book give at best a limited indication of why audiences responded to particular films. How the audience responded is equally difficult to know. We know that they paid to get in, but not what they thought when they came out. Box-office returns and length of run merely help close the circle opened by the production process: the market had been correctly guessed.

In short, an ideological intention and an ideological effect can never be 'proved' because neither is explicit. But the evidence provided by an examination of Warner Brothers during the 1930s is not entirely transparent. In the first place, there is the (inevitable) parallel between the nation's economy and the company's own profit-and-loss sheet, indicating a similar parallel if not an actual causal relationship with the change in the tone of the films produced by the studio either side of 1935. Secondly, there is the evidence of box-office returns: Warners were particularly successful with those films which did come to terms with contemporary reality, indicating an audience response not merely to the choice of subject but to its handling. Most important of all, however, is the clear link between Warners' production methods (the studio system) and the kind of films they produced.

Like any Hollywood studio, Warners drew *on* contemporary reality. Their subject matter was distilled from it, the degree of distillation varying from one movie to another. And the films made by the studio were released *into* contemporary reality, their commercial careers being determined by the accuracy with which the studio had read the trends. In between the distillation from and the release into reality came Burbanking. Warners' studio system was a factory process and, like any factory system, it processed raw material into product. The raw material of Hollywood was of two distinct kinds: a material one – celluloid – and an intangible one – reality. The process of the studio/factory was thus film production and the representation of reality. The material part of this process remained basically the same throughout the period, perfected and tightened as the decade pro- gressed, allowing a little more flexibility towards the end, before beginning to break down and alter in the decade that followed. The studio system made films, and developed particularly efficient, conventional methods of doing so. But if I have devoted comparatively little space to specifically cinematic devices – type of shot, camera

253

movements, editing transitions – it is because others have analysed the 'classic' Hollywood style, and above all because it is the aim of that style to place cinematic devices at the service of narrative – to mask them in it. In the context of the present survey, Hollywood is the stories it told.

The second part of the process necessarily changed as the reality that was being represented itself changed. In a sentence, the system remained standard, while the throughput varied. But the two facets of the production process were undoubtedly related. To make the material process of film production as economical as possible, a standard code of practice was adopted in terms of decision-taking, planning, scripting, shooting, editing, publicity and release. This necessarily involved fitting the variable story material into as regular a narrative pattern and cinematic style as possible, with the crux of the plot – whether it was a social problem, a scientist's life or the career of a medieval outlaw – illuminated through a central character whose response to physical obstacles was action and whose experience of emotional life was romantic. Both sets of problems were resolved in the final reel; whether happily or sadly makes little difference. Obviously there is a number of variables (though not an infinite number) in this structure, but it has not been basically with the structure, and even less with the elaboration of a syntagmatic system for analysing it, that this book has been concerned: its concern has been with the relationship between the production system and the films produced.

I hope some of that relationship has been shown. It is not one that can be reduced to a formula or to a flow diagram. But without the particular production system – the studio system as exemplified and illustrated by Warner Brothers in the 1930s – the films would have had different – or differently slanted – plots, and their relationship with contemporary ideology would have been less demonstrable. The New Deal in Entertainment would have been otherwise. The studio system was a carefully regulated form of industrial production, massively integrated and highly efficient. Inevitably, it left an indelible mark on the films produced under it. And those films marked both contemporary audiences in their attitude to the world and, in a different way, subsequent ideas of what is or is not a 'good' film. The orthodoxy of the New Deal itself still exerts a strong influence on American domestic politics. The orthodoxy of the New Deal in Entertainment continues to mark the cinema just as strongly.

Notes

1 Hollywood

1. Cf., *inter alia*, Malcolm Le Grice, *Abstract Film and Beyond*, London, Studio Vista, 1977; and Peter Gidal (ed.), *Structural Film Anthology*, London, British Film Institute, 1976.
2. Hortense Powdermaker, *Hollywood: the Dream Factory*, Boston, Little, Brown and Co., 1950.
3. Hans Magnus Enzensberger, *Raids and Reconstructions*, London (trans.), Pluto Press, 1976.
4. The most recent biography of Edison, which looks at his business practices as well as his inventions, is: Ronald W. Clark, *Edison: The Man who Made the Future*, London, Macdonald and Jane's, 1977.
5. Tino Balio (ed.), *The American Film Industry*, Madison, University of Wisconsin Press, 1976, p.105.
6. Cf., *inter alia*, Balio, op. cit.; Benjamin B. Hampton, *The History of the American Film Industry*, New York, Dover, 1970; Anthony Slide, *Early American Cinema*, London/New York, Tantivy/Barnes, 1970.
7. For a survey of film theories, see: J. Dudley Andrew, *The Major Film Theories*, New York, Oxford University Press, 1976; Andrew Tudor, *Theories of Film*, London, Secker and Warburg/British Film Institute, 1974; Peter Wollen, *Signs and Meaning in the Cinema*, 2nd ed., London, Secker and Warburg/British Film Institute, 1972; Gerald Mast and Marshall Cohen, *Film Theory and Criticism*, New York, Oxford University Press, 1974.
8. For a particularly violent polemic on this subject, see the article by Lindsay Anderson in the *Guardian*, 2 March 1981.

2 Warner Brothers and the Studio System

1. From the souvenir programme to Warner Brothers' *The Desert Song* (1929).
2. For a much fuller analysis of Warners' economic strategies, see J. Douglas Gomery, 'Writing the History of the American Film Industry: Warner Bros. and sound', *Screen*, Vol. 17, No. 1, Spring 1976, pp. 40-53.
3. The history of Warner Brothers is covered with varying degrees of thoroughness in: Charles Higham, *Warner Brothers*, New York, Scribner's, 1975; Clive Hirschhorn, *The Warner Bros. Story*, London, Octopus, 1979; Roy Pickard, *The Hollywood Studios*, London, Muller, 1978. Cf. also William R. Meyer, *Warners Brothers Directors*, New Rochelle, Arlington House, 1978; Ted Sennett, *Warner Brothers Presents*, New Rochelle, Arlington House, 1971; and the (partly ghosted) autobiographies of Jack L. Warner and Hal B. Wallis (see below, notes 6 and 7).
4. For a full list of Warners' Broadway theatres, see Appendix II.

5. From an interview conducted by the author at Wallis' home in Rancho Mirage, California, in September 1981 (subsequently referred to as 'Wallis interview'). An edited version of this interview has appeared in *Stills*, No.6, pp. 78-9.

6. Jack Warner (with Dean Jennings), *My First Hundred Years in Hollywood*, New York, Random House, 1964.

7. This is obviously one of Wallis' favourite stories. It turned up in my interview with him, it figures in his autobiography (Hal Wallis and Charles Higham, *Starmaker*, New York, Macmillan, 1980), and I have come across it on at least one other occasion.

8. For an extremely readable account of Zanuck's career, see Mel Gussow, *Zanuck: Don't Say Yes Until I Finish Talking*, New York, Doubleday, 1971.

9. Wallis interview.

10. Warner Brothers production files, University of Southern California (subsequently referred to as 'WB/USC'), *The Fighting 69th* file, memo from Bryan Foy to Jack L. Warner, 10 April 1939.

3 Anthony Adverse: A Casebook

1. Hervey Allen, *Anthony Adverse*, New York, 1933. The novel is still in print in paperback on both sides of the Atlantic, in Britain as a Penguin Classic (Harmondsworth, 1980), and in the United States in a 3-volume edition published by Warner Books (1978).

2. For a discussion of *The World Changes* and *Oil for the Lamps of China*, see below, Chapter 11. On the box-office reception of *A Midsummer Night's Dream*, see Wallis and Higham, op. cit., p. 43: 'A Midsummer Night's Dream wasn't a block-buster. It didn't make records at the box office, but it was reasonably successful and earned us unlimited prestige.'

3. The 'Merrie England' pictures are discussed in Chapter 12.

4. See Appendix II.

5. The 'Best Assistant Director' nomination was discontinued after 1936.

6. See Appendix I for fuller details.

7. See below, Chapter 11.

8. There were two 'little boys' in Goldwyn's *Dark Angel* (1935): George Breakstone, who stood in for Mickey Rooney in *A Midsummer Night's Dream* when the young star had broken his leg in a tobogganing accident, and Denis Chaldecott. It seems likely that Wallis would have recalled Breakstone's name, so the odds are he meant Chaldecott.

9. A puzzle. Rin-Tin-Tin proper died in 1932. A successor, dubbed Rin-Tin-Tin Jr, appeared in *Law of the Wild* (1934), a serial, and *The Adventures of Rex and Rinty* (1935), a feature, both co-directed for Mascot by B. Reeves ('Breezy') Eason, who frequently worked at Warners as a 2nd unit director on action sequences (e.g. *The Charge of the Light Brigade* and *Sergeant York*). Rin-Tin-Tin Jr also appeared in a 1936 MGM film, *Tough Guy*. It is possible that Jackman did process work for one of these; if so, it is almost certain to have been *Tough Guy*.

10. See below, p. 142.

11. See below, p. 142, for comments on Michael Curtiz being 'self-indulgent'. Cf. also Wallis and Higham, op. cit., p. 51, for an anecdote about Wyler.

12. The studio memo forms, however, are printed with a permanent enjoinder: VERBAL MESSAGES CAUSE MISUNDERSTANDINGS AND DELAYS (PLEASE PUT THEM IN WRITING).

13. *Los Angeles Times*, 30 July 1936.

14. The voting in the 1936 Poll was as follows: 1. *Mutiny on the Bounty*, MGM, 416; 2. *Mr Deeds Goes to Town*, Columbia, 372; 3. *The Great Ziegfeld*, MGM, 345; 4. *San Francisco*, MGM, 264; 5. *Dodsworth*, Goldwyn, 254; 6. *The Story of Louis Pasteur*, Warner Brothers, 250; 7. *A Tale of Two Cities*, MGM, 235; 8. *Anthony Adverse*, 231; 9. *The Green Pastures*, Warner Brothers, 197; 10. *A Midsummer Night's Dream*, Warner Brothers, 166.

4 From the Crash to Pearl Harbor

1. There is no shortage of books about Roosevelt and the New Deal. My chief source has been William E. Leuchtenburg, *Franklin D. Roosevelt and the New Deal, 1932-1940*, New York, Harper and Row, 1963, though I would not want to make him responsible for any of my conclusions about the relationship between Warners Brothers and the New Deal. I should also like to cite a *Time* Magazine cover story, 'F.D.R.'s disputed legacy' by Otto Friedrich, Ruth Mehrtens Galvin, Hays Gorey, John Kohan and Arthur White, which appeared in the 1 February 1982 issue, and re-examined the New Deal from the standpoint of Reagan's America – a key perspective, since Reagan has frequently claimed to be inspired by FDR, his 'boyhood idol'.

2. See below, pp. 147-9.

3. See below, p. 193.

4. The idea of a 'market group' is slightly problematic when talking about Hollywood in the 1930s, since the basic philosophy was that the market – the audience – was a single, indivisible one, comprising the Great American Public. Nevertheless, there can be no doubt that certain films were aimed more at one group than another. Extreme examples would be provided by *A Midsummer Night's Dream* (1935) and a John Wayne Western like *The Telegraph Trail* (1933). An alternative way of classifying the studio's output may be found in John Davis' ingenious 'Warners' genres of the '30s and '40s', *Velvet Light Trap*, 15.

5 Crime Thrillers and Newspaper Pictures

1. Wallis interview.

2. Ibid.

3. The 1949 re-release of *G-Men* – the print generally available from 16mm film libraries – is preceded by a prologue in which a group of flat-top Feds are attending an FBI training session. *G-Men* is shown to them as a piece of history – and to the audience as, presumably, propaganda.

4. Robert Warshow, *The Immediate Experience*, New York, Doubleday, 1962.

5. For a historical survey of the social role of the outlaw, see Eric Hobsbawm, *Bandits*, Harmondsworth, Penguin, 1972.

6. *Los Angeles Times*, 20 June 1931.

7. Ibid., 9 February 1934.
8. Ibid., 28 October 1931.

6 Gangster Movies

1. *Los Angeles Times*, 29 November 1930.
2. Cf. Henry Cohen, introduction to the screenplay of *The Public Enemy*, Madison, University of Wisconsin Press, 1981, pp. 27-8.
3. Introduction to the screenplay of *Little Caesar*, Madison, University of Wisconsin Press, 1981, p. 18.
4. *Los Angeles Times*, 26 September 1935.
5. See below, Chapter 12.
6. Mordaunt Hall, review of *Taxi!*, *New York Times*, 8 January 1932.
7. Franklin D. Roosevelt, First Inaugural Address, 1933, in Samuel Rosenman (ed.), *The Public Papers and Addresses of Franklin D. Roosevelt*, New York, Russell and Russell, 1969, 13 vols., 1938-1950, Vol. II, pp. 11-15.
8. Edward G. Robinson, the only other contender for the title, had had a distinguished stage career, dating back to 1915, and could thus scarcely be described as a 'discovery'. Cagney's stage career had been both briefer and less distinguished.

7 Rehabilitation

1. *I Am a Fugitive From a Chain Gang*, Madison, University of Wisconsin Press, 1981, pp. 38-41.
2. Ibid, pp. 185-7. There is a slight change in the dialogue in the film as released.
3. See below, p. 183.
4. *Penrod and Sam* (1931), with Leon Janney and Junior Coghlan; a remake in 1937, with Billy Mauch; *Penrod and his Twin Brother* and *Penrod's Double Trouble*, both 1938 and both starring the Mauch twins. To these can perhaps be added another Tarkington adaptation, *Father's Son*, made in 1931 with Leon Janney and in 1941 with Billy Dawson.
5. See below, Chapter 12.
6. WB/USC, *Angels with Dirty Faces* file, Harry M. Warner to Hal Wallis, 10 October 1938.
7. Ibid., Walter MacEwen to R.J. Obringer, 2 June 1938.
8. The percentage system, standard in billing contracts, refers to the size of the typeface in relation to the largest type used in the advertisement, usually for the film's title. Obviously, it is a 'not less than' provision, since 10% of the title type in a newspaper advertisement would be too small to read. It referred mainly to posters.
9. The part was eventually taken by Ann Sheridan.
10. Non-contract performers.
11. Robert M. Haas, the Art Director.
12. This was, in fact, almost literally true. According to Wallis (Wallis interview), Curtiz 'never ate lunch, he never had a lunch hour. The company

would go, and he'd be pacing up and down waiting for them to come back. And then, if they came back and fluffed their lines or were a little slow or what not, he would call them "lunch bums".'

8   Racism, Fascism and Other Issues

1.   See above, p. 13.
2.   8 February 1930.
3.   For an extended discussion of *Knute Rockne – All American*, see below, pp. 203-7.
4.   An equally plausible explanation for this device is that it saved a lot of money, since there would be no need to call day-rate extras for the scenes thus covered.
5.   There were, in fact, a number of alternative endings tried out on preview audiences – a further indication that this was not a standard Warners production. The film is discussed in great detail by Nick Browne of UCLA in 'System of production/System of representation: Industry context and ideological form in Capra's *Meet John Doe*', a paper presented at the 1982 Ancona/Pesaro conference, 'Hollywood/Lo studio system/Il caso Warner Brothers'. Browne's paper is due to be published (in Italian) by the Mostra Internazionale Nuovo Cinema.

9   Foreign Biopics

1.   See below, Chapter 12.
2.   In 1940, *Santa Fe Trail*, *The Sea Hawk*, *The Story of Dr Ehrlich's Magic Bullet*, *Virginia City*, *The Letter* and *All This and Heaven Too*; in 1941, *The Sea Wolf*, *Sergeant York* and *They Died With Their Boots On*.
3.   13 October 1929.
4.   He made three more Hollywood films (not for Warner Brothers), before moving to Britain in 1935. He made seven films there, and retired from the screen when his wife lost her sight in 1937.
5.   Wallis interview: 'Unless it was about something or had a message . . . he wouldn't do it.' Cf. also: 'Finally, it became too difficult to find material for Muni because he would only play very important historical characters or roles with social significance.' (Wallis and Higham, op. cit., p. 64). There is evidence in the studio files that other production executives found Muni not so much admirable as downright irritating.
6.   27 February 1936.
7.   WB/USC, *The Life of Emile Zola* file, Henry Blanke to Hal Wallis, 18 November 1936.
8.   Ibid., Hal Wallis to Perc Westmore, 2 March 1937.
9.   Ibid., Henry Blanke to Morris Ebenstein, 11 December 1936.
10.   Ibid., Robert M. Schless to Henry Blanke, 22 February 1937.
11.   Ibid., note attached to a 'Synopsis of a film dealing with Zola's life – his fight for liberty and right, and the Dreyfus scandal', 15 July 1936.
12.   Summarised in a memo from Henry Blanke to Morris Ebenstein, ibid., 21 January 1937.

13. Ibid., copy of a letter from Joseph I. Breen to Jack L. Warner, 12 February 1937.
14. *Film Daily*, 30 August 1937, p. 2.
15. WB/USC, *Juarez* file. J.B. Wilkinson to J.L. Warner, 22 September 1938; Annie Laurie Williams to Jacob Wilk, 7 October 1938; and a series of letters sent by Dieterle's secretary to Walter MacEwen on 24 January 1939 from Mrs George Meier of Indianapolis, Eric Mann of New York City, Maroa Bailey of Narberth, Pa., Mrs George S. Nalle of Austin, Tx., Willis N. Thorn of the Flint, Michigan, *Journal*, L.A. Cole of Philadelphia, Emma Lieber of Indianapolis, Mrs Ralph Lieber of Indianapolis and Mrs Gertrude Atherton of San Francisco.
16. Ibid., Henry Blanke to Hal Wallis, 4 October 1937.
17. The WB/USC file contains several hundred documents – four separate folders – relating to Torres' proposed $1,000,000 law suit and the various ways of combating it.
18. Ibid., Hermann Lissauer to Arthur Zellner, 6 March 1939; Henry Blanke to Tenny Wright, 9 June 1938; Anton Grot to Tenny Wright, 30 September 1938.
19. Ibid., cable from Presidente Cardenas to J.L. Warner: REFIEROME MENSAJE DIRIGIOME 15 ACTUAL DE NUEVAYORK SENOR S CHARLES EINFELD PUNTO DESEOLES TODO EXITO ESPERANDO QUE OBRA RESPONDA ESFUERZO REALIZADO Y HAGA HONOR A LA OBRA MORALIZ Y SOCIAL DEL GRAN MEXICANO DON BENITO JUAREZ PUNTO AFFECTUOSAMENTE = PRESIDENTE CARDENAS.
20. Wallis interview.
21. WB/USC, *Juarez* file, 24 September 1938.
22. Ibid., publicity file.

10 American History

1. The fact that the second male lead, Ronald Reagan, plays George Armstrong Custer is not really significant: the Custer of *Santa Fe Trail* is just another young officer, not a major historical figure.
2. Gary Cooper was certainly an established star, but he was not a Warners contract artist.
3. Cf. Wallis and Higham, op. cit., p. 69.
4. *New York Times*, 21 December 1940.
5. The early 1940s saw some major reshuffles among top production executives and the emergence of the semi-independent producer. Most notably in the present context, Hal Wallis became semi-independent at Warners in 1942, and subsequently moved to Paramount in 1945.
6. WB/USC, *Sergeant York* file, letter from R.J. Obringer to a New York attorney called Berkowitz, 12 December 1941.
7. Ibid., Daily Production and Progress Report for 19 February 1941.
8. Ibid., Report for 3 February 1941.
9. Ibid., Report for 20 February 1941.
10. Ibid., Report for 30 April 1941.
11. *Variety*, 12 February 1936.
12. Cf. in particular *Flirtation Walk* and *Here Comes the Navy* (1934), *Devil Dogs of the Air* and *Shipmates Forever* (1935) and *The Fighting 69th* (1940).

11 Epics and other Prestige Productions

1. See Appendix II. Of *General Crack*, Edwin Schallert wrote in the *Los Angeles Times* (17 December 1929): 'The production is a superior adventure into the costume realm. In quality of settings and dramatic effectiveness it is practically the best feature of this type so far produced in the talkies.' And of *The Man from Blankleys* he wrote (3 May 1930) rather more guardedly: 'John Barrymore dons the antic manner in *The Man from Blankleys* at Warners Brothers' Hollywood Theater, and those who wish to can have a grand time watching his monkeyshines and listening in on them.'
2. *The Green Goddess* (1930) was a comedy in which Arliss played an Oriental despot in a kind of Shangri-La.
3. See above, p. 181.
4. This is, of course, a personal judgment, as are all critical evaluations of films in this book. In the case of *The Sea Wolf*, however, I have encountered violent disagreement with my low opinion of the result and feel I should probably say so. Some people whose opinions I respect seem to like the film a lot. I should also like to take this opportunity to thank – I think that is the word – Vincent Porter for pointing out to me that I tend to equate films I like with 'typical' Warner Brothers movies. He is probably right; but the fact remains that I don't like *The Sea Wolf* and I don't think it is typical.
5. See above, p. 216.
6. I am grateful to Patricia King Hanson for this piece of information.
7. A reference to the Company's habit of putting little brass plaques on the furniture in Company houses.
8. Cf. also MGM's *The Hollywood Revue*, *Fox Movietone Follies* and *Paramount on Parade* (all 1929).
9. The Joe E. Brown comedy *Hold Everything* (1930).
10. *New York Times*, 10 October 1935.
11. WB/USC, *A Midsummer Night's Dream* file, copy of a letter from Will H. Hays to Dr A.S.W. Rosenbach, 25 September 1935.
12. Introduction to the screenplay, Madison, University of Wisconsin Press, 1979, pp. 28-9.

12 Merrie England

1. For the origins of this analysis of the Flynn character, I should acknowledge Olivier Eyquem: 'Sherwood, U.S.A.: (à propos des *Aventures de Robin des Bois*)', *Positif*, 205, pp. 3-7.
2. In *Alibi Ike* and *The Irish in Us* (both 1935).
3. Quoted in Paul Leggett, 'The noble cynic: Michael Curtiz', *Focus on Film*, 23, pp. 15-19.
4. *New York Times*, 6 May 1937.
5. Madison, University of Wisconsin Press, 1979.
6. Wallis interview.
7. See above, p. 142.
8. Behlmer, op. cit., p. 18.

Conclusion   The Burbanking of America

1. *The Thin Man* (1934), *After the Thin Man* (1936), *Another Thin Man* (1939), *Shadow of the Thin Man* (1941), *The Thin Man Goes Home* (1944), *Song of the Thin Man* (1947).
2. Karl Marx and Friedrich Engels, *Collected Works*, Vol. I, London, Lawrence and Wishart, 1975, p. 182.
3. Not always, though, as witness one of the best books on Hollywood to come out during the 1970s, Todd McCarthy and Charles Flynn (editors), *Kings of the Bs: Working within the Hollywood System*, New York, Dutton, 1975.
4. See above, p. 139.
5. See above, p. 194.
6. Wallis interview.

Appendix I   Awards, Polls and Nominations

The following list covers three main areas in which Warner Brothers' films received acclaim: the Awards and nominations for Awards by the Academy of Motion Picture Arts and Sciences (Oscars); the *Film Daily* annual Critics' Poll; and the annual Awards made by the National Board of Review (NBR).

The Academy Awards information is taken from Robert Osborne, *50 Golden Years of Oscar: The Official History of the Academy of Motion Picture Arts and Sciences*, La Habra, Ca., 1979. The *Film Daily* Poll and the NBR listings are both taken from the *Film Daily Year Book*, 1930-42.

The *Film Daily* Poll, as its name implies, was a poll of newspaper and magazine critics throughout the United States. The number of critics polled increased annually: 327 in 1929, 333 in 1930; 340 in 1931; 368 in 1932; 384 in 1933; 424 in 1934; 451 in 1935; 523 in 1936; 531 in 1937; 536 in 1938; 542 in 1939; 546 in 1940; 548 in 1941. Each year, the 'Ten Best' films were given a page each; after that, all films receiving ten votes or more were listed in an 'Honor Roll'. Films appeared in the poll in the year in which they were released, rather than (if there was a difference) the year in which they were premiered. This makes an exact comparison between the various Awards difficult. A year-to-year comparison is difficult too, since the NBR regularly changed its categories as, to a lesser extent, did the Academy. The NBR did not start putting its choices for the various categories in preferential order until 1936; before that, they are listed alphabetically.

1929

ACADEMY
Award: Frank Lloyd, Direction (*The Divine Lady*, *Weary River*, *Drag*).
Nomination: John Seitz, Cinematography (*The Divine Lady*).

FILM DAILY
Ten Best: *Disraeli* (1st, 192); *Gold Diggers of Broadway* (5th, 139).
Honor Roll: *The Desert Song* (47), *Drag* (35), *On With the Show* (29), *Noah's Ark* (26), *Sonny Boy*, *Weary River* (22), *Young Nowheres* (19), *Show of Shows* (16), *The Divine Lady*, *The Barker* (10).

NATIONAL BOARD OF REVIEW
Ten Best: *Disraeli*.
Best Players: Richard Barthelmess (only player listed for four films: *Scarlet Seas*, *Weary River*, *Drag*, *Young Nowheres*).
Ten Best Directors: Lloyd Bacon, Frank Lloyd.

1930

ACADEMY
Award: George Arliss, Best Actor (*Disraeli*).
Nominations: *Disraeli*, Best Picture; Julian Josephson, Writing (*Disraeli*); Jack Okey, Art Direction (*Sally*); George Groves, Sound Recording (*Song of the Flame*)

FILM DAILY
Ten Best: *Old English* (10th, 87).
Honor Roll: *The Dawn Patrol* (78), *Outward Bound* (73), *General Crack* (37), *The Green Goddess* (28), *Doorway to Hell* (16), *Moby Dick* (14), *The Man from Blankleys* (13).

NATIONAL BOARD OF REVIEW
Ten Best: *The Man from Blankleys.*
Ten Best Directors: Alfred E. Green, Roy Del Ruth, Frank Lloyd.

1931

ACADEMY
Award: John Monk Saunders, Writing – Original Story (*The Dawn Patrol*).
Nominations: Francis Faragoh and Robert N. Lee, Writing – Adaptation (*Little Caesar*); Rowland Brown, Writing – Original story (*Doorway to Hell*); John Bright and Kubec Glasmon, Writing – Original Story (*The Public Enemy*); Lucien Hubbard and Joseph Jackson, Writing – Original Story (*Smart Money*); Barney McGill, Cinematography (*Svengali*); Jack Okey, Art Direction (*Svengali*).

FILM DAILY
Ten Best: *Five Star Final* (7th, 138).
Honor Roll: *Little Caesar* (97), *Alexander Hamilton* (65), *Outward Bound* (57), *The Public Enemy* (56), *The Millionaire* (45), *Star Witness, Smart Money, Svengali* (15), *Night Nurse* (12), *Viennese Nights* (10).

NATIONAL BOARD OF REVIEW
Supplementary Ten: *Little Caesar, The Public Enemy.*

1932

ACADEMY
Nominations: *Five Star Final*, Best Picture; Lucien Hubbard, Writing – Original Story (*The Star Witness*).

FILM DAILY
Honor Roll: *The Man Who Played God* (75), *Blessed Event* (68), *Union Depot* (21), *So Big* (18), *Tiger Shark* (15), *One Way Passage, The Mouthpiece* (13), *Cabin in the Cotton* (10).

NATIONAL BOARD OF REVIEW
Ten Best: *I Am a Fugitive from a Chain Gang* ('not only the best feature film of the year, but one of the best ever made in this country').

1933

ACADEMY
Awards: Robert Lord, Writing – Original Story (*One Way Passage*).
Nominations: *42nd Street, I Am a Fugitive from a Chain Gang*, Best Picture; Paul Muni, Best Actor (*I Am a Fugitive from a Chain Gang*); Nathan Levinson, Sound Recording (*42nd Street, Gold Diggers of 1933, I Am a Fugitive from a Chain Gang*).

FILM DAILY
Ten Best: *42nd Street* (2nd, 209); *I Am a Fugitive from a Chain Gang* (8th, 156).

264

Honor Roll: *Footlight Parade* (59), *Voltaire* (48), *Gold Diggers of 1933* (38), *The Silver Dollar* (33).

NATIONAL BOARD OF REVIEW
No mentions.

1934

ACADEMY
Nominations: *Flirtation Walk*, *Here Comes the Navy*, Best Picture; Nathan Levinson, Sound Recording (*Flirtation Walk*).

FILM DAILY
Honor Roll: *As the Earth Turns* (25), *Hi, Nellie!* (18), *British Agent* (11), *Here Comes the Navy* (10).

NATIONAL BOARD OF REVIEW
No mentions.

1935

ACADEMY
Awards: Bette Davis, Best Actress (*Dangerous*); Hal Mohr, Cinematography (*A Midsummer Night's Dream*); Harry Warren and Al Dubin, Music – Song ('Lullaby of Broadway', *Gold Diggers of 1935*); Bobby Connolly, Dance Direction ('Latin from Manhattan', *Go into Your Dance*; 'Playboy from Paree', *Broadway Hostess*).
Nominations: *Captain Blood*, *A Midsummer Night's Dream*, Best Picture; Busby Berkeley, Dance Direction ('Lullaby of Broadway' and 'The Words are in My Heart', *Gold Diggers of 1935*).

FILM DAILY
Honor Roll: *G-Men* (80), *Oil for the Lamps of China* (64), *Black Fury* (59).

NATIONAL BOARD OF REVIEW
Top Ten (Popular Appeal): *A Midsummer Night's Dream*.

1936

ACADEMY
Awards: Paul Muni, Best Actor (*The Story of Louis Pasteur*); Gale Sondergaard, Best Supporting Actress (*Anthony Adverse*); Pierre Collings and Sheridan Gibney, Writing – Original Story and Writing – Screenplay (*The Story of Louis Pasteur*); Gaetano Gaudio, Cinematography (*Anthony Adverse*); Ralph Dawson, Film Editing (*Anthony Adverse*); Leo Forbstein and Erich Wolfgang Korngold, Music – Score (*Anthony Adverse*); Jack Sullivan, Assistant Director (*The Charge of the Light Brigade*).
Nominations: *Anthony Adverse*, *The Story of Louis Pasteur*, Best Picture; Anton Grot, Art Direction (*Anthony Adverse*); Nathan Levinson, Sound Recording (*The Charge of the Light Brigade*); Leo Forbstein and Max Steiner, Music – Score (*The Charge of the Light Brigade*); William Cannon, Assistant Director (*Anthony Adverse*); Busby Berkeley, Dance Direction ('Love and War', *Gold Diggers of 1937*); Bobby Connolly, Dance Direction ('1000 Love Songs', *Cain and Mabel*).

FILM DAILY
Ten Best: *The Story of Louis Pasteur* (6th, 250), *Anthony Adverse* (8th, 231), *The Green Pastures* (9th, 197), *A Midsummer Night's Dream* (10th, 166).
Honor Roll: *Captain Blood* (94), *The Petrified Forest* (93), *Ceiling Zero* (17), *China Clipper* (10).

NATIONAL BOARD OF REVIEW
Ten Best (Exceptional Photoplays): *The Story of Louis Pasteur* (2nd), *Ceiling Zero* (7th), *The Green Pastures* (10th).
Ten Best (Popular Appeal): *The Story of Louis Pasteur* (3rd), *Anthony Adverse* (6th), *The Green Pastures* (8th).
Ten Best (Young Reviewers and 4-Star Clubs [Ages 8-17]): *Anthony Adverse* (2nd), *The Charge of the Light Brigade* (5th), *The Story of Louis Pasteur* (7th).

1937

ACADEMY
Awards: *The Life of Emile Zola*, Best Picture; Joseph Schildkraut, Best Supporting Actor (*The Life of Emile Zola*); Heinz Herald, Geza Herczeg and Norman Reilly Raine, Writing – Screenplay (*The Life of Emile Zola*).
Nominations: Paul Muni, Best Actor (*The Life of Emile Zola*); William Dieterle, Direction (*The Life of Emile Zola*); Robert Lord, Writing – Original Story (*Black Legion*); Heinz Herald and Geza Herczeg, Writing – Original Story (*The Life of Emile Zola*); Anton Grot, Art Direction (*The Life of Emile Zola*); Harry Warren and Al Dubin, Music – Song ('Remember Me', *Mr Dodd Takes the Air*); Leo Forbstein and Max Steiner, Music – Score (*The Life of Emile Zola*); Russ Saunders, Assistant Director (*The Life of Emile Zola*).

FILM DAILY
Ten Best: *The Life of Emile Zola* (1st, 453).
Honor Roll: *They Won't Forget* (57), *The Charge of the Light Brigade* (36), *The Prince and the Pauper* (31), *Kid Galahad* (30), *Black Legion* (22), *Marked Woman* (21), *Green Light* (20).

NATIONAL BOARD OF REVIEW
Ten Best (Exceptional Photoplays): *The Life of Emile Zola* (2nd), *Black Legion* (3rd), *They Won't Forget* (7th).
Ten Best (Popular Appeal): *The Life of Emile Zola* (2nd).
Ten Best (Young Reviewers): *The Life of Emile Zola* (5th).
Outstanding Artists: Humphrey Bogart (*Black Legion*).

1938

ACADEMY
Awards: Bette Davis, Best Actress (*Jezebel*); Fay Bainter, Best Supporting Actress (*Jezebel*); Carl Jules Weyl, Art Direction (*The Adventures of Robin Hood*); Ralph Dawson, Film Editing (*The Adventures of Robin Hood*); Erich Wolfgang Korngold, Music – Original Score (*The Adventures of Robin Hood*).
Special Award to Harry M. Warner in recognition of patriotic service in the production of historical short subjects presenting significant episodes in the early struggle of the American people for liberty.

Nominations: *The Adventures of Robin Hood, Four Daughters, Jezebel*, Best Picture; James Cagney, Best Actor (*Angels with Dirty Faces*); Fay Bainter, Best Actress (*White Banners*); John Garfield, Best Supporting Actor (*Four Daughters*); Michael Curtiz, Direction (*Angels with Dirty Faces* and *Four Daughters*); Rowland Brown, Writing – Original Story (*Angels with Dirty Faces*); Lenore Coffee and Julius J. Epstein, Writing – Screenplay (*Four Daughters*); Ernest Haller, Cinematography (*Jezebel*); Phil Craig and Arthur Quenzer, Music – Song ('Jeepers Creepers', *Going Places*); Max Steiner, Music – Scoring (*Jezebel*).

FILM DAILY
Ten Best: *The Adventures of Robin Hood* (7th, 218).

Honor Roll: *Four Daughters* (168), *Jezebel* (115), *White Banners* (47), *Tovarich* (46), *The Sisters* (44), *Brother Rat* (38), *A Slight Case of Murder* (31), *The Amazing Dr Clitterhouse* (17).

NATIONAL BOARD OF REVIEW
Ten Best (Exceptional Photoplays): *Jezebel* (8th)

Ten Best (Popular Appeal): *The Adventures of Robin Hood* (7th), *Four Daughters* (10th).

Ten Best (Young Reviewers): *The Adventures of Robin Hood* (6th), *Four Daughters* (8th).

Performances: James Cagney (*Angels with Dirty Faces*), John Garfield (*Four Daughters*).

1939

ACADEMY
Nominations: *Dark Victory*, Best Picture; Bette Davis, Best Actress (*Dark Victory*); Brian Aherne, Best Supporting Actor (*Juarez*); Erich Wolfgang Korngold, Music – Scoring (*The Private Lives of Elizabeth and Essex*); Sol Polito and W. Howard Greene, Cinematography – Color (*The Private Lives of Elizabeth and Essex*); Byron Haskin and Nathan Levinson, Special Effects (*The Private Lives of Elizabeth and Essex*).

FILM DAILY
Ten Best: *Dark Victory* (5th, 280), *Juarez* (8th, 216), *The Old Maid* (10th, 166).

Honor Roll: *Dodge City* (36), *Daughters Courageous* (31), *Confessions of a Nazi Spy* (30), *Angels with Dirty Faces* (29), *The Dawn Patrol* (22), *The Roaring Twenties* (15), *Dust be My Destiny* (12).

NATIONAL BOARD OF REVIEW
Ten Best (Exceptional Photoplays): *Confessions of a Nazi Spy* (1st – 'Best film of the year from any country').

Ten Best (Popular Appeal): *The Old Maid* (5th), *Dark Victory* (7th), *Juarez* (8th).

Performances: James Cagney (*The Roaring Twenties*), Bette Davis (*Dark Victory* and *The Old Maid*), Francis Lederer and Paul Lukas (*Confessions of a Nazi Spy*).

1940

ACADEMY
Awards: Special Award to Colonel Nathan Levinson for his outstanding

service to the industry and the Army during the past nine years, which has made possible the present efficient mobilisation of the motion picture industry facilities for the production of Army training films.

Nominations: *All This and Heaven Too, The Letter*, Best Picture; Bette Davis, Best Actress (*The Letter*); James Stephenson, Best Supporting Actor (*The Letter*); Barbara O'Neill, Best Supporting Actress (*All This and Heaven Too*); William Wyler, Direction (*The Letter*); Byron Haskin and Nathan Levinson, Special Effects (*The Sea Hawk*); Norman Burnside, Heinz Herald and John Huston, Writing – Original Screenplay (*The Story of Dr Ehrlich's Magic Bullet*); Warren Low, Film Editing (*The Letter*); Gaetano Gaudio, Cinematography – Black and white (*The Letter*); Nathan Levinson, Sound Recording (*The Sea Hawk*); Anton Grot, Art Direction (*The Sea Hawk*); Erich Wolfgang Korngold, Music – Scoring (*The Sea Hawk*); Max Steiner, Music – Original Score (*The Letter*).

FILM DAILY

Ten Best: *All This and Heaven Too* (5th, 230).

Honor Roll: *Knute Rockne – All American* (136), *The Story of Dr Ehrlich's Magic Bullet* (121), *We Are Not Alone* (61), *The Fighting 69th* (55), *The Private Lives of Elizabeth and Essex*, *The Sea Hawk* (44), *City for Conquest*, *They Drive by Night* (19), *A Dispatch from Reuters* (17), *No Time for Comedy* (15).

NATIONAL BOARD OF REVIEW

Ten Best (Popular Appeal – Review Committee): *All This and Heaven Too* (8th).

Ten Best (Popular Appeal – Motion Picture Councils): *All This and Heaven Too* (2nd), *Knute Rockne – All American* (6th).

Performances: Jane Bryan and Flora Robson (*We Are Not Alone*).

1941

ACADEMY

Awards: Gary Cooper, Best Actor (*Sergeant York*); Mary Astor, Best Supporting Actress (*The Great Lie*); William Holmes, Film Editing (*Sergeant York*).

Nominations: *The Maltese Falcon, One Foot in Heaven, Sergeant York*, Best Picture; Walter Brennan, Best Supporting Actor (*Sergeant York*); Sydney Greenstreet, Best Supporting Actor (*The Maltese Falcon*); Margaret Wycherley, Best Supporting Actress (*Sergeant York*); Howard Hawks, Direction (*Sergeant York*); Harold Arlen and Johnny Mercer, Music – Song ('Blues in the Night', *Blues in the Night*); Max Steiner, Music – Scoring of a Dramatic Picture (*Sergeant York*); Heinz Roemheld, Music – Scoring of a Musical Picture (*The Strawberry Blonde*); Richard Connell and Robert Presnell, Writing – Original Story (*Meet John Doe*); Harry Chandlee, Abem Finkel, John Huston and Howard Koch, Writing – Original Screenplay (*Sergeant York*); John Huston, Writing – Screenplay (*The Maltese Falcon*); Sol Polito, Cinematography – Black and white (*Sergeant York*); Bert Glennon, Cinematography – Color (*Dive Bomber*); John Hughes and Fred Maclean, Art direction – black and white (*Sergeant York*); Nathan Levinson, Sound recording (*Sergeant York*).

FILM DAILY

Ten Best: *Sergeant York* (2nd, 413), *Meet John Doe* (9th, 218).

Honor Roll: *The Letter* (92), *The Maltese Falcon* (57), *The Great Lie* (49), *Dive Bomber* (25), *High Sierra* (22), *The Bride Came C.O.D.* (20), *The Strawberry Blonde* (19), *The Sea Wolf* (14), *Shining Victory* (10).

NATIONAL BOARD OF REVIEW

Ten Best (Exceptional Photoplays): *High Sierra* (6th).

Ten Best (Popular Appeal – Review Committee): *Sergeant York* (2nd), *Meet John Doe* (8th), *One Foot in Heaven* (9th).

Ten Best (Popular Appeal – Motion Picture Councils): *Sergeant York* (1st), *Meet John Doe* (5th), *One Foot in Heaven* (6th).

Best Performances: Mary Astor (*The Great Lie* and *The Maltese Falcon*), Humphrey Bogart (*High Sierra* and *The Maltese Falcon*), Gary Cooper (*Sergeant York*), James Gleason (*Meet John Doe*), Ida Lupino (*High Sierra*), James Stephenson (*The Letter* and *Shining Victory*).[1]

1. Best Performances are listed in alphabetical order.

Appendix II   Main First-Run Engagements in New York and Los Angeles, 1929-41

The following material is taken from the entertainments pages of the *New York Times* and the *Los Angeles Times* between January 1929 and December 1941. Only Warner Brothers first-run theatres have been covered on a systematic basis, but I have also included films which were premiered in theatres belonging to other companies and, in the case of Los Angeles, films which received gala premieres at Warner theatres not normally used as first-run houses.

The New York theatres which figure regularly in the following lists are:

– the Strand (seating capacity 2,758) at 1577 Broadway, which was Warners' regular grind house at the beginning of the period and, from early 1932, their only Broadway theatre in continuous use as a first-run house;
– the Warner (seating capacity 1,286) at 1664 Broadway, which was used for roadshows in 1929 and 1930, but thereafter became a second-run house screening films made by Warners and other companies;
– the Winter Garden (seating capacity 1,671) at 1646 Broadway, which was a major roadshow theatre from 1929 to 1932, but thereafter declined into a second-run grind house and closed in April 1933;
– the Hollywood (seating capacity 1,800) at Broadway and 51st, a custom-built movie palace which opened on 22 April 1932 with *Hold Everything*, was in regular but by no means constant use as a roadshow theatre up to the end of 1933, and was then used for only a few weeks in most years to premiere prestige productions (for the rest of the year, it housed live stage shows);
– the Central (seating capacity 922), a small theatre at Broadway and 47th, leased by First National and not used for first runs beyond 1930.

Other major New York theatres which appear from time to time are: the RKO Music Hall (seating capacity 6,000) at Radio City, which was used to premiere certain major Warners pictures in the second half of the decade; the Astor (seating capacity 1,141) at 1531 Broadway, and the Rivoli (seating capacity 2,122) at 1620 Broadway.

In Los Angeles, the theatres logged are:

– the Warners Hollywood (seating capacity 2,756) at Hollywood and Wilcox, which remained the company's major Los Angeles showcase throughout the period;
– the Warners Downtown (seating capacity 2,500) at 7th and Hill, which opened on 26 September 1929 as a roadshow theatre, ran the same programme as the Hollywood from October 1930 until January 1932, fluctuated between duplicating the Hollywood programme and following it one week behind for the next three and a half years, then from the end of August 1935 regularly ran the same programme as the Hollywood;
– the Warners Western (seating capacity 2,500) at Wilshire and Western,

which opened with the West Coast premiere of *Alexander Hamilton* on 7 October 1931 but was used as a first-run theatre for a bare three months before first combining with the Downtown to show the previous week's programme from the Hollywood for most of 1932, then becoming an ordinary neighbourhood theatre for the rest of the decade; it was renamed the Wiltern in 1934.

Other Los Angeles theatres referred to below are: Grauman's Chinese (seating capacity 2,028) at Hollywood and Highland, where *Gold Diggers of 1933* was premiered; the Carthay Circle (seating capacity 1,734) at the Carthay Center, which was used to premiere *Anthony Adverse* and *The Life of Emile Zola*; the RKO Hill Street (seating capacity 2,916) at 8th and Hill, which doubled with the Warners Hollywood from September 1934 until August 1935, replacing the Downtown as the company's main city-centre showcase; Loew's State at 7th and Broadway (seating capacity 2,242); the Paramount (seating capacity 3,347) at 6th and Hill, used to premiere certain films early in the period; and Warners Beverly Hills Theatre on Wilshire (seating capacity 1,620), a neighbourhood theatre which was used for the gala West Coast premiere of *A Midsummer Night's Dream* in 1935 (and is the only Warners theatre of all those mentioned still to be operating as a movie theatre under its original name).

A 'run' is taken as being from the day the film was first shown at a theatre until the day before the next programme came in. This involves certain problems in the first half of the decade, when films were often premiered in both cities at the last evening show (sometimes the midnight show), with the previous week's programme being played for the two or three matinee shows. But since this practice was also applied at the other end of the film's run, it makes little difference to the length of the engagement, which is what the tables are concerned with. Finally, it is highly probable that, without my being aware of it, one or more theatres in both cities were, on various days during the 13-year period, closed as a result of strikes, power cuts or other unforeseen circumstances.

The following tables include all Warners films which ran for two weeks or more in either city. The figures before the double oblique stroke (//) are for New York, those after for Los Angeles, irrespective of the city in which the film was premiered. The figure in the right-hand column is the two-city total. Where films transferred from a roadshow theatre to another theatre generally used for first runs (i.e., in New York, from the Hollywood to the Strand) – something which happened regularly in 1929 but only occasionally thereafter – I have included both engagements.

A clear pattern of exhibition exists at the beginning of the period. Big pictures are given roadshows, then transferred to the grind house – an exhibition practice common in the silent period and essentially carried over from the legitimate theatre. This pattern begins to change from late 1932 onwards into something much more familiar to present-day moviegoers: a run of one or more weeks, with the changeover day remaining the same for several months at a time. By the end of the decade, the changeover day was all but inflexible: Fridays at the Strand, Thursdays at the Hollywood and Downtown.

1929

Disraeli (Warner, 2 October – 1 December / Central, 2 December – 27 March 1930 / Strand, 4-17 April 1930 // Hollywood, 7 November – 1 December)   215

On with the Show (Winter Garden, 28 May – 29 August / Strand, 13-19 September // Hollywood, 20 May – 23 June)   136

Gold Diggers of Broadway (Winter Garden, 30 August – 17 November / Strand, 5-19 December // Downtown, 26 September – 3 November)   133

Weary River (Central, 24 January – 1 April / Strand, 13-26 April // Paramount, 28 February – 6 March)   89

General Crack (Warner, 3 December – 29 January 1930 / Strand, 28 February – 6 March 1930 // Hollywood, 16 December – 2 January 1930)   83

Say it with Songs (Warner, 6 August – 1 October / Strand, 18-24 October // Hollywood, 7-22 October)   80

Sally (Winter Garden, 23 December – 12 February 1930 / Strand, 7-13 March 1930 // Hollywood, 12-30 January 1930)   78

The Desert Song (Warner, 1 May – 3 June / Strand 15-21 June // Hollywood, 8 April – 12 June)   76

Show of Shows (Winter Garden, 20 November – 22 December / Strand, 17-30 January 1930 // Downtown, 6 January – 1 February 1930)   74

Fast Life (Central, 15 August – 30 September / Strand, 11-17 October // Hollywood, 12-22 September)   65

Drag (Warner, 20 June – 3 August / Strand, 9-15 August // Paramount, 18-24 July)   59

The Squall (Central, 9 May – 19 June / Strand, 29 June – 5 July // RKO Hill Street, 29 June – 5 July)   56

His Captive Woman (Central, 2 April – 8 May / Strand, 18-24 May // Loew's State, 30 May – 6 June)   51

Young Nowheres (Central, 1 October – 5 November / Strand, 15-21 November // Loew's State, 7-13 November)   50

The Redeeming Sin (Warner, 15 February – 7 March / Strand, 6-12 April // Hollywood, 28 January – 17 February)   49

Broadway Babies (Central, 21 June – 22 July / Strand, 16-22 August // ??)   47?

Sonny Boy (Warner, 1-14 March / Strand, 23-29 March // Hollywood, 18 March – 7 April)   42

Paris (Central, 7 November – 1 December / Strand, 27 December – 2 January 1930 // Downtown, 23-29 December)   40

Honky Tonk (Warner, 4-19 June // Hollywood, 22 July – 4 August)   30

Smiling Irish Eyes (Central, 23 July – 14 August // Loew's State, 26 September – 2 October)   30

The Argyle Case (Strand, 30 August – 5 September // Hollywood, 19 August – 1 September)   21

Conquest (Strand, 9-15 February // Hollywood, 18 February – 3 March)   21

Footlights and Fools (Strand, 8-14 November // Downtown, 18 November – 1 December)   21

The Gamblers (Strand, 23-29 August // Hollywood, 8-21 July)   21

The Hottentot (Strand, 6-12 September // Hollywood, 5-18 August)   21

Is Everybody Happy? (Strand, 1-7 November // Downtown, 4-17 November)   21

Queen of the Night Clubs (Strand, 16-22 March // Downtown, 4-17 March)   21

1930

Old English (Warner, 21 August – 28 October / Strand, 21-26 November // Hollywood, 29 August – 11 September)   89

Outward Bound (Hollywood, 17 September – 29 October / Warner, 30 October – 25 November // Hollywood, 5-15 January 1931)   74

The Dawn Patrol (Winter Garden, 10 July – 10 September // Hollywood, 26 September – 2 October)   70

The Green Goddess (Winter Garden, 13 February – 2 April/ Strand, 23-29 May // Hollywood, 21 February – 6 March)   70

Hold Everything (Hollywood, 22 April – 20 May / Strand, 13-16 June // Hollywood, 20 March – 13 April)   67

The Office Wife (Winter Garden, 25 September – 6 November // Downtown, 19 September – 2 October)   64

Mammy (Warner, 27 March – 5 May / Strand, 6-12 June // Downtown, 24 April – 8 May)   62

Moby Dick (Hollywood, 14 August – 16 September / Strand, 3-9 October // Downtown, 15 August – 4 September)   62

Song of the Flame (Warner, 6 May – 13 June / Strand, 18-24 July // Hollywood, 20 April – 1 May)   58

Viennese Nights (Warner, 26 November – 6 January 1931 / Strand, 13-19 February 1931 // Hollywood, 6-12 March 1931)   56

Son of the Gods (Warner, 30 January – 26 February / Strand, 14-27 March // Downtown, 2-14 February)   55

Kismet (Hollywood, 30 October – 7 December / Strand, 6-12 February 1931 // Hollywood, 2-14 February 1931)   53

Song of the West (Warner, 27 February – 26 March / Strand, 18-24 April // Downtown, 9-20 March)   47

Bride of the Regiment (Hollywood, 21 May – 13 June / Strand, 8-14 August // Hollywood, 1-12 June)   43

Under a Texas Moon (Winter Garden, 3 April – 1 May // Downtown, 28 March – 10 April)   43

The Life of the Party (Winter Garden, 7 November – 3 December // Hollywood and Downtown, 31 October – 13 November)   41

The Man from Blankleys (Central, 28 March – 28 April // Hollywood, 2-10 May)   41

Numbered Men (Winter Garden, 7 June – 9 July // Downtown, 9-15 May)   40

Doorway to Hell (Strand, 31 October – 20 November // Hollywood and Downtown, 28 November – 11 December)   35

Mothers Cry (Winter Garden, 4-30 December // Downtown, 23-29 January 1931)   34

The Lash (Winter Garden, 31 December – 15 January 1931 // Hollywood and Downtown, 2-15 January 1931)   30

Bright Lights (Warner, 7-20 February 1931 // Downtown, 4-17 July)   28

No, No, Nanette (Strand, 3-16 January // RKO Hill Street, 4-17 January)   28

Three Faces East (Strand, 5-18 September // Downtown, 18-31 July)   28

Show Girl in Hollywood (Winter Garden, 2-20 May // Hollywood, 20-26 June)   26

Courage (Winter Garden, 21 May – 6 June // Hollywood, 11-18 May)   25

She Couldn't Say No (Strand, 14-20 February // Downtown, 22 February – 8 March)   22

The Bad Man (Strand, 26 September – 2 October // Downtown, 5-18 September) 21

Big Boy (Winter Garden, 11-24 September // Hollywood, 3-9 October) 21

The Girl of the Golden West (Strand, 24-30 October // Hollywood, 12-25 September) 21

The Gorilla (Warner, 21 February – 6 March 1931 // Downtown, 14-20 November) 21

The Matrimonial Bed (Strand, 22-28 August // Hollywood, 1-14 August) 21

Maybe It's Love (Strand, 17-23 October // Hollywood, 17-30 October) 21

Scarlet Pages (Strand, 5-11 December // Downtown, 1-14 August) 21

Top Speed (Strand, 29 August – 4 September // Hollywood, 15-28 August) 21

The Way of All Men (Strand, 19-25 September // Hollywood, 18-31 July) 21

Sweethearts and Wives (Strand, 27 June – 10 July // Hollywood, 26-31 May) 20

Nancy from Naples (also known as *Oh! Sailor, Behave!* (?? // Hollywood, 4-17 July) 14?

1931

Five Star Final (Winter Garden, 10 September – 4 November // Western, 27 October – 18 November / Downtown, 19-25 November) 86

Alexander Hamilton (Hollywood, 16 September – 22 October / Strand, 23-29 October // Western, 7-27 October / Downtown, 28 October – 4 November) 72

Smart Money (Winter Garden, 18 June – 5 August // Hollywood and Downtown, 18 June – 1 July) 63

The Star Witness (Winter Garden, 3 August – 9 September // Hollywood and Downtown, 27 August – 9 September) 52

The Millionaire (Winter Garden, 9 April – 13 May // Hollywood and Downtown, 1-14 May) 49

Svengali (Hollywood, 1 May – 11 June // Hollywood and Downtown, 22-28 May) 49

Bought (Hollywood, 14 August – 15 September // Hollywood and Downtown, 13-26 August) 46

Illicit (Winter Garden, 16 January – 16 February // Hollywood and Downtown, 20 February – 5 March) 46

The Mad Genius (Hollywood, 23 October – 22 November // Western, 19 November – 2 December) 45

Little Caesar (Strand, 9 January – 5 February // Hollywood and Downtown, 30 January – 12 February) 42

The Public Enemy (Strand, 24 April – 28 May // Hollywood and Downtown, 15-21 May) 42

Chances (Hollywood, 12 June – 5 July // Hollywood and Downtown, 10-16 July) 37

Safe in Hell (Warner, 31 December – 28 January 1932 // Hollywood and Downtown, 26 November – 2 December) 36

Manhattan Parade (Winter Garden, 25 December – 14 January 1932 // Hollywood and Downtown, 24-30 December) 29

Sit Tight (Winter Garden, 17 February – 10 March // Hollywood and Downtown, 13-19 March) 29

The Finger Points (Strand, 27 March – 16 April // Hollywood and Downtown, 17-23 April) 28

The Maltese Falcon (Winter Garden, 28 May – 17 June // Hollywood and Downtown, 5-11 June) 28
Night Nurse (Strand, 17-30 July // Hollywood and Downtown, 23 July – 5 August) 28
The Ruling Voice (Winter Garden, 5-25 November // Hollywood and Downtown, 21-28 October) 28
Kiss Me Again (Warner, 7-23 January // Hollywood and Downtown, 20-26 March) 24
50 Million Frenchmen (Winter Garden, 25 March – 8 April // Hollywood and Downtown, 10-16 April) 22
Blonde Crazy (Strand, 4-17 December // Hollywood and Downtown, 5-11 November) 21
Going Wild (Warner, 24 January – 6 February // Hollywood and Downtown, 16-22 January) 21
The Last Flight (Strand, 21 August – 3 September // Hollywood, 10-16 September) 21
The Road to Singapore (Strand, 2-15 October // Hollywood and Downtown, 8-14 October) 21

1932

The Man Who Played God (Warner, 10 February – 10 March // Western, 10 February – 2 March) 52
Life Begins (Hollywood, 25 August – 11 September / Strand, 16-29 September // Hollywood, 28 October – 9 November) 45
The Crowd Roars (Winter Garden, 23 March – 20 April // Hollywood, 28 April – 11 May) 43
Taxi! (Strand, 7-28 January / Warner, 29 January – 9 February // Hollywood, 7-13 January) 42
Tiger Shark (Winter Garden, 23 September – 20 October // Hollywood, 22 September – 5 October) 42
Blessed Event (Strand, 2-15 September // Hollywood, 1-21 September) 35
The Hatchet Man (Winter Garden, 4 February – 2 March // Hollywood, 28 January – 3 February) 35
The Mouthpiece (Winter Garden, 21 April – 18 May // Hollywood, 21-27 April) 35
I Am a Fugitive from a Chain Gang (Strand, 11 November – 7 December // Hollywood and Downtown, 10-16 November) 34
The Dark Horse (Winter Garden, 9-29 June // Hollywood, 22-29 June) 29
Two Seconds (Winter Garden, 19 May – 8 June // Hollywood, 26 May – 1 June) 28
Winner Take All (Strand, 17 June – 7 July // Hollywood, 7-13 July) 28
Alias the Doctor (Winter Garden, 3-22 March // Hollywood, 25 February – 2 March) 27
Union Depot (Winter Garden, 15 January – 3 February // Hollywood, 21-27 January) 27
You Said a Mouthful (Winter Garden, 17 November – 6 December // Hollywood and Downtown, 17-23 November) 27
Silver Dollar (Strand, 23 December – 8 January 1933 // Hollywood and Downtown, 29 December – 4 January 1933) 24

1933

1934

Wonder Bar (Strand, 1-23 March // Hollywood and Downtown, 15 March – 4 April) 44

Dames (Strand, 16 August – 13 September // Hollywood and Downtown, 31 August – 14 September) 43

20 Million Sweethearts (Strand, 26 April – 16 May // Hollywood and Downtown, 2-16 May) 35

Here Comes the Navy (Strand, 21 July – 9 August // Hollywood and Downtown, 2-15 August) 34

Flirtation Walk (Strand, 29 November – 16 December // Hollywood and RKO Hill Street, 29 November – 12 December) 32

Fashions of 1934 (Hollywood, 29 January – 11 February // Hollywood and Downtown [as *Fashion Follies of 1934*], 22-28 February) 31

Massacre (Strand, 17-31 January // Hollywood and Downtown, 25-31 January) 22

The St Louis Kid (Strand, 31 October – 14 November // Hollywood and RKO Hill Street, 29 November – 5 December) 22

Fog Over Frisco (Strand, 7-20 June // Hollywood and Downtown, 7-13 June) 21

Happiness Ahead (Strand, 11-24 October // Hollywood and RKO Hill Street, 26 January – 1 February 1935) 21

Hi, Nellie! (Strand, 1-14 February // Hollywood and Downtown, 8-14 February) 21

Mandalay (Strand, 15-28 February // Hollywood and Downtown, 1-7 March) 21

1935

A Midsummer Night's Dream (Hollywood, 9 October – 5 January 1936 / Strand, 3-16 October 1936 // Beverly Hills, 16 October – 30 November / Hollywood and Downtown, 21-27 October 1936) 163

G-Men (Strand, 1 May – 5 June // Hollywood and RKO Hill Street, 25 April – 8 May) 50

Captain Blood (Strand, 25 December – 17 January 1936 // Hollywood and Downtown, 1-21 January 1936) 45

Frisco Kid (Strand, 23 November – 13 December // Hollywood and Downtown, 28 November – 11 December) 35

Bordertown (Strand, 23 January – 6 February // Hollywood and RKO Hill Street, 12-25 January) 29

The Irish in Us (Strand, 31 July – 14 August // Hollywood and RKO Hill Street, 8-21 August) 29

Black Fury (Strand, 10-30 April // Hollywood and RKO Hill Street, 23-29 May) 28

Oil for the Lamps of China (Strand, 6-19 June // Hollywood and RKO Hill Street, 6-19 June) 28

Special Agent (Strand, 18 September – 1 October // Hollywood and Downtown, 25 September – 8 October) 28

Devil Dogs of the Air (Strand, 7-20 February // Hollywood and RKO Hill Street, 9-21 February) 27

Page Miss Glory (Strand, 29 August – 11 September // Hollywood and Downtown, 30 August – 10 September) 26

Dr Socrates (Strand, 2-16 October // Hollywood and Downtown, 30 October – 6 November)   23

Shipmates Forever (Strand, 17-31 October // Hollywood and Downtown, 9-16 October)   23

Gold Diggers of 1935 (Strand, 14-27 March // Hollywood and RKO Hill Street, 18-24 April)   21

In Caliente (Strand, 27 June – 10 July // Hollywood and RKO Hill Street, 4-10 July)   21

Sweet Music (Strand, 21 February – 6 March // Hollywood and RKO Hill Street, 22-28 February)   21

1936

Anthony Adverse (Strand, 26 August – 25 September // Carthay Circle, 29 July – 21 September / Hollywood and Downtown, 26 November – 9 December)   100

Three Men on a Horse (Strand, 25 November – 24 December // Hollywood and Downtown coupled with *Fugitive in the Sky*, 25 December – 7 January 1937)   44

The Charge of the Light Brigade (Strand, 31 October – 24 November // Hollywood and Downtown c/w *Smart Blonde*, 16-27 January 1937)   37

Ceiling Zero (Strand, 18 January – 7 February // Hollywood and Downtown, 29 January – 11 February)   35

Bullets or Ballots (Strand, 26 May – 11 June // Hollywood and Downtown, 28 May – 3 June)   31

The Petrified Forest (RKO Music Hall, 6-19 February // Hollywood and Downtown, 12-25 February)   28

The Story of Louis Pasteur (Strand, 8-21 February // Hollywood and Downtown, 26 February – 10 March)   28

China Clipper (Strand, 12-25 August // Hollywood and Downtown, 27 August – 18 September)   27

The Green Pastures (RKO Music Hall, 16-29 July // Hollywood and Downtown, 14-26 August)   27

Colleen (Strand, 7-20 March // Hollywood and Downtown, 11-19 March)   23

Gold Diggers of 1937 (Strand, 25 December – 8 January 1937 // Hollywood and Downtown c/w *King of Hockey*, 8-15 January 1937)   23

Public Enemy's Wife (Strand, 8-21 July // Hollywood and Downtown c/w *Two Against the World*, 9-17 July)   23

The White Angel (Strand, 24 June – 7 July // Hollywood and Downtown, 25 June – 3 July)   23

Cain and Mabel (Strand, 17-30 October // Hollywood and Downtown c/w *The Case of the Black Cat*, 4-11 November)   22

The Singing Kid (Strand, 4-17 April // Hollywood and Downtown, 9-16 April)   22

I Married a Doctor (Strand, 18 April – 1 May // Hollywood and Downtown, 17-23 April)   21

1937

The Life of Emile Zola (Hollywood, 11 August – 7 November / Strand, 24 November – 21 December // Carthay Circle, 9 September – 24 October / Hollywood and Downtown, 18-31 December)   177

Kid Galahad (Strand, 26 May – 15 June // Hollywood and Downtown, c/w
That Man's Here Again, 2-15 June)   42
Green Light (Strand, 12 February – 4 March // Hollywood and Downtown,
4-16 March)   34
The Prince and the Pauper (Strand, 6-25 May // Hollywood and Downtown,
12-25 May)   34
Marked Woman (Strand, 10 April – 5 May // Hollywood and Downtown, 14-20
April)   33
That Certain Woman (Strand, 15 September – 1 October // Hollywood and
Downtown c/w *Over the Goal*, 14-27 October)   31
Alcatraz Island (Strand, 13-26 October // Hollywood and Downtown, 18
November – 1 December, c/w *Sh! The Octopus* in the first week and *It's Love
I'm After* in the second)   28
The King and the Chorus Girl (Strand, 27 March – 9 April // Hollywood and
Downtown, 31 March – 13 April)   28
The Singing Marine (Strand, 30 June – 13 July // Hollywood and Downtown
c/w *The Devil is Driving*, 30 June – 13 July)   28
Varsity Show (Strand, 1-14 September // Hollywood and Downtown c/w *Wine,
Women and Horses*, 2-15 September)   28
They Won't Forget (Strand, 14 July – 3 August // Hollywood and Downtown
c/w *Love is on the Air*, 28 October – 3 November)   27
Tovarich (RKO Music Hall, 30 December – 12 January 1938 // Hollywood
and Downtown, 1-12 January 1938)   25
Submarine D-1 (Strand, 29 December – 11 January 1938 // Hollywood and
Downtown c/w *Torchy Blane, the Adventurous Blonde*, 2-8 December)   23
Black Legion (Strand, 16-29 January // Hollywood and Downtown c/w *Women
of Glamor*, 18-24 February)   21
Confession (Strand, 18-31 August // Hollywood and Downtown c/w *Dance,
Charlie, Dance*, 30 September – 6 October)   21
Ever Since Eve (RKO Music Hall, 24-30 June // Hollywood and Downtown
c/w *The Case of the Stuttering Bishop*, 14-27 July)   21
The Perfect Specimen (Strand, 27 October – 9 November // Hollywood and
Downtown c/w *Escape by Night*, 4-10 November)   21
It's Love I'm After (Strand, 10-23 November // Hollywood and Downtown c/w
Alcatraz Island, 25 November – 1 December)   21
Ready, Willing and Able (Strand, 13-26 March // Hollywood and Downtown
c/w *Midnight Court*, 24-30 March)   21

1938

Angels with Dirty Faces (Strand, 25 November – 21 December // Hollywood
and Downtown, 24 November – 9 December)   44
The Adventures of Robin Hood (RKO Music Hall, 12 May – 1 June // Hollywood
and Downtown, 12 May – 1 June)   42
The Amazing Dr Clitterhouse (Strand, 20 July – 9 August // Hollywood and
Downtown c/w *Mr Chump*, 28 July – 9 August)   36
The Dawn Patrol (Strand, 23 December – 5 January 1939 // Hollywood and
Downtown c/w *Nancy Drew, Detective*, 17 December – 6 January 1939)   35
The Sisters (Strand, 14 October – 3 November // Hollywood and Downtown

The Oklahoma Kid (Strand, 10-23 March // Hollywood and Downtown c/w *The Adventures of Jane Arden*, 16-29 March)   28
We Are Not Alone (RKO Music Hall, 30 November – 13 December // Hollywood and Downtown c/w *Private Detective*, 30 November – 13 December)   28
You Can't Get Away with Murder (Strand, 24 March – 6 April // Hollywood and Downtown c/w *The Man in the Iron Mask*, 3-16 August)   28
They Made Me a Criminal (Strand, 20 January – 2 February // Hollywood and Downtown, 26 January – 6 February)   26
Dead End Kids on Dress Parade (Strand, 27 October – 9 November // Wiltern, 6-12 December)   21
Dust Be My Destiny (Strand, 6-19 October // Hollywood and Downtown c/w *Nancy Drew and the Hidden Staircase*, 28 September – 4 October)   21
Espionage Agent (Strand, 22 September – 5 October // Hollywood and Downtown c/w *Everybody's Happy*, 21-27 September)   21
Invisible Stripes (Strand, 12-25 January 1940 // Hollywood and Downtown, 28 December – 3 January 1940)   21
The Kid from Kokomo (Strand, 19 May – 1 June // Hollywood and Downtown c/w *Sons of Liberty*, 29 June – 5 July)   21

1940

The Fighting 69th (Strand, 26 January – 22 February // Hollywood and Downtown c/w *Calling Philo Vance*, 27 January – 14 February)   47
The Sea Hawk (Strand, 9 August – 5 September // Hollywood and Downtown, 24 August – 11 September)   47
The Letter (Strand, 22 November – 19 December // Hollywood and Downtown, 19 November – 2 December)   42
All This and Heaven Too (RKO Music Hall, 4-31 July // Hollywood and Downtown, 26 September – 4 October)   37
Santa Fe Trail (Strand, 20 December – 9 January 1941 // Hollywood and Downtown, 31 December – 15 January 1941)   37
Torrid Zone (Strand, 17 May – 6 June // Hollywood and Downtown, 23 May – 5 June)   35
Brother Orchid (Strand, 7-27 June // Hollywood and Downtown c/w *Sandy is a Lady*, 21 June – 3 July)   34
City for Conquest (Strand, 27 September – 10 October // Hollywood and Downtown c/w *Nobody's Sweetheart*, 17-28 October)   33
Knute Rockne – All American (Strand, 18 October – 7 November // Hollywood and Downtown c/w *Slightly Tempted*, 5-16 October)   33
Virginia City (Strand, 22 March – 4 April // Hollywood and Downtown, 21 March – 8 April)   33
Four Mothers (Strand, 10-23 January 1941 // Hollywood and Downtown c/w *South of Suez*, 17-30 December)   28
No Time for Comedy (Strand, 6-26 September // Hollywood and Downtown c/w *Service with the Colors*, 19-25 September)   28
The Story of Dr Ehrlich's Magic Bullet (Strand, 23 February – 7 March // Hollywood and Downtown c/w *Blondie on a Budget*, 29 February – 13 March) 28
They Drive By Night (Strand, 26 July – 8 August // Hollywood and Downtown c/w *Scatterbrain*, 27 July – 9 August)   28

It All Came True (Strand, 5-18 April // Hollywood and Downtown c/w *King of the Lumberjacks*, 9-17 April)   23
My Love Came Back (Strand, 12-25 July // Hollywood and Downtown c/w *Murder in the Air*, 11-19 July)   23
Saturday's Children (Strand, 3-16 May // Hollywood and Downtown c/w *The Man with Nine Lives*, 2-8 May)   21
Three Cheers for the Irish (Strand, 8-21 March // Hollywood and Downtown c/w *The Lone Wolf Strikes*, 14-20 March)   21
'Til We Meet Again (Strand, 19 April – 2 May // Hollywood and Downtown c/w *Teddy, the Rough Rider*, 18-24 April)   21
Tugboat Annie Sails Again (Strand, 8-21 November // Hollywood and Downtown c/w *Hit Parade of 1941*, 5-11 November)   21

1941

Sergeant York (Astor, 3 July – 11 August / Hollywood, 12 August – 5 October / Strand, 17 October – 12 November // Hollywood and Downtown, 18 September – 22 October)   163
Meet John Doe (Hollywood and Rivoli, 13 March – 1 April, then at the Rivoli alone until 25 April // Hollywood and Downtown, 13 March – 9 April)   72
The Great Lie (Strand, 11 April – 8 May // Hollywood and Downtown c/w *The Case of the Black Parrot*, 24 April – 7 May)   42
The Bride Came C.O.D. (Strand, 25 July – 14 August // Hollywood and Downtown, 3-16 July)   35
Dive Bomber (Strand, 29 August – 18 September // Hollywood and Downtown, 21 August – 3 September)   35
Manpower (Strand, 4-24 July // Hollywood and Downtown, 17-30 July)   35
The Sea Wolf (Strand, 21 March – 10 April // Hollywood and Downtown c/w *The Great Mr Nobody*, 10-23 April)   35
The Strawberry Blonde (Strand, 21 February – 13 March // Hollywood and Downtown c/w *Father's Son*, 13-26 February)   35
They Died With Their Boots On (Strand, 20 November – 10 December // Hollywood and Downtown, 31 December – 14 January 1942)   35
Bad Men of Missouri (Strand, 15-28 August // Hollywood and Downtown c/w *Angels with Broken Wings*, 31 July – 13 August)   28
High Sierra (Strand, 24 January – 6 February // Hollywood and Downtown c/w *She Couldn't Say No*, 23 January – 5 February)   28
The Maltese Falcon (Strand, 3-16 October // Hollywood and Downtown c/w *Target for Tonight*, 20 November – 3 December)   28
Million Dollar Baby (Strand, 6-19 June // Hollywood and Downtown, 29 May – 11 June, c/w *Singapore Woman* for the first week and a revival of *Devil Dogs of the Air* for the second)   28
Navy Blues (Strand, 19 September – 2 October // Hollywood and Downtown, 4-17 September)   28
Out of the Fog (Strand, 20 June – 3 July // Hollywood and Downtown c/w *They Met in Argentina*, 12-20 June)   23
Blues in the Night (Strand, 11-24 December // Hollywood and Downtown c/w *You Belong to Me*, 13-19 November)   21
Footsteps in the Dark (Strand, 14-20 March // Hollywood and Downtown c/w

Here Comes Happiness, 27 February – 12 March)   21
Honeymoon for Three (Strand, 7-20 February // Hollywood and Downtown c/w a
revival of *Here Comes the Navy*, 16-22 January)   21
One Foot in Heaven (RKO Music Hall, 13-19 November // Hollywood and
Downtown, 4-17 December, c/w *The Tanks are Coming* for the first week of the
run only)   21
The Wagons Roll at Night (Strand, 9-22 May // Hollywood and Downtown c/w
Sis Hopkins, 8-14 May)   21

Changing exhibition patterns throughout the period

Number of long runs (in weeks)

	20+	15+	10+	9+	8+	7+	6+	5+
1929	2	1	6	1	1	3	2	2
1930	-	-	4	2	4	2	3	4
1931	-	-	2	1	-	3	5	2
1932	-	-	-	-	-	1	4	3
1933	1	-	1	-	-	1	2	2
1934	-	-	-	-	-	-	2	1
1935	1	-	-	-	-	1	1	1
1936	-	-	1	-	-	-	1	2
1937	1	-	-	-	-	-	1	-
1938	-	-	-	-	-	-	2	3
1939	-	-	-	1	1	-	-	7
1940	-	-	-	-	-	-	3	3
1941	1	-	1	-	-	-	1	6

Filmography

The information contained in this filmography is taken from prints of the films themselves, supplemented by material from published and unpublished sources. The unpublished sources are those in the Warners Archives at the University of Southern California; the published ones consist of contemporary trade papers and certain of the magazines and books (notably the *Films of . . .* series) listed in the bibliography.

The filmography covers only those films discussed in detail in this book. A complete but much less detailed filmography of all Warners pictures can be found in *The Warner Bros. Golden Anniversary Book* (New York, Dell, 1973).

Between 1929 and 1941, all films were released under the Warner Brothers banner, but variously registered as Warner Brothers, First National or (occasionally) Cosmopolitan pictures. Which of these three applies is indicated immediately after the title of each film. Since the aim is to provide information rather than to reproduce the terminology of contemporary credits, I have standardised certain of the production credits: 'Associate producer' includes the earlier 'Supervisor'; 'Screenplay' includes the earlier 'Adaptation by'; 'Photography' covers both 'Cameraman', which was standard in the early years, and 'Director of Photography' which began to appear towards the end of the decade; 'Costumes' also includes 'Gowns', used on films where only certain of the (women's) costumes were specially made; 'Orchestrations' covers both that credit and 'Orchestral arrangements by'; 'Musical director' includes the earlier credit of 'Vitaphone Orchestra conducted by'.

Since the credits included here relate to specific films, I have omitted Hal Wallis' 'Executive Producer' credit, which appeared regularly in the second half of the decade. For the same reason I have also omitted the credit 'Jack L. Warner in charge of production', which often appeared on the first title card.

The running time given is, as far as I have been able to ascertain, that of the first American release. Re-release prints and British releases were often shorter. The date of first showing is that (again, as far as I have been able to ascertain) on which the film received its first advertised public performance, not that of the first complete studio screening, the sneak preview (not a common practice at Warners), the trade show or the 'official' studio preview at Warners Hollywood Theatre.

The only reviews listed are those in *Variety* and the *New York Times*. The *Los Angeles Times*, which I have quoted fairly frequently in the text, reviewed all releases between 1929 and 1933, and most of the major releases between then and 1941, but the paper is not generally available in libraries, even on microfilm, outside Southern California.

The following abbreviations are used:

A.d.	Art director	Orch.	Orchestrations
Ass.d.	Assistant director	Ph.	Photography
Ass.p.	Associate producer	R.t.	Running time (minutes)
Cost.	Costumes	Sc.	Screenplay
D.	Director	Sd.	Sound

284

Dial.d.	Dialogue director	2nd d.	Second unit director
Ed.	Film editor	Sfx.	Special effects
M.	Music composed by	Tech.ad.	Technical adviser
M.d.	Musical director	U.m.	Unit manager
NYT	*New York Times*	V	*Variety*

The Adventures of Robin Hood
First National
Ass.p–Henry Blanke. U.m–Al Alborn. D–Michael Curtiz, William Keighley.
Ass.d–Lee Katz, Jack Sullivan. Dial.d–Irving Rapper. 2nd.d–Reeves Eason.
Sc–Norman Reilly Raine, Seton I. Miller. Ph–Tony Gaudio (Technicolor),
Sol Polito. Photographic Representative, Technicolor Corporation–W.
Howard Greene. Technicolor Color Director–Natalie Kalmus. Technicolor
Associate–Morgan Padelford. Ed–Ralph Dawson. A.d–Carl Jules Weyl.
Cost–Milo Anderson. Make-up–Perc Westmore. M–Erich Wolfgang
Korngold. Orch–Hugo Friedhofer, Milan Roder. Sd–C.A. Riggs. Tech.ad–
Louis Van den Ecker. Archer–Howard Hill. Fencing master–Fred Cavens.

Errol Flynn (*Sir Robin of Locksley*), Olivia De Havilland (*Maid Marian*), Basil
Rathbone (*Sir Guy of Gisbourne*), Claude Rains (*Prince John*), Ian Hunter
(*Richard the Lionhearted*), Eugene Pallette (*Friar Tuck*), Alan Hale (*Little John*),
Melville Cooper (*High Sheriff of Nottingham*), Patric Knowles (*Will Scarlet*),
Herbert Mundin (*Much, the Miller's Son*), Una O'Connor (*Bess*), Montagu
Love (*Bishop of Black Canon*), Robert Noble (*Sir Ralf*), Robert Warwick (*Sir
Geoffrey*), Lester Matthews (*Sir Ivor*), Howard Hill (*Captain of Archers*),
Leonard Willey (*Sir Essex*), Kenneth Hunter (*Sir Mortimer*), Colin Kenny (*Sir
Baldwin*), Harry Cording (*Dickon Malbete*), Ivan Simpson (*Tavern Proprietor*),
Charles McNaughton (*Crippen*), Lionel Belmore (*Humility Prin*), Janet Shaw
(*Prin's Daughter*), Crauford Kent (*Sir Norbett*), Ernie Stanton, Olaf Hytten,
Peter Hobbes (*Outlaws*), Hal Brazeale (*Sheriff's Squire*), Leonard Mudie (*Town
Crier*), Phyllis Coghlan (*Saxon Girl*), Leyland Hodges (*Norman Officer*),
Reginald Sheffield (*Herald*), Holmes Herbert (*Referee*), Wilson Benge (*Monk*),
Nick de Ruiz (*Hangman*), Dick Rich (*Soldier*), Austin Fairman (*Sir Nigel*), Val
Stanton, Alec Harford, Edward Dean, Sidney Baron (*Outlaws*), John Sutton,
Paul Power, Ivo Henderson, Jack Deery (*Knights with Richard*), Martin
Lamont (*Sir Guy's Squire*), Dennis d'Auburn, Cyril Thornton, Gerald Rogers,
Charles Irwin (*Saxons*), Connie Leon (*Saxon Woman*), Herbert Evans (*Sene-
chal*), Frank Hagney, James Baker (*Soldiers*), Joe North (*Monk*), Jack
Richardson (*Serf*), Claude Wisberg (*Blacksmith's Apprentice*), Harold
Entwhistle (*Tailor*), Leyland Hodgson (*Norman Officer*), Harold Howard
(*Beggar*), Bob Stevenson (*Soldier*), Bob St. Angelo (*Pierre de Caen*), Frank
Baker (*Prison Guard*), Lowden Adams (*Vieux Croisé*), Charles Bennett (*Ped-
dlar*), James Baker (*Philip d'Arras*), D'Arcy Corrigan (*Villager*).

R.t. 105.
Copyright, 14 March 1938.
First shown, Radio City Music Hall, New York, 12 May 1938.
Reviews, V, 27 April 1938 (Flin), NYT, 13 May 1938 (Frank S. Nugent).

Alcatraz Island
First National/A Cosmopolitan Production
Producer–Bryan Foy. D–William K. McGann. Dial.d–Harry Seymour. Sc–Crane Wilbur, from his own story. Ph–L.W. O'Connell. Ed–Frank Dewar. A.d–Esdras Hartley. Cost–Howard Shoup. Sd–Francis J. Scheid.

John Litel (*Gat Brady*), Ann Sheridan (*Flo Allen*), Mary Maguire (*Annabel Brady*), Gordon Oliver (*George Drake*), Dick Purcell (*David 'Harp' Santell*), Ben Welden (*Red Carroll*), Addison Richards (*Fred MacLane*), George E. Stone (*Tough Tony Burke*), Vladimir Sokoloff (*The Flying Dutchman*), Peggy Bates (*Miss Tolliver*), Doris Lloyd (*Miss Marquand*), Charles Trowbridge (*Warden Jackson*), Veda Ann Borg (*The Redhead*), Anderson Lawler (*Whitney Edwards*), Edward Keane (*Crandall*), Walter Young (*Federal Judge*), Ed Stanley (*U.S. Attorney*), Ellen Clancy, Matty Fain, Lane Chandler.

R.t. 63.
Copyright, 27 September 1937.
First shown, Strand, New York, 13 October 1937.
Reviews, V, 13 October 1937 (Char), NYT, 14 October 1937 (Frank S. Nugent).

Alexander Hamilton
Warner Brothers
D–John G. Adolfi. Ass.d–Ben Silvey. Sc–Julian Josephson, Maude Howell, from the play by George Arliss and Mary Hamlin. Ph–James Van Trees. Ed–Owen Marks. A.d–Esdras Hartley. Cost–Earl Luick. M.d–David Mendoza. Settings supervised by W. and J. Sloane.

George Arliss (*Alexander Hamilton*), Doris Kenyon (*Betsy Hamilton*), Dudley Digges (*Senator Timothy Roberts*), June Collyer (*Mrs Reynolds*), Montagu Love (*Thomas Jefferson*), Ralf Harolde (*Mr Reynolds*), Lionel Belmore (*General Schuyler*), Alan Mowbray (*George Washington*), John T. Murray (*Count Talleyrand*), Morgan Wallace (*Senator James Munroe*), John Larkin (*Zekial*), Gwendolyn Logan (*Martha Washington*), Charles Evans (*Whalen*), Russell Simpson (*1st ex-soldier*), James Durkin (*2nd ex-soldier*), Evelyn Hall (*Mrs Bingham*), Charles Middleton (*Chief Justice Jay*).

R.t. 71.
Copyright, 10 September 1931.
First shown, Hollywood, New York, 16 September 1931.
Reviews, NYT, 17 September 1931 (Mordaunt Hall), V, 22 September 1931 (Rush).

The Amazing Dr Clitterhouse
First National
Producer–Anatole Litvak. Ass.p–Robert Lord. D–Anatole Litvak. Ass.d–Jack Sullivan. Dial.d–Jo Graham. Sc–John Wexley, John Huston, based on the play by Barré Lyndon. Ph–Tony Gaudio. Ed–Warren Low. A.d–Carl Jules Weyl. Cost–Milo Anderson. M–Max Steiner. Orch–George Parish. Sd–C.A. Riggs. Tech.ad–Dr Leo Schulman.

Edward G. Robinson (*Dr Clitterhouse*), Claire Trevor (*Jo Keller*), Humphrey Bogart (*Rocks Valentine*), Allen Jenkins (*Okay*), Gale Page (*Nurse Randolph*),

Donald Crisp (*Inspector Lane*), Maxie Rosenbloom (*Butch*), Curt Bois (*Rabbit*), Bert Hanlon (*Pal*), Billy Wayne (*Candy*), Vladimir Sokoloff (*Popus*), Henry O'Neill (*Judge*), Robert Homans (*Lieutenant Johnson*), Ward Bond (*Tug*), John Litel (*Prosecuting Attorney*), Thurston Hall (*Grant*), Irving Bacon (*Jury Foreman*), William Worthington (*Guest*), Ed Mortimer (*Guest*), William Haade (*Watchman*), Thomas Jackson (*Connors*), Edward Gargan (*Sergeant*), Ray Dawe (*Policeman*), Bob Reeves (*Policeman*), Winifred Harris (*Mrs Ganswoort*), Eric Stanley (*Dr Ames*), Lois Cheaney (*Nurse Donor*), Wade Boteler (*Captain McLevy*), Larry Steers (*Guest*), Libby Taylor (*Mrs Jefferson*), Edgar Dearing (*Patrolman*), Sidney Bracy (*Chemist*), Vera Lewis (*Woman Juror*), Bruce Mitchell (*Bailiff*).

R.t. 87.
Copyright, 17 June 1938.
First shown, Strand, New York, 20 July 1938.
Reviews, NYT, 21 July 1938 (Frank S. Nugent), V, 22 July 1938 (Wear).

Angels with Dirty Faces
First National
Ass.p–Sam Bischoff. U.m–Frank Mattison. D–Michael Curtiz. Ass.d–Sherry Shourds. Dial.d–Jo Graham. Sc–John Wexley, Warren Duff, from the story by Rowland Brown. Ph–Sol Polito. Camera–Al Greene, Frankie Evans. Ed–Owen Marks. Scriptman–Francis Kowalski. A.d–Robert Haas. Properties–Herbert Plews. Cost–Orry-Kelly. Make-up–Monty Westmore. M–Max Steiner. Orch– Hugo Friedhofer. M.d–Leo F. Forbstein. Song–'Angels with Dirty Faces' by Fred Fisher, Maurice Spitahy. Sd–Everett A. Brown. Tech.ad–Father J.J. Devlin.

James Cagney (*Rocky Sullivan*), Pat O'Brien (*Jerry Connolly*), Humphrey Bogart (*James Frazier*), Ann Sheridan (*Laury Ferguson*), George Bancroft (*Mac Keefer*), Billy Halop (*Soapy*), Bobby Jordan (*Swing*), Leo Gorcey (*Bim*), Bernard Punsley (*Hunky*), Gabriel Dell (*Pasty*), Huntz Hall (*Crab*), Joe Downing (*Steve*), Edward Pawley (*Guard Edwards*), Adrian Morris (*Blackie*), Frankie Burke (*Rocky as a boy*), William Tracey (*Jerry as a boy*), Marilyn Knowlden (*Laury as a child*), Oscar O'Shea (*Guard Kennedy*), William Pawley (*Bugs*), John Hamilton (*Police Captain*), Earl Dwire (*Priest*), Jack Perrin (*Death Row Guard*), Mary Gordon (*Mrs Patrick*), Vera Lewis (*Soapy's Mother*), William Worthington (*Warden*), James Farley (*Railroad yard watchman*), Chuck Stubbs (*Red*), Eddie Syracuse (*Maggione boy*), Robert Homans (*Policeman*), Harris Berger (*Basketball Captain)*, Harry Hayden (*Pharmacist*), Dick Rich, Steven Darrell, Joe A. Devlin (*Gangsters*), William Edmunds (*Italian storekeeper*), Charles Wilson (*Buckley*), Frank Coghlan Jr, David Durand (*Boys in Poolroom*), Bill Cohee, Lavel Lund, Norman Wallace, Gary Carthew, Bibby Mayer (*Church Basketball Team*), Belle Mitchell (*Mrs Maggione*), Eddie Brian (*Newsboy*), Billy McLain (*Janitor*), Wilbur Mack (*Croupier*), Poppy Wilde (*Girl at Gaming Table*), George Offerman Jr (*Adult Boy*), Charles Trowbridge (*Norton J. White*), Ralph Sanford (*City Editor 'Press'*), Wilfred Lucas (*Police Officer*), Lane Chandler (*Guard*), Elliott Sullivan (*Cop*), Lottie Williams, George Mori, Dick Wessel, John Harron, Vince Lombardi, Al Hill, Thomas Jackson, Jeffrey Sayre, St. Brendan's Church Choir.

R.t. 97.
Copyright, 14 September 1938.
First shown, Warners Hollywood and Warners Downtown, Los Angeles, 24 November 1938.
Reviews, V, 26 October 1938 (Hobe), NYT, 26 November 1938 (Frank S. Nugent).

Anthony Adverse
Warner Brothers
Ass.p–Henry Blanke. U.m–Al Alborn. D–Mervyn LeRoy. Ass.d–Bill Cannon (1st), Art Lucker (2nd). Sc–Sheridan Gibney, from the novel by Hervey Allen. Ph–Tony Gaudio. Camera–Carl Guthrie. Special photographic effects–Fred Jackman. Ed–Ralph Dawson. Continuity–Irva Ross. A.d–Anton Grot. Associate a.d–Charles M. Novi. Set decorators–Harold Richmond, John Ewing. Properties–Eddie Edwards. Cost–Milo Anderson. Cosmetician–Perc Westmore. Hair styles–Joan St. Oegger. M–Erich Wolfgang Korngold. M.d–Leo F. Forbstein. Operas–Monteverdi (Leghorn), Aldo Franchetti (Paris). Sd–Nathan Levinson, Al Riggs. Tech.ad–Dwight Franklin. Opera sequences staged by Natale Carossio.

Fredric March (*Anthony Adverse*), Olivia De Havilland (*Angela Guessippi*), Donald Woods (*Vincent Nolte*), Anita Louise (*Maria*), Edmund Gwenn (*John Bonnyfeather*), Claude Rains (*Don Luis*), Louis Hayward (*Denis Moore*), Gale Sondergaard (*Faith*), Steffi Duna (*Neleta*), Billy Mauch (*Anthony aged ten*), Akim Tamiroff (*Carlo Cibo*), Ralph Morgan (*Debrulle*), Henry O'Neill (*Father Xavier*), Pedro De Cordoba (*Brother François*), Luis Alberni (*Tony Guessippi*), Fritz Leiber (*Ouvrard*), Joseph Crehan (*Captain Elisha Jorham*), Rafaela Ottiano (*Signora Bovina*), Rollo Lloyd (*Napoleon Bonaparte*), Leonard Mudie (*De Borrienne*), Marilyn Knowlden (*Florence Udney*), Mathilde Comont (*Cook Guessippi*), Eily Malyon (*Mother Superior*), J. Carrol Naish (*Major Doumet*), Scotty Beckett (*Little Anthony*), Paul Sotoff (*Ferdinand*), Frank Reicher (*Coach driver to Paris*), Clara Blandick (*Mrs Jorham*), Addison Richards (*Captain Matanza*), William Ricciardi (*Coachman in Leghorn*), Grace Stafford (*Lucia*), Boris Nicholai (*Courier*).

R.t. 140.
Copyright, 15 July 1936.
First shown, Carthay Circle, Los Angeles, 29 July 1936.
Reviews, NYT, 27 August 1936 (Frank S. Nugent), V, 2 September 1936 (Kauf).

Black Fury
First National
Ass.p–Robert Lord. D–Michael Curtiz. Ass.d–Russ Saunders. Dial.d–Frank McDonald. Sc–Abem Finkel, Carl Erickson, from the story 'Jan Volkanik' by Judge M.A. Musmanno and the play 'Bohunk' by Harry R. Irving. Ph–Byron Haskins. Ed–Thomas Richards. A.d–John Hughes. M.d–Leo F. Forbstein.

Paul Muni (*Joe Radek*), Karen Morley (*Anna Novak*), William Gargan (*Slim Johnson*), Barton MacLane (*McGee*), John T. Qualen (*Mike Kumansky*), J. Carrol Naish (*Steve*), Vince Barnett (*Kubanda*), Tully Marshall (*Tommy Poole*),

Henry O'Neill (*John W. Hendricks*), Joe Crehan (*Johnny Farrell*), Mae Marsh (*Mary Novak*), Sarah Haden (*Sophie*), Willard Robertson (*Walsh*), Effie Ellsler (*The Bubitschka*), Wade Boteler (*Mulligan*), Egon Brecher (*Alec Novak*), George Pat Collins (*Lefty*), Ward Bond (*Mac*), Akim Tamiroff (*Sokolsky*), Purnell Pratt (*Jenkins*), Eddie Shubert (*Butch*).

R.t. 94.
Copyright, 24 April 1935.
First shown, Strand, New York, 10 April 1935.
Reviews, NYT, 11 April 1935 (Andre Sennwald), V, 17 April 1935 (Abel Green).

Black Legion
Warner Brothers
Ass.p–Robert Lord. D–Archie L. Mayo. Ass.d–Jack Sullivan. Sc–Abem Finkel, William Wister Haines, from a story by Robert Lord. Ph–George Barnes. Ed–Owen Marks. A.d–Robert Haas. Cost–Milo Anderson. M–Bernhard Kaun. Sd–C.A. Riggs. Sfx–Fred Jackman, H.F. Koenekamp.

Humphrey Bogart (*Frank Taylor*), Dick Foran (*Eddie Jackson*), Erin O'Brien-Moore (*Ruth Taylor*), Ann Sheridan (*Betty Grogan*), Helen Flint (*Pearl Danvers*), Robert Barrat (*Brown*), Joseph Sawyer (*Cliff Moore*), Clifford Soubier (*Mike Grogan*), Alonzo Price (*Alf Hargrave*), Paul Harvey (*Billings*), Dickie Jones (*Buddy Taylor*), Samuel Hinds (*Judge*), Addison Richards (*Prosecuting Attorney*), Eddie Acuff (*Metcalf*), Dorothy Vaughan (*Mrs Grogan*), John Litel (*Tommy Smith*), Henry Brandon (*Joe Dumbrowski*), Pat C. Flick (*Nick Strumpas*), Francis Sayles (*Charlie*), Paul Stanton (*Barman*), Harry Hayden (*Jones*), Egon Brecher (*Dumbrowski*), Charles Halton (*Osgood*).

R.t. 83.
Copyright, 29 December 1936.
First shown, Strand, New York, 16 January 1937.
Reviews, NYT, 18 January 1937 (Frank S. Nugent), V, 20 January 1937 (Odec).

Blessed Event
Warner Brothers
Ass.p–Ray Griffith. D–Roy Del Ruth. Sc–Howard J. Green, from the play by Manuel Seff and Forrest Wilson. Ph–Sol Polito. Ed–James Gibbons. A.d–Robert Haas. M.d–Leo F. Forbstein.

Lee Tracy (*Alvin Roberts*), Mary Brian (*Gladys Price*), Dick Powell (*Bunny Harmon*), Allen Jenkins (*Frankie Wells*), Ruth Donnelly (*Miss Stevens*), Edwin Maxwell (*Sam Goebel*), Emma Dunn (*Mrs Roberts*), Ned Sparks (*George Moxley*), Walter Walker (*Louis Miller*), Frank McHugh (*Reilly*), Milton Maxwell (*Moskowitz*), Isabel Jewell (*Dorothy Lane*), Ruth Hall (*Miss Bauman*), George Chandler (*Hanson*), Tom Dugan (*Cooper*), William Halligan (*Herbert Flint*), George Meeker (*Church*), Jesse De Vorska (*Shapiro*), Walter Miller (*Boldt*), Harold Waldridge.

R.t. 83.
Copyright, 7 September 1932.
First shown, Warners Hollywood, Los Angeles, 1 September 1932.

Reviews, NYT, 3 September 1932 (Mordaunt Hall), V, 6 September 1932 (Rush).

Bordertown
Warner Brothers
Ass.p–Robert Lord. D–Archie L. Mayo. Ass.d–Leo Katz. Sc–Laird Doyle, Wallace Smith, from a story by Robert Lord, suggested by a novel by Carroll Graham. Ph–Tony Gaudio. Ed–Thomas Richards. A.d–Jack Okey. Cost–Orry-Kelly. M.d–Leo F. Forbstein.

Paul Muni (*Johnny Ramirez*), Bette Davis (*Marie Roark*), Margaret Lindsay (*Dale Elwell*), Eugene Pallette (*Charlie Roark*), Robert Barrat (*Padre*), Hobart Cavanaugh (*Drunk*), Gavin Gordon (*Brook Mandville*), William Davidson (*Dr Carter*), Arthur Stone (*Manuel Diego*), Vivian Tobin (*Dale's friend*), Soledad Jimenez (*Mrs Ramirez*), Henry O'Neill (*Mr Elwell*), Nella Walker (*Mrs Elwell*), Oscar Apfel, Samuel S. Hinds, Chris Pin Martin, Frank Puglia, Jack Norton.
R.t. 90.
Copyright, 15 December 1934.
First shown, general release, 5 January 1935.
Reviews, NYT, 24 January 1935 (Andre Sennwald), V, 29 January 1935 (Kauf).

Brother Orchid
Warner Brothers
Ass.p–Mark Hellinger. D–Lloyd Bacon. Ass.d–Dick Mayberry. Dial.d–Hugh Cummings. Sc–Earl Baldwin, from a story by Richard Connell (published in *Colliers*). Ph–Tony Gaudio. Ed–William Holmes. A.d–Max Parker. Cost–Howard Shoup. Make-up–Perc Westmore. M–Heinz Roemheld. Orch–Ray Heindorff. Sd–C.A. Riggs. Sfx–Byron Haskin, Willard Van Enger, Edwin B. Du Par. Montages–Don Siegel, Robert Burke.

Edward G. Robinson (*Little John Sarto*), Ann Sothern (*Flo Addams*), Humphrey Bogart (*Jack Buck*), Donald Crisp (*Brother Superior*), Ralph Bellamy (*Clarence Fletcher*), Allen Jenkins (*Willie the Knife Corson*), Charles D. Brown (*Brother Wren*), Cecil Kellaway (*Brother Goodwin*), Morgan Conway (*Philadelphia Powell*), Richard Lane (*Mugsy O'Day*), Joseph Crehan (*Brother MacEwen*), Dick Wessel (*Buffalo Burns*), Granville Bates (*Superintendent*), Paul Phillips (*French Frank*), Nanette Vallon (*Fifi*), Tommy Baker (*Joseph*), Paul Guilfoyle (*Red Martin*), John Ridgeley (*Texas Pearson*), Wilfred Lucas (*Brother MacDonald*), Tom Tyler (*Curly Matthews*), Don Rowan (*Al Muller*), Joe Caites (*Handsome Harry Edwards*), Tim Ryan (*Turkey Malone*), Pat Gleason (*Dopey Perkins*), G. Pat Collins (*Tim O'Hara*), John T. Qualen (*Mr Pigeon*), Leonard Mudie (*Englishman*), Charles Coleman (*Englishman*), Edgar Norton (*Meadows*), Jean Del Val (*Frenchman*), Armand Kaliz (*Frenchman*), Charles De Ravenne (*Stable boy*), Gino Corrado (*Artist*), Paul Porcasi (*Warehouse manager*), George Sorel (*Casino Attendant*), Georges Renevent (*Cable Office clerk*), De Wolfe Hopper (*First Reporter*), George Heywood (*Second Reporter*), Creighton Hale (*Third Reporter*), Mary Gordon (*Mrs Sweeney*), Frank Faylen (*Superintendent of service*), Lee Phelps (*Policeman*), Sam McDaniel (*Janitor*), James Flavin (*Parking attendant*).

R.t. 91.
Copyright, 8 June 1940.
First shown, Strand, New York, 7 June 1940.
Reviews, V, 29 May 1940 (Walt), NYT, 8 June 1940 (Bosley Crowther).

Bullets or Ballots
First National
Ass.p–Lou Edelman. D–William Keighley. Ass.d–Chuck Hansen. Sc–Seton I.
Miller, from a story by Martin Mooney and Seton I. Miller. Ph–Hal Mohr.
Ed–Jack Killifer. A.d–Carl Jules Weyl. M–Heinz Roemheld. Sd–Oliver S.
Garretson. Sfx–Fred Jackman, Fred Jackman Jr, Warren E. Lynch.

Edward G. Robinson (*Johnny Blake*), Joan Blondell (*Lee Morgan*), Barton
MacLane (*Al Kruger*), Humphrey Bogart (*Nick 'Bugs' Fenner*), Frank McHugh
(*Herman*), Joseph King (*Captain Dan McLaren*), Richard Purcell (*Ed Driscoll*),
George E. Stone (*Wires*), Joseph Crehan (*Grand Jury Spokesman*), Henry O'Neill
(*Bryant*), Henry Kolker (*Hollister*), Gilbert Emory (*Thorndyke*), Herbert
Rawlinson (*Caldwell*), Louise Beavers (*Nellie La Fleur*), Norman Willis (*Vinci*),
William Pawley (*Crail*), Ralph Remley (*Kelly*), Frank Faylen (*Gatley*), Wallace
Gregory (*Lambert*), Frank Bruno (*Ben*), Rosalind Marquis (*Dancer*), Alice
Lyndon (*Old lady*), Victoria Vinton (*Ticket seller*), Addison Richards
(*Announcer's voice*), Harry Watson (*Second kid*), Jerry Madden (*Third kid*),
Herman Marks (*First man*), Benny the Gouge (*Second man*), Ray Brown
(*Proprietor*), Al Hill (*First man*), Dutch Schlickenmeyer (*Second man*), Eddie
Shubert (*Truck driver*), George Lloyds (*First man*), Jack Gardner (*Second man*),
Saul Gross (*Third man*), Max Wagner (*Actor playing Kruger*), Ed Stanley (*Judge*),
Milton Kibbee (*Jury Foreman*), Jack Goodrich (*Cigar clerk*), Alma Lloyd (*First
beauty attendant*), Ralph M. Benley (*Kelly*), Ann Nagel, Gordon Elliott (*Bank
secretaries*), Carlyle Moore Jr (*Kruger's secretary*), Virginia Dabney (*Mary*).

R.t. 70.
Copyright, 15 June 1936.
First shown, Strand, New York, 26 May 1936.
Reviews, NYT, 27 May 1936 (Frank S. Nugent), V, 3 June 1936 (Kauf).

Captain Blood
First National
Ass.p–Harry Joe Brown. U.m–Gordon Hollingshead. D–Michael Curtiz.
Ass.d–Sherry Shourds. Dial.d–Stanley Logan. Sc–Casey Robinson, from the
novel by Rafael Sabatini. Ph–Hal Mohr. Additional photography–Ernest
Haller. Ed–George Amy. A.d–Anton Grot. Cost–Milo Anderson. M–Erich
Wolfgang Korngold. Orch–Hugo Friedhofer, Ray Heindorf. M.d–Leo F.
Forbstein. Sd–C.A. Riggs. Sfx–Fred Jackman.

Errol Flynn (*Peter Blood*), Olivia De Havilland (*Arabella Bishop*), Lionel Atwill
(*Colonel Bishop*), Basil Rathbone (*Levasseur*), Ross Alexander (*Jeremy Pitt*), Guy
Kibbee (*Hagthorpe*), Henry Stephenson (*Lord Willoughby*), Robert Barrat
(*Wolverstone*), Hobart Cavanaugh (*Dr Bronson*), Donald Meek (*Dr Whacker*),
Jessie Ralph (*Mrs Barlow*), Forrester Harvey (*Honesty Nutall*), Frank McGlynn
Sr (*Reverend Ogle*), Holmes Herbert (*Captain Gardner*), David Torrence
(*Andrew Baynes*), J. Carrol Naish (*Cahusac*), Pedro De Cordoba (*Don Diego*),

291

George Hassell (*Governor Steed*), Harry Cording (*Kent*), Leonard Mudie (*Baron Jeffreys*), Ivan Simpson (*Prosecutor*), Stuart Casey (*Captain Hobart*), Dennis d'Auburn (*Lord Gilroy*), Mary Forbes (*Mrs Steed*), E.E. Clive (*Clerk of the Court*), Colin Kenny (*Lord Chester Dyke*), Maude Leslie (*Mrs Baynes*), Gardner James (*Slave*), Vernon Steele (*King James*).

R.t. 120.
Copyright, 31 December 1935.
First shown, Strand, New York, 25 December 1935.
Reviews, NYT, 27 December 1935 (Andre Sennwald), V, 8 January 1936 (Abel).

The Charge of the Light Brigade
Warner Brothers
Ass.p–Sam Bischoff. D–Michael Curtiz. Dial.d–Stanley Logan. 2nd.d–B. Reeves Eason. Sc–Michael Jacoby, Rowland Leigh, from a story by Michael Jacoby, inspired by the poem by Alfred Lord Tennyson. Ph–Sol Polito. Special photographic effects–Fred Jackman. Ed–George Amy. A.d–Jack Hughes. Cost–Milo Anderson. M–Max Steiner. Orch–Hugo Friedhofer. M.d–Leo F. Forbstein. Sd–C.A. Riggs. Sfx–Fred Jackman, H.F. Koenekamp. Tech.ad. on Military Drills and Tactics–Major Sam Harris, Ret'd. A.L.H. 'We gratefully acknowledge the technical advice of Captain E. Rochfort-John, formerly of the Royal Engineers.'

Errol Flynn (*Captain, later Major Geoffrey Vickers*), Olivia De Havilland (*Elsa Campbell*), Patric Knowles (*Captain Perry Vickers*), Henry Stephenson (*Sir Charles Macefield*), Nigel Bruce (*Sir Benjamin Warrenton*), Donald Crisp (*Colonel Campbell*), David Niven (*Captain Randall*), C. Henry Gordon (*Surat Khan*), George P. Huntley Jr (*Major Jowett*), Robert Barrat (*Count Igor Volonoff*), Spring Byington (*Lady Octavia Warrenton*), J. Carrol Naish (*Subahdar-Major Puran Singh*), Walter Holbrook (*Cornet Barclay*), Princess Baigum (*Prema's mother*), Charles Sedgwick (*Cornet Pearson*), Scotty Beckett (*Prema Singh*), George Regas (*Wazir*), Helen Sanborn (*Mrs Jowett*), E.E. Clive (*Sir Humphrey Harcourt*), Lumsden Hare (*Colonel Woodward*), Colin Kenny (*Major Anderson*), Gordon Hart (*Colonel Coventry*), Holmes Herbert (*General O'Neill*), Boyd Irwin (*General Dunbar*), Reginald Sheffield (*Bentham*), Georges Renevent (*General Canrobert*), Charles Croker King (*Lord Cardigan*), Brandon Hurst (*Lord Raglan*).

R.t. 115.
Copyright, 4 November 1936.
First shown, Strand, New York, 31 October 1936.
Reviews, NYT, 2 November 1936 (Frank S. Nugent), V, 4 November 1936 (Wear).

Confessions of a Nazi Spy
First National
Ass.p–Robert Lord. D–Anatole Litvak. Sc–Milton Krims, John Wexley, from the articles 'Storm over America' by Leon Turrou. Ph–Sol Polito. Ed–Owen Marks. A.d–Carl Jules Weyl. Cost–Milo Anderson. M.d–Leo F.Forbstein. Sd–Robert B.Lee. Tech.ad–Leon G. Turrou. Narrator–John Deering.

Edward G. Robinson (*Edward J. Renard*), Paul Lukas (*Dr Kassel*), Francis Lederer (*Schneider*), George Sanders (*Schlager*), Henry O'Neill (*D.A. Kellog*), Lya Lys (*Erika Wolff*), Grace Stafford (*Mrs Schneider*), James Stephenson (*British agent*), Sig Rumann (*Krogman*), Fred Tozere (*Phillips*), Dorothy Tree (*Hilda Keinhauer*), Celia Sibelius (*Mrs Kassel*), Joe Sawyer (*Renz*), Lionel Royce (*Huntze*), Hans von Twardowsky (*Wildebrandt*), Henry Victor (*Heildorf*), Frederick Vogeding (*Captain Richter*), George Rosener (*Klauber*), Robert Davis (*Straubel*), John Voigt (*Westphal*), Willy Kaufman (*Greutwald*), William Vaughn (*Captain von Eichen*), Jack Mower (*McDonald*), Robert Emmett Keane (*Harrison*), Eily Malyon (*Mrs McLaughlin*), Frank Mayo (*Staunton*), Lucien Prival (*Kranz*), Frederick Burton (*Judge*), Alec Craig (*Postman*), Jean Brook (*Kassel's nurse*), Ward Bond (*American Legionnaire*), Charles Trowbridge (*U.S. Intelligence man*), John Ridgeley (*Army Hospital clerk*), Emmett Vogan (*Hotel man*), Edward Keane (*FBI Man*), Martin Kosleck (*Goebbels*), Selmer Jackson (*Customs official*), Egon Brecher (*Nazi agent*), Bodil Rosing (*Passenger on boat*), Nicolai Yoshkin, Charles Sherlock.

R.t. 102.
Copyright, 6 May 1939.
First shown, Strand, New York, 28 April 1939.
Reviews, NYT, 29 April 1939 (Frank S. Nugent), V, 3 May 1939 (Land).

Crime School

First National
Producer–Bryan Foy. D–Lewis Seiler. Ass.d–Fred Tyler. Dial.d–Vincent Sherman. Sc–Crane Wilbur, Vincent Sherman, from a story by Crane Wilbur. Ph–Arthur Todd. Ed–Terry Morse. A.d–Charles Novi. Cost–Miss McKenzie. M–Max Steiner. Orch–Hugo Friedhofer, George Parrish. Sd–Francis J. Scheid.

Humphrey Bogart (*Mark Braden*), Gale Page (*Sue Warren*), Billy Halop (*Frankie Warren*), Bobby Jordan (*Squirt*), Huntz Hall (*Goofy*), Leo Gorcey (*Spike Hawkins*), Bernard Punsley (*Fats Papadopolo*), Gabriel Dell (*Bugs Burke*), Paul Porcasi (*Nick Papadopolo*), Al Bridge (*Mr Burke*), Helen MacKellar (*Mrs Burke*), James B. Carson (*Schwartz*), George Offerman Jr (*Red*), Milburn Stone (*Joe Delaney*), Frank Otto (*Junkie*), Cy Kendall (*Morgan*), Weldon Heyburn (*Cooper*), Charles Trowbridge (*Judge Clinton*), Jack Mower (*John Brower*), Harry Cording (*Guard*), Spencer Charters (*Old Doctor*), Donald Briggs (*New Doctor*), Frank Jaquet (*Commissioner*), Sibyl Harris (*Mrs Hawkins*), Ed Gargan (*Officer Hogan*).

R.t. 86.
Copyright, 24 March 1938.
First shown, Strand, New York, 10 May 1938.
Reviews, V, 4 May 1938 (Flin), NYT, 11 May 1938 (Frank S. Nugent).

A Dispatch from Reuters (UK: This Man Reuter)

Warner Brothers
Ass.p–Henry Blanke. D–William Dieterle. Ass.d–Jack Sullivan. Sc–Milton Krims, from a story by Valentine Williams and Wolfgang Wilhelm. Dial.d–Jo Graham. Ph–James Wong Howe. Ed–Warren Low. A.d–Anton Grot. M–Max

Steiner. Orch–Hugo Friedhofer. M.d–Leo F. Forbstein. Sfx–Byron Haskin, Robert Burke.

Edward G. Robinson (*Julius Reuter*), Edna Best (*Ida Magnus*), Eddie Albert (*Max Wagner*), Albert Basserman (*Franz Geller*), Gene Lockhart (*Bauer*), Otto Kruger (*Dr Magnus*), Nigel Bruce (*Sir Randolph Persham*), Montagu Love (*Delane*), James Stephenson (*Carew*), Walter Kingsford (*Napoleon III*), David Bruce (*Bruce*), Dickie Moore (*Reuter as a boy*), Billy Dawson (*Max as a boy*), Richard Nichols (*Herbert, aged 5*), Lumsden Hare (*Chairman of the Anglo-Irish Telegraph Company*), Alec Craig (*Grant*), Hugh Sothern (*American Ambassador*), Egon Brecher (*Reingold*), Frank Jaquet (*Stein*), Walter O. Stahl (*Von Danstedt*), Paul Irving (*Josephat Benfey*), Edward McWade (*Chemist*), Gilbert Emory (*Lord Palmerston*), Robert Warwick (*Opposition Speaker*), Ellis Irving (*Speaker*), Henry Roguemore (*Otto*), Paul Weigel (*Gauss*), Josef Stefani (*Assistant*), Mary Anderson (*Girl*), Wolfgang Zilzer (*Post Office clerk*), Frederic Mellinger (*Man*), Stuart Holmes (*Attendant*), Sunny Boyne (*Companion*), Ernst Hansman (*Heinrich*), Grace Stafford (*Young Woman*), Theodor von Eltz (*Actor*), Kenneth Hunter, Holmes Herbert, Leonard Mudie, Laurence Grant (*Members of Parliament*), Pat O'Malley (*Workman*), Cyril Delevanti, Norman Ainsley, Bobby Hale (*News vendors*).

R.t. 89.
Copyright, 18 October 1940.
First shown on general release, 19 October 1940.
Reviews, V, 25 September 1940 (Walt), NYT, 12 December 1940 (TMP).

Disraeli
Warner Brothers
D–Alfred E. Green. Sc–Julian Josephson, from the play by Louis Napoleon Parker. Ph–Lee Garmes. Ed–Owen Marks. Orch–Louis Silvers.

George Arliss (*Benjamin Disraeli*), Doris Lloyd (*Mrs Travers*), Joan Bennett (*Lady Clarissa Pevensy*), Florence Arliss (*Lady Beaconsfield*), Anthony Bushell (*Charles, Lord Deeford*), Michael Visaroff (*Count Bosrinov*), David Torrence (*Lord Probert, Governor of the Bank of England*), Ivan Simpson (*Hugh Meyers*), Gwendolen Logan (*Duchess of Glastonbury*), Charles E. Evans (*Potter*), Cosmo Kyrle Bellew (*Mr Terle*), Jack Deery (*Bascot*), Norman Cannon (*Foljambe*), Henry Carvill (*Duke of Glastonbury*), Shayle Gardner (*Dr Williams*), Powel York (*Flookes*), Margaret Mann (*Queen Victoria*), Helena Phillips (*Lady Probert*).

R.t. 88.
Copyright, 8 October 1929.
First shown, Warner, New York, 2 October 1929.
Reviews, NYT, 8 October 1929 (Mordaunt Hall), V, 9 October 1929 (Land).

Doorway to Hell
Warner Brothers
D–Archie L. Mayo. Sc–George Rosener, from the story 'A Handful of Clouds' by Rowland Brown. Ph–Barney McGill. Ed–Robert Crandall. Cost–Earl Luick. M–Louis Silvers. M.d–Erno Rapee.

Lew Ayres (*Louis Ricarno*), Charles Judels (*Sam Margoni*), Dorothy Matthews

294

(*Doris*), Leon Janney (*Jackie Lamarr/Ricarno*), Robert Elliott (*Captain O'Grady*), James Cagney (*Steve Mileaway*), Kenneth Thompson (*Captain of the Military Academy*), Jerry Mandy (*Joe*), Noel Madison (*Rocco*), Edwin Argus (*The Midget*), Eddie Kane (*Dr Morton*), Tom Wilson, Dwight Frye (*Gangsters*).

R.t. 79.
Copyright, 6 October 1930.
First shown, Strand, New York, 31 October 1930.
Reviews, NYT, 1 November 1930 (Mordaunt Hall), V, 5 November 1930 (Sid).

Each Dawn I Die
First National
Ass.p–David Lewis. D–William Keighley. Ass.d–Frank Heath. Sc–Norman Reilly Raine, Warren Duff, Charles Perry, from a novel by Jerome Odlum. Ph–Arthur Edeson. Ed–Thomas Richards. A.d–Max Parker. Cost–Howard Shoup. Make-up–Perc Westmore. M–Max Steiner. M.d–Leo F. Forbstein. Sd–E.A. Brown. Tech.ad–William Buckley. Narrator–John Conte.

James Cagney (*Frank Ross*), George Raft (*Hood Stacey*), Jane Bryan (*Joyce Conover*), George Bancroft (*John Armstrong*), Maxie Rosenbloom (*Fargo Red*), Stanley Ridges (*Mueller*), Alan Baxter (*Polecat Carlisle*), Victor Jory (*W.J. Grayce*), John Wray (*Pete Kassock*), Edward Pawley (*Dale*), Willard Robertson (*Lang*), Emma Dunn (*Mrs Ross*), Paul Hurst (*Garsky*), Joe Downing (*Limpy Julien*), Louis Jean Heydt (*Joe Lassiter*), Thurston Hall (*D.A. Jesse Hanley*), William Davidson (*Bill Mason*), Clay Clement (*Stacey's Attorney*), Charles Trowbridge (*Judge*), Harry Cording (*Temple*), John Harron (*Lew Keller*), John Ridgeley (*Jerry Poague*), Selmer Jackson (*Patterson*), Robert Homans (*Mac*), Abner Biberman (*Snake Edwards*), Napoleon Simpson (*Mose*), Stuart Holmes (*Accident witness*), Marie Wrixon (*Girl in car*), Garland Smith, Arthur Gardner (*Men in car*), James Flavin (*Policeman*), Max Hoffman Jr (*Gate guard*), Walter Miller (*Turnkey*), Fred Graham (*Guard in cell*), Wilfred Lucas (*Bailiff*), Vera Lewis (*Woman on jury*), Emmett Vogan (*Prosecutor*), Earl Dwire (*Judge Crowder*), Bob Perry (*Bud*), Al Hill (*Johnny*), Elliott Sullivan (*Convict*), Chuck Hamilton (*Court Officer*), Nat Carr, Wedgewood Nowell, Frank Mayo, Dick Rich, Lee Phelps, Jack Wise, Granville Bates.

R.t. 92.
Copyright, 19 August 1939.
First shown, Strand, New York, 21 July 1939.
Reviews, V, 19 July 1939 (Wear), NYT, 22 July 1939 (Bosley Crowther).

Five Star Final
First National
D–Mervyn LeRoy. Ass.d–Gordon Hollingshead (1st), Bill Carr (2nd). Sc–Byron Morgan, Robert Lord, from the play by Louis Weitzenkorn. Ph–Sol Polito. Ed–Frank Ware. Continuity–Irva Ross. A.d–Jack Okey. Cost–Earl Luick. M.d–Leo F. Forbstein.

Edward G. Robinson (*Joseph Randall*), Marian Marsh (*Jenny Townsend*), H.B. Warner (*Michael Townsend*), Anthony Bushell (*Phillip Weeks*), George E. Stone (*Ziggie Feinstein*), Frances Starr (*Nancy Voorhees Townsend*), Ona Munson (*Kitty Carmody*), Boris Karloff (*T. Vernon Isopod*), Aline MacMahon (*Miss Taylor*),

Oscar Apfel (*Bernard Hinchecliffe*), Purnell Pratt (*Robert French*), Robert Elliott (*Brannegan*), Harold Waldridge (*Arthur Goldberg*), Evelyn Hall (*Mrs Weeks*), Polly Walters (*Telephonist*), James Donlin (*Reporter*), Frank Darren (*Schwartz*).

R.t. 89.
Copyright, 8 September 1931.
First shown, Winter Garden, New York, 10 September 1931.
Reviews, NYT, 11 September 1931 (Mordaunt Hall), V, 15 September 1931 (Bige).

Fog over Frisco
First National
Ass.p–Henry Blanke. D–William Dieterle. Dial.d–Daniel Reed. Sc–Robert N. Lee, from a story by George Dyer adapted by Robert N. Lee and Eugene Solow. Ph–Tony Gaudio. Ed–Harold McLernon. A.d–Jack Okey. Cost–Orry-Kelly. M.d–Leo F. Forbstein.

Bette Davis (*Arlene Bradford*), Donald Woods (*Tony Stirling*), Margaret Lindsay (*Valkyr Bradford*), Lyle Talbot (*Spencer Carleton*), Hugh Herbert (*Izzy*), Arthur Byron (*Everett Bradford*), Robert Barrat (*Thorne*), Henry O'Neill (*Oren Porter*), Irving Pichel (*Jake Bello*), Douglass Dumbrille (*Joshua Mayard/Arthur Burchard*), Alan Hale (*Chief O'Malley*), Gordon Westcott (*Joe*), Charles Wilson (*O'Hagan*), Harold Minjir (*Archie Van Ness*), William Demarest (*Spike*), Douglas Cosgrove (*Lieutenant Davis*), William Davidson (*Joe Hague*), George Chandler (*Driver*).

R.t. 68.
Copyright, 22 May 1934.
First shown on general release, 2 June 1934.
Reviews, NYT, 7 June 1934 (Mordaunt Hall), V, 12 June 1934 (Char).

Frisco Kid
Warner Brothers
Ass.p–Sam Bischoff. D–Lloyd Bacon. Ass.d–Jack Sullivan. Sc–Warren Duff, Seton I. Miller. Ph–Sol Polito. Ed–Owen Marks. A.d–John Hughes. Cost–Orry-Kelly. Make-up–Perc Westmore. M.d–Leo F. Forbstein. Sd–James Thompson.

James Cagney (*Bat Morgan*), Margaret Lindsay (*Jean Barrat*), Ricardo Cortez (*Paul Morra*), Lili Damita (*Belle Morra*), Donald Woods (*Charles Ford*), Barton MacLane (*Spider Burke*), George E. Stone (*Solly*), Joseph King (*James Daley*), Addison Richards (*William T. Coleman*), Robert McWade (*Judge Crawford*), Joseph Crehan (*McClanahan*), Robert Strange (*Graber*), Joseph Sawyer (*Slugs Crippen*), Fred Kohler (*Shanghai Duck*), Edward McWade (*Tupper*), Claudia Coleman (*Jumping Whale*), John Wray (*The Weasel*), Ivar McFadden (*First lookout*), Lee Phelps (*Second lookout*), William Wagner (*Evangelist*), Don Barclay (*Drunk*), Jack Curtis (*Captain*), Walter Long (*Miner*), James Farley (*Man*), Milton Kibbee (*Shop man*), Harry Seymour (*Salesman*), Claire Sinclair (*Madame*), Alan Davis (*Young drunk*), Karl Hackett (*Dealer*), Wilfred Lucas (*First policeman*), John T. Dillon (*Second policeman*), Edward Mortimer (*First man*), William Holmes (*Second man*), Don Downer (*Usher*), Mrs Wilfred North

(*Mrs Crawford*), Charles Middleton (*Speaker*), Joe Smith Marba (*Man*), Landers Stevens (*Doctor*), Frank Sheridan (*Mulligan*), J.C. Morton, Harry Tenbrook (*Men*), Lew Harvey (*Dealer*), Eddie Sturges (*Rat Face*), William Desmond (*Vigilante captain*), Jessie Perry (*Maid*), Edward Keane, Edward Le Saint (*Contractors*), Robert Dudley, Dick Rush (*Vigilante leaders*), John Elliott (*Doctor*), Helene Chadwick, Bill Dale, Dick Kerr, Alice Lake, Vera Stedman, Jane Tallent.

R.t. 80.
Copyright, 12 November 1935.
First shown, Strand, New York, 23 November 1935.
Reviews, NYT, 25 November 1935 (Andre Sennwald), V, 27 November 1935 (Bige).

G-Men
First National
Ass.p–Lou Edelman. U.m–Frank Mattison. D–William Keighley. Ass.d–Chuck Hansen. 2nd.d–William K. McGann. Sc–Seton I. Miller, from his own story 'Public Enemy No. 1'. Ph–Sol Polito. Camera–Al Green. Ed–Jack Killifer. Script–Beulah Ashley. A.d–John J. Hughes. Properties–Bill Kuehl. Cost–Orry-Kelly. M.d–Leo F. Forbstein. Song–'You bother me an awful lot' by Sammy Fain and Irving Kahal. Sd–Stanley Jones. Night club number choreographed by Bobby Connolly.

James Cagney (*James 'Brick' Davis*), Margaret Lindsay (*Kay McCord*), Ann Dvorak (*Jean Morgan*), Robert Armstrong (*Jeff McCord*), Barton MacLane (*Brad Collins*), Lloyd Nolan (*Hugh Farrell*), William Harrigan (*McKay*), Russell Hopton (*Gerard*), Edward Pawley (*Danny Leggett*), Noel Madison (*Durfee*), Monte Blue (*Analyst*), Regis Toomey (*Eddie Buchanan*), Harold Huber (*Venke*), Addison Richards (*Bruce J. Gregory*), Raymond Hatton (*The Man*), Louise Allen, Vivian Faulkner, Emily Fitzpatrick, Margaret Fitzpatrick, Wilma Holly, Iris Meyers, Donna Massin, Sheila Rae, Betty Wood, Elizabeth Cooke, Jean Ashton, Bobbi Cronin, Florence d'Aquin, Emily Renard, Lee Bailey, Valerie Trayler, Virginia Ray (*Dancers*), Mary Treen (*Gregory's secretary*), Adrian Morris (*Accomplice*), Edwin Maxwell (*Joseph Kratz*), Emmett Vogan (*Bill*), James Flavin (*Agent*), Ed Keane (*Bank cashier*), Stanley Blystone, Pat Flaherty (*Cops*), James T. Mack (*Agent*), Jonathan Hale (*Congressman*), Charles Sherlock (*Short man*), Wheeler Oakman (*Henchman at Lodge*), Eddie Dunn (*Police broadcaster*), Gordon 'Bill' Elliott (*Intern*), Perry Irvins (*Doctor at store*), Gertrude Short (*Collins' moll*), Marie Astaire (*Gerard's moll*), Florence Dudley (*Durfee's moll*), Frances Morris (*Moll*), Al Hill (*Hood*), Huey White (*Gangster*), Glen Cavender (*Headwaiter*), John Impolito (*Tony*), Bruce Mitchell (*Sergeant*), Monte Vandergrift (*Deputy Sheriff*), Frank Shannon (*Chief*), Frank Bull (*Announcer*), Marta Merrill (*Nurse*), Gene Morgan (*Lounger*), Joseph De Stefani (*Florist*), George Daly, Ward Bond (*Machine gunners*), Tom Wilson (*Police guard*), Henry Hall (*Police driver*), Lee Phelps (*McCord's aide*), Marc Lawrence (*Hood at Lodge*), Brooks Benedict (*Man*), Frank Marlowe (*Hood shot at Lodge*).

R.t. 84.
Copyright, 18 May 1935.

First shown, Warners Hollywood and RKO Hill Street, Los Angeles, 25 April 1935.
Reviews, NYT, 2 May 1935, V, 8 May 1935 (Kauf).
(A prologue was added for the 1949 re-release to mark the 25th anniversary of the Federal Bureau of Investigation, featuring David Brian as The Chief and Douglas Kennedy as an Agent).

The Green Pastures

Warner Brothers
Ass.p–Henry Blanke. D–William Keighley, Marc Connelly. Ass.d–Sherry Shourds. Sc–Marc Connelly, Sheridan Gibney, from the play by Marc Connelly, based on the novel 'Ol' Man Adam an' His Chillun' by Roark Bradford. Ph–Hal Mohr. Special photographic effects–Fred Jackman. Ed–George Amy. A.d–Allen Sallburg, Stanley Fleischer. Cost–Milo Anderson. Choral music arranged by Hall Johnson and performed by The Hall Johnson Choir. M.d–Leo F. Forbstein. Sd–Nathan Levinson.

Rex Ingram (*De Lawd/Adam/Hezdrel*), Oscar Polk (*Gabriel*), Eddie Anderson (*Noah*), Frank Wilson (*Moses*), George Reed (*Mr Deshee*), Abraham Gleaves (*Archangel*), Myrtle Anderson (*Eve*), Al Stokes (*Cain*), Edna M. Harris (*Zeba*), James Fuller (*Cain the Sixth*), George Randol (*High Priest*), Ida Forsyne (*Noah's Wife*), Ray Martin (*Shem*), Charles Andrews (*Flatfoot*), Dudley Dickerson (*Ham*), Jimmy Burgess (*Japheth*), William Cumby (*Abraham/Head Magician/King of Babylon*), George Reed (*Isaac*), Ivory Williams (*Jacob*), David Bethea (*Aaron*), Ernest Whitman (*Pharaoh*), Reginald Fenderson (*Joshua*), Slim Thompson (*Master of Ceremonies*), Clinton Rosemond (*Prophet*), The Hall Johnson Choir.

R.t. 92.
Copyright, 15 July 1936.
First shown, RKO Music Hall, New York, 16 July 1936.
Reviews, NYT, 17 July 1936 (Bosley Crowther), V, 22 July 1936 (Abel).

The Hatchet Man (UK: The Honourable Mr Wong)

First National
D–William A. Wellman. Sc–J. Grubb Alexander, from the play 'Honorable Mr Wong' by Achmed Abdullah and David Belasco. Ph–Sid Hickox. Camera–Richard Towers. Ed–Owen Marks. A.d–Anton Grot. Cost–Earl Luick. M.d–Leo F. Forbstein. Sd–Robert Lee.

Edward G. Robinson (*Wong Low Get*), Loretta Young (*Toya San*), Dudley Digges (*Nag Hong Fah*), Leslie Fenton (*Harry En Hai*), Edmund Breese (*Yu Chang*), Tully Marshall (*Long Sen Yat*), J. Carrol Naish (*Sun Yet Ming*), Charles Middleton (*Li Hop Fat*), E. Allyn Warren (*Soo Lat the Bootmender*), Eddie Piel (*Foo Ming*), Noel Madison (*Charles Kee*), Blanche Frederici (*Madame Si-Si*), Toshia Mori (*Miss Ling*), Otto Yamicka (*Chung Ho*), Ralph Ince (*Malone*), Evelyn Selbie (*Wah Li*), Willie Fung (*Fung Loo the Notary*), Anna Chang (*Sing Girl*), James Leong (*Tong member*).

R.t. 74.
Copyright, 28 January 1932.
First shown, Warners Hollywood, Los Angeles, 28 January 1932.
Reviews, NYT, 5 February 1932 (Mordaunt Hall), V, 9 February 1932 (Sid).

High Sierra
First National
Ass.p–Mark Hellinger. D–Raoul Walsh. Dial.d–Irving Rapper. Sc–John
Huston, W.R. Burnett, from the latter's novel. Ph–Tony Gaudio. Ed–Jack
Killifer. A.d–Ted Smith. Cost–Milo Anderson. Make-up–Perc Westmore.
M–Adolph Deutsch. Orch–Arthur Lange. Sd–Dolph Thomas. Sfx–Byron
Haskin, H.F. Koenekamp.

Ida Lupino (*Marie Garson*), Humphrey Bogart (*Roy Earle*), Alan Curtis (*Babe
Kozak*), Arthur Kennedy (*Red Hattery*), Joan Leslie (*Velma*), Henry Hull (*Doc
Banton*), Henry Travers (*Pa Goodhue*), Jerome Cowan (*Healy*), Minna Gombell
(*Mrs Baughman*), Donald MacBride (*Big Mac*), Willie Best (*Algernon*), Barton
MacLane (*Jake Kranmer*), Elisabeth Risdon (*Ma Goodhue*), Cornel Wilde (*Louis
Mendoza*), Paul Harvey (*Mr Baughman*), Isabel Jewell (*Blondie*), Spencer
Charters (*Ed*), George Meeker (*Pfiffer*), Robert Strange (*Art*), Sam Hayes
(*Announcer*), John Eldredge (*Lon Preiser*), Zero (*Pard*).

R.t. 100.
Copyright, 25 January 1941.
First shown, Warners Hollywood and Warners Downtown, Los Angeles, 23
January 1941.
Reviews, V, 22 January 1941 (Scho), NYT, 25 January 1941 (Bosley
Crowther).

Hi, Nellie!
Warner Brothers
Ass.p–Robert Presnell. D–Mervyn LeRoy. Sc–Abem Finkel, Sidney Suther-
land, from a story by Roy Chanslor. Ph–Sol Polito. Ed–Bill Holmes.
A.d–Robert Haas. Cost–Orry-Kelly. M.d–Leo F. Forbstein.

Paul Muni (*Samuel N. Bradshaw*), Glenda Farrell (*Gerry Krayle*), Ned Sparks
(*Shammy*), Robert Barrat (*Beau Brownell*), Berton Churchill (*John L. Graham*),
Kathryn Sergava (*Grace*), Hobart Cavanaugh (*Fullerton*), Douglass Dumbrille
(*Harvey Dawes*), Edward Ellis (*O'Connell*), Donald Meek (*Durkin*), Marjorie
Gateson (*Mrs Canfield*), George Meeker (*Sheldon*), Pat Wing (*Sue*), Frank
Reicher (*Nate Natham*), George Chandler (*Danny*), John T. Qualen (*Steve*),
Sidney Miller (*Louie*), James Donlan (*Evans*), Dorothy Lebaire (*Rosa*), Harold
Huber (*Leo*), Paul Kaye, Allen Vincent, George Humbert.

R.t. 75.
Copyright, 24 January 1934.
First shown, Strand, New York, 31 January 1934.
Reviews, NYT, 1 February 1934 (Mordaunt Hall), V, 6 February 1934 (Char).

I Am a Fugitive from a Chain Gang (UK: I Am a Fugitive from the Chain
Gang)
Warner Brothers
U.m–Al Alborn. D–Mervyn LeRoy. Ass.d–Chuck Hansen. Sc–Sheridan
Gibney, Brown Holmes, from the book 'I Am a Fugitive from a Georgia Chain
Gang' by Robert E. Burns. Ph–Sol Polito. Ed–William Holmes. A.d–Jack
Okey. Make-up–Ray Romero. Sd–Al Riggs. Tech.ad–S.H. Sullivan, Jack
Miller.

Paul Muni (*James Allen*), Glenda Farrell (*Marie Allen*), Helen Vinson (*Helen*), Noel Francis (*Linda*), Preston S. Foster (*Pete*), Allen Jenkins (*Barney Sykes*), Berton Churchill (*The Judge*), Edward Ellis (*Bomber Wells*), David Landau (*Warden*), Hale Hamilton (*Reverend Robert Clinton Allen*), Sally Blane (*Alice*), Louise Carter (*Mrs Allen*), Willard Robertson (*Prison Board Chairman*), William LeMaire (*Texas*), Edward J. McNamara (*Second Warden*), Sheila Terry (*Allen's Secretary*), John Wray (*Nordine*), James Bell (*Red*), Robert McWade (*Ramsay*), Everett Brown (*Sebastian T. Yale*), Edward Arnold (*Lawyer*), Oscar Apfel (*Chairman of the Chamber of Commerce*), Erville Alderson (*Sheriff*), George Pat Collins (*Wilson*), William Pawley (*Doggy*), Reginald Barlow (*Parker*), Jack La Rue (*Ackerman*), Henry Woods (*Guard*), Douglass Dumbrille (*District Attorney*), Robert Warwick (*Fuller*), Roscoe Karns, Spencer Charters, Edward Le Saint, Charles Middleton, Charles Sellon, Lew Kelly, George Cooper, Wallis Clark, Irving Bacon, Lee Shumway, J. Frank Glendon, Dennis O'Keefe.

R.t. 93.
Copyright, 1 November 1932.
First shown, Warners Hollywood and Warners Downtown, Los Angeles, 10 November 1932.
Reviews, NYT, 11 November 1932 (Mordaunt Hall), V, 15 November 1932 (Abel).

Juarez
Warner Brothers
Ass.p–Henry Blanke. U.m–Al Alborn. D–William Dieterle. Ass.d–Jack Sullivan. Dial.d–Irving Rapper. Sc–John Huston, Wolfgang Reinhardt, Aeneas MacKenzie, from a play by Franz Werfel and the novel 'The Phantom Crown' by Bertita Harding. Ph–Tony Gaudio. Camera–Carl Guthrie, Buddy Weiler. Ed–Warren Low. Assistant film editor–Rudi Fair. A.d–Anton Grot. Assistant art director–Leo Kinder. Properties–Pat Patterson. Cost–Orry-Kelly. Make-up–Perc Westmore. Hair styles–Margaret Donovan. M–Erich Wolfgang Korngold. Orch–Hugo Friedhofer, Milan Roder. M.d–Leo F. Forbstein. Sd–C.A. Riggs. Tech.ad–Ernesto Romero.

Paul Muni (*Benito Pablo Juarez*), Bette Davis (*Carlotta*), Brian Aherne (*Maximilian*), Claude Rains (*Napoleon III*), John Garfield (*Porfirio Diaz*), Donald Crisp (*Maréchal Bazaine*), Joseph Calleia (*Alejandro Uradi*), Gale Sondergaard (*Empress Eugénie*), Gilbert Roland (*Colonel Miguel Lopez*), Henry O'Neill (*Miguel Miramon*), Pedro De Cordoba (*Riva Palacio*), Montagu Love (*Jose de Montares*), Henry Davenport (*Dr Samuel Basch*), Walter Fenner (*Achille Fould*), Alex Leftwich (*Drouyn de Lhuys*), Georgia Caine (*Countess Battenberg*), Robert Warwick (*Major Du Pont*), Gennaro Curci (*Señor de Leon*), Bill Wilkerson (*Tomas Mejia*), John Miljan (*Mariano Esobedo*), Hugh Sothern (*John Bigelow*), Fred Malatesta (*Señor Salas*), Carlos de Valdez (*Tailor*), Irving Pichel (*Carbajal*), Frank Lackteen (*Coachman*), Walter O. Stahl (*Senator del Valle*), Frank Reicher (*Duc de Morny*), Holmes Herbert (*Marshall Randon*), Walter Kingsford (*Prince Metternich*), Egon Brecher (*Baron von Magnus*), Monte Blue (*Lerdo de Tejada*), Louis Calhern (*Le Marc*), Manuel Diaz (*Pepe*), Mickey Kuhn (*Augustine Hurbide*), Lillian Nicholson (*Josefa Hurbide*), Noble Johnson (*Regules*), Martin Garralaga (*Negroni*), Vladimir Sokoloff (*Camito*), Douglas Wood (*Mr

Hartman), Grant Mitchell (*Mr Harris*), Charles Halton (*Mr Roberts*), William Edmunds (*Italian Minister*), Gilbert Emory (*Ambassador*).

R.t. 130.
Copyright, 10 June 1939.
First shown, Hollywood Theatre, New York, 25 April 1939.
Reviews, NYT, 26 April 1939 (Frank S. Nugent), V, 26 April 1939 (Flin).

Knute Rockne – All American (UK: A Modern Hero)
Warner Brothers
Ass.p–Robert Fellows. D–Lloyd Bacon. Sc–Robert Buckner, based upon the private papers of Mrs Rockne and reports of Rockne's intimate associates and friends. Ph–Tony Gaudio. Ed–Ralph Dawson. A.d–Robert Haas. Cost–Milo Anderson. Make-up–Perc Westmore. Orch–Ray Heindorf. M.d–Leo F. Forbstein. Sd–Charles Lang. Sfx–Byron Haskin, Rex Wimpy. Tech.ad–Nick Lukats, J.A. Haley.

Pat O'Brien (*Knute Rockne*), Gale Page (*Bonnie Skiles Rockne*), Ronald Reagan (*George Gipp*), Donald Crisp (*Father John Callahan*), Albert Bassermann (*Father Julius Nieuwland*), Owen Davis Jr (*Gus Dorais*), Nick Lukats (*Harry Stuhldreher*), Kane Richmond (*Elmer Layden*), William Marshall (*Don Miller*), William Byrne (*James Crowley*), John T. Qualen (*Lars Rockne*), John Litel (*Committee Chairman*), Henry O'Neill (*Doctor*), Dorothy Tree (*Martha Rockne*), John Sheffield (*Knute at age 7*), Howard Jones, Glenn 'Pop' Warner, Alonzo Stagg, William 'Bill' Spaulding, Bob Byrne, William Marshall, Ruth Robinson, Cliff Clark, Richard Clayton, George Haywood, Carlyle Moore Jr, Peter Ashley, Michael Harvey, Gaylord Pendleton, George Irving, Charles Trowbridge, Charles Wilson, Bill Sheffield, John Ridgeley, The Moreau Choir of Notre Dame.

R.t. 98.
Copyright, 5 October 1940.
First shown, Warners Hollywood and Warners Downtown, Los Angeles, 5 October 1940.
Reviews, V, 9 October 1940 (Walt), NYT, 19 October 1940 (Bosley Crowther).

Life Begins
First National
Ass.p–Ray Griffith. D–James Flood, Elliott Nugent. Sc–Earl Baldwin, from the play by Mary McDougal Axelson. Ph–James van Trees. Ed–George Marks. A.d–Esdras Hartley. Cost–Orry-Kelly. M.d–Leo F. Forbstein. Tech.ad–Dr Harry Martin MD.

Loretta Young (*Grace Sutton*), Eric Linden (*Jed Sutton*), Aline MacMahon (*Miss Bowers*), Glenda Farrell (*Florette*), Clara Blandick (*Mrs West*), Preston S. Foster (*Dr Brett*), Frank McHugh (*Ringer Banks*), Walter Walker (*Dr Tubby*), Hale Hamilton (*Dr Cramm*), Vivienne Osborne (*Mrs MacGilvary*), Dorothy Peterson (*Psychopathic Patient*), Gilbert Roland (*Tony*), Herbert Mundin (*Mr MacGilvary*), Gloria Shea (*Mrs Banks*), Elizabeth Patterson (*Mrs Tubby*), Dorothy Tree (*Rita*), Helena Phillips, Reginald Mason, Ruthelma Stevens,

Terrence Ray, Mary Phillips.

R.t. 72.

Copyright, 5 September 1932.

First shown, Hollywood Theatre, New York, 25 August 1932.

Reviews, NYT, 26 August 1932 (Mordaunt Hall), V, 30 August 1932 (Sid).

The Life of Emile Zola

Warner Brothers

Ass.p–Henry Blanke. U.m–Al Alborn. D–William Dieterle. Ass.d–Russ Saunders (1st), Les Guthrie, C.E. Archer (2nd). Dial.d–Irving Rapper. Sc–Norman Reilly Raine, Heinz Herald, Geza Herczeg, from a story by Heinz Herald and Geza Herczeg.* Ph–Tony Gaudio. Camera–Carl Guthrie, Frank Gaudio. Ed–Warren Low. Script clerk–Irva Ross. A.d–Anton Grot. Interior decorations–Albert C. Wilson. Properties–Pat Patterson. Cost–Milo Anderson, Ali Hubert. Make-up artist–Perc Westmore. Hair styles–Tillie Starriett. M–Max Steiner. M.d–Leo F. Forbstein. Sd–E.A. Brown. Tech.ad–Ali Hubert.

Paul Muni (*Emile Zola*), Gale Sondergaard (*Lucie Dreyfus*), Joseph Schildkraut (*Captain Alfred Dreyfus*), Gloria Holden (*Alexandrine Zola*), Donald Crisp (*Maitre Labori*), Erin O'Brien-Moore (*Nana*), John Litel (*Charpentier*), Henry O'Neill (*Colonel Picquart*), Morris Carnovsky (*Anatole France*), Louis Calhern (*Major Dort*), Ralph Morgan (*Pellieux, Commandant of Paris*), Robert Barrat (*Major Walsin-Esterhazy*), Vladimir Sokoloff (*Paul Cézanne*), Grant Mitchell (*Georges Clemenceau*), Henry Davenport (*General Boisdeffre, Chief of Staff*), Robert Warwick (*Major Henry*), Charles Richman (*M. Delagorgue*), Gilbert Emory (*General Mercier, Minister of War*), Walter Kingsford (*Colonel Sandherr*), Paul Everton (*General Gonse, Assistant Chief of Staff*), Montagu Love (*M. Cavignac*), Frank Sheridan (*M. van Cassell*), Lumsden Hare (*Mr Richards*), Marcia Mae Jones (*Helen Richards*), Florence Roberts (*Madame Zola*), Dickie Moore (*Pierre Dreyfus*), Rolla Gourvitch (*Jeanne Dreyfus*), Galan Galt (*Court Attendant*), Scotty Mattraw (*Assistant Judge*), Walter O. Stahl (*Kestner*), Wilfred Lucas (*Court Attendant*).

R.t. 116.

Copyright, 14 July 1937.

First shown, Hollywood Theatre, New York, 11 August 1937.

Reviews, V, 30 June 1937 (Flin), NYT, 12 August 1937 (Frank S. Nugent).

* After a threatened lawsuit, the following was added to the script credit: 'Source material, Matthew Josephson's *Zola and His Time*'.

Little Caesar

First National

D–Mervyn LeRoy. Sc–Francis Edwards Faragoh, from the novel by W.R. Burnett, adapted by Robert W. Lee. Ph–Tony Gaudio. Ed–Ray Curtiss. A.d–Anton Grot. M.d–Erno Rapee.

Edward G. Robinson (*Caesar Enrico Bandello*), Douglas Fairbanks Jr (*Joe Massara*), Glenda Farrell (*Olga Strassoff*), Sidney Blackmer (*The Big Boy*), Thomas Jackson (*Police Sergeant Tom Flaherty*), Ralph Ince (*Diamond Pete Montana*), Wm. Collier Jr (*Tony Passa*), Maurice Black (*Little Arnie Lorch*), Stanley Fields (*Sam Vettori*), George E. Stone (*Otero*), Armand Kaliz (*De Voss*),

Noel Madison (*Peppi*), Nick Bela (*Ritz Colonna*), Lucille LaVerne (*Ma Magdalena*), Ben Hendricks Jr (*Kid Bean*), Al Hill (*Waiter*), Ernie S. Adams (*Cashier*), Larry Steers (*Café guest*), George Daly (*Machine gunner*), Landers Stevens (*Gabby*).

R.t. 80.
Copyright, 29 December 1930.
First shown, Strand, New York, 9 January 1931.
Reviews, NYT, 10 January 1931 (Mordaunt Hall), V, 14 January 1931 (Bige).

The Maltese Falcon
Warner Brothers
Ass.p–Henry Blanke. D–John Huston. Ass.d–Claude Archer. Dial.d–Robert Foulk. Sc–John Huston, from the novel by Dashiell Hammett. Ph–Arthur Edeson. Ed–Thomas Richards. A.d–Robert Haas. Cost–Orry-Kelly. Make-up–Perc Westmore. M–Adolph Deutsch. Orch–Arthur Lange. Sd–Oliver S. Garretson.

Humphrey Bogart (*Samuel Spade*), Mary Astor (*Brigid O'Shaughnessy*), Peter Lorre (*Joel Cairo*), Gladys George (*Iva Archer*), Barton MacLane (*Lieutenant of Detectives Dundy*), Lee Patrick (*Effie Perrine*), Sydney Greenstreet (*Kasper Gutman*), Ward Bond (*Detective Tom Polhaus*), Jerome Cowan (*Miles Archer*), Elisha Cook Jr (*Wilmer Cook*), James Burke (*Luke*), Murray Alper (*Frank Richman*), John Hamilton (*D.A. Bryan*), Emory Parnell (*Mate of the La Palma*), Walter Huston (*Captain Jacobi*), Jack Mower (*Announcer*), Hank Mann (*Reporter*), William Hopper (*Reporter*), Charles Drake (*Reporter*), Creighton Hale (*Stenographer*).

R.t. 100.
Copyright, 18 October 1941.
First shown, Strand, New York, 3 October 1941.
Reviews, V, 1 October 1941 (Walt), NYT, 4 October 1941 (Bosley Crowther).

Marked Woman
First National
Ass.p–Lou Edelman. D–Lloyd Bacon. Ass.d–Dick Mayberry. Sc–Robert Rossen, Abem Finkel. Ph–George Barnes. Ed–Jack Killifer. A.d–Max Parker. Cost–Orry-Kelly. M–Bernhard Kaun, Heinz Roemheld. M.d–Leo F. Forbstein. Songs–'My Silver Dollar Man' by Harry Warren and Al Dubin; 'Mr and Mrs Dooks' by M.K. Jerome and Jack Scholl. Sd–Everett A. Brown. Sfx–James Gibbons, Robert Burks.

Bette Davis (*Mary Dwight*), Humphrey Bogart (*David Graham*), Lola Lane (*Gabby Marvin*), Isabel Jewell (*Emmy Lou Egan*), Eduardo Cianelli (*Johnny Vanning*), Rosalind Marquis (*Florrie Liggett*), Mayo Methot (*Estelle Porter*), Jane Bryan (*Betty Dwight*), Allen Jenkins (*Louie*), John Litel (*Gordon*), Ben Welden (*Charlie*), Damian O'Flynn (*Ralph Krawford*), Henry O'Neill (*Arthur Sheldon*), Raymond Hatton (*Lawyer at jail*), Carlos San Martin (*Head waiter*), William B. Davidson (*Bob Crandall*), Kenneth Harlan (*Eddie*), Robert Strange (*George Beler*), James Robbins (*Bell Captain*), Arthur Aylesworth (*John Truble*), John Sheehan (*Vincent*), Sam Wren (*Mac*), Edwin Stanley (*Detective Casey*), Alan Davis (*Henchman*), Allen Matthews (*Henchman*), Guy Usher (*Detective Ferguson*),

Gordon Hart (*Judge at first trial*), Pierre Watkin (*Judge at second trial*), Herman Marks (*Joe*).

R.t. 95.
Copyright, 19 February 1937.
First shown, Strand, New York, 10 April 1937.
Reviews, NYT, 12 April 1937 (Frank S. Nugent), V, 16 April 1937 (anon).

Massacre
First National
Ass.p–Robert Presnell. D–Alan Crosland. Sc–Ralph Block, Sheridan Gibney, from a story by Robert Gessner. Ph–George Barnes. Ed–Terry Morse. A.d–John Hughes. Cost–Orry-Kelly. M.d–Leo F. Forbstein.

Richard Barthelmess (*Chief Joe Thunder Horse*), Ann Dvorak (*Lydia*), Dudley Digges (*Elihu P. Quissenbery*), Claire Dodd (*Norma*), Henry O'Neill (*J.R. Dickinson*), Robert Barrat (*Dawson*), Arthur Hohl (*Doc Turner*), Sidney Toler (*Shanks*), Clarence Muse (*Sam*), Wallis Clark (*Cochran*), Wm. V. Mong (*Mr Grandy*), De Witt Jennings (*Sheriff Jennings*), Frank McGlynn Sr (*Missionary*), Agnes Nascha (*Jennie*), Douglass Dumbrille (*Chairman*), Charles Middleton, Tully Marshall, Juliet Ware, James Eagles, Philip Faversham, George Blackwood, Samuel Hinds.

R.t. 70.
Copyright, 16 January 1934.
First shown, Strand, New York, 17 January 1934.
Reviews, NYT, 18 January 1934 (Mordaunt Hall), V, 23 January 1934 (Bige).

Meet John Doe
A Frank Capra Production
D–Frank Capra. Ass.d–Arthur S. Black. Sc–Robert Riskin, from the story 'The Life of John Doe' by Richard Connell and Robert Presnell. Ph–George Barnes. Ed–Daniel Mandell. A.d–Stephen Goosson. Cost–Natalie Visart. M–Dimitri Tiomkin. Choral arrangements–Hall Johnson. M.d–Leo F. Forbstein. Sd–C.A. Riggs. Sfx–Jack Cosgrove. Montage effects–Slavko Vorkapich.

Gary Cooper (*Long John Willoughby/'John Doe'*), Barbara Stanwyck (*Ann Mitchell*), Edward Arnold (*D.B. Norton*), Walter Brennan (*The Colonel*), Spring Byington (*Mrs Mitchell*), James Gleason (*Henry Connell*), Gene Lockhart (*Mayor Lovett*), Rod La Rocque (*Ted Sheldon*), Irving Bacon (*Beany*), Regis Toomey (*Bert Hansen*), J. Farrell MacDonald (*Sourpuss Smithers*), Warren Hymer (*Angel-face*), Harry Holman (*Mayor Hawkins*), Andrew Tombes (*Spencer*), Pierre Watkin (*Hammett*), Stanley Andrews (*Weston*), Mitchell Lewis (*Bennett*), Charles Wilson (*Charlie Dawson*), Vaughan Glaser (*Governor*), Sterling Holloway (*Dan*), Mike Frankovich (*Radio Announcer*), Knox Manning (*Radio Announcer*), John B. Hughes (*Radio Announcer*), Russell Simpson (*Barrington*), Pat Flaherty (*Mike*), Gene Morgan (*Mug*), Mrs Gardner Crane (*Mrs Webster*), Anne Doran (*Mrs Hansen*), Sarah Edwards (*Mayor's wife*), Aldrich Bowker (*Pop Dwyer*), Ed Stanley (*Political Manager*), Bennie Bartlett (*Red the office boy*), Bess Flowers (*Mattie*), Gary Owen (*Signpainter*), Carlotta Jelm, Tina Thayer (*Ann's sisters*), Cyril Thornton (*Butler*), Edward Earle (*Radio M.C.*), Emma Tansey

(*Mrs Delaney*), Billy Curtis, Johnny Fern (*Midgets*), Vernon Dent (*Man*), Suzanne Carnahan, Marie Wrixon (*Autograph hunters*), Hank Mann (*Photographer*), Walter Soderling (*Barrington*), Lafe McKee (*Mr Delaney*), Selmer Jackson (*Radio Announcer*), Lucia Carroll, Ed Stanley, Ed Herne, Charles K. French, Cyril Ring, Edward McWade, Gail Nembray, Eddie Cobb, Inez Gray, Frank Moran, the Hall Johnson Choir.

R.t. 129.
Copyright, 5 May 1941.
First shown, Hollywood and Rivoli Theatres, New York, 12 March 1941.
Reviews, NYT, 13 March 1941 (Bosley Crowther), V, 19 March 1941 (Flin).
Meet John Doe was re-released in 1950 as *John Doe Dynamite*.

A Midsummer Night's Dream
Warner Brothers
Ass.p–Henry Blanke. U.m–Al Alborn. D–Max Reinhardt, William Dieterle. Ass.d–Sherry Shourds, Russell Saunders. Dial.d–Stanley Logan. Arranged for the screen by Charles Kenyon and Mary C. McCall Jr from the play by William Shakespeare. Ph–Hal Mohr. Camera–Robert Surtees, Thomas Brannigan. Special photographic effects–Fred Jackman, Byron Haskin, H.F. Koenekamp. Ed–Ralph Dawson. Assistant film editor–Warren Low. Continuity–Fred Applegate. A.d–Anton Grot. Set decorator–Ben Bone. Properties–Emmett Emerson, John More. Cost–Max Ree, Milo Anderson. Cosmetician–Perc Westmore. Hair styles–Fay Hanlin. M–Felix Mendelssohn. Orch–Erich Wolfgang Korngold. M.d–Leo F. Forbstein. Ballets–Bronislava Nijinska. Sd–Dave Forrest. Interpreter–Marie Hayes.

Ian Hunter (*Theseus, Duke of Athens*), Verree Teasdale (*Hippolyta, Queen of the Amazons*), Hobart Cavanaugh (*Philostrate*), Dick Powell (*Lysander*), Ross Alexander (*Demetrius*), Olivia De Havilland (*Hermia*), Jean Muir (*Helena*), Grant Mitchell (*Egeus*), Frank McHugh (*Quince the Carpenter*), Dewey Robinson (*Snug the Joiner*), James Cagney (*Bottom the Weaver*), Joe E. Brown (*Flute the Bellows-mender*), Hugh Herbert (*Snout the Tinker*), Otis Harlan (*Starveling the Tailor*), Arthur Treacher (*Epilogue/Ninny's Tomb*), Victor Jory (*Oberon, King of the Fairies*), Anita Louise (*Titania, Queen of the Fairies*), Nini Theilade (*Fairy*), Mickey Rooney (*Puck*), Katherine Frey (*Pease-Blossom*), Helen Westcott (*Cobweb*), Fred Sale Jr (*Moth*), Billy Barty (*Mustard Seed*), Sheila Brown (*Indian Prince*), Sara Haden (*Bottom's wife*), Miriam Dawn.

R.t. 132.
Copyright, 16 October 1935.
First shown, Hollywood Theatre, New York and Adelphi Cinema, London, 9 October 1935.
Reviews, NYT, 10 October 1935 (Andre Sennwald), V, 16 October 1935 (Flin).

Moby Dick
Warner Brothers
D–Lloyd Bacon. Sc–J. Grubb Alexander, from the novel by Herman Melville, adapted by Oliver H.P. Garrett. Ph–Robert Kurrle. Ed–Desmond O'Brien.

M.d–Louis Silvers, Erno Rapee. Sd–David Forrest. Technical effects–Fred Jackman.

John Barrymore (*Captain Ahab*), Joan Bennett (*Faith Mapple*), Lloyd Hughes (*Derek*), May Boley (*Whale Oil Rosie*), Walter Long (*Stubbs*), Tom O'Brien (*Starbuck*), Nigel de Brulier (*Elijah*), Noble Johnson (*Queequeg*), William Walling (*Blacksmith*), Virginia Sale (*Old maid*), Jack Curtis (*First mate*), John Ince (*Reverend Mapple*).

R.t. 70.
Copyright, 26 August 1930.
First shown, Hollywood Theatre, New York, 14 August 1930.
Reviews, NYT, 15 August 1930 (Mordaunt Hall), V, 20 August 1930 (Sime).

The Mouthpiece
Warner Brothers
Ass.p–Lucien Hubbard. D–James Flood, Elliott Nugent. Ass.d–Bill Cannon. Sc–Joseph Jackson, from the play by Frank Collins. Adaptation and dialogue–Earl Baldwin. Ph–Barney McGill. Ed–George Amy. A.d–Esdras Hartley. Cost–Earl Luick. M.d–Leo F. Forbstein.

Warren William (*Vincent Day*), Sidney Fox (*Celia Faraday*), Aline MacMahon (*Miss Hickey*), John Wray (*Barton*), Mae Madison (*Elaine*), Ralph Ince (*J.B.*), Morgan Wallace (*A.E. Smith*), Guy Kibbee (*Paddy the bartender*), J. Carrol Naish (*Tony*), Walter Walker (*Forbes*), Stanley Fields (*Pondapolis*), Murray Kinnell (*Jarvis*), Noel Francis (*Miss De Vere*), William Janney (*Johnny Morris*), Polly Walters (*Gladys*), Jack La Rue (*Garland*), Emerson Tracey (*Wilson*).

R.t. 86.
Copyright, 18 April 1932.
First shown, Winter Garden, New York, 21 April 1932.
Reviews, NYT, 22 April 1932 (Mordaunt Hall), V, 26 April 1932 (Rush).

Night Nurse
Warner Brothers
D–William A. Wellman. Sc–Oliver H.P. Garrett, from a novel by Dora Macy (Grace Parkins Oursier). Dialogue–Oliver H.P. Garrett, Charles Kenyon. Ph–Chick McGill. Ed–Ed McDermott. A.d–Max Parker. Cost–Earl Luick. M.d–Leo F. Forbstein. Tech.ad–Dr Harry Martin.

Barbara Stanwyck (*Lora Hart*), Ben Lyon (*Mortie*), Joan Blondell (*Maloney*), Clark Gable (*Nick*), Blanche Frederici (*Mrs Maxwell*), Charlotte Merriam (*Mrs Richey*), Charles Winninger (*Dr Bell*), Edward Nugent (*Eagan*), Vera Lewis (*Miss Dillon*), Ralf Harolde (*Dr Ranger*), Walter McGrail (*Drunk*), Allan Lane (*Intern*), Betty May (*Nurse*), Marcia Mae Jones (*Nanny*), Betty Jane Graham (*Desney*).

R.t. 72.
Copyright, 10 July 1931.
First shown, Strand, New York, 16 July 1931.
Reviews, NYT, 17 July 1931 (Mordaunt Hall), V, 21 July 1931 (Sid).

Oil for the Lamps of China
Cosmopolitan
Ass.p–Robert Lord. D–Mervyn LeRoy. Ass.d–Lee Katz. Sc–Laird Doyle, from the novel by Alice Tisdale Hobart. Ph–Tony Gaudio. Ed–William Clemens. A.d–Robert Haas. Cost–Orry-Kelly. M.d–Leo F. Forbstein.

Pat O'Brien (*Stephen Chase*), Josephine Hutchinson (*Hester Adams*), Jean Muir (*Alice Wellman*), Lyle Talbot (*Jim*), Arthur Byron (*No. 1 Boss*), John Eldredge (*Don Wellman*), Donald Crisp (*McCargar*), Willie Fung (*Kin*), Tetsun Komai (*Ho*), Henry O'Neill (*Hartford*), Ronnie Cosby (*Bunsy Wellman*), William Davidson (*Swaley*), George Meeker (*Kendall*), Joseph Crehan (*Clements*), Christian Rub (*Dr Jorgen*), Willard Robertson (*Speaker*), Edward McWade (*Dan*), Florence Fair (*Miss Cunningham*), Keye Luke (*Young Chinese*).

R.t. 110.
Copyright, 4 June 1935.
First shown, Strand, New York, 5 June 1935.
Reviews, NYT, 6 June 1935 (Andre Sennwald), V, 12 June 1935 (Kauf).

Old English
Warner Brothers
D–Alfred E. Green. Sc–Walter Anthony, Maude T. Howell, from the novel 'The Stoic' by John Galsworthy. Ph–James van Trees. Ed–Owen Marks. Cost–Earl Luick. M.d–Louis Silvers, Erno Rapee. Sd–Clare A. Riggs.

George Arliss (*Sylvanus Heythrop*), Doris Lloyd (*Mrs Rosamond Larne*), Harrington Reynolds (*Farney*), Reginald Sheffield (*Bob Pillin*), Betty Lawford (*Phyllis Larne*), Murry Kinnell (*Charles Ventnor*), Ivan Simpson (*Joe Pillin*), Leon Janney (*Jock*), Ethel Griffies (*Adela Heythrop*), Joan Maclean (*Molly*), Henry Morrell (*Meller*), Henrietta Goodwin (*Letty Booth*), Herbert Brunston (*Mr Brownley*), Charles Evans (*Appleby*), Barry Winton (*First clerk*), Powell York (*Clerk*), Horace Cooper (*Westgate*), Clive Morgan (*Winkley*), John Rogers (*Budgeon*), Wilfred Noy (*Batterson*), Robert Hunter (*Director*).

R.t. 85.
Copyright, 13 September 1930.
First shown, Warner Theatre, New York, 21 August 1930.
Reviews, NYT, 22 August 1930 (Mordaunt Hall), V, 27 August 1930 (Sime).

The Prince and the Pauper
First National
Ass.p–Robert Lord. D–William Keighley. Ass.d–Chuck Hansen. Sc–Laird Doyle, from the story by Mark Twain (dramatised version by Catherine Chisholm Cushing). Ph–Sol Polito. Ed–Ralph Dawson. A.d–Robert Haas. M–Erich Wolfgang Korngold. Orch–Hugo Friedhofer, Milan Roder. M.d–Leo F. Forbstein. Sd–Oliver S. Garretson. Sfx–Willard Van Enger, James Gibbons.

Errol Flynn (*Miles Hendon*), Claude Rains (*Earl of Hertford*), Henry Stephenson (*Duke of Norfolk*), Barton MacLane (*John Canty*), Billy Mauch (*Tom Canty*), Bobby Mauch (*Prince Edward*), Alan Hale (*Captain of the Guard*), Eric Portman (*First Lord*), Lionel Pape (*Second Lord*), Leonard Willey (*Third Lord*), Murray Kinnell (*Hugo*), Halliwell Hobbes (*Archbishop*), Phyllis Barry (*Barmaid*), Ivan

Simpson (*Clemens*), Montagu Love (*Henry VIII*), Fritz Leiber (*Father Andrew*), Elspeth Dudgeon (*Grandmother Canty*), Mary Field (*Mrs Canty*), Forrester Harvey (*Meaty man*), Helen Valkir (*Lady Jane Seymour*), Lester Matthews (*St. John*), Robert Adair (*First guard*), Harry Cording (*Second guard*), Robert Warwick (*Lord Warwick*), Holmes Herbert (*First doctor*), Robert Evans (*Rich man*), Ian MacLaren (*Second doctor*), Ann Howard (*Lady Jane Grey*), Gwendolyn Jones (*Lady Elizabeth*), Lionel Braham (*Ruffler*), Harry Beresford (*The Watch*), Lionel Belmore (*Innkeeper*), Ian Wolf (*Proprietor*), The St. Luke's Choristers.

R.t. 120.
Copyright, 11 March 1937.
First shown, Strand, New York, 5 May 1937.
Reviews, NYT, 6 May 1937 (Frank S. Nugent), V, 12 May 1937 (Flin).

The Private Lives of Elizabeth and Essex
Warner Brothers
Ass.p–Robert Lord. U.m–Frank Mattison. D–Michael Curtiz. Ass.d–Sherry Shourds. Dial.d–Stanley Logan. Sc–Norman Reilly Raine, Aeneas MacKenzie, from the play 'Elizabeth the Queen' by Maxwell Anderson. Ph–Sol Polito (Technicolor). Technicolor associate–W. Howard Greene. Technicolor color director–Natalie Kalmus. Technicolor associate–Morgan Padelford. Ed–Owen Marks. A.d–Anton Grot. Cost–Orry-Kelly. Make-up–Perc Westmore. M–Erich Wolfgang Korngold. Orch–Hugo Friedhofer, Milan Roder. M.d–Leo F. Forbstein. Sd–C.A. Riggs. Sfx–Byron Haskin, H.F. Koenekamp. Tech.ad–Ali Hubert.

Bette Davis (*Queen Elizabeth*), Errol Flynn (*Robert Devereux, Earl of Essex*), Olivia De Havilland (*Lady Penelope Gray*), Donald Crisp (*Sir Francis Bacon*), Alan Hale (*Earl of Tyrone*), Vincent Price (*Sir Walter Raleigh*), Henry Stephenson (*Lord Burghley*), Henry Daniell (*Sir Robert Cecil*), James Stephenson (*Sir Thomas Egerton*), Nanette Fabares [Fabray] (*Mistress Margaret Radcliffe*), Ralph Forbes (*Lord Knollys*), Robert Warwick (*Lord Mountjoy*), Leo G. Carroll (*Sir Edward Coke*), Rosella Towne, Marie Wrixon, John Sutton, Guy Bellis, Doris Lloyd, Forrester Harvey.

R.t. 106.
Copyright, 11 November 1939.
First shown, Warners Hollywood and Warners Downtown, Los Angeles, 16 November 1939.
Reviews, V, 4 October 1939 (anon), NYT, 2 December 1939 (Frank S. Nugent).

The Public Enemy (UK: Enemies of the Public)
Warner Brothers
D–William A. Wellman. Sc–Harvey Thew, from the story 'Beer and Blood: The story of a Couple o' Wrong Guys' by Kubec Glasmon and John Bright. Ph–Dev Jennings. Ed–Ed McCormick. A.d–Max Parker. Cost–Earl Luick. Make-up–Perc Westmore. M.d–David Mendoza.

James Cagney (*Tom Powers*), Jean Harlow (*Gwen Allen*), Edward Woods (*Matt Doyle*), Joan Blondell (*Mamie*), Donald Cook (*Mike Powers*), Leslie Fenton

(*Nails Nathan*), Beryl Mercer (*Ma Powers*), Robert Emmett O'Connor (*Paddy Ryan*), Murray Kinnell (*Putty Nose*), Mae Clarke (*Kitty*), Mia Marvin (*Jane*), Ben Hendricks Jr (*Bugs Moran*), Rita Flynn (*Molly Doyle*), Clark Burroughs (*Dutch*), Snitz Edwards (*Hack Miller*), Adele Watson (*Mrs Doyle*), Frank Coghlan Jr (*Tom as a boy*), Frankie Darro (*Matt as a boy*), Purnell Pratt (*Officer Powers*), Ward Bond (*Machine-gunner*), Robert E. Homans (*Officer Pat Burke*), Dorothy Gee (*Nails' girl*), Lee Phelps (*Steve the bartender*), Helen Parrish, Dorothy Grey, Nancy Price (*Little girls*), Ben Hendricks III (*Bugs as a boy*), George Daly (*Machine-gunner*), Eddie Kane (*Joe the headwaiter*), Charles Sullivan (*Mug*), Douglas Gerrard (*Assistant tailor*), Sam McDaniels (*Black headwaiter*), William H. Strauss (*Pawnbroker*).

R.t. 96.
Copyright, 4 April 1931.
First shown, Strand, New York, 23 April 1931.
Reviews, NYT, 24 April 1931 (Andre Sennwald), V, 29 April 1931 (Sid).

The Roaring Twenties
Warner Brothers
Ass.p–Sam Bischoff. D–Raoul Walsh. Ass.d–Dick Mayberry. Dial.d–Hugh Cummings. Sc–Jerry Wald, Richard Macaulay, Robert Rossen, from the story 'The World Moves On' by Mark Hellinger. Ph–Ernest Haller. Ed–Jack Killifer. Continuity–Virginia Moore. A.d–Max Parker. Cost–Milo Anderson. Make-up–Perc Westmore. M–Heinz Roemheld, Ray Heindorf. Orch–Ray Heindorf. M.d–Leo F. Forbstein. Songs–'My Melancholy Baby' by Ernie Burnett and George A. Norton; 'I'm Just Wild About Harry' by Eubie Blake and Noble Sissle; 'It Had to be You' by Isham Jones and Gus Kahn; 'In a Shanty in Old Shanty Town' by Jack Little, Joseph Young and John Siras. Sd–Everett A. Brown. Sfx–Byron Haskin, Edwin B. Du Par. Montages–Don Siegel. Narrator–John Deering.

James Cagney (*Eddie Bartlett*), Priscilla Lane (*Jean Sherman*), Humphrey Bogart (*George Hally*), Gladys George (*Panama Smith*), Jeffrey Lynn (*Lloyd Hart*), Frank McHugh (*Danny Green*), Paul Kelly (*Nick Brown*), Elizabeth Risdon (*Mrs Sherman*), Vera Lewis (*Mrs Gray*), Ed Keane (*Pete Henderson*), Joe Sawyer (*Sergeant Pete Jones*), Joseph Crehan (*Mr Fletcher*), George Meeker (*Masters*), John Hamilton (*Judge*), Robert Elliott (*First Detective*), Eddie Chandler (*Second Detective*), Max Wagner (*Lefty*), Abner Biberman, Elliott Sullivan (*Eddie's cellmates*), Bert Hanlon (*Piano Accompanist*), Murray Alper (*First Mechanic*), Dick Wessell (*Second Mechanic*), George Humbert (*Luigi*), Ben Welden (*Tavern proprietor*), Clay Clement (*Bramfield*), Don Thaddeus Kerr (*Bobby Hart*), Ray Cooke (*Orderly*), Norman Willis (*Bootlegger*), Pat O'Malley (*Jailer*), Arthur Loft (*Proprietor of Still*), Al Hill, Raymond Bailey, Lew Harvey (*Ex-cons*), Joe Devlin, Jeffrey Sayre (*Order-takers*), Paul Phillips (*Mike*), Jack Norton (*Drunk*), Alan Bridge (*Captain*), Fred Graham (*Henchman*), James Blaine (*Doorman*), Henry C. Bradley, Lotte Williams (*Couple in restaurant*), John Harron (*Soldier*), Lee Phelps (*Bailiff*), Nat Carr (*Waiter*), Wade Boteler (*Policeman*), Creighton Hale (*Customer*), Ann Codee (*Saleswoman*), Eddie Acuff, Milton Kibbee, John Ridgeley (*Cab drivers*), James Flavin, Oscar O'Shea, Frank Wilcox, The Jane Jones Trio, Harry Hollingsworth, Frank Mayo, Emory Parnell, Billy Wayne, Philip Morris, Maurice Costello, John St. Clair.

R.t. 104.
Copyright, 28 October 1939.
First shown on general release, 28 October 1939.
Reviews, V, 25 October 1939 (Scho), NYT, 11 November 1939 (Frank S. Nugent).

The St. Louis Kid (UK: A Perfect Weekend)
Warner Brothers
Ass.p–Sam Bischoff. D–Ray Enright. Dial.d–Stanley Logan. Sc–Warren Duff, Seton I. Miller, from the story 'A Perfect Weekend' by Frederick Hazlitt Brennan. Ph–Sid Hickox. Ed–Clarence Kolster. A.d–Jack Okey. Cost–Orry-Kelly. Make-up–Perc Westmore. Orch–Leo F. Forbstein.

James Cagney (*Eddie Kennedy*), Patricia Ellis (*Ann Reid*), Allen Jenkins (*Buck Willetts*), Robert Barrat (*James Benson*), Hobart Cavanaugh (*Richardson*), Spencer Charters (*Pop Messeldopp*), Addison Richards (*Brown*), Dorothy Dare (*Gracie*), Arthur Aylesworth (*Judge Jeremiah Jones*), Charles Wilson (*Harris*), William Davidson (*Joe Hunter*), Harry Woods (*Louie*), Gertrude Short (*The girlfriend*), Eddie Shubert (*Pete*), Russell Hicks (*Gorman*), Guy Usher (*Sergeant*), Cliff Saum, Bruce Mitchell (*Cops*), Wilfred Lucas (*Policeman*), Rosalie Roy (*Girl*), Mary Russell (*Office girl*), Ben Hendricks (*Motor cop*), Harry Tyler (*Mike*), Milton Kibbee (*Paymaster*), Tom Wilson (*Cook*), Alice Marr, Victoria Vinton (*Secretaries*), Lee Phelps (*Farmer*), Louise Seidel (*Girl in car*), Mary Treen (*Giddy girl*), Nan Grey (*First girl*), Virginia Grey (*Second girl*), Martha Merrill (*Third girl*), Charles Middleton (*Sheriff*), Douglas Cosgrove (*Prosecutor*), Monte Vandergrift (*First deputy*), Jack Cheatham (*Second deputy*), Stanley Mack (*Driver*), Grover Liggen (*Attendant*), Frank Bull (*Broadcast officer*), Wade Boteler (*Sergeant*), Frank Fanning (*Policeman*), Gene Strong (*Second Policeman*), Edna Bennett (*Flora*), Clay Clement (*Man*), James Burtis (*Detective*), Eddie Fetherstone, Joan Barclay.

R.t. 66.
Copyright, 16 November 1934.
First shown, Strand, New York, 31 October 1934.
Reviews, NYT, 1 November 1934 (Andre Sennwald), V, 6 November 1934 (Bige).

Santa Fe Trail
First National
Ass.p–Robert Fellows. D–Michael Curtiz. Dial.d–Jo Graham. Sc–Robert Buckner. Ph–Sol Polito. Ed–George Amy. A.d–John Hughes. Cost–Milo Anderson. Make-up–Perc Westmore. M–Max Steiner. Orch–Hugo Friedhofer. M.d–Leo F. Forbstein. Sd–Robert B. Lee. Sfx–Byron Haskin, H.F. Koenekamp.

Errol Flynn (*J.E.B. Stuart*), Olivia De Havilland (*Kit Carson Halliday*), Raymond Massey (*John Brown*), Ronald Reagan (*George Armstrong Custer*), Alan Hale (*Tex Bell*), William Lundigan (*Bob Halliday*), Van Heflin (*Rader*), Gene Reynolds (*Jason Brown*), Henry O'Neill (*Cyrus K. Halliday*), Guinn 'Big Boy' Williams (*Windy Brody*), Alan Baxter (*Oliver Brown*), John Litel (*Martin*), Moroni Olsen (*Robert E. Lee*), David Bruce (*Phil Sheridan*), Hobart Cavanaugh

(*Barber Doyle*), Charles D. Brown (*Major Sumner*), Joe Sawyer (*Kitzmiller*), Frank Wilcox (*James Longstreet*), Ward Bond (*Townsley*), Russell Simpson (*Shoubel Morgan*), Charles Middleton (*Gentry*), Erville Alderson (*Jefferson Davis*), Spencer Charters (*Conductor*), Suzanne Carnahan (*Charlotte Davis*), William Marshall (*George Pickett*), George Haywood (*John Hood*), Wilfred Lucas (*Weiner*), Russell Hicks (*J. Royce Russell*).

R.t. 109.
Copyright, 28 December 1940.
First shown, Strand, New York, 20 December 1940.
Reviews, NYT, 21 December 1940 (Bosley Crowther), V, 18 December 1940 (Wear).

The Sea Hawk
Warner Brothers
Ass.p–Henry Blanke. U.m–Frank Mattison. D–Michael Curtiz. Ass.d–Jack Sullivan. Dial.d–Jo Graham. Sc–Seton I. Miller, Howard Koch. Ph–Sol Polito. Ed–George Amy. A.d–Anton Grot. Cost–Orry-Kelly. Make-up–Perc Westmore. M–Erich Wolfgang Korngold. M.d–Leo F. Forbstein. Sd–Francis J. Scheid. Sfx–Byron Haskin, H.F. Koenekamp. Tech.ad–Ali Hubert.

Errol Flynn (*Francis Thorpe*), Brenda Marshall (*Dona Maria*), Claude Rains (*Don Alvarez*), Donald Crisp (*Sir John Burleson*), Flora Robson (*Queen Elizabeth*), Alan Hale (*Carl Pitt*), Henry Daniell (*Lord Wolfingham*), Montagu Love (*King Philip II*), Gilbert Roland (*Captain Lopez*), Una O'Connor (*Miss Latham*), William Lundigan (*Danny Logan*), Robert Warwick (*Frobisher*), Guy Hawkins (*Hawkins*), J.M. Kerrigan (*Eli Matson*), Julien Mitchell (*Oliver Scott*), Clyde Cook (*Walter Boggs*), James Stephenson (*Abbott*), Herbert Anderson (*Eph Winters*), Ian Keith (*Peralta*), Frederick Worlock (*Darnell*), Ivar McFadden (*Hormiston*), Clifford Brooke (*William Tuttle*), Francis McDonald (*Kroner*), David Bruce (*Martin Burke*), Frank Wilcox (*Barrett*), Alec Craig (*Chartmaker*), Ellis Irving (*Monty Preston*), Halliwell Hobbes (*Astronomer*), Edgar Buchanan (*Ben Rollins*), Pedro de Cordoba (*Captain Mendoza*), Frank Lackteen (*Captain Ortiz*), Jack La Rue (*Lieutenant Ortega*), Fritz Leiber (*Inquisitor*), Victor Varconi (*General Aguirre*), Harry Cording (*Slavemaster*), Charles Irwin (*Arnold Cross*), Max Carmel.

R.t. 127.
Copyright, 3 September 1940.
First shown, Strand, New York, 9 August 1940.
Reviews, NYT, 10 August 1940 (Bosley Crowther), V, 24 July 1940 (Walt).

The Sea Wolf
Warner Brothers
Ass.p–Henry Blanke. D–Michael Curtiz. Ass.d–Sherry Shourds. Dial.d–Jo Graham. Sc–Robert Rossen, from the novel by Jack London. Ph–Sol Polito. Ed–George Amy. A.d–Anton Grot. Make-up–Perc Westmore. M–Erich Wolfgang Korngold. Orch–Hugo Friedhofer. M.d–Leo F. Forbstein. Sfx–Byron Haskin, H.F. Koenekamp.

Edward G. Robinson (*Wolf Larsen*), Ida Lupino (*Ruth Webster*), John Garfield (*George Leach*), Alexander Knox (*Humphrey Van Weyden*), Gene Lockhart (*Dr

Louie Prescott), Barry Fitzgerald (*Cookie*), Stanley Ridges (*Johnson*), Francis McDonald (*Svenson*), Howard Da Silva (*Harrison*), Frank Lackteen (*Smoke*), David Bruce (*Young sailor*), Wilfred Lucas (*Helmsman*), Louis Mason (*Sailor*), Ralf Harolde (*Agent*), Dutch Hendrian (*Crewman*), Cliff Clark (*1st detective*), William Gould (*2nd detective*), Charles Sullivan (*First mate*), Ernie Adams (*Pickpocket*), Jeane Cowan (*Singer*), Ethan Laidlaw (*Crewman*).

R.t. 98.
Copyright, 22 February 1941.
First shown, Strand, New York, 21 March 1941.
Reviews, NYT, 22 March 1941 (Bosley Crowther), V, 26 March 1941 (Walt).

Sergeant York
Warner Brothers
Executive co-producers–Jesse L. Lasky, Hal B. Wallis. U.m–Eric Stacey. D–Howard Hawks. Ass.d–Jack Sullivan. 2nd.d–B. Reeves Eason. Sc–Abem Finkel, Harry Chandlee, Howard Koch, John Huston, from the books 'The War Diary of Sergeant York' and 'Sergeant York and his People', by Sam K. Cowan, and 'Sergeant York, Last of the Long Hunters' by Tom Skeyhill. Ph–Sol Polito. Camera–Al Greene. Battle sequences photographed by Arthur Edeson. Ed–William Holmes. Assistant film editor–Tom Reilly. Continuity– Eugene Busch. A.d–John Hughes. Set decorator–Fred MacLean. Properties– Lou Hafley. Make-up–Perc Westmore. Hair styles–Edith Westmore. M–Max Steiner. Orch–Hugo Friedhofer. M.d–Leo F. Forbstein. Sd–Oliver S. Garretson. Tech.ad–Donoho Hall, Captain Paul Walters, F.A.R., William Yetter.

Gary Cooper (*Alvin C. York*), Walter Brennan (*Pastor Rosier Pile*), Joan Leslie (*Gracie Williams*), Stanley Ridges (*Major Buxton*), George Tobias (*Michael T. 'Pusher' Ross*), Ward Bond (*Ike Botkin*), Margaret Wycherley (*Mother York*), June Lockhart (*Rosie York*), Noah Beery Jr (*Buck Lipscomb*), Clem Bevans (*Zeke*), Dickie Moore (*George York*), Charles Trowbridge (*Cordell Hull*), Howard Da Silva (*Lem*), David Bruce (*Burt Thomas*), Harvey Stephens (*Captain Danforth*), Joseph Sawyer (*Sergeant Early*), Charles Esmond (*German Major*), Robert Porterfield (*Zeb Andrews*), Guy Wilkerson (*Tom*), James Anderson (*Eb*), Lasses White (*Luke, the target keeper*), Erville Alderson (*Nate Tomkins*), Tully Marshall (*Uncle Lige*), Victor Killian (*Mr Andrews*), Pat Flaherty (*Sergeant Harry Parsons*), Lane Chandler (*Corporal Savage*), Jack Pennick (*Corporal Cutting*), Don Douglas (*Captain Tillman*), George Erving (*Mr Harrison*), Ed Keane (*Oscar of the Waldorf*), William Forrest (*Officer*), Frank Wilcox (*Sergeant in trench*), James Bush (*Private in trench*), Douglas Wood (*Major Hylan*), Frank Marlowe (*Beardsley*), Arthur Aylesworth (*Bartender at the Blind Tiger*), Elisha Cook Jr (*Piano player at the Blind Tiger*), Frank Orth (*Drummer*), Joseph Gerard (*General Pershing*), Jane Isbell (*Gracie's sister*), Rita La Roy, Lucia Carroll, Kay Sutton (*Girls in saloon*), William Haade (*Card player*), Jody Gilbert (*Fat woman*), Frank Faylen, Murray Alper (*Butt boys*), Gaylord Pendleton, Charles Drake (*Scorers*), Theodore Von Eltz (*Prison Camp Commandant*), Roland Drew (*Officer*), Russell Hicks (*General*), Jean Del Vale (*Marshall Foch*), Selmer Jackson (*General Duncan*), Byron Barr [Gig Young] (*Soldier*), Si. Jenks, Ray Teal, Kit Guard, Dick Simmons.

R.t. 134.
Copyright, 27 September 1941.
First shown, Astor, New York, 2 July 1941.
Reviews, NYT, 3 July 1941 (Bosley Crowther), V, 2 July 1941 (Flin).

Show of Shows
Warner Brothers
D—John G. Adolfi. Technical director—Louis Geib. Ph—Barney McGill (86% Technicolor). Electrical effects—Frank N. Murphy. Cost—Earl Luick. M.d— Louis Silvers. Dance ensembles—Larry Ceballos and Jack Haskell. Songs— 'Singing in the Bathtub' by Ned Washington, Herb Magdison and Michael Cleary; 'Lady Luck' by Ray Perkins; 'Motion Picture Pirates' by M.K. Jerome; 'If I Could Learn to Love' by Herman Ruby and M.K. Jerome; 'Pingo Pongo' and 'If Your Best Friends Won't Tell You' by Al Dubin and Joe Burke; 'The Only Song I Know' and 'My Sister' by J. Keirn Brennan and Ray Perkins; 'Your Mother and Mine' by Joe Goodwin and Gus Edwards; 'You Were Meant For Me' by Arthur Freed and Nacio Herb Brown; 'Just an Hour of Love', 'Li-Po-Li' and 'Military March' by Al Bryan and Ed Ward; 'Rock-A-Bye Your Baby with a Dixie Melody' by Joe Young, Sam Lewis and Jean Schwartz; 'Jumping Jack' by Bernie Seaman, Herman Ruby, Marvin Smolev and Rube Bloom; 'Your Love is All I Crave' by Al Dubin, Perry Bradford and Jimmy Johnson. Sd—George R. Groves. Special material—Frank Fay, J. Keirn Brennan.

Frank Fay (*Master of Ceremonies*), William Courtenay (*The Minister*), H.B. Warner (*The Victim*), Hobart Bosworth (*The Executioner*), Marion Nixon, Sally O'Neill, Myrna Loy, Alice Day, Patsy Ruth Miller, Lila Lee (*The Floradora Sextette*), Ben Turpin (*Waiter*), Heinie Conklin (*Iceman*), Lupino Lane (*Street Cleaner*), Lee Moran (*Plumber*), Bert Roach (*Father*), Lloyd Hamilton (*Hansom Cabby*), Noah Beery, Tully Marshall, Wheeler Oakman, Bull Montana, Kalla Pasha, Anders Randolf, Philo McCullough, Otto Mattieson, Jack Curtis (*Pirates*), Johnny Arthur (*Hero*), Carmel Myers, Ruth Clifford, Sally Eilers, Viola Dana, Shirley Mason, Ethlyne Clair, Frances Lee, Julianne Johnson (*Ladies*), Douglas Fairbanks Jr (*Ambrose*), Chester Conklin (*Traffic cop*), Grant Withers, William Collier Jr, Jack Mulhall, Chester Morris, William Bakewell (*Boys*), Lois Wilson, Gertrude Olmstead, Pauline Garon, Edna Murphy, Jacqueline Logan (*Girls*), Monte Blue (*Condemned Man*), Albert Green, Noah Beery, Lloyd Hamilton, Tully Marshall, Kalla Pasha, Lee Moran (*Soldiers*), Armida, John Barrymore, Richard Barthelmess, Sally Blane, Irene Bordoni, Anthony Bushell, Marion Byron, Georges Carpentier, James Clemmons, Betty Compson, Dolores Costello, Helene Costello, Marceline Day, Louise Fazenda, Alexander Gray, Beatrice Lillie, Winnie Lightner, Hariette Luke, Lila Lee, Ted Lewis, Nick Lucas, Molly O'Day, Rin-Tin-Tin, E.J. Radcliffe, Sid Silvers, Sojin, Lola Vendrill, Ada Mae Vaughn, Alberta Vaughn, Ted Williams, Adagio Dancers, Alice White, Loretta Young.

R.t. 124.
Copyright, 7 December 1929.
First shown, Winter Garden, New York, 20 November 1929.
Reviews, NYT, 21 November 1929 (Mordaunt Hall), V, 27 November 1929 (Sid).

Smart Money
Warner Brothers
D–Alfred E. Green. Sc–Kubec Glasmon, John Bright, Lucien Hubbard, Joseph Jackson, from the story 'The Idol' by Kubec Glasmon and John Bright. Ph–Robert Kurrle. Ed–Jack Killifer. A.d–Robert Haas. Cost–Earl Luick. Make-up–Perc Westmore. M.d–Leo F. Forbstein.

Edward G. Robinson (*Nick Venezelos*), James Cagney (*Jack*), Evalyn Knapp (*Irene Graham*), Ralf Harolde (*Sleepy Sam*), Noel Francis (*Marie*), Margaret Livingston (*D.A.'s girl*), Maurice Black (*Greek barber*), William House (*Salesman*), Paul Porcasi (*Alexander Amenoppopolus*), Gladys Lloyd (*Cigar stand girl*), Morgan Wallace (*D.A. Black*), Clark Burroughs (*Back-to-back Schultz*), Edwin Argus (*Two-time Phil*), Boris Karloff (*Sport Williams*), Mae Madison (*Small-town girl*), Walter Percival (*Dealer Barnes*), John Larkin (*Snake-eyes*), Polly Walters (*Lola*), Ben Taggart (*Hickory Short*), Clinton Rosemond (*George*), Charles Lane (*Desk clerk*), Eulalie Jackson (*Matron*), Edward Hearn (*Reporter*), Eddie Kane (*Tom*), Charles O'Malley (*Machine-gunner*), Gus Leonard (*Joe*), Wallace Macdonald (*Cigar stand clerk*), John George (*Dwarf on train*), Harry Semels (*Gambler*), Charlotte Merriam (*Girl at gaming table*), Allan Lane (*Suicide*), Larry McGrath, Spencer Bell.

R.t. 81.
Copyright, 3 June 1931.
First shown, Winter Garden, New York and Warners Hollywood and Warners Downtown, Los Angeles, 18 June 1931.
Reviews, NYT, 19 June 1931 (Mordaunt Hall), V, 23 June 1931 (Bige).

Son of the Gods
First National
D–Frank Lloyd. Sc–Bradley King, from the story by Rex Beach. Ph–Ernest Haller (including Technicolor sequence). M.d–Leo F. Forbstein. Song–'Pretty Like You' by Ben Ryan and Sol Violinsky.

Richard Barthelmess (*Sam Lee*), Constance Bennett (*Allana Wagner*), Anders Randolf (*Wagner*), E. Alyn Warren (*Lee Ying*), Claude King (*Bathurst*), Frank Albertson (*Kicker*), King Hoo Chang (*Moy*), Mildred Van Dorn (*Eileen*), Barbara Leonard (*Mabel*), Jimmy Eagles (*Spud*), Geneva Mitchell (*Connie*), Ivan Christie (*Café manager*), George Irving (*Attorney*), Dickie Moore (*Boy Sam*), Robert Homans (*Dugan*).

R.t. 90.
Copyright, 17 March 1930.
First shown, 30 January 1930, Warner Theatre, New York.
Reviews, NYT, 31 January 1930 (Mordaunt Hall), V, 5 February 1930 (Land).

Special Agent
Cosmopolitan
Ass.p–Sam Bischoff. D–William Keighley. Ass.d–Chuck Hansen. Sc–Laird Doyle, Abem Finkel, from a story idea by Martin Mooney. Ph–Sid Hickox. Ed–Clarence Kolster. A.d–Esdras Hartley. M.d–Leo F. Forbstein.

Bette Davis (*Julie Gardner*), George Brent (*Bill Bradford*), Ricardo Cortez (*Alexander Carston*), Jack La Rue (*Jake Andrews*), Henry O'Neill (*D.A. Walter Quinn*), Robert Strange (*Waxy Armitage*), Joseph Crehan (*Chief of Police*), J. Carrol Naish (*Durrell*), Joseph Sawyer (*Rich*), William Davidson (*Charley Young*), Robert Barrat (*Head of the Internal Revenue Department*), Paul Guilfoyle (*Secretary to the D.A.*), Joseph King (*Wilson*), Irving Pichel (*U.S. District Attorney*), J. Farrell MacDonald, Walter Walker, DeWitt Jennings, Huntley Gordon, Adrian Rosley, Georges Renevent, Grace Hale, Selmer Jackson, Gordon Westcott.

R.t. 76.
Copyright, 20 September 1935.
First shown on general release, 14 September 1935.
Reviews, NYT, 19 September 1935 (anon), V, 25 September 1935 (Land).

The Star Witness
Warner Brothers
D–William A. Wellman. Sc–Lucien Hubbard. Ph–James Van Trees. Ed–Harold McLernan. A.d–John J. Hughes. M.d–Leo F. Forbstein.

Walter Huston (*District Attorney Whitlock*), Frances Starr (*Ma Leeds*), Grant Mitchell (*Pa Leeds*), Sally Blane (*Sue Leeds*), Ralph Ince (*Maxey Campo*), Edward J. Nugent (*Jackie Leeds*), Dickie Moore (*Ned Leeds*), Nat Pendleton (*Big Jack*), George Ernest (*Donny Leeds*), Russell Hopton (*Deputy Thorpe*), Charles 'Chic' Sayle (*Gramps*), Robert Elliott, Noel Madison, Tom Dugan.

R.t. 67.
Copyright, 8 August 1931.
First shown, Winter Garden, New York, 3 August 1931.
Reviews, NYT, 4 August 1931 (Mordaunt Hall), V, 4 August 1931 (Sid).

The Story of Dr Ehrlich's Magic Bullet
Warner Brothers
Ass.p–Wolfgang Reinhardt. D–William Dieterle. Ass.d–Jack Sullivan. Dial.d–Irving Rapper. Sc–John Huston, Heinz Herald, Norman Burnside, based on biographical material in the possession of the Ehrlich family. Ph–James Wong Howe. Ed–Warren Low. A.d–Carl Jules Weyl. M–Max Steiner. Sd–Robert B. Lee. Special microscopic effects–Robert Burks.

Edward G. Robinson (*Dr Paul Ehrlich*), Ruth Gordon (*Heidi Ehrlich*), Otto Kruger (*Dr Emil von Behring*), Donald Crisp (*Minister Althoff*), Maria Ouspenskaya (*Franziska Speyer*), Montagu Love (*Professor Hartmann*), Sig Rumann (*Dr Hans Wolfert*), Donald Meek (*Mittelmeyer*), Henry O'Neill (*Dr Lentz*), Albert Bassermann (*Dr Robert Koch*), Edward Norris (*Dr Morgenroth*), Harry Davenport (*Judge*), Louis Calhern (*Dr Brockdorf*), Louis Jean Heydt (*Dr Kunze*), Charles Halton (*Sensenbrenner*), Irving Bacon (*Becker*), Douglas Wood (*Speidler*), Theodor von Eltz (*Dr Kraus*), Hermine Sterler (*Miss Marquandt*), John Hamilton (*Hirsch*), Paul Harvey (*Defence Attorney*), Frank Reicher (*Old Doctor*), Torben Meyer (*Kadereit*), Louis Arco (*Dr Bertheim*), Wilfred Hari (*Dr Hata*), John Henrick (*Dr Bucher*), Ann Todd (*Marianne*), Polly Stewart (*Steffi*), Ernst Hausman (*Hans Weisgart*), Stuart Holmes (*Male nurse*), Frank Lackteen

(*Arab man*), Herbert Anderson (*Assistant*), Egon Brecher (*Martl*), Robert Strange (*Koerner*), Cliff Clark (*Haupt*).

R.t. 103.
Copyright, 2 March 1940 (as *Dr Ehrlich's Magic Bullet*).
First shown, Strand, New York, 23 February 1940.
Reviews, V, 7 February 1940 (anon), NYT, 24 February 1940 (Frank S. Nugent).

The Story of Louis Pasteur
First National
D–William Dieterle. Ass.d–Frank Shaw. Dial.d–Gene Lewis. Sc–Sheridan Gibney, Pierre Collings. Ph–Tony Gaudio. Ed–Ralph Dawson. A.d–Robert Haas. Cost–Milo Anderson. M.d–Leo F. Forbstein. Sd–Nathan Levinson.

Paul Muni (*Louis Pasteur*), Josephine Hutchinson (*Marie Pasteur*), Anita Louise (*Annette Pasteur*), Donald Woods (*Dr Jean Martel*), Fritz Leiber (*Dr Charbonnet*), Henry O'Neill (*Dr Emile Roux*), Porter Hall (*Dr Rossignol*), Raymond Brown (*Dr Radisse*), Akim Tamiroff (*Dr Zaranoff*), Halliwell Hobbes (*Dr Lister*), Frank Reicher (*Dr Pfeiffer*), Dickie Moore (*Joseph Meister*), Ruth Robinson (*Mrs Meister*), Walter Kingsford (*Napoleon III*), Iphigenie Castiglione (*Empress Eugénie*), Herbert Corthell (*Louis Adolphe Thiers, First President of the Republic of France*).

R.t. 85.
Copyright, 31 January 1936.
First shown, Strand, New York, 8 February 1936.
Reviews, NYT, 10 February 1936 (Frank S. Nugent), V, 12 February 1936 (Kauf).

Taxi!
Warner Brothers
D–Roy Del Ruth. Ass.d–William Cannon. Sc–Kubec Glasmon, John Bright, from the play 'Blind Spot' by Kenyon Nicholson. Ph–James Van Trees. Ed–James Gibbons. A.d–Esdras Hartley. Make-up–Perc Westmore. M.d–Leo F. Forbstein.

James Cagney (*Matt Nolan*), Loretta Young (*Sue Reilly*), George E. Stone (*Skeats Nolan*), Guy Kibbee (*Pop Reilly*), Leila Bennett (*Ruby*), Dorothy Burgess (*Marie Costa*), David Landau (*Buck Gerard*), Ray Cooke (*Danny Nolan*), Matt McHugh (*Joe Silva*), George MacFarlane (*Father Nulty*), Nat Pendleton (*Truck Driver*), Berton Churchill (*Judge West*), George Raft (*William Kenney*), Polly Walters (*Polly*), Hector V. Sarno (*Monument salesman*), Aggie Herring (*Cleaning Lady*), Lee Phelps (*Onlooker*), Harry Tenbrook (*Cabbie*), Robert Emmett O'Connor (*Irish cop*), Eddie Fetherstone (*Dance judge*), Russ Powell (*Dance judge*), Ben Taggart (*Cop*), The Cotton Club Orchestra.

R.t. 70.
Copyright, 9 January 1932.
First shown, Strand, New York and Warners Hollywood, Los Angeles, 7 January 1932.
Reviews, NYT, 8 January 1932 (Mordaunt Hall), V, 12 January 1932 (Sid).

316

They Died With Their Boots On
Warner Brothers
Ass.p–Robert Fellows. D–Raoul Walsh. Ass.d–Russell Saunders. Dial.d–
Edward A. Blatt. Sc–Wally Kline, Aeneas MacKenzie. Ph–Bert Glennon.
Ed–William Holmes. A.d–John Hughes. Cost–Milo Anderson. Make-up–Perc
Westmore. M–Max Steiner. M.d–Leo F. Forbstein. Sd–Dolph Thomas.
Tech.ad–Lieutenant-Colonel J.G. Taylor, US Army Ret'd.

Errol Flynn (*George Armstrong Custer*), Olivia De Havilland (*Elizabeth Bacon/Beth
Custer*), Arthur Kennedy (*Ned Sharp*), Charley Grapewin (*California Joe*), Gene
Lockhart (*Samuel Bacon*), Anthony Quinn (*Crazy Horse*), Stanley Ridges (*Major
Romulus Taipe*), John Litel (*General Phil Sheridan*), Walter Hampden (*William
Sharp*), Sydney Greenstreet (*General Winfield Scott*), Regis Toomey (*Fitzhugh Lee*),
Hattie McDaniel (*Callie*), George P. Huntley Jr (*Lieutenant Butler*), Joe Sawyer
(*Sergeant Doolittle*), Frank Wilcox (*Captain Webb*), Selmer Jackson (*Captain
McCook*), Minor Watson (*Senator Smith*), DeWolf Hopper Jr (*Lieutenant Frazier*),
Joseph Crehan (*President Grant*), Irving Bacon (*Salesman*), Eddie Acuff (*Colonel
Smith*), George Eldredge (*Corporal Riley*), Spencer Charters (*Station Master*),
Hobart Bosworth (*Clergyman*), Russell Hicks (*Corporal of First Michigan*), Hugh
Sothern (*Major Smith*), John Ridgeley (*Lieutenant Davis*), Gig Young (*Lieutenant
Roberts*), Aileen Pringle (*Mrs Sharp*), Anna Q. Nilsson (*Mrs Taipe*), Frank
Ferguson (*Grant's Secretary*).

R.t. 140.
Copyright, 3 January 1942.
First shown, Strand, New York, 20 November 1941.
Reviews, V, 19 November 1941 (Flin), NYT, 21 November 1941 (T.M.P.).

They Won't Forget
First National/A Mervyn LeRoy Production
D–Mervyn LeRoy. Sc–Robert Rossen, Abem Kandel, from the novel 'Death in
the South' by Ward Greene. Ph–Arthur Edeson. Ed–Thomas Richards.
A.d–Robert Haas. Cost–Miss MacKenzie. M–Adolph Deutsch. M.d–Leo F.
Forbstein.

Claude Rains (*D.A. Andy Griffin*), Gloria Dickson (*Sybil Hale*), Edward Norris
(*Robert Hale*), Otto Kruger (*Mike Gleason*), Allyn Joslyn (*Bill Brock*), Elisha
Cook Jr (*Joe Turner*), Lana Turner (*Mary Clay*), Linda Perry (*Imogene Mayfield*),
Cy Kendall (*Detective Lancart*), Clinton Rosemond (*Tump Redwine*), E. Alyn
Warren (*Carlisle P. Buxton*), Elizabeth Risdon (*Mrs Hale*), Clifford Soubier (*Jim
Timberlake*), Granville Bates (*Detective Pindar*), Ann Shoemaker (*Mrs Mountford*),
Paul Everton (*Governor Thomas Mountford*), Donald Briggs (*Harmon*), Sybil
Harris (*Mrs Clay*), Trevor Bardette (*Shattuck Clay*), Elliott Sullivan (*Luther
Clay*), Wilmer Hines (*Ransom Scott Clay*), Eddie Acuff (*Drugstore clerk*), Frank
Faylen (*Reporter*), Leonard Mudie (*Judge Moore*), Henry Davenport, Harry
Beresford, Edward McWade (*Confederate soldiers*).

R.t. 95.
Copyright, 4 October 1937.
First shown, Strand, New York, 14 July 1937.
Reviews, V, 30 June 1937 (Bert), NYT, 15 July 1937 (Frank S. Nugent).

20,000 Years in Sing Sing

First National

Ass.p–Ray Griffith. D–Michael Curtiz. Ass.d–Stanley Logan. Sc–Wilson Mizner, Brown Holmes, from the book by Warden Lewis E. Lawes, adapted by Courtenay Terrett and Robert Lord. Ph–Barney McGill. Ed–George Amy. A.d–Anton Grot. Cost–Orry-Kelly. M–Bernard Kaun. M.d–Leo F. Forbstein.

Spencer Tracy (*Tommy Connors*), Bette Davis (*Fay Wilson*), Arthur Byron (*Warden Paul Long*), Lyle Talbot (*Bud Saunders*), Warren Hymer (*Hype*), Louis Calhern (*Joe Finn*), Grant Mitchell (*Psychiatrist, Dr Ames*), Sheila Terry (*Billie*), Spencer Charters (*Daniels*), Edward J. McNamara (*Chief of Guards*), Sam Godfrey (*Second Reporter*), Nella Walker (*Warden Long's Wife*), Harold Huber (*Tony*), William LeMaire (*Black Jack*), Arthur Hoyt (*Dr Meeker*), George Pat Collins (*Mike*), Rockliffe Fellows, Lucille Collins, Clarence Wilson, Jimmie Donlon.

R.t. 78.

Copyright, 23 December 1932.

First shown, Strand, New York, 9 January 1933.

Reviews, NYT, 10 January 1933 (Mordaunt Hall), V, 17 January 1933 (Char).

Voltaire

Warner Brothers

D–John G. Adolfi. Sc–Paul Green, Maude T. Howell, from the novel by George Gibbs and E. Lawrence Dudley. Ph–Tony Gaudio. Ed–Owen Marks. A.d–Anton Grot. Cost–Orry-Kelly. M.d. Leo F. Forbstein.

George Arliss (*Voltaire*), Doris Kenyon (*Mme de Pompadour*), Margaret Lindsay (*Nanette Calas*), Alan Mowbray (*Count de Sarnac*), Reginald Owen (*King Louis XV*), Theodore Newton (*François Chaumont*), David Torrence (*Doctor Tranchon*), Murray Kinnell (*Emile*), Doris Lloyd (*Mme Louise Denis*), Ivan Simpson (*Voltaire's servant*), Gordon Westcott, Douglass Dumbrille, Helena Phillips, Leonard Mudie.

R.t. 72.

Copyright, 24 July 1933.

First shown on general release, 28 July 1933.

Reviews, NYT, 23 August 1933 (Mordaunt Hall), V, 29 August 1933 (Chic).

Weary River

First National

Ass.p–Richard A. Rowland. D–Frank Lloyd. Sc–Bradley King, from the story by Courtney Riley Cooper. Dialogue–Tom O. Geraghty. Titles (silent version)–Paul Perez. Ph–Ernest Haller. Special photography–Alvin Knechtel. Ed–Edward Schroeder, James Gibbon. A.d–John J. Hughes. Cost–Max Ree. M.d–Louis Silvers. Song–'Weary River' by Louis Silvers and Grant Clarke.

Richard Barthelmess (*Jerry Larrabee*), Betty Compson (*Alice*), William Holden (*Warden*), Louis Natheaux (*Spadoni*), George E. Stone (*Blackie*), Raymond Turner (*Elevator boy*), Gladden James (*Manager*), Robert Emmett O'Connor.

R.t. 88.

Copyright, 14 March 1929.

First shown, Central, New York, 24 January 1929.
Reviews, NYT, 25 January 1929 (Mordaunt Hall), V, 30 January 1929 (Land).

Wild Boys of the Road (UK: Dangerous Age)
First National
Ass.p–Robert Presnell. D–William A. Wellman. Sc–Earl Baldwin, from a story by Daniel Ahearn. Ph–Arthur Todd. Ed–Thomas Pratt. A.d–Esdras Hartley. M.d–Leo F. Forbstein.

Frankie Darro (*Eddie Smith*), Dorothy Coonan (*Sally*), Rochelle Hudson (*Grace*), Edwin Phillips (*Tommy*), Ann Hovey (*Lola*), Arthur Hohl (*Dr Heckel*), Grant Mitchell (*Mr Smith*), Claire McDowell (*Mrs Smith*), Sterling Holloway (*Ollie*), Robert Barrat (*Judge White*), Shirley Dunsted (*Harriet*), Minna Gombell (*Aunt Carrie*), Charles Grapewin, Ward Bond, Adrian Morris, Willard Robertson.

R.t. 77.
Copyright, 26 September 1933.
First shown, Hollywood Theatre, New York, 21 September 1933.
Reviews, NYT, 22 September 1933 (Frank S. Nugent), V, 26 September 1933 (Rush).

The World Changes
First National
Ass.p–Robert Lord. D–Mervyn LeRoy. Sc–Edward Chodorov, from the story 'America Kneels' by Sheridan Gibney. Ph–Tony Gaudio. Ed–William Holmes. A.d–Robert Haas. Cost–Earl Luick. M.d–Leo Forbstein.

Paul Muni (*Orin Nordholm Jr*), Aline MacMahon (*Anna Nordholm*), Mary Astor (*Virginia Claflin*), Donald Cook (*Richard Nordholm*), Jean Muir (*Selma Peterson II*), Guy Kibbee (*James Claflin*), Patricia Ellis (*Natalie Nordholm*), Theodore Newton (*Paul*), Margaret Lindsay (*Jennifer Clinton*), Gordon Westcott (*John Nordholm*), Alan Dinehart (*Ogden Jarrett*), Henry O'Neill (*Orin Nordholm Sr*), Anna Q. Nilsson (*Mrs Petersen*), Arthur Hohl (*Patten*), William Janney (*Orin Nordholm III*), Mickey Rooney (*Otto Petersen as a child*), Douglass Dumbrille (*Buffalo Bill*), Marjorie Gateson (*Mrs Clinton*), Oscar Apfel (*Mr Krauss*), Alan Mowbray (*Sir Philip Ivor*), William Burress (*Mosley*), Wallis Clark (*Mr McCord*), Clay Clement (*Captain Custer*), Willard Robertson (*Mr Petersen*), Philip Faversham (*Clerk*), Sidney Toler (*Hodgens*), Jackie Searle (*John as a boy*), George Meeker.

R.t. 90.
Copyright, 21 November 1933.
First shown, Hollywood Theatre, New York, 25 October 1933.
Reviews, NYT, 26 October 1933 (Mordaunt Hall), V, 31 October 1933 (Abel).

Bibliography

Sections 1 and 2 of this Bibliography are heavily selective: there is far more material on the American film industry and on film and society than I have listed here. Sections 3 and 4 are as complete a list as I have been able to compile of published material on Warner Brothers (together with selected material on some of the people who worked there) and on the films discussed in this book.

1 The American Film Industry

Tino BALIO (ed.), *The American Film Industry*, University of Wisconsin Press, 1976.
    United Artists, the company built by the stars, University of Wisconsin Press, 1975.
John BAXTER, *Hollywood in the thirties*, Zwemmer/Barnes, 1968.
Bosley CROWTHER, *The lion's share: the story of an entertainment empire*, Dutton, 1957.
Richard CORLISS, *Talking Pictures*, Avon Books, 1975.
Philip FRENCH, *The movie moguls*, Weidenfeld and Nicolson, 1969.
Ezra GOODMAN, *The fifty year decline and fall of Hollywood*, Simon and Schuster, 1961.
Benjamin B. HAMPTON, *The history of the American film industry*, Dover, 1970.
Lewis JACOBS, *The rise of the American film*, Teacher's College Press, 1970.
Gertrude JOBES, *Motion picture empire*, Archon Books, 1966.
Arthur KNIGHT, *The liveliest art*, Macmillan, 1957.
Howard T. LEWIS, *The motion picture business*, D. Van Nostrand Co., 1933.
Colin McARTHUR, *Underworld USA*, Secker & Warburg/British Film Institute, 1972.
Olga J. MARTIN, *Hollywood's motion picture commandments*, H.H. Wilson & Co., 1937.
Richard Dyer McCANN, *Hollywood in transition*, Houghton, Miflin, 1962.
Hortense POWDERMAKER, *Hollywood, the dream factory*, Grosset and Dunlap, 1950.
David ROBINSON, *Hollywood in the twenties*, Zwemmer/Barnes, 1968.
Leo C. ROSTEN, *Hollywood: the movie colony, the movie makers*, Harcourt, Brace, 1941.
Andrew SARRIS, *The American Cinema*, Dutton, 1968.
Richard SCHICKEL, *Movies: the history of an art and an institution*, Basic Books, 1964.
Jack SHADOIAN, *Dreams and dead ends: The American crime gangster film*, MIT Press, 1977.
Edward WAGENKNECHT, *The movies in the age of innocence*, University of Oklahoma Press, 1962.
Norman ZIEROLD, *The Hollywood tycoons*, Hamish Hamilton, 1969.

2 Film and Society

Andrew BERGMAN, *We're in the money*, Harper & Row, 1972.
Herbert BLUMER, *Movies and conduct*, Macmillan, 1933.
R.G. BURNETT and E.D. MARTELL, *The devil's camera*, Epworth Press, 1932.

Stanley CAVELL, *The world viewed*, enlarged ed., Harvard University Press, 1979.

John G. CAWELTI, *Adventure, mystery and romance*, University of Chicago Press, 1976.

W.W. CHARTERS, *Motion pictures and youth*, Macmillan, 1933.

Edgar DALE, *The content of motion pictures*, Macmillan, 1935.

Leo A. HANDEL, *Hollywood looks at its audience*, University of Illinois Press, 1950.

Molly HASKELL, *From reverence to rape: the treatment of women in the movies*, Holt, Rinehart and Winston, 1974.

Richard HOFSTADTER, *Anti-intellectualism in American life*, Random House, 1966.

George A. HUACO, *The sociology of film art*, Basic Books, 1965.

William HUNTER, *Scrutiny of cinema*, Wishart and Co., 1932.

Ruth INGLIS, *Freedom of the movies*, University of Chicago Press, 1947.

Lewis JACOBS, *The movies as medium*, Farrar, Strauss & Giroux, 1970.

I.C. JARVIE, *Movies and society*, Basic Books, 1970.

Garth JOWETT, *Film: the democratic art*, Little, Brown & Co., 1976.

Orrin E. KLAPP, *Heroes, villains and fools: the changing American character*, Prentice Hall, 1962.

F.D. KLINGENDER and Stuart LEGG, *Money behind the screen*, Lawrence & Wishart, 1937.

Max KNEPPER, *Sodom and Gomorrah*, 1935.

Richard Dyer McCANN, *Film and society*, Scribner's, 1964.

Broadus MITCHELL, *Depression decade*, M.E. Sharpe, 1977.

Raymond MOLEY, *Are we movie made?*, Macy-Marcus, 1938.

Payne Fund Studies of Motion Pictures and Social Values, 1933-39, Arno Press/New York Times, 1970.

W. PERLMAN (ed.), *Movies on trial*, Macmillan & Co., 1936.

Charles PETERS, *Motion pictures and standards of morality*, Macmillan & Co., 1933.

Martin QUIGLEY, *Decency in motion pictures*, Macmillan & Co., 1937.

Quentin REYNOLDS, *Leave it to the people*, Random House, 1949.

W.R. ROBINSON, *Man and the movies*, Louisiana State University Press, 1967.

Marjorie ROSEN, *Popcorn Venus: women, movies and the American dream*, Avon Books, 1974.

Constance ROURKE, *The roots of American culture and other essays*, Harcourt, Brace and Co., 1942.

Gilbert SELDES, *The movies come from America*, Scribner's, 1937.
  The public arts, Simon and Schuster, 1964.

Robert SKLAR, *Movie-made America*, Random House, 1975.

Margaret Farrar THORP, *America at the movies*, Yale University Press, 1939.

Andrew TUDOR, *Image and influence*, Allen & Unwin, 1974.

G. WAGNER, *Parade of pleasure: a study of popular iconography in the USA*, D. Verschoyle, 1954.

Alexander WALKER, *Stardom: the Hollywood phenomenon*, Michael Joseph, 1970.

Robert WARSHOW, *The immediate experience*, Doubleday, 1962.

Raymond WILLIAMS, *Communications*, Penguin, 1976.

Michael WOOD, *America in the movies*, Secker & Warburg, 1975.

3 Warner Brothers

James N. BEAVER Jr, *John Garfield, his life and films*, Barnes/Yoseloff, 1978.

Rudy BEHLMER, 'Erich Wolfgang Korngold', *Films in Review*, February 1967.

Spencer M. BERGER, *'The film career of John Barrymore'*, *Films in Review*, December 1952.

Jean-Pierre BLEYS, 'Les films criminels de la Warner Bros : classement thématique', *Cahiers de la Cinémathèque*, 25, Summer 1978.

'William Keighley, Raoul Walsh et le "style Warner"', idem.

Ronald BOWERS, 'Gale Sondergaard', *Films in Review*, August-September 1978.

Edward BUSCOMBE, 'Walsh and Warner Brothers' in Phil HARDY (ed), *Raoul Walsh*, Edinburgh Film Festival, 1974.

James CAGNEY, *Cagney by Cagney*, Doubleday, 1976.

Russell CAMPBELL, 'Warner Brothers in the thirties', *Velvet Light Trap*, 1.

'Warners, the Depression and FDR', *Velvet Light Trap*, 4.

Kingsley CANHAM, 'Curtiz : cynicism, cinema and Casablanca' in *The Hollywood professionals*, Vol. 1, Barnes/Tantivy, 1973.

Mervyn LeRoy : star-making, studio systems and style' in *The Hollywood professionals*, Vol. 5, Barnes/Tantivy, 1976.

'Raoul Walsh : the rugged individualist' in *The Hollywood professionals*, Vol. 1, Tantivy/Barnes, 1973.

Mitchell COHEN, 'Hawks in the 30s', *Take One*, IV, 12.

Elizabeth DALTON, 'Women at work : Warners in the thirties', *Velvet Light Trap*, 6.

John DAVIS, 'Notes on Warner Brothers' foreign policy, 1918-1948', *Velvet Light Trap*, 4.

'Warners genres of the '30s and '40s', *Velvet Light Trap*, 15.

Donald DESCHNER, 'Anton Grot, Warners art director 1927-1948', *Velvet Light Trap*, 15.

The films of Spencer Tracy, Citadel Press, 1968.

Homer DICKENS, *The films of James Cagney*, Citadel Press, 1972.

The films of Gary Cooper, Citadel Press, 1970.

Neil DOYLE, 'Olivia De Havilland', *Films in Review*, February 1962.

Michael B. DRUXMAN, *Paul Muni, his life and his films*, Barnes/Yoseloff, 1974.

Tom FLINN, 'William Dieterle : the Plutarch of Hollywood', *Velvet Light Trap*, 15.

Errol FLYNN, *My wicked, wicked ways*, Puttnam's, 1959.

Gene FOWLER, *Good night, sweet Prince : the life and times of John Barrymore*, Viking Press, 1944.

John GALLAGHER, 'William Wellman', *Films in Review*, May and June-July 1982.

George GELTZER, 'William Keighley', *Films in Review*, October 1974.

J. Douglas GOMERY, 'Writing the history of the American film industry - Warner Bros and sound', *Screen*, Spring 1976.

Joel GREENBERG, 'Writing for the movies : Casey Robinson', *Focus on Film*, 32.

Harry HAUN and George RABORN, 'Max Steiner', *Films in Review*, June-July 1961.

Charles HIGHAM, *Warner Brothers*, Scribner's, 1975.

Charles HIGHAM and Joel GREENBERG, 'Irving Rapper' in *The celluloid muse, Hollywood directors speak*, Regnery, 1969.

Clive HIRSCHHORN, *The Warner Bros story*, Octopus, 1979.

John HUSTON, *An open book*, Knopf, 1980.

Stuart KAMINSKY, *John Huston : maker of magic*, Angus & Robertson, 1978.

Karyn KAY and Gerald PEARY, 'Talking to Pat O'Brien', *Velvet Light Trap*, 15.

John KOBAL, 'Interview with Joan Blondell', *Focus on Film*, 24.

Jerome LAWRENCE, *Actor : the life and times of Paul Muni*, Puttnam's, 1974.

Mervyn LEROY, (as told to Dick Kleiner), *Take one*, Hawthorn Books, 1974.

Joseph McBRIDE (ed.), *Focus on Howard Hawks*, Prentice Hall, 1972.

Clifford McCARTY, *Bogey : The films of Humphrey Bogart*, Citadel Press, 1965.

Patrick McGILLIGAN, *Cagney : The actor as auteur*, Barnes/Tantivy, 1975.

William R. MEYER, *Warner Brothers directors*, Arlington House, 1978.

Joyce NELSON, 'Warner Brothers' deviants', *Velvet Light Trap*, 15.

David NIVEN, *The moon's a balloon*, Hamish Hamilton, 1971.
Bring on the empty horses, Hamish Hamilton, 1975.

Rui NOGUEIRA, '400 films, 1 producteur : Hal Wallis', *Cinéma 70*, November 1970.

Rui NOGUEIRA and Bertrand TAVERNIER, 'Entretien avec John Huston', *Postif*, 116, May 1970.

Pat O'BRIEN, *The wind at my back*, Doubleday, 1964.

James Robert PARISH and Alvin H.MARILL, *The cinema of Edward G. Robinson*, Barnes/Tantivy, 1972.

Alfonso PINTO and Francisco RIALP, 'The films of William Dieterle', *Films in Review*, April 1957.

Lawrence J. QUIRK, 'Bette Davis', *Films in Review*, December 1955.

Jeffrey RICHARDS, 'In praise of Claude Rains', *Films & Filming*, February and March 1982.

Edward G. ROBINSON (with Leonard Spigelgass), *All my yesterdays - an autobiography*, Hawthorn, 1973.

Nick RODDICK, 'The man who was Warners', *Stills*, 6.

Arthur SACKS, 'An analysis of the gangster movies of the early thirties', *Velvet Light Trap*, 1.

Ted SENNETT, *Warner Brothers presents*, Castle Books, 1971.

Graham SHIRLEY, 'Interview with Byron Haskin', *Cinema Papers*, March-April 1975.

Jeanne STEIN, 'Aline MacMahon', *Films in Review*, December 1965.
'Claude Rains', *Films in Review*, November 1963.

Whitney STINE, *Mother Goddam : the story of the career of Bette Davis (with a running commentary by Bette Davis)*, Hawthorn, 1974.

Bertrand TAVERNIER, 'Entretien avec Edward Chodorov', *Postif*, 108, September 1969.

Tony THOMAS, *The films of Ronald Reagan*, Citadel Press, 1980.
'Hugo Friedhofer', *Films in Review*, October 1965.

Tony THOMAS, Rudy BEHLMER and Clifford McCARTY, *The films of Errol Flynn*, Citadel Press, 1967.

Frank T. THOMPSON, *Nothing sacred : The motion pictures of William A. Wellman*, Scarecrow Press, 1982.

Hal WALLIS and Charles HIGHAM, *Starmaker : The autobiography of Hal Wallis*, Macmillan, 1980.

Raoul WALSH, *Each man in his time : the life and story of a director*, Farrar, Straus & Giroux, 1974.

Jack WARNER (with Dean Jennings), *My first hundred years in Hollywood*, Random House, 1965.

William A. WELLMAN, *A short time for insanity : an autobiography*, Hawthorn, 1974

Frank WESTMORE and Muriel DAVIDSON, *The Westmores of Hollywood*, Lippincott, 1976.

Arthur WILSON (ed.), *The Warner Bros golden anniversary book*, Dell, 1973.

J. L. YECK, 'De Havilland vs. Warner Brothers', *American Classic Screen*, VI, 3.

4 Films

The Adventures of Robin Hood, ed. Rudy Behlmer, University of Wisconsin Press, 1979 (Wisconsin/Warner Bros. Screenplay Series).

Ernest CALLENBACH, 'Comparative anatomy of folk myth films: *Robin Hood* and *Antonio das Mortes*', *Film Quarterly*, Winter 1969-70.

Olivier EYQUEM, 'Sherwood USA (à propos des *Aventures de Robin des Bois*)', *Positif*, 205, March 1978.

Ina Rae HARK, 'The visual politics of *The Adventures of Robin Hood*', *Journal of Popular Film*, V,1,1976.

The Amazing Dr Clitterhouse

American Cinemeditor, Summer/Fall 1982, 'Reviewing the classics: *The Amazing Dr Clitterhouse* and *The Charge of the Light Brigade*'.

Captain Blood

John DAVIS, '*Captain Blood*', *Velvet Light Trap*, 1.

The Charge of the Light Brigade

American Cinemeditor, Summer/Fall 1982, 'Reviewing the classics: *The Amazing Dr Clitterhouse* and *The Charge of the Light Brigade*'.

Confessions of a Nazi Spy

David WOOLF, 'Fact into Film in *Confessions of a Nazi Spy*', *Films*, November 1939.

Doorway to Hell

Gerald PEARY, '*Doorway to Hell*', *Velvet Light Trap*, 16.

Five Star Final

Jeffrey RICHARDS, 'Discovery: *Five Star Final*', *Focus on Film*, 23.

The Green Pastures, ed. Thomas E. Cripps, University of Wisconsin Press, 1979. (Wisconsin/Warner Bros. Screenplay Series).

High Sierra, ed. Douglas Gomery, University of Wisconsin Press, 1979 (Wisconsin/Warner Bros. Screenplay Series).

Kenneth D. ALLEY, '*High Sierra* – swan song for an era', *Journal of Popular Film*, V, 3 & 4, 1976.

John L. SIMONS, 'Henry on Bogie: reality and romance in "Dream Song No. 9" and *High Sierra*', *Literature/Film Quarterly*, Summer 1977.

I Am a Fugitive from a Chain Gang, ed. John E. O'Connor, University of Wisconsin Press, 1981 (Wisconsin/Warner Bros. Screenplay Series).

Russell CAMPBELL, '*I Am a Fugitive from a Chain Gang*', *Velvet Light Trap*, 1 and 2.

Juarez in John GASSNER and Dudley NICHOLS (ed.), *Twenty Best Film Plays*, Crown, 1943.

Allen L. WOLL, 'The dilemma of *Juarez*', *Film and History*, February 1975.

Little Caesar, ed. Gerald Peary, University of Wisconsin Press, 1981 (Wisconsin/Warner Bros. Screenplay Series).

Stuart M. KAMINSKY, '*Little Caesar* and its role in the gangster film genre', *Journal of Popular Film*, Summer 1972.

The Life of Emile Zola in John GASSNER and Dudley NICHOLS (ed.), *Twenty Best Film Plays*, Crown, 1943.

The Maltese Falcon, ed. Richard N. ANOBILE, Darien House, 1974.

Lawrence BENAQUIST, 'Function and index in Huston's *The Maltese Falcon*', *Film Criticism*, Winter 1982.

Gordon GOW, 'Pursuit of the Falcon', *Films & Filming*, March 1974.

Douglas McVAY, '*The Maltese Falcon* and *Casablanca*', *Focus on Film*, 30.

James NAREMORE, 'John Huston and *The Maltese Falcon*', *Literature/Film Quarterly*, Summer 1973.

Virginia Wright WEXMAN, 'Kinesics and film acting: Humphrey Bogart in *The Maltese Falcon* and *The Big Sleep*', *Journal of Popular Film and Television*, VII, 1, 1978.

Marked Woman

Charles W. ECKERT, 'The anatomy of a proletarian film: *Marked Woman*', *Film Quarterly*, Winter 1973/4.

Mary Beth HARALOVICH and Cathy Root KLAPRAT, '*Marked Woman* and *Jezebel*: the spectator on the trailer', *Enclitic*, Fall 81/Spring 82.

Karyn KAY, 'Sisters of the night: *Marked Woman*', *Velvet Light Trap*, 6.

Massacre

Karyn KAY, 'Happy days are here again: *Massacre* (1934)', *Velvet Light Trap*, 4.

Meet John Doe

Glenn A. PHELPS, 'Frank Capra and the political hero: a new reading of *Meet John Doe*', *Film Criticism*, Winter 1981.

Dudley ANDREW, '*Meet John Doe*', *Enclitic*, Fall 81/Spring 82.

A Midsummer Night's Dream

W.E. WILLIAMS, 'Film and Literature', *Sight & Sound*, Winter 1935-6.

Robert F. WILLSON Jr., 'Ill met by moonlight: Reinhardt's *A Midsummer Night's Dream* and Musical/Screwball Comedy', *Journal of Popular Film*, V, 3-4, 1976.

Moby Dick

Edward STONE, 'Ahab gets the girl, or Herman Melville goes to the movies', *Literature/Film Quarterly*, Spring 1975.

Old English

William K. EVERSON, 'Rediscovery', *Films in Review*, April 1979.

The Public Enemy, ed. Henry Cohen, University of Wisconsin Press, 1981 (Wisconsin/Warner Bros. Screenplay Series).

Santa Fe Trail

Linda PEPPER and John DAVIS, 'John Brown's body lies a' rolling in his grave',

Velvet Light Trap, 8.

Smart Money
Allen EYLES, 'Discovery: *Smart Money*', *Focus on Film*, 21.

The Story of Louis Pasteur in Lorraine NOBLE (ed.), *Four-star scripts*, Doubleday, Doran, 1936.

20,000 Years in Sing Sing
Albert MORAN, '*Twenty Thousand Years in Sing Sing*', *Australian Journal of Film Theory*, 3, 1977.
Jack SHADOIAN, 'Michael Curtiz's *Twenty Thousand Years in Sing Sing*', *Journal of Popular Film*, Spring 1973.

Wild Boys of the Road
Russell CAMPBELL, 'Wild Bill's *Wild Boys*', *Velvet Light Trap*, 15.
Gillian KLEIN, 'Wellman's *Wild Boys of the Road*: the rhetoric of a Depression movie', *Velvet Light Trap*, 15.

Index